D1325827

Language and Dialect Contact in Ireland

Edinburgh University Press is one of the leading university presses in the UK. We publish academic books and journals in our selected subject areas across the humanities and social sciences, combining cutting-edge scholarship with high editorial and production values to produce academic works of lasting importance. For more information visit our website: edinburghuniversitypress.com

Edinburgh University Press Ltd
The Tun – Holyrood Road, 12(2f) Jackson's Entry, Edinburgh EH8 8PJ

Typeset in 10.5/12 Janson by
Servis Filmsetting Ltd, Stockport, Cheshire
and printed and bound by CPI Group (UK) Ltd, Croydon, CR0 4YY

A CIP record for this book is available from the British Library

ISBN 978 1 4744 5290 8 (hardback)
ISBN 978 1 4744 5292 2 (webready PDF)
ISBN 978 1 4744 5293 9 (epub)

Contents

List of figures and tables   viii
Acknowledgements   ix
List of abbreviations   x

1 Introduction   **1**
   1.1   About this book   1
   1.2   What is Mid-Ulster English?   1
   1.3   The phonological origins of Mid-Ulster English   5
   1.4   Sources and methods   8
   1.5   Structure of this book   10

2 Background   **13**
   2.1   Preliminaries   13
   2.2   English in Ulster before the seventeenth century   14
   2.3   The Plantation of Ulster and its associated settlements   16
     2.3.1   Antrim and Down   17
     2.3.2   The escheated counties   18
     2.3.3   The origins of the English and Scottish settlers   18
     2.3.4   Later settlements   21
     2.3.5   Other settlements in Ireland   21
     2.3.6   The Irish   22
   2.4   Demographic and linguistic transformation in the seventeenth and early eighteenth centuries   23
   2.5   Ulster in subsequent centuries   26
   2.6   The decline of Irish in Ulster   30
   2.7   The ethno-religious dimension   35
   2.8   The linguistic history of Ulster   37

3 Consonants   **40**
   3.1   The consonants of MUE   40
   3.2   The dorsal and glottal fricatives   42
   3.3   Velar Palatalisation   47
     3.3.1   Velar Palatalisation in MUE   47
     3.3.2   Broad and slender dorsal stops in Irish   49
     3.3.3   Velar Palatalisation in English   51

	3.3.4	Velar Palatalisation in Scots	54
	3.3.5	The origins of Velar Palatalisation in MUE	55
3.4		The palato-alveolars and Palatal Velarisation	56
3.5		Pre-R Dentalisation	61
3.6		Intervocalic /t/-Voicing	63
3.7		Dental fricatives	66
	3.7.1	/θ/ and /ð/ in IrE	66
	3.7.2	Stopping of /θ/ before /r/ in MUE	66
	3.7.3	Debuccalisation of /θ/	67
	3.7.4	Changes affecting foot-internal /ð/	69
	3.7.5	Summary	70
3.8		Rhoticity, /r/ realisation and Post-/r/ Retraction	70
	3.8.1	Rhoticity	71
	3.8.2	/r/ realisation	72
	3.8.3	Post-/r/ Retraction	74
3.9		The distribution and realisation of /l/	74
	3.9.1	The lexical distribution of /l/	74
	3.9.2	The realisation of /l/	76
3.10		Epenthesis	82
3.11		Consonant cluster simplification	84
	3.11.1	Deletion of /t/	84
	3.11.2	Deletion of /d/ after /l/	86
	3.11.3	Deletion of /d/ after /n/	88
	3.11.4	Deletion of /b/ and /g/	90
	3.11.5	Summary	91
3.12		Other consonantal features	92
	3.12.1	Aspiration and voicing	92
	3.12.2	Glottalisation and glottal replacement	93
	3.12.3	Simplification of /kn/ and /wr/	93
	3.12.4	Interchange of /s/ and /ʃ/	95
	3.12.5	Realisation of /kl/ and /gl/ as [tl] and [dl]	95
	3.12.6	/z/ and /ʒ/	96
3.13		Summary	96
4	**Vowels**		**100**
4.1		The MUE vowels	100
4.2		Vowel quality in MUE	101
	4.2.1	Lowering and centralisation of the KIT and STRUT vowels	103
	4.2.2	Lowering of the DRESS vowel	106
	4.2.3	Backing of the TRAP/BATH vowel	107
	4.2.4	Unrounding of the LOT vowel	108
	4.2.5	Fronting of the GOOSE vowel and the second component of the MOUTH diphthong	110
	4.2.6	The FACE vowel	111
	4.2.7	Variation in the PRICE vowel	113
4.3		Vowel quantity in MUE	114

	4.3.1	The MUE patterns	114
	4.3.2	Vowel quantity in USc, SUE and SIrE	116
	4.3.3	The origins of MUE vowel quantity	118
	4.3.4	SVLR conditioning	119
	4.3.5	The VE and PFL	120
	4.3.6	The VE and PFL in Scots	122
	4.3.7	The origins of the VE and PFL in MUE	125
4.4	Lexical distribution		125
	4.4.1	The lexical distribution of the MUE vowels	125
	4.4.2	*top* and *off*	131
	4.4.3	The PRICE diphthongs	132
	4.4.4	/wë-/ > /wɔ̈-/	135
	4.4.5	The FOOT lexical set	136
	4.4.6	The THOUGHT vowels	138
4.5	Summary		140
	4.5.1	Vowel quality	140
	4.5.2	Vowel quantity	141
	4.5.3	Vowel lexical distribution	142

5	**Discussion**		**145**
5.1	Preliminaries		145
5.2	Contact with Irish		147
	5.2.1	Reinforcement	151
	5.2.2	Lexis and syntax	156
	5.2.3	Summary	159
5.3	The English input to MUE		161
	5.3.1	The English input and New Dialect Formation	161
	5.3.2	Conservatism	166
5.4	The Scots input to MUE		171

| **6** | **Conclusions** | **178** |

| *Bibliography* | 189 |
| *Index* | 201 |

Abbreviations

BVE	Belfast Vernacular English
D1	First Dialect
D2	Second Dialect
EDG	*The English Dialect Grammar* (Wright 1905)
EModE	Early Modern English
IPA	International Phonetic Alphabet
IrE	Irish English
L1	First Language
L2	Second Language
LAS3	*Linguistic Atlas of Scotland*, Vol. 3 (Mather and Speitel 1986)
MBC	Morpheme Boundary Constraint
ME	Middle English
ModSc	Modern Scots
MUE	Mid-Ulster English
NDF	New Dialect Formation
OE	Old English
OSc	Older Scots
PFL	Pre-Fricative Lengthening
PPR	Pre-Palatal Raising
PreRD	Pre-R Dentalisation
PV	Palatal Velarisation
RP	Received Pronunciation
RRE	/r/-Realisation Effect
SED	*Survey of English Dialects* (Orton and Dieth 1962–71)
SIrE	Southern Irish English
SSE	Scottish Standard English
StE	Standard English
SUE	Southern Ulster English
SVLR	Scottish Vowel Length Rule
SwTE	South-west Tyrone English
TL	Target Language
TRS	*Tape Recorded Survey of Hiberno-English Speech* (Barry 1981a)
USc	Ulster Scots
VE	Voicing Effect
VP	Velar Palatalisation

1 Introduction

1.1 About this book

This book presents an investigation into the phonological origins of Mid-Ulster English (MUE), one of the primary dialects of English on the island of Ireland. Specifically it is an analysis of the development of the segmental phonology of the dialect and the input to this from English, Scots and Irish. Like other varieties of Irish English (IrE), MUE is an extra-territorial, new dialect of English, albeit one which has a history of over 400 years, making it one of the oldest 'new' dialects of the language. It developed in a context of contact between English, Scots and Irish in Ulster, the northernmost province of Ireland, as a result of English and Scottish migration to the island, especially during the Plantation of Ulster and its associated settlements in the seventeenth and early eighteenth centuries. Understanding the phonological development of MUE therefore requires us to take into account the nature of the contact that occurred between English, Scots and Irish in Ulster. In turn, an analysis of the phonological origins of MUE can help us to clarify aspects of this linguistic history, since the dialect which developed is one of the chief witnesses of it. This study, then, seeks not only to determine the phonological origins of MUE, but also to understand why the dialect developed the way it did and what the phonology of the dialect can tell us about the nature of contact between the input language varieties (English, Scots and Irish). In doing so, it demonstrates the kinds of analysis that are required to explain the development of colonial dialects in complex situations of contact, and provides a useful testing-ground for models of new dialect formation.

1.2 What is Mid-Ulster English?

Mid-Ulster English is a distinctive dialect (or group of similar dialects) of English spoken across much of the Irish province of Ulster, mostly but not exclusively within the bounds of Northern Ireland, including in the two largest cities in the region, Belfast and (London)Derry.[1] There is a considerable degree of variation within MUE, covering as it does working-class Belfast Vernacular English, middle-class non-regional and 'standardised' Northern Irish English (see Barry 1981b; Kingsmore 1995: 29), and traditional rural dialects in places like the author's native county, Tyrone, which were, until recent decades, the varieties spoken by most people in rural parts of the MUE region. It is these traditional forms of MUE with which this book is primarily concerned, as they tell us most about the phonological origins of the dialect (as opposed to ongoing variation and change in it).

Despite this internal variation, MUE stands in contrast to other varieties of IrE, not least in terms of its segmental phonology. Although MUE shares various features in common with other dialects of IrE (many of which are discussed in this book), it is also different from them in important respects. For example, Southern Irish English (SIrE) dialects usually have dental or alveolar stops where other dialects of English, including MUE, have dental fricatives (e.g. in *thin* and *this*). Similarly, there are significant divergences in vowel quality and quantity between MUE and other varieties of IrE. For example, the vowel system of SIrE dialects contrast phonemically short and long vowels, whilst vowel length in MUE is in large part allophonic (see Section 4.3).

These differences are a result of the unique history of the province. MUE is one of the earliest extra-territorial varieties of English, one which formed in a situation of contact between Irish, English (in various forms) and Scots as a result of the migration of large numbers of English and Scots speakers to Ulster, especially during the Plantation of Ulster and its associated settlements in the seventeenth and early eighteenth centuries. As such, it provides a useful case study for understanding the formation of a new dialect in situations of settlement colonisation (see Section 5.3.1) and for determining whether theories of new dialect formation (see Siegel 1985 and, particularly, Trudgill 2004) can be applied to older 'new' varieties of English in complex situations of contact between different languages (English and Irish), different dialects of the same language (dialects of English; dialects of Scots), and between divergent dialect groups of the same language or, alternatively, between two closely related languages (English and Scots). A central aim of this book is to show that it is possible to explain the phonological origins of older extra-territorial varieties of English such as MUE in much the same way as we can explain the origins of more recently developed varieties such as New Zealand English (Gordon *et al.* 2004; Trudgill 2004). Furthermore, the study of the phonological origins of MUE is not only important for understanding the development of English in Ireland. Speakers of MUE were a substantial component of the populations that gave rise to various other extra-territorial Englishes, especially in North America, Australia and New Zealand. An exploration of the dialect's phonological development is crucial, then, for understanding the potential input it and, at a further remove, the English, Scots and Irish dialects which contributed to it have had to these varieties.

Mid-Ulster English is not the only long-standing non-Irish variety spoken in Ulster. Ulster Scots (USc), which may be interpreted as a group of dialects of Scots or as a language in its own right (see Kallen 1999; Mac Póilin 1999; Montgomery 1999), developed in Ulster as a result of immigration of speakers of Scots dialects in the seventeenth and early eighteenth centuries (see Section 2.3.3). It became established as the vernacular speech of those areas of Ulster with the densest Scottish settlement, i.e. northern and eastern County Down, most of County Antrim, northern County (London)Derry and the Laggan area of County Donegal, and has retained close similarity with dialects of Scots in west and south-west Scotland. The geographical distribution of USc in the mid twentieth century was documented in Gregg (1972, 1985). Gregg surveyed the traditional rural dialect of 125 locations in Counties Down, Antrim, (London)Derry and Donegal in order to determine the location and nature of the border between USc and MUE. In his extensive analysis, he selected 665 individual words covering more than twenty key phonological and morphological features that are known to distinguish Scots and English. A subset of these data (fifty-two representative words) were used to determine the proportion of 'Scots' and 'English' variants at each location, with the striking result that informants were almost all very consistent in producing variants of one type or the other. This allowed Gregg to draw a sharp boundary between what he called 'Scotch-Irish' (i.e. USc) and 'Ulster Hiberno-English' (i.e. MUE) dialects. The result was Gregg's well-known 'Scotch-Irish Dialect Boundaries in Ulster' map (Gregg 1972: 132–3, 1985: Map 1), which has been used as a basis for maps of dialect boundaries in Ulster ever since (see, for example, Corrigan 2010: 16; Harris 1984: 117; Hickey 2007a: 442; Kingsmore 1995: 21; McCafferty 2001: Map 1; Robinson 1997: 17).

Gregg's important work has contributed enormously to understanding the dialect geography of Ulster, and the results of his survey are incorporated into the map in Figure 1.1 of this book, which, rather than repeating the dialect borders from Gregg's map, shows the locations he classified as USc and those he classified as MUE. One reason for this representation is that the dialect border drawn by Gregg is not

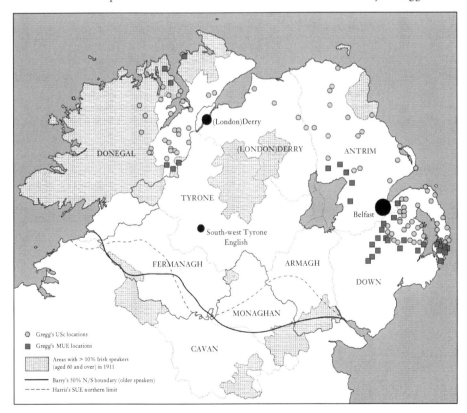

Fig. 1.1 The linguistic geography of Ulster.

Note: The outline of this map was drawn using the DMAP program (Morton 1993–2005).

unproblematic. Although his network of locations is often dense, the placement of the MUE–USc boundary involves a fair amount of (no doubt informed) guesswork, especially in Counties Antrim, (London)Derry and Donegal. In addition, Gregg's boundary line assumes an either/or distinction between USc and MUE, but at least two of his locations suggest that intermediate dialects exist (Gregg 1985: 87–8), and without a similar survey of locations across the 'MUE' area we cannot be sure that dialects with substantial evidence of Scots input don't lie further to the south and west (see ibid.: 14 and Harris 1984: 116 for some comments on this issue). Certainly, some of the features which Gregg identifies as USc and not MUE are common in traditional MUE dialects (see Section 1.4) such as South-west Tyrone English and the locations surveyed in the third volume of the *Linguistic Atlas of Scotland* (Mather and Speitel 1986), as is amply illustrated in the analyses in Chapters 3 and 4 of this book. And of course the two dialects share many other phonological features in common that were excluded from Gregg's analysis. The investigation in this book demonstrates that the input from Scots to the development of MUE was extensive, and it is possible that Gregg's boundary represents a sharpening of the distinction between USc and MUE in recent times rather than a long-standing distinction between areas of Scots and English speech.

To the south of the MUE dialect area lies SIrE, which in its various forms covers the provinces of Munster, Leinster, Connacht, and parts of Ulster. The boundary between northern and southern forms of IrE was investigated by Barry (1980), who used data from the 1970s *Tape Recorded Survey of Hiberno-English Speech* (TRS; Barry 1981a). This survey recorded free conversation and answers to 379 questions designed to elicit phonetic and phonological features of IrE accents across Ireland on a 20km^2 grid, collecting data from three informants (one child, one middle-aged adult and one older adult) at each location. Whilst the TRS was not strictly a survey of traditional dialect, the older age group in particular represents conservative forms of speech at the time. Barry analysed the distributions of twenty-five phonological features which showed north–south variation, calculating the percentage of 'Northern' vs 'Southern' answers at each location for each age group. The results of his analysis were a series of isogloss maps for individual features and overall percentage maps of northern forms for each age group. Although the boundary between areas with northern and southern forms was not sharp in the same way as between MUE and USc, clear patterns emerged from Barry's analysis. For the older speakers, a line at the 50 per cent northern/southern boundary ran from Carlingford Lough in the east to Upper Lough Erne and from there to Bundoran on the south Donegal coast, taking in all but the mostly southerly part of County Armagh, and most of Counties Monaghan, Fermanagh and Donegal, but excluding most of County Cavan. Surrounding this line is a transition zone, rather narrow to the north but more diffuse to the south, with some 'Northern' forms extending south towards Dublin and the Irish Midlands. The two younger age groups show a similar pattern, with some usually minor variation in the placement of various features and the 50 per cent line. Barry's 50 per cent line for his older speakers is shown on Figure 1.1.

Harris (1984, 1985) also mapped the boundary between northern and southern forms of IrE, but suggested a three-way division between MUE, 'Southern Ulster English' (SUE), and 'Southern Hiberno-English' (i.e. SIrE). SUE is a transitional dialect, roughly equivalent in geographical distribution to Barry's 50–75 per cent 'Northern' zone, though Harris defines SUE in a rather different way. Harris (1985: 15) states that SUE

> can be seen as a transitional dialect between southern H[iberno]E[nglish] on the one hand and U[lster]S[cots] and MUE on the other, since it combines the English dichotomous pattern of phonemic vowel length found in southern HE with some typically northern features of vowel quality.

The northern limits of his SUE zone (i.e. the southern boundary of MUE) is also indicated on Figure 1.1.

The dialects of English and Scots in Ulster have largely replaced Irish, which was once spoken throughout the province (see Section 2.6). Outside of Donegal, Irish survived longest in Rathlin Island and the Glens of Antrim, in the Sperrin Mountains of north Tyrone and south (London)Derry, and in pockets of south Ulster from Armagh to Cavan (see FitzGerald 2003), eventually dying out as a native language in the early to mid twentieth century. In Donegal, the language survived much better into the twentieth century, and continues to be spoken as a native language in parts of the county today. The areas identified in FitzGerald (2003) with over 10 per cent survival of Irish amongst those aged sixty and over in the 1911 census are indicated in the map in Figure 1.1.

In areas where Irish still survives or did so until recent decades, particular forms of English are spoken that are likely to show obvious evidence of influence from Irish in the same way that English spoken in the Gaeltacht areas in Connacht and Munster do (Gregg 1985: 11; Harris 1985: 15). Unfortunately these varieties of Ulster English have been little studied, though see Ní Ghallchóir (1981) and the data for the locations in the Glens of Antrim and the Sperrins in Henry (1958) and Mather and Speitel (1986). Gregg (1985: 11) suggests that this Gaeltacht English 'may be self-perpetuating in a few areas after the disappearance of Gaelic, although its ultimate fate would seem to be levelling under the pressure of U[lster]H[iberno] E[nglish]' (i.e. MUE). This study concerns itself with the long-established forms of MUE found in most of lowland Ulster, from Belfast in the east to Donegal Bay in the west, rather than these recent contact varieties, and assesses the impact of Irish on the dialect more generally rather than in the rather special cases where Irish survived into the twentieth century (and beyond in Donegal) and where speakers of English are, or were until recently, bilingual in Irish and English.

1.3 The phonological origins of Mid-Ulster English

MUE is phonologically rather different from varieties of English in Britain, and whilst it is distinct from other varieties of IrE, it also shares a not insignificant number of phonological features with them. Key questions are why the phonology of MUE is the way it is, and what has caused its distinctiveness.

One thing that's obviously different about MUE, and which may help to explain its similarities with other varieties of English in Ireland, is that it has been in contact with Irish. Since we know that languages in contact can influence each other (see, for example, Matras 2009; Thomason 2001; Thomason and Kaufman 1988), a possible explanation for the distinctiveness of MUE is that its phonology has been affected by Irish (e.g. by speakers of that language imperfectly learning English). This is indeed a common explanation for distinctive linguistic features of IrE dialects, including MUE (see Section 5.2), and given that we know that Irish and English have been in contact for centuries and that certain transparently Irish lexical and syntactic features have become established in IrE, it is not an unreasonable hypothesis.

However, this book in part grew out of a recognition that an Irish explanation for divergent phonological features of MUE and other dialects of IrE cannot be assumed, as it often has been. In numerous cases described in Chapters 3 and 4 of this book, explanations of phonological features of MUE (and other varieties of IrE) have invoked contact with Irish, often as a result of superficial similarity between the two languages in some respect(s), without a detailed examination of the evidence or a consideration of alternative hypotheses. In other words, Irish influence has been *assumed* to be the explanation for divergent phonological patterns in IrE without proper evidence being brought to bear on the issue. It could be that Irish has been involved in the development of some of these features, but it is not enough to assume that this is the case. Some examples, discussed later in this book, are:

- Clear [l] in IrE, including in MUE, has its origins in contact with Irish. Clear [l] occurs in all positions as the realisation of /l/ in MUE and other varieties of IrE, in contrast to mainstream varieties of English in Britain and elsewhere, which have dark [ɫ] in at least coda position. Kingsmore (1995: 18–19) states that

  > To some degree, Irish Gaelic has influenced all Ulster speech, particularly in outlying areas where there was greater contact between English and Irish. For example, all areas of Ulster tend to use a clear or nonvelarized /l/ in post-vocalic position.

  In other words, she (and she is not the only one, as noted in Section 3.9.2) explains the occurrence of clear [l] as the result of Irish influence on English in Ireland, including Ulster. But no explanation is offered as to why Irish, which has a complex system of palatalised and velarised laterals (see Section 3.1) should have caused clear [l] to occur in all environments in IrE. Furthermore, clear [l] in all positions is a feature of various dialects of English (and Scots) in Britain. This is particularly associated with Tyneside and Norfolk, but was once characteristic of much of England, as is apparent from descriptions of traditional dialects in sources such as the *Survey of English Dialects* (SED; Orton and Dieth 1962–71). Why, then, have some scholars assumed an Irish origin for the feature? It may be that Irish has played a role, but potential inputs from English (and Scots) also need to be evaluated and the possibility that the feature has a British origin in whole or in part should also be considered.

- Dental realisation of general English alveolar stops before /r/ and /ər/ are the result of Irish influence. These realisations are found in most conservative varieties of IrE, including traditional MUE, so that [t̪] and [d̪] occur in *try, dry, better* and *border*. Lunny (1981a: 166) recorded this 'Pre-R Dentalisation' (PreRD; see Maguire 2012a and Section 3.5 for discussion) in the English dialect of Ballyvourney in Cork (he used the symbols /T/ and /D/ for /t̪/ and /d̪/), noting that '[i]n Ballyvourney English in a cluster with mixed quality (according to Irish phonology), the quality of the final consonant still often determines whether the cluster is to be palatal or non-palatal and the appropriate consonant is substituted accordingly'. In other words, the feature is a consequence, in Lunny's view, of the application of an Irish phonological rule to the English learned by Irish speakers. As is discussed in Maguire (2012a), Lunny is not alone in this view. Lunny further added that

> [i]nitial /tr/ and /dr/ have become /tθr/, /θr/, /dðr/ and /ðr/ in some dialects of northern England … but it is not possible to establish any useful connection between this phenomenon and the appearance of dental /T/ and /D/ in similar contexts in Ballyvourney English.

In fact, an examination of descriptions of traditional northern dialects of English in sources such as the SED reveals *exactly* the same PreRD pattern as occurs in IrE. Why, then, must an Irish origin of the feature be assumed and an English origin ruled out? It is not enough to assume an Irish origin for a feature of IrE just because it is not typical of mainstream varieties of English in Britain and elsewhere, and a detailed analysis of the history and precise nature of the phenomenon, taking all of the input varieties into account, is required.

- Epenthesis in liquid+sonorant clusters, especially in /lm/, is of Irish origin. Perhaps the most famous IrE pronunciation of them all, also shared by MUE, is the insertion of an epenthetic vowel in the cluster /lm/ in words like *film* (e.g. ['fɪləm]). Given that a similar epenthesis also occurs in this cluster in Irish, a contact explanation has almost universally been assumed (see Maguire 2018 and Section 3.10). But as anyone who has lived in north-east England or Scotland can tell you, epenthesis in words like *film* is not restricted to Irish English. Indeed, as Maguire (2018) showed, it was found across Lowland Scotland and much of England in the mid twentieth century and has a long history in both English and Scots. Why, then, is contact with Irish a preferred explanation to inheritance from English (and Scots in Ulster), given that no such explanation is possible for the feature in English dialects? Again, an analysis of the sort reported in Maguire (2018) is required to determine the nature and history of the phenomenon so that a proper assessment of the likely roles of the input varieties can be made.

It may well be the case that Irish has been instrumental in the development of these and other phonological features of MUE (and of other varieties of IrE). But unless a detailed investigation is made, bringing in evidence from all of the input varieties and going beyond noticing superficial similarities, it should not be assumed. The role of historical and non-standard varieties of English and Scots, which were characterised by many features not found in mainstream present-day varieties of English in Britain and elsewhere, must also be assessed and should not be underestimated.

It may be that Irish has *not* played a role in the development of many distinctive phonological features of MUE or other varieties of IrE. If this is the case, we need to explain why contact between English and Irish in this part of Ireland has not led to contact-induced change. And denying Irish contact as an explanation for IrE phonological features is in no way a denial of the importance of Irish in Ireland, including in Ulster, neither in the past nor in the present. Regardless of what community we come from, some of our ancestors spoke Irish in the not too distant past, and it remains the language of many people in Ireland, north and south of the border today, as well as being the source of many of our personal names and place-names, and of various dialect words and other features of our Irish dialects of English. It has enormous historical, cultural and linguistic value across the island of Ireland. The loss of the language across the province and beyond is a linguistic and social tragedy, but this should not influence our search for the origins of the phonology of MUE and other dialects of IrE.

There has also been an assumption, especially amongst less linguistically informed commentators on the dialect, that MUE has some special relationship with Elizabethan English and the language of Shakespeare (see Section 5.3.2). For example, the nineteenth-century Belfast-born author St. John Greer Ervine 'advised his readers to go to Ulster if they wanted to hear English spoken as it was in Shakespeare's day' (Braidwood 1964: 46). Features given in evidence of such a connection include the forms *hit* for 'it' and *ax* for 'ask', both of which were used by Shakespeare and which are indeed found in the dialect (the former in particular being common amongst more conservative speakers). But as anyone who has studied Shakespeare in school in Ulster can tell you, speaking MUE, even in its more traditional forms, is not much help in understanding the works of the Bard. Is this claim of a connection between MUE and Elizabethan and Shakespearean English simply a myth, or are there aspects of the historical phonology of the dialect which back up such a hypothesis? Only a detailed investigation of the phonological origins of English in Ulster, covering a wide range of features, can hope to answer such a question, one which I return to in Chapter 5.

1.4 Sources and methods

The phonologies of the traditional dialects of English, Scots and Irish have been relatively well documented in various studies of individual dialects and in general surveys, in particular in Ellis (1889), Joseph Wright's *The English Dialect Grammar* (EDG; Wright 1905), the SED, the third volume of the *Linguistic Atlas of Scotland* (LAS3; Mather and Speitel 1986), and the *Linguistic Atlas and Survey of Irish Dialects* (Wagner 1958–64). There is of course much that we don't know about particular dialects and phonological features but the records that have been made and published provide us with a rich insight into the synchronic and diachronic phonologies of these languages.

The same is not true for dialects of IrE, including varieties of MUE. Very few monograph-length phonological descriptions have been published; notable exceptions include the description of the north Roscommon dialect in Henry (1957) and the analysis of the phonology of Belfast Vernacular English (BVE) in Harris (1985). And although there have been two surveys that have recorded data from traditional English dialects from across Ireland (*A Linguistic Survey of Ireland*, as described in Henry 1958, and the TRS, as reported in Barry 1981a), in neither case has the data been published, nor is the full extent of data collection clear. The TRS was not, in fact, a survey of traditional forms of Irish English, though doubtless its older participants often spoke traditional varieties. The survey of IrE accents detailed in Hickey (2004) contains much useful information on modern accents of MUE but does not usually contain data from more conservative speakers of the dialect. Dialects of Ulster Scots have received rather more attention (especially in the surveys reported in Gregg 1972, 1985 and in LAS3; see further below), though the coverage has been patchy and somewhat limited in scope.

That is not to say there is no information available on traditional dialects of MUE outside of Belfast. Information on the phonology of these dialects is scattered across many publications, as the analyses in Chapters 3 and 4 indicate. Harris (1985) is a particularly useful source of information, not only on BVE but also on various aspects of the phonology of traditional rural MUE dialects. Other key sources of information include the works of G. B. Adams (especially Adams 1948, 1950, 1966, 1967, 1986) and the MUE data contained in Gregg (1985) and in LAS3. The latter is a particularly good source of information on the phonology of traditional dialects of MUE. Although LAS3 is primarily a survey of Scottish dialects, it includes data from fifteen locations in Ulster (six in Co. Down, five in Co. Antrim, three in Co. Armagh and one in Co. (London)Derry). Most of these survey locations were, not surprisingly, characterised by Ulster Scots forms of speech. But the dialect recorded at Glenshesk in Co. Antrim was a variety of MUE influenced by USc and Irish (i.e. a form of post-Gaeltacht Ulster English), whilst the dialect recorded at Kilrea in Co. (London)Derry was a form of MUE obviously influenced by USc (Gregg 1985 recorded an USc dialect at the same location). Although the dialect recorded at Drumintee in south Armagh was a variety of SUE, the dialects recorded at Loughinisland and Annalong in Co. Down and Poyntzpass and Mount Norris in Co. Armagh were typical conservative MUE varieties and thus provide important sources of information on traditional MUE phonology. LAS3 provides a substantial amount of data on the consonant and, especially, vowel phonology of these dialects. Furthermore, the unpublished fieldworkers' notebooks for these locations (see Maguire 2020a) provide even more information on the phonetics and phonology of these traditional MUE dialects.

In addition to these, there is another very substantial (but as yet unpublished) source of information on the phonology of traditional MUE. This is a corpus of audio recordings collected by the current author of his native south-west Tyrone MUE dialect (for the location of this dialect, see Figure 1.1). This dialect is referred to in this book as 'South-west Tyrone English' (SwTE). From the start of the twenty-first century, I have been recording older Protestant and Catholic speakers of SwTE from the rural area south of Omagh in conversation and in various questionnaire and elicitation tasks. To this corpus has been added a small amount of recorded material of older speakers from the same area from the late 1980s and early 1990s. To date, this corpus consists of over forty hours of audio recordings, involving around thirty speakers, most of whom were born between 1900 and 1950.[2] The dialect recorded in the SwTE corpus is of a traditional MUE type (though some speakers are rather more traditional than others), and it is similar in general terms to other MUE dialects recorded in the sources described above. Although data collection is ongoing and analysis of the recordings is only at a preliminary stage, it is clear that the SwTE corpus provides a very substantial amount of information on the phonology of traditional MUE, constituting as it does the largest collection of data for any traditional Ulster dialect to date. Although this book does not present an analysis of SwTE, it does contain some analyses of subsets of the data and draws on it generally for describing and understanding phonological patterns in traditional rural MUE.

In order to explore and explain the phonological origins of MUE, data from these sources is compared in this book with historical and modern phonological patterns in English, Scots and Irish. Whilst the phonological history of English is fairly well understood and described (as, for example, in Dobson 1957; Lass 1992, 2000; Luick 1940; Minkova 2014; Wyld 1927), this is mostly in reference to the ancestor of Standard English (StE).[3] A great deal of further information on the phonological history of English can be gained from analysis of phonological patterns in non-standard dialects. As is discussed in Maguire (2012a), for example, the widespread IrE (and MUE) feature 'Pre-R Dentalisation' (PreRD; see Section 3.5) is hardly attested in the English historical record, but is well recorded, in a form which is essentially identical to what is found in Ireland, in traditional nineteenth- and twentieth-century dialects of English. The data from these modern dialects of English is crucial for understanding the history of the feature in the language, and comparison of MUE with traditional English dialects as documented in sources such as the SED reveals many such parallels which inform the analysis in this book. The same is true of Scots, the phonological development of which is detailed in Aitken and Macafee (2002) in particular. When combined with information from modern studies and surveys (see especially LAS3, including the unpublished data underlying the survey described in Maguire 2020a, and Johnston 1997b), this provides a detailed picture of the historical phonology of the language. The historical phonology of Irish has been subject to rather less analysis (though see, for example, the chapters in McCone *et al.* 1994; Ó Maolalaigh 1997), but the data that we do have for the phonology of the language, both in general terms and for its modern dialects, permits the same kinds of comparison, as the analyses in Chapters 3 and 4 of this book repeatedly demonstrate.

1.5 Structure of this book

This book is structured as follows. Chapter 2 reviews the linguistic history of northern Ireland, concentrating in particular on the Plantation of Ulster and its associated settlements in the seventeenth and early eighteenth centuries and the subsequent shift from Irish to English in the province. It also examines the issue of whether the ethno-religious dimension has played a role in the phonological development of MUE. Whilst the history of Ulster is obviously crucial for understanding the phonological development of MUE, there are various aspects of it which remain uncertain, and I suggest that the linguistic features of MUE itself provide useful evidence for the linguistic history of the province. Chapters 3 and 4 consist of a wide-ranging analysis of the phonological origins of MUE, with features of the dialect compared in detail to diachronic and synchronic patterns in English, Scots and Irish. Although much can be learned from examining the origins of a single phonological feature (see, for example, Maguire 2018 for the case of epenthesis in liquid+sonorant clusters), a central point in this book is that in order to understand the phonological origins of this (or any other) dialect, and to assess the importance of the English, Scots and Irish input to it, a large number of features should be examined. In this way, the risk of cherry-picking the data in order to confirm a particular hypothesis (cf. the discussion of possible Irish influence in Section 5.2) can be avoided. In examining a large number of features which have not been specifically chosen to highlight the contribution of any one input variety, a better understanding of the various roles of the English, Scots and Irish inputs will be possible. Thus in Chapter 3 I analyse the origins of thirty-six consonantal features in MUE, covering much of the consonantal system and the distributions and realisations of its members, whilst in Chapter 4 I analyse the origins of the quality, quantity and lexical distribution of the dialect's vowel system. The analyses in these two chapters reveal three general patterns which would not be apparent from examination of a small number of features. Firstly, the input from Irish to the dialect's phonology has been slight, mostly consisting of possible reinforcement of features already present in the English and Scots inputs. Secondly, the dialect is of a somewhat conservative, non-regional Midland and/or southern English type in key respects, particularly in terms of the lexical distribution of its vowels and in its consonantal realisations. Thirdly, the Scots input has had a noticeable impact on the realisation of the dialect's vowels, in terms of both their quality and quantity, whilst it has also played a role in the development of its consonant system and of specific aspects of the lexical distribution of vowels. These patterns are discussed in Chapter 5 in reference to theories of language contact and shift, reinforcement, koinéisation, new dialect formation and colonial lag. It will be seen that the three general patterns identified in the analysis of consonantal and vocalic features in MUE can be explained through a combination of (largely) unidirectional bilingualism, a gradual, long-term language shift from Irish, the mixed origin of the English settlers and their dialects, the geographical and socio-political peripheralisation of the dialect, and through adult speakers of Scots learning English in Ulster in the seventeenth and early eighteenth centuries. In Chapter 6, the approach and analysis presented in this book are reviewed, and its contribution towards an explanation of the formation of English in Ulster and in Ireland, and of extra-territorial varieties more generally, is highlighted.

Notes

1. The name of the city and county to which the latter refers is infamously contentious. I follow McCafferty (2001: 6) in using the format '(London)Derry', in this case for both the city and the county regardless of the historical period under discussion.
2. Speakers in the SwTE corpus are identified as either Catholic (C) or Protestant (P), female (F) or male (M), and by the year of their birth in the twentieth century. So, for example, PM43 is a Protestant male born in 1943.
3. Throughout this book I use the term 'Standard English' (StE) to refer, in a phonological context, to varieties of (British) English which are phonologically similar to Received Pronunciation (RP), particularly in terms of the lexical distribution of vowel phonemes. RP is a specific accent or range of accents of StE. In referring to the phonological history of StE and to the phonology of Early Modern

(varieties of) StE, I refer to those relatively non-regional forms of speech that were characteristic of educated speakers (including orthoepists and grammarians) of the periods under discussion, which were distinct from the phonologically divergent regional dialects of English, and which fed into, or were similar to those varieties which fed into, the phonology of modern RP English and other varieties of present-day (British) StE.

2 Background

2.1 Preliminaries

The linguistic geography of Ulster and the unique nature of the Mid-Ulster dialect of English spoken there are products of the complicated history of the province. As was noted in Chapter 1, MUE is a 'new' dialect of English that developed in a context of contact between English, Scots and Irish in northern Ireland as a result of migration from England and Scotland to Ulster, and the purpose of this chapter is to examine what this contact involved. Key questions for understanding the phonological development of MUE are:

1. When and in what varieties were English and Scots brought to Ulster, and how significant were the populations that spoke them?
2. What were the circumstances of contact with Irish, how did the shift from Irish to English happen, and what was the timescale of this shift?
3. Does the ethno-religious divide, which has been so important in the history of the province, have any relevance for understanding the phonological development of MUE?

This chapter reviews the history of English, Scots and Irish in Ulster in order to begin to answer these questions. The chapter is structured as follows. In Section 2.2, I review the history of Ulster between the twelfth and the sixteenth centuries, assessing the extent to which English was likely to have been present in the province. In Section 2.3, I examine the seventeenth-century Plantation of Ulster and its associated settlements, including the nature of the settlements, the geographical origins of the settlers, the effects of the Plantation on the native Irish, and continued settlement into the early eighteenth century. In Section 2.4, I consider the demographic and linguistic effects of these settlements and their importance for understanding the phonological origins of MUE, whilst in Section 2.5 I review aspects of the history of the province in subsequent centuries that may also have had important linguistic consequences. In Sections 2.6 and 2.7, I examine in detail two issues which relate to the history of the province in the centuries since the Plantation: the decline of Irish in Ulster and the linguistic effects of the ethno-religious divide. Both of these are profoundly important for understanding the linguistic and social history of the province, but their impact on the phonological development of MUE is less certain, and I return to them throughout this book, especially in Chapter 5. I offer concluding remarks to this review of the linguistic history of Ulster in Section 2.8.

It should be pointed out at this stage, however, that there is much about the linguistic history of the province that remains unknown and which may never be recoverable, including, for example, the degree of survival of pre-Plantation English in Ulster, the precise linguistic varieties spoken by Scottish settlers, the extent to which settlers learned Irish, and the exact origins of the English tenants during the Plantation of Ulster. We can make educated guesses about all of these and other points of interest (as I do throughout this chapter), but it will inevitably be the case that a great deal of uncertainty remains. Nevertheless, it will also be seen that the history of language in the province suggests particular relationships between the varieties that have been in contact, and these relationships help to explain the phonological origins of MUE.

2.2 English in Ulster before the seventeenth century

The first significant introduction of English to Ireland came with the Anglo-Norman intrusion into Leinster and the subsequent invasion of the island in the second half of the twelfth century AD (see Cosgrove 1987 for a history of this period). Although the initial areas of Anglo-Norman control centred on Dublin, Wexford and Waterford, it was not long before this was extended northwards to Ulster. In 1177, John de Courcy undertook an invasion of the province, and over the following years he established Anglo-Norman rule in most of Counties Antrim and Down, founding settlements at strategic points, especially at Carrickfergus on the shore of Belfast Lough. However, Bardon (1992: 38) notes that 'there was no exten-sive colonisation' in this period, and that 'the great majority in the earldom were Irish and for the most part it was they who farmed the land' (ibid.: 46). Nevertheless, it was the beginning of four centuries of fitful English rule in Ulster that was only secured with the Elizabethan conquest in the second half of the sixteenth century. Throughout this period, small numbers of settlers and their descendants occupied manors and towns in the east and north of the province, especially in and around Carrickfergus, Coleraine, Downpatrick and Newry. In addition to the English, there was also settlement and incursion from Scotland at various points in this period, for example from Galloway (ibid.: 41–2, 67), and the Bruce invasion of Ireland (includ-ing Scots-speaking soldiers from the Lowlands) between 1315 and 1318, which marked the beginning of a decline in the English colony in Ulster lasting until the Tudor period. During most of the fourteenth and fifteenth centuries, there was little effective English rule in Ulster, and the colony ultimately dwindled to the bastion of Carrickfergus, mirroring the similar retraction of English power further south in Ireland to the Pale around Dublin.

The extent to which English was spoken in Ulster throughout this period is uncer-tain. It must have been present in the chief settlements, but these constituted a much more limited colony than what existed further south in Ireland, in the Pale around Dublin and beyond. Outside of this area, the 'English' settlers often 'nativised'. As Bardon (1992: 54) puts it,

[o]ther lords of Norman origin, who for generations had intermarried with the Irish, adopted Gaelic speech and customs. Seeming to fit the description 'more Irish than the Irish themselves' . . . they showed scant regard for weakening royal authority and ruled great tracts of the Irish countryside as independent warlords.

The same process of nativisation occurred amongst some of the 'Old English' (i.e. these early English settlers and their descendants) in Ulster too (Corrigan 2010: 114). It is unlikely that much English survived in the declining colony outside of Carrickfergus, which was 'described in 1468 as "a garrison of war . . . surrounded by Irish and Scots, without succour of the English for sixty miles"' (Bardon 1992: 67). Bliss (1977: 26) argues that 'by the end of the fifteenth century little English was heard except in the Pale . . . and in the towns' (see also Filppula 1999: 4–6 for a useful summary). However, Kallen (2013: 18–19) expresses the opinion that Bliss's view is overly pessimistic and argues that

> [i]f we understand these towns as focal points for networks of English speakers with common political and economic interests as well as a common language, we can suggest that they had a stronger linguistic significance than their strict population numbers would imply.

Whether such an argument can be made for Ulster outside of Carrickfergus, in towns like Coleraine and Newry, is another matter.

Some Scots must also have been spoken in Ulster during this period (e.g. by 'Lowland spearmen' of the Bruce invasion, as noted in Bardon 1992: 49), but this is unlikely to have been a significant element in the linguistic landscape of these centuries, and was no doubt dwarfed by Gaelic input from Scotland (e.g. from the MacDonnells of Islay and Kintyre, who settled in County Antrim at the start of the sixteenth century).

In the sixteenth century, the Tudor governors in Ireland began to reassert the power of the Crown in Ulster, though mostly via punitive actions from areas to the south under secure English control (see Moody *et al.* 1976 and Bardon 1992: 69–114 for the history of this period). Nevertheless, the results were significant and had important consequences for the later history of the province. Ulster lords submitted to the authority of the English Crown and were persuaded 'to drop their traditional Gaelic titles and give up their lands, receiving them back from the king with English titles' (Bardon 1992: 71). This meant that any lord who repudiated English authority was in rebellion against the Crown, and could, theoretically at least, lose his lands and titles. It was inevitable, then, that some of the Gaelic lords of Ulster, determined to maintain their independence and power, should find themselves in conflict with their supposed feudal masters. Throughout the second half of the sixteenth century, the forces of Queen Elizabeth sought to dominate the lords of Ulster in a series of brutal campaigns that ultimately led to the end of the Gaelic order in Ulster. The presence of garrisons of English soldiers at places like Armagh, (London)Derry and Newry was the first step in the transformation of the linguistic geography of the province that would result from the large-scale colonial settlements of the following century. As early as the 1570s there were attempts at settlement in east Ulster (see Section 2.3.1), as part of a growing English philosophy that the only way to pacify

Ireland was to transport large numbers of loyal English citizens to the island, though these came to nothing due to the unstable political situation in the province. But they were a sign of the way things were heading, and it was only a matter of time before British dominance was achieved in Ulster and full-scale plantation began.

2.3 The Plantation of Ulster and its associated settlements

When the Gaelic lords of Ulster submitted to the English Crown in the late sixteenth century, their lands were granted to them on condition of loyalty and due service. But because of their resentment of their British masters, in no small part due to aggravations engineered by the English themselves, many of the Gaelic lords turned to rebellion. The inevitable consequence was their loss of title and land, most notably as a result of the 'Flight of the Earls' in 1607, in which some of the most prominent members of the Ulster Gaelic aristocracy quit the province rather than face imprisonment or death.

The Flight of the Earls and the crushing of Sir Cahir O'Doherty's rebellion in the north of the province meant that most of Ulster outside of Antrim and Down (which were already being colonised, as described in Section 2.3.1) fell directly under the control of the Crown. In 1603 this passed to James VI of Scotland, who also became James I of England and Ireland, uniting the Crowns and preparing the way for Lowland Scottish as well as English involvement in Ulster. The situation in the province provided James with the ideal opportunity not only to reap economic benefit from Ulster, but also to install Protestant British owners and tenants on the land who would be loyal to the Crown. In order to bring about these circumstances, a grand scheme of Plantation was drawn up (see Bardon 2011: 111–41).

The aim of the Plantation of Ulster and its associated settlements was to establish a population in the province that was British in politics and Protestant in religion. This was to be done not only for economic benefit, but to secure it from the Irish and from the threat of invasion, via the Irish 'back door', from elsewhere in Europe (see Bardon 2011: 20, 27–37). The Plantation was a process of what is termed 'settlement colonisation' (Mufwene 2001: 9). Schneider (2007: 25), refining Mufwene's definition, describes settlement colonisation (in the context of European settlement of other parts of the globe) as a process whereby

> large numbers of Europeans migrated to new continents to settle there, typically carrying out manual, mostly agricultural, labor themselves, and due to their ever-increasing numbers and their military and economical superiority they established themselves as the dominant power and marginalized indigenous peoples.

Schneider contrasts this with what he terms 'plantation colonies', in which 'European settlers imported laborers from elsewhere and reserved ownership and managerial roles to themselves' (ibid.).

The Plantation of Ulster was only one such scheme in Ireland, and not the first, though it was the most successful by far. In addition to the failed settlements in the Ards and Clandeboye in east Ulster in the 1570s (see Section 2.3.1), there was the Plantation of Laois (renamed 'Queen's County') and Offaly (renamed 'King's County') in the 1550s and the Plantation of Munster in the 1580s. The less than successful Plantation of Laois and Offaly was 'an ambitious scheme to colonise these two counties with loyal subjects' in which '[t]he Gaelic nobles were either executed or expelled, but a proposal to drive out or slaughter all the native Irish inhabitants of the counties had been rejected' (Bardon 2011: 6). The Plantation of Munster followed the defeat of the rebelling FitzGerald lords of the province, who forfeited their territory (much of which was depopulated by war and famine), and was a scheme 'to settle people of English birth on the confiscated lands' (ibid.: 19). This involved the division of the forfeited lands 'into portions of between four thousand and twelve thousand acres, each granted to an "undertaker", that is, a man who undertook to bring in a specified number of families to work the land' (ibid.: 19). There were to be no Irish tenants of these lands. Despite the granting of estates to undertakers and some English settlement, the Plantation of Munster failed due to the size of the estates, which meant that the tenants who did come were not numerous enough to farm the lands, and the subsequent Nine Years' War, which drove most of the settlers from the plantation estates.

2.3.1 Antrim and Down

In 1571, Sir Thomas Smith, Provost of Eton and a vice-chancellor of Cambridge, was granted lands in Counties Antrim and Down by Queen Elizabeth, and he set about planning a plantation of his new territory with British Protestants who were loyal to the Crown (Bardon 2011: 1). A second plantation, led by Walter Devereux, Earl of Essex, also attempted to establish a British Protestant presence in these counties in 1573 (ibid.: 2). Both of these early attempts at plantation failed due to insufficient numbers of settlers, poor planning and an underestimation of the hardships involved, resistance from the Irish and a fair measure of bad luck.

Counties Antrim and Down were not included in the official scheme for the Plantation of Ulster, but they were, nevertheless, subject to large-scale settlement from Britain. In order to escape imprisonment, Conn Mac Néill O'Neill, Lord of Upper Clandeboye, agreed to a deal in 1605 to divide his vast territories in Antrim and Down between himself and his Scottish benefactors, Hugh Montgomery and James Hamilton. These men began the plantation of Protestant settlers from Britain in Ulster, a condition of their grants from the Crown (Bardon 2011: 77), and it was not long before other Irish lords in the two counties followed suit and 'made room for servitors and colonisers in return for a secure title in English law to their estates' (Bardon 1992: 121). For example, Sir Randal MacDonnell, once a major enemy of the Elizabethan forces in Ireland, submitted to the English throne in 1602, and was given royal grant of his large estates in north Antrim in 1604. A condition of this grant was that he should organise his territory along plantation lines, dividing it into manors. Randal invited large numbers of Protestant Lowland Scots to settle on his estates, despite himself being a Gaelic-speaking Catholic and one-time enemy of the Crown. He also included (Gaelic-speaking) Catholics from the Hebrides and Kintyre amongst the planters on his estates, who mostly settled in the Glens of Antrim (Bardon 2011: 80–5). However, most plantation settlers in Counties Antrim and Down came from south-west Scotland, as a result of the origins of the landowners and the close proximity of this part of Ulster to their home country, though

Belfast and the Lagan Valley in particular attracted many English landowners and settlers.

2.3.2 The escheated counties

The official plantation of the 'escheated counties' (i.e. Cavan, Armagh, (London) Derry, Donegal, Fermanagh and Tyrone, which defaulted to the Crown with the removal of most of the Gaelic aristocracy) began with surveys of the lands and division of them into portions, the best of which were to be bid for by Scottish and English Protestant undertakers. These undertakers were required to be resident on their portions for five years, after which they could sell them if they wished, but only to Protestants. In addition, lands were granted to 'servitors' (British veterans of the wars in Ulster) and to Irish landowners who had remained loyal to the British Crown (though their allotted portions often did not equate with the lands that they had previously held), whilst substantial areas were retained by or given over to the Church, educational establishments, the towns, and the City of London (Bardon 2011: 137–8). All of these were to be subject to plantation too. It was a theoretical requirement of the grants to undertakers that they not only settle their lands with Protestants but that they remove the Irish from their estates. The same requirement was not placed on the servitors, though their rents were lower if they followed suit.

The establishment of corporate towns (or boroughs) across Ulster was a major component of the Plantation (see Robinson 1984: 150–71 for discussion). Towns served various purposes, included acting as commercial, military, legal, religious and educational centres, and supplying (Protestant) burgesses for the Dublin parliament. The Plantation plan of 1611 was for there to be twenty-four boroughs in Ulster, some building on older urban settlements, others new, though not all of them ended up as incorporated boroughs. Many other, usually smaller, market towns without corporate status also developed in Ulster in this period, so that there were over 100 towns in Ulster by the middle of the seventeenth century. The population of most of these towns was low (at least by modern standards), all but four of them having populations of fewer than 500 adults by 1659. The four biggest were (London)Derry (with 1,052 adult residents), Carrickfergus (with 962 adult residents), Coleraine (with 633 adult residents) and Belfast (with 589 adult residents). Nevertheless, together they formed an important component in the landscape and contained a substantial proportion of the population, which was otherwise distributed across the province in villages and farmsteads (indeed, many tenants dispersed to the farmlands after settlement despite it being a requirement of Plantation that they live in towns and villages; see ibid.: 158–61). The towns were settled by merchants, traders and artisans, drawn from both England and Scotland (though not necessarily in equal measure in any given place), and acted as important locations for the establishment of English and Scots in Ulster and for contact between different input dialects.

2.3.3 The origins of the English and Scottish settlers

The English Plantation undertakers and servitors mostly came from the Midlands and south of England. For example, Robinson (1984: 202–4) lists just over thirty

English undertakers in the early years of the Plantation, of whom eleven were from East Anglia, six from the north and west Midlands (Leicestershire, Nottinghamshire, Staffordshire and Shropshire), with others from Bedfordshire, London, Oxfordshire and Somerset. Braidwood (1964) gives details of undertakers across Ulster through-out the Plantation period from Bedfordshire, Cambridgeshire, Cheshire, Devon, Essex, Gloucestershire, Lancashire, London, Middlesex, Norfolk, Nottinghamshire, Oxfordshire, Shropshire, Somerset, Staffordshire, Suffolk, Surrey, Warwickshire and Yorkshire. Undertakers from different parts of England were present in the same counties in Ulster. For example, Braidwood (1964: 11–14) lists English estate owners in south Antrim from Cheshire, Devon, Gloucestershire, Lancashire, Warwickshire and Yorkshire, whilst he lists undertakers in Tyrone from Devon, Essex, Oxfordshire, Staffordshire and Suffolk (ibid.: 28–30).

These undertakers attracted tenants to their plantation portions from their estates and adjoining lands, and sometimes from elsewhere in England (Bardon 2011: 146). For example, Sir George Rawdon from the Leeds area brought in tenants from his Yorkshire estates to the Moira and Ballynahinch areas in County Down (Braidwood 1964: 14), whilst Sir Thomas Ridgeway of Devon 'brought tenants from London and Devon' to his lands in the Clogher Valley in Tyrone (ibid.: 28). Given the origins of the undertakers, the majority of these English tenants in Ulster are likely to have come from East Anglia, the Midlands and the south of England rather than from areas further to the north, but with no one place of origin dominating. To these were added other English migrants later in the seventeenth century, including substan-tial numbers from the north-west of England, who settled in the Lagan Valley and Armagh (Bardon 2011: 296). The English settlers would have spoken a wide variety of Early Modern East Anglian, southern, Midland and north-west English dialects, whilst early forms of StE and supraregional varieties of English must also have been spoken by landowners and settlers.

The Scottish undertakers came from across Lowland Scotland, includ-ing Kincardineshire in the north-east, Haddingtonshire in the south-east and Wigtonshire in the south-west, but especially from the Lothians, around the Clyde, and Ayrshire (Perceval-Maxwell 1973: 92–106, 368). However, the several dozen Scottish undertakers (ibid.: 317–58) were of course vastly outnumbered by their Scottish tenants; Perceval-Maxwell (1973: 289) estimates that during the Jacobite Plantation some 14,000 adult Scottish settlers came to Ulster. These predominantly came 'from the eight counties which lay either along the border with England, or up the west coast to Argyll' (ibid.). This distribution is illustrated in map form in Fischer (1989: 619), which shows a scattering of tenants coming from across Lowland Scotland, but the vast majority of them from Renfrewshire, Ayrshire and Wigtonshire, with substantial input also from Argyll and Bute, Lanarkshire, Kirkcudbrightshire, Dumfriesshire, Roxburghshire and Berwickshire. However, tenants from these different areas were not distributed evenly across Ulster. For example, settlers with surnames associated with the Scottish Borders were particularly common in Fermanagh and Tyrone, whilst the other coun-ties received the majority of their Scottish settlers from the west and south-west counties, especially Renfrewshire, Lanarkshire, Ayrshire and Wigtonshire, though Borderers were present there too (Perceval-Maxwell 1973: 287–9). That said, there was also a fair degree of internal movement of settlers once they came to Ulster, complicating the picture further. As is described in Section 2.3.4, Scottish settlement increased in the second half of the seventeenth century and into the eighteenth century, dwarfing what had gone before. Given the geographical origins of the Scottish settlers, both in the first and second waves of settlement, the Scots dialects that they brought to Ulster were Early Modern forms of West-Mid, South-Mid and South Scots.

Although Scottish and English settlers predominated in particular areas (see Robinson 1984: 94 for a useful illustration in map form), there was much contact between and intermingling of the two groups. This was the result of a variety of factors. Firstly, Plantation portions within each county were granted to a mix of English and Scottish undertakers. For example, thirteen portions were granted to English undertakers and fifteen to Scottish undertakers in Tyrone (Braidwood 1964: 28; see also Robinson 1978). This meant that even when English and Scottish undertakers settled their estates with planters from their home countries English and Scots settlers were neighbours within the same county. Secondly, there was a considerable degree of mixing of English and Scottish planters within estates, regardless of the origins of the undertakers. Whilst English estates mostly had English tenants and Scottish estates Scottish tenants (see Robinson 1984: 119–23 for examples), there were estates which had a mix of both. A good example is provided by the 'English' Audley estates around Omagh in County Tyrone, which had as many Scottish as English tenants, indeed more of each than was required in the terms of Lord Audley's grants (Braidwood 1964: 28–9), and this was not an isolated case. Thirdly, the initial state of plantation was considerably altered by sales of land and internal migration of settlers within Ulster, so that there was further mixing of planters from the various parts of Britain, and to this were added later waves of settlers from England and Scotland in the late seventeenth and early eighteenth centuries, complicating the demographic (and linguistic) picture further. The result was that although certain areas were more or less Scottish or English, most parts of Ulster had settlers from both backgrounds to one degree or another. Robinson's map of indices of Scottish settlement (Robinson 1984: 110) reveals that in large swathes of the province in the early twentieth century over 50 per cent of the Protestant population were Presbyterian or had surnames of Scottish origin, reflecting the density of Scottish settlement in earlier centuries. But it also obscures more fine-grained patterns, since it uses a 50 per cent cut-off for these distinctions, and the proportion of Protestants who were Presbyterians and/or had Scottish surnames in the predominantly 'English' zone he identifies was far from negligible. This is illustrated by the more fine-grained analysis in Robinson (1974). Although the English were the majority settlers across much of the MUE area, this was only just the case, with most of the province having levels of Scottish surnames of 45 per cent or more. For example, Robinson's map of Scottish surnames in mid-twentieth-century Ulster (ibid.: 192–3) shows that they predominate amongst Protestants not only in the Ulster Scots-speaking areas, but also across most of (London)Derry, north Tyrone and inland Down, and are found at levels of between 45 and 50 per cent across most of the rest of Tyrone, south Down and north Fermanagh, i.e. most of the MUE area. This reflects similar patterns in the mid seventeenth century, mapped in Robinson (1974: 203–4). The same kind of pattern holds for the distribution of Anglican and Presbyterian Protestants in the province in the mid nineteenth century (ibid.: 187–8).

2.3.4 Later settlements

As is typical with settlement colonisation, the Plantation of Ulster took on a life of its own, far outstripping and outlasting the original plans of James I. Settlers from England and Scotland continued to be attracted to Ulster (and other parts of Ireland) throughout the seventeenth century and into the early eighteenth century for a variety of reasons. These included population pressures and poor economic conditions in Britain, the ready availability of cheap land and tenancies in Ulster, the restless nature of many settlers and landowners (who not infrequently sold their lots and moved on), the attraction of a land remote from political, legal and religious authorities, and continuing political instability and land confiscations in the province and elsewhere. After the Cromwellian conquest of Ireland in the middle of the seventeenth century, most of the Catholic landowners who remained in Ulster lost their properties. These lands were granted to those who had supported Cromwell financially or militarily, which, given that Cromwell's Act of Settlement targeted Royalist Presbyterians as well as Catholics, initially attracted new settlers from England rather than from Scotland (see Bardon 2011: 286–91). However, with the abandonment of punitive measures against the Presbyterians, new waves of Scottish settlers poured into the province. Although the Plantation of Ulster and the plantations in Antrim and Down brought large numbers of Scottish settlers to the province in the first half of the seventeenth century, Scots were more likely to migrate to Poland or Scandinavia in this period (ibid.: 303–5). But in the 1650s, migration of Scots to the continent tailed off, and at the same time Scottish settlement in Ulster began to surge, a trend which continued during and after the Williamite Wars towards the end of the century. Bardon (2011: 306) estimates that somewhere between 60,000 and 100,000 Scots came to Ulster between 1650 and 1700, a figure which is 'between three and four times as many as had migrated in the first half of the century'. This new wave of Scottish settlers came particularly from Glasgow, Wigtonshire and Kirkcudbrightshire, rather than from Ayrshire, which had supplied the majority of earlier tenants. These new arrivals settled widely across Ulster, not concentrating, as many earlier Scottish settlers had, in Antrim and Down, whilst Belfast also received many of this second wave of Scottish migrants (ibid.: 306–8). These Scottish settlers ensured that there was a Protestant majority in Ulster by the early eighteenth century, and it is likely that settlers in Ulster of Scottish origin outnumbered those of English origin as a result of late-seventeenth and early-eighteenth-century migration.

2.3.5 Other settlements in Ireland

The Plantation of Ulster and its associated settlements was part of a wider pattern of British colonisation of Ireland in the late sixteenth century and the seventeenth century, and thus was not an isolated phenomenon, though it was the most extensive and thoroughgoing element of this process. In addition to the long-established

'British' population in Dublin and the Pale, and late-sixteenth-century plantations in Laois, Offaly and Munster (see the introduction to Section 2.3), there were further early-seventeenth-century plantations across the other provinces of Ireland, including in Cork, Laois, Leitrim, Longford, Westmeath and Wexford (Moody *et al.* 1976). Though these plantations did attract settlers from England, they were never as significant as the settlements in Ulster, though they were instrumental in establishing English in southern Ireland beyond its eastern heartlands. The Cromwellian confiscations and settlements also had a significant effect, with many Catholic landowners losing their lands, substantial removal of Catholics to Connacht, and the granting of lands to supporters and thousands of soldiers, though many of these latter 'went native very quickly' (Bardon 2011: 291). Kallen (2013: 25) notes, however, that all of this

> gave further power to the spread of English, not only by providing new populations for whom the L[ow] domain of everyday communication was dominated by English, but by establishing English-dominated H[igh] domains in new relationships of law, administration, and land ownership.

Nevertheless, by 1659, the only county outside of Ulster to have an English population of greater than 20 per cent was Dublin, whilst in other areas the English were concentrated in the towns in counties that were for the most part overwhelmingly inhabited by the Irish (ibid.: 26–7). Just as the Plantation of Ulster was unique in the history of British colonisation of Ireland in terms of the numbers and origins of its settlers, so it was unique in the extent to which Irish was replaced, in the seventeenth century, by the language of the settlers.

2.3.6 The Irish

Although Sir Thomas Smith's plantation of parts of Counties Antrim and Down in the 1570s failed (see Section 2.3.1), his plans contained an unambiguous statement of his attitude towards the Irish that was shared by many of those who took part in the seventeenth-century Plantation of Ulster. Bardon (2011: 1) tells us that 'Smith made it clear that he intended to sweep away the native Irish', except those who were needed for agricultural labour. In a pamphlet, Smith outlined his thoughts as follows: 'Every Irishman shall be forbidden to wear English apparel or weapon upon pain of death. That no Irishman, born of Irish race and brought up Irish, shall purchase land, bear office, be chosen of any jury' (ibid.). The settlement of Ulster was to be a British, Protestant affair, and the Irish, in as much as they had any place in the process at all, were to be relegated to second-class citizens at all levels of society.

The removal of the majority of the Irish Gaelic aristocracy and the carving up of their lands for plantation meant that most landowners in Ulster became British Protestants, though there were some Catholic landowners who had taken the Oath of Supremacy too (e.g. Lord Audley in Tyrone), and a number of Irish lords were granted land (up to 20 per cent of the total), albeit not necessarily their own, often not as much as they had originally owned, and in some cases only for the duration of the owners' lives (Bardon 2011: 137, 159, 161). Undertakers in the official Plantation scheme 'were required to clear natives of all classes completely from their estates' (ibid.: 137), though the same condition was not placed upon the servitors and Irish landowners. In theory this meant that the Irish 'would have to uproot themselves and squeeze into those precincts set aside for servitors and native Irish' (ibid.; see also Bardon 2011: 159), something which would, had it been carried through, have had massive demographic and linguistic (never mind personal and humanitarian) consequences. In fact, although there was some removal of the Irish, most of them stayed put during the Plantation, though they were often subject to considerable changes in status and place of occupation within the estates. There were three main reasons why 'James I's determination to remove all the natives from the estates of the leading planters came to nothing' (ibid.: ix). Firstly, the size of the Plantation estates was usually underestimated, sometimes radically so, so that the number of settlers who came to or could be attracted to the estates was often insufficient to farm the land. The Irish were thus required to ensure continued agricultural production on the Plantation estates, providing as they did substantial menial labour. Secondly, the Irish often refused to leave, preferring to become insecure tenants to Protestant masters than to lose access to the lands they had always farmed. Furthermore, many of the Protestant landowners refused to remove the Irish from their lands. In addition to recognising the strife and suffering this would cause, they knew that the Irish were essential for ensuring the proper functioning of the estates. They also provided crucial rents, which could be set at higher rates and with less secure conditions than those of the settlers. Thus it was the case that 'most of the Irish – reduced in status, with burdensome rents and uncertain tenures – remained to farm the land' (ibid.: ix), at least for the time being, even if they weren't content with their new station in society. But as the seventeenth century wore on and the amount of land owned by Catholics continued to diminish, even these Catholic tenants 'found that they were being forced onto poorer or more inaccessible land' (ibid.: 292–3).

2.4 Demographic and linguistic transformation in the seventeenth and early eighteenth centuries

The Plantation and its associated settlements led to a demographic transformation of Ulster, which was of course one of its primary aims. This dramatic demographic change inevitably led to a significant linguistic transformation of the province, which ultimately gave rise to MUE (and USc). Prior to the Plantation, English settlers can only have made up a small percentage of the population, and English, though an important language politically, was probably confined to small numbers of speakers in the towns and manors in the east of the province. This small 'founding population' (see Section 5.3.1) was swamped by the large numbers of settlers who arrived from England and Scotland throughout the seventeenth and early eighteenth centuries. By 1630, it is estimated that there were around 14,500 British men in Ulster (Robinson 1984: 104), who, together with their families, must have represented a substantial proportion of the population. By around 1659, Robinson (1984: 104–5) estimates, based on the numbers of individuals enumerated in a census 'compiled from poll-tax returns', that there were around 20,000 British males in Ulster. This census, which unfortunately does not distinguish between Scottish and English settlers, only included adult males and married or widowed females, so the absolute numbers are rather less informative than the proportions of British and Irish individuals recorded. Although figures are missing for Tyrone and Cavan, the census reveals that 37 per cent of individuals recorded in the rest of Ulster were British, whilst 63 per cent were Irish. Robinson (1984: 105) gives the following percentages of British individuals for the counties: Antrim, 45 per cent; Armagh, 35 per cent; Donegal, 28 per cent; Down, 43 per cent; Fermanagh, 25 per cent; (London) Derry, 45 per cent; Monaghan, 11 per cent. In other words, British settlers made up a substantial proportion of the population in all counties, in some of them almost half of the population. This represents a massive demographic, political, cultural and linguistic change in Ulster over fifty years, dwarfing the limited British settlements in the province prior to the Plantation. It also shows that the initial idea of clearing the Irish from the settlement lands had never been realised.

The English settlers in Ulster spoke a variety of dialects of English, whilst most of the settlers from Scotland came from the Lowlands and would have spoken Early Modern dialects of Mid and South Scots. Although some of the Scottish settlers, particularly those from Argyll but also some from Galloway (see Adams 1976: 85), must have spoken Scottish Gaelic, this can only have represented a small proportion of the Scottish linguistic input to Ulster, and was massively outnumbered by Scots speakers from the Central Belt, Ayrshire, much of the south-west and from the Borders. The suggestion in Ó Snodaigh (1995: 30; see also p. 32) that the 'Gaelic-speaking element among' Scottish Presbyterian settlers in Ulster 'was a very large one, possibly the majority' is not supported by the known geographical origins of the Scottish settlers or the extent of Gaelic in the seventeenth century, nor by the existence of substantial Gaelic-speaking communities of Scottish settlers in Ulster (see further Livingston 2012 and McCoy 1997: 5). Whilst some Gaelic must indeed have been present amongst the settlers, in specific areas at least, the lack of evidence of influence from the language on USc or MUE also speaks strongly against such prominence. Nevertheless, the settlers, both Scottish and English, were surrounded by speakers of Irish and the development of a degree of bilingualism amongst some of the settlers was inevitable, not only as a communicative necessity, but also because some 'young Protestants learned Irish from nurses, household servants and tenants' (ibid.). But this bilingualism was inhibited by two main factors. Firstly, settler attitudes towards the Irish and their language were often negative, as might be expected in a situation of settlement colonisation (Schneider 2007). McCoy (1997: 60) suggests that many of the settlers viewed the Irish as inferior, and their language as 'backward' and as a 'vehicle of seditious thoughts', and 'equated a knowledge of English with an acceptance of English rule, and the Irish language with anti-English sentiments'. Given the overwhelming cultural and political dominance of English, it is not surprising that '[t]hese attitudes were internalised by many Irish speakers, who were anxious that their children should learn English and abandon the use of Irish' (McCoy 1997: 61). This meant, secondly, that the Irish were much more likely to learn English than the settlers were to learn Irish, so that most of the bilingualism that existed was found amongst the native population. McCoy (1997: 5) makes the important point concerning Irish that 'as the number of monoglots fell, the need and opportunity for newcomers to learn the language declined as a consequence'. Thus widespread bilingualism (of a significant sort at least) in the settler population was unlikely, and indeed became less likely as time went on.

Assuming, as we must, that the (mostly Protestant) English and Scottish Plantation settlers did not learn Irish in large numbers (and mostly did not speak Scottish Gaelic either), and that the (Catholic) Irish were under pressure to learn English from the start of the colonial process, it can be conjectured, given the census figures of the time, that at least around 40 per cent of the population of Ulster spoke English or Scots by 1659, and this figure may have been rather higher if we assume large-scale bilingualism amongst the Irish. Certainly Corrigan (2010: 121) suggests that this was the case in the seventeenth century, with 'stable Irish–English bilingualism' prevailing in 'rural areas near centres of influence like the new market towns established by the British', and with 'unstable bilingualism with Gaelic[1] increasingly recessive (particularly amongst urbanites in more established towns and villages)'. In 1682, William Brooke, in his description of the Barony of Oneilland in north Armagh, observed that 'the few Irish we have amongst us are very much reclaimed of their barbarous customs, the most of them speaking English' (quoted in Bardon 2011: 298). From the start there must, then, have been a fairly strong association in Ulster between Irishness, Catholicism and the Irish language on the one hand, and between Britishness, Protestantism and English/Scots on the other, even if these correlations were never absolute (for example, as a result of small numbers of Catholic settlers and Gaelic-speaking Protestant Scottish settlers, and a degree of conversion and intermarriage, as well as bilingualism amongst the native Irish population in particular).

As is described in Section 2.3.4, British settlement of Ulster continued throughout the seventeenth century and into the early eighteenth century from both England and Scotland. The numbers of settlers and their descendants thus increased substantially, and this is reflected in population figures from 1732, which enumerate the numbers of Protestants and Catholics in Ulster. The account of population changes in the late seventeenth and early eighteenth centuries in Bardon (2011: 306–7) suggests that this increase in the number of Protestants in the province reflects this surge in settlement rather than any large-scale conversion of Catholics to Protestantism (though this must have been a part of the story too, as discussed in Adams 1976: 83–5). To suggest otherwise would be to deny that the massive numbers of later settlers had a significant impact on the demography of the province. Overall in 1732, 61.95 per cent of the population of Ulster was Protestant, a large increase from the 37 per cent (mostly Protestant British settlers) of seventy years before. In all counties except Cavan, Monaghan and Tyrone, Protestants were in the majority, in some cases considerably so. The figures per county (see Bardon 2011: 307, Elliot 2000: map 6; Macafee and Morgan 1981) were: Antrim, 71 per cent; Armagh, 65 per cent; Cavan, 24 per cent; Donegal, 57 per cent; Down, 73 per cent; Fermanagh, 58 per cent; (London)Derry, 76 per cent; Monaghan, 36 per cent; and Tyrone, 48 per cent. Given the fairly strong (but not absolute) correlations between Irish, Catholicism and non-British identity described by McCoy (1997), and the increasing replacement of Irish by English in the province, it is reasonable to suggest that by this date English and Scots were spoken by more than 60 per cent of the population of Ulster, and the figure may have been rather higher than this, depending upon the extent to which English (and potentially Scots) had made substantial inroads into formerly Irish monolingual communities. This is so even if we allow for a degree of bilingualism amongst some settlers and their descendants and for some continued use of Irish amongst Catholics who converted to Protestantism in this period (though this is unlikely to have been sustained for long, as noted in Adams 1976: 84).

Of course, it is not the case that there was a one-to-one equivalence between British identity, Protestantism and lack of knowledge of Irish, nor between Irish identity, Catholicism and knowledge of the Irish language. Catholic settlers, Scottish Gaelic speakers and converts in both directions, as well as a degree of intermarriage and bilingualism, inevitably complicated the picture (see Bardon 1992: 400–1). But these factors must have correlated strongly in the seventeenth and early eighteenth centuries, given that the settlers and their descendants were mostly Protestant speakers of English and Scots, whilst the Irish were mostly Catholics and frequently spoke Irish (whilst at the same time learning English in many cases). As a result, the population figures described above can be used to arrive at a rough upper estimate of the likely levels of Irish speech in Ulster during this period. If 37 per cent of the population is estimated to be British settlers in 1659, then it is reasonable to suggest that no more than about 60 per cent of the population spoke Irish to any significant degree, given that there is little likelihood of substantial bilingualism amongst the settlers and the inevitable need for the Irish to learn English. Likewise, the fact that 62 per cent of the population of Ulster was Protestant in 1732 does not mean that every one of those Protestants was a monolingual English- or Scots-speaking settler or a descendant of settlers. But it does suggest that in the absence of large-scale Protestant bilingualism, conversions and intermingling of the Irish and settler populations in the preceding century (though all of these things occurred to an extent), Irish was unlikely to have been spoken by any more than about 40 per cent of the population, and the figure may be rather lower than this given that many of the Irish would have learned English by this point. It is clear, with these caveats in mind, that the Plantation of Ulster and its associated settlements led not only to a demographic but also a linguistic transformation of the province. It also created the correlations between origins, political affiliation, religion and language that coalesced into the ethno-religious Protestant and Catholic identities of the subsequent centuries.

2.5 Ulster in subsequent centuries

The Plantation and its associated settlements set the scene for the demographic make-up of Ulster and the political tensions that have characterised the province over the centuries. Although there was a strong correlation between religion and settler/native identity in the seventeenth and early eighteenth centuries, and although the two ethno-religious groups in Ulster and Northern Ireland in subsequent centuries have their origins in this division (see Corrigan 2010: 25), this is not the same as saying that there is a direct, genetic continuation between British settlers and Protestants and between Irish natives and Catholics. Even at low levels, several centuries of conversions (often with name changes) and intermarriage, in addition to the 'Old English' and to Catholic and Gaelic-speaking settlers, mean that we are dealing with ethno-religious rather than genetic groups (Bardon 1992: 400–2). Many Protestants (the present author included) have surnames of Irish origin, and many Catholics have surnames of British origin. Nevertheless, we shouldn't take this too far and deny that the two ethno-religious groups have their religious, political and, to an extent, ethnic origins in the Plantation and its associated settlement. In the majority of cases, children would have maintained the religion of their parents and would have married within their own ethno-religious group, as is still the case in Northern Ireland today. The close correlations between settlement history, religion and surnames highlighted in Robinson (1974, 1984) cannot be by chance, nor can they have resulted from conversions and name changes subsequently. Thus the native, Catholic, Irish and settler, Protestant, British identities of the Plantation period transformed into the two distinct ethno-religious groups that have characterised Ulster ever since.

Although the period of settlements came to an end in the early 1700s, the rest of the eighteenth century was a time of considerable change and turmoil for both communities. A series of cattle plagues, harvest failures and severe winters led to famine and disease, most notably in 1728–9 and 1740–1. Bardon (1992: 176) notes that in the 1740–1 famine 'perhaps around three hundred thousand died' across Ireland and that this was 'a death toll in proportion as terrible as the Great Famine of the 1840s'. In Ulster as elsewhere, the people who were hit hardest by the famine were the rural Catholic poor, and this *Bliadhain an Áir* ('Year of Slaughter') can only have accelerated the decline of Irish in Ulster described in Section 2.6. The dreadful conditions in Ulster in this period, combined with the poor quality of much of the land in the province (see ibid.: 179), meant that this new colony did not turn out to be the land of opportunity that many must have hoped it would be. As a result, there was a large-scale departure from Ulster to the colonies in America of those who had the means to do so. As Bardon (1992: 177) puts it:

> The migration across the Atlantic got under way just at the time that the coming of Scots into Ulster had almost completely ceased. Catholics had neither the resources nor the inclination to go to colonies, which were in any case still overwhelmingly Protestant.

Presbyterians in particular departed in large numbers. The scale of this emigration was alarming to those who wished to ensure Protestant domination in Ulster, though it is unlikely that the thousands who left in the late 1720s outnumbered the many thousands of Catholics who must have died in the province in the *Bliadhain an Áir* and the other famines of the period. Nevertheless, the departure of tens of thousands of 'Scotch Irish' from Ulster through the course of the eighteenth century and into the nineteenth century must have had some balancing effect on the demographics of the province, and of course was important in the development of English in the New World, so that the study of the origins of MUE phonology is also, in part, the study of the origins of the phonology of American English (Milroy 1981: 3–4).

Despite these extreme conditions and changes, the economy in Ulster began to boom in the eighteenth century, in large part because of the linen industry (see Bardon 1992: 179–88; see also Ó Gráda 1989: 118–20). The production of linen was carried out across the province, but was particularly characteristic of the 'Linen Triangle' (demarcated by the towns of Lisburn, Armagh and Dungannon; see Boldorf 2015). This densely populated, economically prosperous and mostly Protestant area in County Down, north Armagh and east Tyrone was an important focal point in the MUE dialect territory, and to these can be added the city of Belfast which, by the end of the eighteenth century, had a (mostly Protestant) population of around 18,000 and had become the largest port in Ulster due to its role in the cotton and linen industries (Bardon 1992: 203). The importance and size of Belfast increased even more in the nineteenth century as a result of the industrial revolution (ship-building being the most well-known industry) and migration to the city from across rural Ulster and beyond. By 1850, the population of Belfast had risen to 80,000, and had exploded to 350,000 by the start of the twentieth century (Harris 1985: 139; see also Milroy 1981: 22). A major factor in this population boom was migration of people from rural areas of western Ulster to the city, many of whom were Catholic (Harris 1985: 138). This was of course a response to the opportunities which the industrial revolution gave rise to, but it was fuelled in large part by the continuing hardships of life in the Ulster countryside, most particularly by the catastrophic potato famines of the second half of the 1840s. As a result of the prosperity of the eighteenth century, there had been a considerable increase in the population of the province (see Bardon 1992: 268–71), and most of the population (and their livestock) depended on the potato crop for sustenance. The Great Famine, combined with harsh winters and disease, led to the deaths of around 1,000,000 people across Ireland (Donnelly 1989: 350–3), and although Ulster, especially in the east, was hit less hard than other parts of Ireland, the poorest, often Catholic, communities in rural parts of the province were particularly affected. In addition to deaths by starvation and disease, tens of thousands of people, most of them poor and many of them Catholic, left their homes to escape deprivation, migrating to Belfast and other urban areas, or leaving Ireland altogether, especially for Britain and North America (Bardon 1992: 308–12). In all, the population of Ulster fell by 374,000 (15.7 per cent of the total population) as a result of death and emigration (Bardon 1992: 307–8). This led to a substantial depletion of the population of many areas where Irish was most common, hastening its demise over much of the province (see Section 2.6). Large-scale internal migration to Belfast and other urban areas resulted in a considerable degree of dialect contact, and helped to produced the Belfast Vernacular MUE that we know today (see Milroy 1981; Harris 1985), which is considerably less Scots in character than its location might lead us to expect (Harris 1985: 140; see also Gregg 1972: 132–3). It also helped to shape the ethno-religious geography of Belfast. Harris (1985: 139) notes that

> Episcopalians (Church of Ireland) are concentrated in the south of the city, reflecting the dominance of English settlement in the Lagan Valley. The east and north of the city, which were settled primarily from rural areas where Scottish settlement was densest (i.e. north Down and mid and north Antrim), contain high proportions of Presbyterians. West Belfast is one of the most recently settled areas of the inner city, the population here being predominantly Catholic with a background in south and west Ulster.

The ethno-religious tensions that have characterised Belfast and Northern Ireland in recent decades are, of course, nothing new from a wider Ulster perspective, having as they do their origins in the colonial settlements and wars of the seventeenth century. From the 1641 rebellion (see Bardon 2011: 270–82) and the 1688–91

Williamite Wars (Bardon 1992: 150–65; Simms 1976) through the sectarian strife and rebellion of the 1790s (Bardon 1992: 223–37) to the Home Rule movement and the Ulster Crisis at the end of the nineteenth and start of the twentieth centuries (ibid.: 400–54), distrust, division and conflict has rarely been far away, reflecting and reinforcing the primary ethno-religious social division in the province. Whether this ethno-religious division has had linguistic consequences in considered in Section 2.7, but it is also only part of the story of the history of Ulster. Throughout the centuries since the Plantation, Protestants and Catholics have lived and worked side by side, as they did in most parts of Northern Ireland even during the darkest days of the Troubles in the second half of the twentieth century, and indeed more significant exchanges between the two communities, in the form of conversions and intermarriage, have always characterised the province, as previously noted. In addition, whilst it is true that Ulster Protestants have, by and large, had a British identity and Ulster Catholics have not (ibid.: 402), it shouldn't be assumed that the two communities never had any common ground. Indeed, the political alliances between Catholics and Presbyterians in the late eighteenth century (ibid.: 216–23; see also McDowell 1986), Protestant support for Home Rule (Comerford 1989: 66–7) and Protestant involvement in the Gaelic Revival (Bardon 1992: 419–22; Blaney 1996: 175–82) indicate the complexity of interactions between religion and political identity in the province.

By the time of the Partition of Ireland in 1921 (Bardon 1992: 476–9), a response to the different political and ethno-religious character of much of Ulster, MUE had been in existence for several centuries and was much as we know it, in its traditional forms at least, in recent decades (see, for example, Patterson 1860; Staples 1896; and the data for the MUE locations in LAS3, which were gathered from speakers who were born at the end of the nineteenth and start of the twentieth centuries; several of the oldest speakers in the SwTE corpus were also born before Partition). There is little evidence that the Border has affected the development of MUE significantly, though Harris (1991: 46) suggested that

> it is difficult to avoid the conclusion that unionists and nationalists simply do not share the same set of prestige linguistic norms ... The impression that strikes anyone who is familiar with the sociolinguistic situation in the North is that, for some nationalists, linguistic targets dictating the direction of standardisation appear to be defined at least in part by southern norms.

The effects of standardisation, supraregionalisation and dialect levelling that are particularly characteristic of our modern age of education, communication and travel are likely to be the most important factors in the future development of MUE, but these lie beyond the scope of the investigation in this book. The phonological origins of MUE, then, lie in the centuries before Partition, with the dialect nowadays being spoken not only in Northern Ireland, but also in adjacent parts of Counties Donegal and Monaghan in the Republic of Ireland (see Figure 1.1). By the time of the creation of the Border, Irish was in its last stages of decline in the province outside of Donegal, but for most of its history MUE was in contact with Irish, and the nature of this contact is an important part of the history of the dialect, a topic which is explored in the following section.

2.6 The decline of Irish in Ulster

The discussion in Section 2.4 suggested possible levels of Irish use in Ulster in the mid seventeenth and early eighteenth centuries, though they are rough estimates, if not unreasonable ones, given that these are based on ethnicity and religion rather than on actual figures of language use. Data for the use of Irish in Ulster become rather better for the late eighteenth century and especially the nineteenth. In an important pair of publications, FitzGerald (1984, 2003), building on research by Adams (1964b, 1973, 1974, 1975, 1976, 1979), charted the survival and decline of Irish from 1771 to 1871 across Ireland, including in Ulster. FitzGerald analysed data from 1881 and 1911 in particular, and also used data from the 1851 and 1861 censuses. Unfortunately in neither case does FitzGerald (nor Adams) give figures for the extent to which Irish was used by the two ethno-religious communities, but it is clear from the geographical distribution of Irish speakers, found in areas which were and are strongly Catholic (see Robinson 1982: 20–1), that most speakers of the language were Catholic in this period. For example, Ó Tuathail (1933: xi) reports that McEvoy, in his 1802 'Statistical Survey of County Tyrone', states that

> except through the wilds of Munterloney (chiefly in the barony of Strabane) the English language is most prevalent; indeed throughout the county it is gaining ground every day. The Roman Catholics are the only sect who are fond of speaking the Irish language, and with them too it is wearing off very much.

Similarly, Braidwood (1964: 20) reports that John Dubourdieu recorded in his 1802 'Statistical Survey of the County of Down' that

> [t]he English language is so general that every person speaks it; but, notwithstanding, the Irish language is much used in the mountainous parts, which in this, as well as in most other countries, seem to have been the retreat of the ancient inhabitants.

FitzGerald's analysis of the nineteenth-century census data relied on answers given to the question on Irish language use by successive decennial cohorts. It was in 1881 that this question was properly incorporated into the census, whilst in previous decades it was included as a footnote only, so that it often remained unanswered. This means that the figures for Irish use from the 1851 and 1861 censuses are rather lower than expected, as is revealed by a comparison of equivalent cohorts in the 1881 census on the one hand and the 1851 and 1861 censuses on the other. Since the 1881 census gave a much more reliable indication of Irish use, FitzGerald (1984) extrapolated from these differences to give a better idea of levels of Irish use amongst those born between 1771 and 1791 who were only recorded in the earlier censuses.

As a useful comparison to the nineteenth-century data, FitzGerald (2003) analysed the levels of Irish reported in the 1911 census by those aged 60 and above. This census also provided much more detail on the distribution of Irish, since figures are available for district electoral divisions, unlike the nineteenth-century censuses, which reported figures for the much larger baronies only. These figures thus give an indication of levels of Irish use of those born during or shortly before the Famine (see also Figure 1.1 in this book). The combination of FitzGerald's two analyses

Table 2.1 Percentage of population speaking Irish in Ulster and by county in the nineteenth-century censuses (FitzGerald 1984: 127).

County	1771–81	1801–11	1831–41	1861–71
Antrim	3	2	1	0
Armagh	18	15	8	1
Cavan	39	29	8	0
Donegal	56	53	40	29
Down	3	1	0	0
Fermanagh	16	9	2	0
(London)Derry	10	7	4	1
Monaghan	33	28	11	1
Tyrone	19	14	7	3
Total	19	15	8	4

Table 2.2 Percentage of the population aged 60 and over speaking Irish in the 1911 census (FitzGerald 2003: 281).

County	%	Monoglots
Antrim	1.6	
Armagh	5.8	
Belfast	1.4	
Cavan	6.6	
Donegal	46.8	6.4
Down	0.7	
Fermanagh	1.6	
(London)Derry	2.9	
Monaghan	9.1	
Tyrone	8.9	
Total	9.8	0.9

allows us to see how Irish survived and declined in Ulster in the late eighteenth and throughout the nineteenth century in detail.

Tables 2.1 and 2.2 give the percentage of Irish survival for each county in Ulster (and for Belfast in the 1911 census) and for the province as a whole as reported in FitzGerald's two analyses. Table 2.1 provides figures for selected decades in his study of the nineteenth-century censuses, the figures for 1771–81 relying on extrapolation based on differences between equivalent cohorts in the 1881 census and the 1851 and 1861 censuses as noted previously. Table 2.2 gives figures from his analysis of the 1911 census, and includes the numbers of monoglot Irish speakers (found only in Donegal).

These figures show that there were significant numbers of Irish speakers in most counties of Ulster in the late eighteenth century, but that the language had almost entirely disappeared from most of the province by the late nineteenth century. County Donegal stands out as the stronghold of Ulster Irish, and this is reflected in the survival of the language there into the twenty-first century. Elsewhere in Ulster levels of Irish were lower, often much lower. In Counties Antrim and Down in particular, levels of Irish use were negligible even in the late eighteenth century, despite the survival of the language in the Glens of Antrim and on Rathlin Island into the first half of the twentieth century (Holmer 1940, 1942). Armagh, Fermanagh, (London)Derry and Tyrone lie between these extremes, with levels of Irish of between 10 and 19 per cent in the late eighteenth century falling to negligible levels in the late nineteenth century, though Irish continued to be spoken in parts of (London)Derry, Armagh and, especially, Tyrone into the early and mid twentieth century (Sommerfelt 1929; Wagner and Ó Baoill 1969: 285–6, 288–94; Stockman and Wagner 1965). Counties Cavan (outside of the MUE area) and Monaghan (only the northern third of which falls in the MUE area) represent cases of a sharp decline in Irish over this century.

Figure 2.1, based on FitzGerald's eighteenth- and nineteenth-century figures in Table 2.1, shows the trend of decline in Irish in Counties Antrim, Armagh, Down, Fermanagh, (London)Derry and Tyrone, which between them cover most of the MUE and USc area (Donegal also has areas of MUE and USc speech, but is a rather different case with regard to the survival of Irish, as noted above).

The trend is generally the same in all of these counties, regardless of the 1771–81 levels of Irish use, with Irish being steadily lost throughout this period across the province. The figures from FitzGerald's analysis of the 1911 census (Table 2.2) fit well into this trend. The loss of Irish in Fermanagh is particularly sharp, though it did not fare much better in Tyrone and, especially, Armagh. That

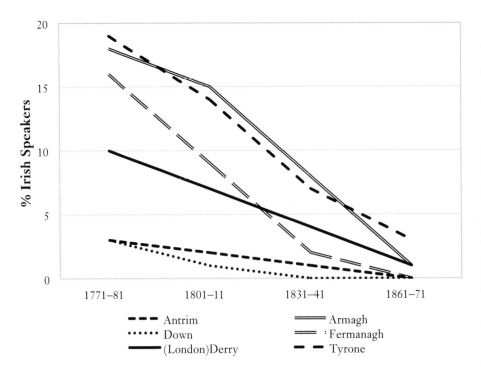

Fig. 2.1 Decline of Irish between 1771 and 1871 in Counties Antrim, Armagh, Down, Fermanagh, (London)Derry and Tyrone.

said, the 1771 levels of Irish use in all of these counties was already fairly low, so that this doesn't so much represent a sudden cliff-edge drop in Irish use but rather the end of a longer, gradual decline of the language across most of the MUE (and USc) area.

The analyses of levels of Irish use by county provide a useful summary of trends, but they also obscure important patterns of survival of the language in the MUE and USc areas. FitzGerald (1984, 2003) maps the data from these censuses (by barony for the nineteenth-century censuses and by dispensary districts and district electoral divisions for the 1911 census). The maps in FitzGerald (2003) in particular illustrate in fine detail the survival of the language into the mid nineteenth century (see also Figure 1.1 in this book). Outside of Donegal, there are four main areas of Irish survival in Ulster, all of them in peripheral rural, often upland areas with relatively low populations. In the north-east, surrounded by USc-speaking territory, Irish survived in the Glens of Antrim and Rathlin Island, at levels of 100 per cent in Rathlin and up to 50 per cent in the Glens of Antrim for speakers aged 60 or over in the 1911 census. In two areas in the SUE zone, south Armagh and south Monaghan on the one hand, and west Cavan on the other, Irish also survived to an extent, at levels of up to 50 per cent (and occasionally higher) amongst speaker aged 60 or over in 1911. The only area of significant Irish survival in the mid nineteenth century in the MUE zone was in the Sperrin Mountains, in north Tyrone and south (London)Derry. Here, Irish was spoken at levels of over 90 per cent in a few district electoral divisions in the middle of this area, and at lower levels in surrounding divisions, by speakers aged 60 or over in 1911. But the high levels in these parts of Tyrone and elsewhere were atypical of Ulster (outside of Donegal) more generally, especially in lowland and urban areas, as the figures in Table 2.2 indicate. Otherwise, Irish was almost entirely absent from the MUE area, with only isolated pockets of low-level Irish use (typically less than 10 per cent) reported in the 1911 census in these and the other counties of Ulster (outside of Donegal). Perhaps the most striking thing about the maps in FitzGerald (2003) is not how much Irish had survived in Ulster but how much white space (i.e. no Irish) there was across most of the province in the mid nineteenth century, a pattern which continues the trends seen in the maps of the nineteenth-century data provided in FitzGerald (1984). It is fair to say that most MUE speakers outside of Donegal would not have been much exposed to Irish, never mind have spoken the language, throughout most of the nineteenth century, and this was true for many of them even in the late eighteenth century.

Although figures for levels of Irish use in the seventeenth and early eighteenth centuries are not available, the population figures discussed in Section 2.4 can, as discussed previously, be used to give us a very rough guide to the likely state of the language and its change from the Plantation period onwards. As noted in Section 2.4, an estimated 37 per cent of the population of Ulster were of British origin in 1659, and they were unlikely to have learned Irish (or have spoken Scottish Gaelic) in significant numbers. Thus we can assume that around 40 per cent of the population did not speak Irish in 1659, and the figure may have been higher given that the native population may already have begun to abandon Irish in and around the new settlement towns (see Corrigan 2010: 121).

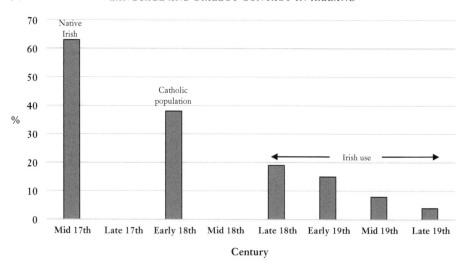

Fig. 2.2 Percentages of native Irish, Catholics and Irish speakers in Ulster.

By the time we get to 1732, 62 per cent of the population of Ulster was Protestant, a figure which, Bardon (2011) suggests, was mostly the consequence of continued settlement throughout the seventeenth century and into the early eighteenth century rather than a result of widespread conversion of the Irish to Protestantism. As was argued in Section 2.4, this figure implies that no more than 40 per cent of the population of the province was likely to have spoken Irish by this time, and indeed the figure may have been rather lower given the ongoing loss of Irish amongst the Irish/Catholic population, especially in urban and lowland areas.

When we add to these rough estimates the figures for Irish usage from the later census data described above, interesting patterns emerge, as illustrated in Figure 2.2 (there are no equivalent figures for the late seventeenth or mid eighteenth centuries, but these periods are included so as not to obscure the trend in the data). Given the rough correlations between language use, population and religion described in this chapter, Figure 2.2 indicates that the loss of Irish in Ulster was firstly a consequence of the large numbers of non-Irish-speaking settlers in the province in the seventeenth century and the lack of substantial language shift to Irish by the Protestant 'British' population in the eighteenth century, and secondly the decline of Irish amongst the Catholic population throughout this period. The eighteenth century was an important period of change, no doubt connected with the famines that hit the poorest (i.e. rural Catholic) part of the population hardest, and the fall in the proportion of the population speaking Irish that must have resulted was only partially offset by the large-scale migration of Ulster Protestants to the New World (see Section 2.5). Even where Irish was maintained bilingualism with English was the norm, so that by the nineteenth century the language had mostly disappeared outside of its upland strongholds (mostly in Donegal). At no point was there a 'cliff-edge' in this loss of Irish whereby a majority of the Irish-speaking population (never mind the population as a whole) suddenly shifted to English. Rather the change was gradual, with Irish receding from the towns and lowlands, with bilingualism permeating the Irish-speaking communities, and with the language slowly contracting into the uplands until it became extinct in most areas.

2.7 The ethno-religious dimension

The division between the two 'ethno-religious' groups, Catholics and Protestants (for overviews of the issue, see Corrigan 2010: 25–7; McCafferty 2001: 67–129), has, in one form or another, played a fundamental role in the history of Ulster over the last four centuries. It would be surprising if it has not also had linguistic consequences given the differing histories, and places and practices of worship, marriage, education, employment, commerce, socialisation and celebration, never mind differences in politics, ideology and identity, that have characterised the two communities, even when they live side by side.

However, much linguistic work on Ulster English has either side-stepped the issue or has failed to find significant ethno-religious linguistic differences, despite anecdotal evidence that such a difference exists. For example, Harris (1991: 46) states that 'the local wisdom is that "Catholics speak differently from Protestants"', and presumably this involves more than the stereotype that Protestants say 'aitch' for the letter <h>, whilst Catholics say 'haitch' (Kingsmore 1995: 35). Indeed, that such a difference might exist has been denied by some researchers. For example, Henry (1995: 7–8) states that

> [o]ne of the interesting characteristics of Belfast English is that, although Belfast is known to be in many ways a divided society, with often little contact between the Protestant and Catholic communities, Belfast English is not distinguished, either pho-nologically or grammatically, along religious lines ... where there is any distinction in usage, it is between working- and middle-class speakers or older and younger speakers, rather than along religious lines. It is simply not possible to tell to which community persons belong by how they speak English.

This failure to identify ethno-religious differences has been dubbed the 'Belfast Paradox' (McCafferty 2001: 42): how is it that the two communities, which are so distinct in many other ways, appear to differ little linguistically, and indeed appear 'to be undergoing a process of increased focusing that goes against the grain of greater ethnic polarisation in the society in question' (ibid.)?

In fact, some studies of English in Ulster *have* revealed linguistic differences between the speech of Catholics and Protestants, though these are statistical rather than categorical differences. McCafferty (2001: 35–66) reviews the evidence from a range of studies and finds that 'ethnicity does appear to be a factor that affects the spread of linguistic change between neighbourhoods in Belfast ... The ethnic dimension is an important factor in relation to change in Northern Ireland's largest, most influential speech community' and that 'ethnicity may be a factor in determining the use of (conservative) dialect forms in rural communities as well' (McCafferty 2001: 63, 64).

Of particular importance in this respect is McCafferty's own research on the MUE dialect of (London)Derry (McCafferty 1999, 2001). McCafferty sought to determine the social factors involved in linguistic variation in this divided city. He analysed the pronunciation of a range of phonological variables (see McCafferty 2001: 136–66) in the speech of a large sample of speakers, each of whom was categorised as older or younger, working class or middle class, and Protestant or Catholic. McCafferty found that age, class and ethno-religious group all impacted on the linguistic behaviour of people from (London)Derry, and that these factors interacted. For example, the [ʌ] variant of the FOOT[2] vowel was much more characteristic of working-class speech than of middle-class speech (where [ʉ] was common), though Protestant middle-class speakers were somewhat more likely to use [ʉ] (at levels of around 60 per cent) than Catholic middle-class speakers (at levels of around 50 per cent). The use of the [iə] diphthong in the FACE lexical set was, on the other hand, primarily a function of the ethno-religious divide, with working- and middle-class Protestant adults using it between 15 and 17 per cent of the time, whilst Catholic adults and Catholic working-class teenagers barely used it at all, and Catholic middle-class teenagers only used it at a level of 8 per cent. Conversely, the use of [l] for intervocalic /ð/ was found at low levels in the speech of working-class adults from both communities, but at much higher levels in the speech of Catholic teenagers in particular (all middle-class speakers except for Catholic teenagers avoided the feature altogether).

McCafferty identified a number of trends that emerged from his analysis. Middle-class speakers are more likely to use standard (that is, Northern Irish standard), less local pronunciations than working-class speakers. These standard and supra-regional features, which are probably relatively new in (London)Derry English, typically have their source in middle-class Belfast speech. Catholics, regardless of social class, are more likely to retain local and non-standard pronunciation variants than Protestants, whereas Protestants are more likely to use incoming supralocal and standard pronunciations than Catholics, even when they are working class. In other words, there *are* differences between the speech of Catholics and Protestants in (London)Derry, and these reflect differing attitudes towards local and incoming, and non-standard and standard variants. However, none of the differences identified by McCafferty have anything to do with Irish influence on MUE, as none of the variants of these features have their origins in Irish (see Sections 3.7.4, 4.2.6 and 4.4.5 for discussion). The same is probably true of most of the features analysed in the other studies reviewed by McCafferty. So what, if anything, does the ethno-religious divide have to do with the phonological origins of MUE? Is it possible that some differences between the speech of Protestants and Catholics *are* connected with Irish influence on MUE?

As was discussed in Section 2.4, the 'Protestant' ethno-religious group in Ulster in the centuries since the Plantation has its roots in the Protestant, English/Scots-speaking British settlers in Ulster, whilst the 'Catholic' ethno-religious group in the province has its origins in the Catholic, Irish-speaking native and 'Old English' population. These correlations are important not only for understanding the origins of the two ethno-religious groups, but also for understanding the history of language in Ulster. As long as Irish was, in the main, the speech of the Catholic population (of whatever origin), as is argued in Sections 2.4 and 2.6, it is not unlikely that any Irish influence on English would be most obvious, at least to begin with, in the speech of that part of the population which was bilingual (i.e. rural Catholics) and, further-more, that these Irish-influenced forms of English may also have been stigmatised. It is of course possible that any such correlation between Catholic speech and Irish-influenced English in the past has not persisted into the twentieth and twenty-first centuries, given the early loss of Irish over most of Ulster and its low levels of survival in the late nineteenth and early twentieth centuries even in its heartlands (see Section 2.6), as well as centuries of interaction and interchange between the two ethno-religious groups.

However, one linguist has suggested that the correlations between ethno-religious group and ethno-linguistic background are important for understanding the origins and nature of MUE. Todd (1984, 1989) claimed not only that there are obvious overall differences, especially in pronunciation, between the speech of Catholics and Protestants in Northern Ireland, but crucially that 'these marked differences . . . can be attributed mainly to the facts that Catholic English (CE) owes much to Gaelic, whereas Protestant English (PE) derives from non-standard Scottish and English and from the blending of the two' (Todd 1984: 162). That is, Catholic speech essen-tially derives from the English learnt by native speakers of Irish, whilst Protestant speech descends from the native-speaker dialects of the English and Scots settlers. If this is true, this has important consequences for understanding the phonological origins of MUE, since Catholic speech is much more likely to show the effects of influence from Irish than Protestant speech. Indeed, Todd's hypothesis suggests that there is not one, but rather two forms of MUE, and these two forms of the dialect have different phonological origins and histories.

Whether Todd's hypothesis is tenable or not (and Kingsmore 1995: 34, McCafferty 1994 and Millar 1987 argue that it is not) depends not only on the extent to which Protestant and Catholic speech differs, but also on the features which instantiate these differences. It is not enough that Catholic and Protestant speech should differ (as we know it does in some cases, statistically anyway). The differences must relate to features which have their origins in Irish influence on the dialect. Thus an impor-tant part of the investigation of the phonological origins of MUE is first to deter-mine which features (if any) are of Irish origin. Many of the phonological features listed in Todd (1984, 1989) are discussed further in Chapters 3 and 4 of this book, and the extent to which Irish influence has played a role in the development of the phonology of MUE is a central theme of this study. Whilst a sociolinguistic study of phonological features of MUE to determine whether they exhibit ethno-religious differences is beyond the scope of this book, some discussion of this matter is given in crucial cases. In addition to the case studies in Chapters 3 and 4, I return to this issue in Chapter 5.

2.8 The linguistic history of Ulster

The history of Ulster is a history of linguistic contact. There was contact between Norman French, English, Irish and Scottish Gaelic in the province before the sev-enteenth century, contact between different dialects of English, between different dialects of Scots, and between English, Scots and Irish as a result of the Plantation of Ulster and its associated settlements, and ongoing contact between MUE, USc, Irish and other varieties of English, including StE, in the centuries since the Plantation. MUE originated and developed in the context of these situations of linguistic contact and thus constitutes ones of the earliest contact varieties of English outside of Britain. But the exact effects of these various kinds of contact need to be unravelled, and it is the purpose of this book to do so from one important perspective, that of the phonology of the dialect. What role, if any, did these various situations of contact play in the phonological development of MUE? For example, did the pre-seventeenth-century English-speaking population serve as a 'founding population' for the future development of the language in Ulster, or was it too insignificant compared to what came after to have any input? What contributions did the English and Scots settlements of the seventeenth and early eighteenth century make to MUE, and how were the differences between the various dialects of each, and indeed between English and Scots more generally, resolved? What effects did the long-term shift from Irish to English in Ulster have, can input to MUE from Irish as a result of this be detected, and what is the nature of this input? Has the continuing ethno-religious divide in Ulster and Northern Ireland affected the phonological development of the dialect, and if so, how?

The purpose of the rest of this book is to investigate the phonological origins of MUE with these questions and the history outlined in this chapter in mind. In addition to analysing phonological patterns in MUE using the kinds of data source described in Section 1.4, features of the dialect are compared in detail to phonological patterns in dialects (historical and current) of English, Scots and Irish. It will be seen that this close comparison of phonological patterns in MUE, English, Scots and Irish reveals consistent patterns of similarity and difference which suggest the relative importance of the various input varieties in the formation of the phonology of the dialect. These patterns make sense given what we know about the linguistic history of Ulster as described in this chapter, especially when combined with theories of koinéisation and new dialect formation, as explored in Chapter 5. But they also provide another line of evidence for understanding the nature of the linguistic contacts that have occurred in the province, and this highlights an important aspect of this study. It is not just the case that the history of Ulster helps to explain why MUE is the way it is. The converse is also true. The linguistic shape of MUE, including its phonology, can tell us a great deal about the linguistic history of the province, and it will be seen through the analyses presented in Chapters 3 and 4 and discussed further in Chapter 5 that the phonological patterns of MUE suggest particular things about the nature and extent of the input to the dialect from English, Scots and Irish which help us to understand the interaction between them in earlier centuries. Just to take a single example: features of English origin in MUE are of a non-regional Midland and southern English type, rather similar to the phonology of Early Modern StE in fact. This suggests that input from northern England in the formation of the dialect was minimal and, furthermore, that English settlers came from across the Midlands and south of the country and that no one group of settlers predominated and contributed more to the phonological development of the dialect. I return to this issue throughout Chapters 3 and 4 and, especially, Chapter 5. It will be seen from examples like this that we can, in light of what we *do* know about the history of Ulster, make informed assumptions about the population history of the province and of the varieties spoken by those who lived there in the past.

Notes

1. I.e. Irish.
2. Throughout this book I make use of the lexical set labels (in small caps, e.g. FACE) described in Wells (1982).

3 Consonants

3.1 The consonants of MUE

In some ways there is a not a great deal of variation between dialects of English (or Scots) in terms of their consonant systems, with the same phonemes found in most dialects. The consonant system of MUE, which is not exceptional in this respect, is given in Table 3.1.

The status of [ŋ] in MUE is uncertain, as it is in other dialects of English, and one possible analysis of it is as an allophone of /n/ before /g/ (which is often deleted in this position) and /k/. The phoneme /x/ (see Section 3.2) is not found in most varieties of English but is shared with Scottish Standard English (SSE), Scots and SIrE. It is often realised as uvular [χ] rather than velar [x]. Traditional MUE also has the sound [ʍ] (as in *where*), which is phonologised in this book as /hw/, just as [ç] (e.g. in *huge*) is phonologised as /hj/ (see Section 3.2). Although some previous analyses of MUE phonology have added dental and palatal stops and nasals to the inventory in Table 3.1 (see Harris 1997 for a critical review), these are in most cases transparently sub-phonemic variants of the alveolar and velar series, as is discussed in Sections 3.3 and 3.5.

But this overall uniformity in consonantal systems between dialects of English and Scots contrasts with considerable variation in how these consonants are distributed and, especially, how they are realised, and much of this chapter will concern

Table 3.1 The consonant phonemes of MUE.

	Labial	Dental	Alveolar	Palato-alveolar	Palatal	Velar	Glottal
Voiceless stops/affricates	p		t	tʃ		k	
Voiced stops/affricates	b		d	dʒ		g	
Voiceless fricatives	f	θ	s	ʃ		x	h
Voiced fricatives	v	ð	z	ʒ			
Nasals	m		n			(ŋ)	
Liquids			l	rª			
Semi-vowels	wᵇ				j		

Notes:
a Post-alveolar rather than palato-alveolar.
b Labio-velar rather than labial.

Table 3.2 The consonants of Irish.

	Broad labial	Slender labial	Broad coronal	Slender coronal	Slender velar	Broad velar	Glottal
Voiceless stops	p	p′	t	t′	k′	k	
Voiced stops	b	b′	d	d′	g′	g	
Voiceless fricatives	f	f′	s	s′	x′	x	h
Voiced fricatives	v	v′			ɣ′	ɣ	
Tense nasals	m	m′	N	N′	ŋ′	ŋ	
Lax nasals	(ṽ)ᵃ	(ṽ′)	n	n′			
Tense laterals			L	L′			
Lax laterals			l	l′			
Tense rhotics			R				
Lax rhotics			r	r′			

Note:
a The nasalised fricatives /ṽ/ and /ṽ′/ were found in earlier stages of the language but have been merged with /v/ and /v′/ in most modern dialects.

itself with the various ways that MUE differs from mainstream varieties of English in these respects. Although the MUE consonant system shares much in common with those of English and Scots, it also diverges from them in significant ways, and one of the purposes of this chapter is to determine what role, if any, contact with Irish has played in their development. Not unexpectedly, the consonant system of Irish differs considerably from that of English and Scots, in the phonemes it has, in the positional distributions of these phonemes and in their realisation. The consonant system of Irish is given in Table 3.2 (see Ó Baoill 2009: 164–8; Ó Siadhail 1989: 67–104), though there is degree of diachronic and diatopic variation in the language.

It can be seen from Table 3.2 that the Irish consonant system is radically different from the English/Scots one. Notable features include:

1. A distinction between 'broad' (plain or velarised) consonants (usually unmarked in phonemic transcriptions, though in phonetic transcriptions they may be indicated by the diacritic [ˠ]) and 'slender' (palatalised) consonants, typically marked with the symbol ′ in phonemic transcriptions, though the IPA symbol [ʲ] is also used;
2. Pairs of tense and lax sonorants (capital letters are conventionally used to represent the tense sonorants), though the distinction between these is not maintained in all modern dialects of Irish; the tense sonorants are typically longer and more firmly articulated than the lax ones;
3. Grammatically conditioned alternations between consonants, including lenition, eclipsis and palatalisation (for overviews, see Ó Baoill 2009; Ó Siadhail 1989).

There are also correlations between broad/slender consonant quality, on the one hand, and the quality of neighbouring vowels on the other, as is discussed in Sections 3.3.2 and 3.9.2 of this chapter and in Section 4.2.1 of Chapter 4.

It might be expected, then, that if contact with Irish has been important in the development of the phonology of MUE aspects of this very different consonant system should occur in the dialect, as has not infrequently been claimed in previous analyses (discussed throughout this chapter). In order to provide an understanding of the origins of consonantal features of MUE, this chapter examines a wide range of characteristic features of the dialect, which are compared to apparently similar patterns in English, Scots and Irish. Sections 3.2 to 3.4 deal with dorsal and palatal consonants, whilst Sections 3.5 to 3.9 discuss coronal consonants, including the liquids /r/ and /l/. Sections 3.10 and 3.11 deal with the treatment of consonant clusters in MUE, whilst a number of other consonantal features of the dialect are discussed in Section 3.12. The findings of this chapter are summarised in Section 3.13. It will be seen that evidence for direct influence on the consonant phonology of the dialect from Irish is in fact slight, and in almost all cases where we suspect Irish to have played a role this has at most involved reinforcement of patterns already present in the English and Scots input to the province. Instead, the consonantal features of MUE are of a somewhat conservative English type, many of which are also shared by Scots. These findings have important consequences for understanding the phonological history of MUE, and I return to them in Chapter 5.

3.2 The dorsal and glottal fricatives

Like English and Scots, MUE has the glottal fricative /h/ ([h]), confined for the most part (but see below) to onset position. Except in unstressed function words (as is commonly the case in English), /h/ is not generally dropped in MUE, though it can be absent in a small number of words which vacillated between /h/-full and /h/-less pronunciations in the history of English (Dobson 1957: 991), for example, *habitual*, *hospital*, *hotel* and *humble* (de Rijke 2015: 208–9; Lass 2000: 118–19; Robinson 1997: 36–7; Wells 1982: 255), and may be omitted post-consonantally in compounds such as *bill-hook* and *hen-house*. The glottal fricative also occurs intervocalically, usually before an unstressed vowel, in borrowings from Irish (Harris 1985: 59), e.g. *Cathal* ['cähəl], *Monaghan* ['mɒnəhən] (Irish *Muineachán*).

In MUE, /h/ also occurs in the sequences /hw/ (e.g. *white*, typically [ʍ]) and /hj/ (e.g. *huge*, often [ç]), at least if these are interpreted as clusters (as they are here) rather than unitary phonemes. The first of these is traditional in the dialect, though it is now being lost rapidly in MUE (Braidwood 1964: 75; Corrigan 2010: 46; Harris 1984: 130, 1985: 57; Wells 1982: 446). Although [ʍ] is the default pronunciation, [χʍ] can also occasionally be heard in traditional SwTE. Merger with /f/, for example under [ɸ] (as may be the case in SIrE, see Wells 1982: 434), is not reported for MUE. The sequence /hj/ is uncommon in MUE, as it is in English generally, and is subject to various, often lexically specific, changes in traditional MUE. As can be the case in old-fashioned RP and in SIrE (Wells 1982: 230, 432), *humour* may be pronounced with an initial [j], but initial /nj/ is also common in this word (i.e. ['ɲʉmə˞]). The name *Hugh* and, occasionally, the word *human* may be pronounced with [c] (/kj/) rather than [ç] in traditional MUE (cf. Adams 1950: 300; Todd 1984: 167–8). The origins of [ɲ] in *humour* and of [c] in *Hugh* and *human* are uncertain. Todd (1984: 167–8) suggests that since [ç] (/x'/) alternates with [c] (/k'/) in lenition contexts in Irish, phrases such as *a human* [ə ˈçʉmən] could have been interpreted as involving lenition (of *[ˈcʉmən]) by Irish learners of English, who then produced [ˈcʉmən] as a result of hypercorrection.[1] Whether such a development is likely, given the lack of any evidence of this kind of development in other aspects of MUE phonology, is questionable. It may be that the uncommon and thus marked sound [ç] was simply subject to various changes, as it has been in some dialects of English and Scots. In north-east England, where [h] is generally retained in initial position, the initial sequence /hj/ is sometimes simplified to /j/, for example (see *home* and *humour* in Rydland 1998). And in Mid Scots dialects across the Central Belt, /hj/ in *Hugh(ie)* and *human* may be realised as [ʃ], thus merging with /ʃ/ (Johnston 1997b: 509), a feature which Todd (1984: 167) claims is also found in Protestant speech in Ulster, though this is not reported in other sources.

In retaining /h/ before vowels in initial position, MUE groups with varieties of Scots (and English) in Scotland, with varieties of StE in England and with most extra-territorial varieties in North America and the southern hemisphere. But it contrasts with most non-standard dialects of English in England which, outside of the north-east, East Anglia and parts of the south-west, generally have /h/-dropping (Anderson 1987: 144; Wells 1982: 253–6). /h/-dropping in England has a long history, with common examples from the Midlands and south in the Middle English (ME) period, and with widespread written and orthoepic evidence from the sixteenth century (Dobson 1957: 991–2; Lass 1992: 61–3, 2000: 118–19; Minkova 2014: 105–8). But from the seventeenth century onwards, /h/-dropping became stigmatised in English, and /h/ was ultimately restored for the most part in StE where it occurred etymologically or in spelling (Minkova 2014: 107), though /h/-dropping remained a feature of most non-standard English dialects. Given the history of /h/-dropping in English, it is surprising that the feature is not found in MUE or indeed in most other extra-territorial varieties. It could be that the Scots input in Ulster swung the balance in favour of /h/-retention in the dialect, in a similar way to how Trudgill (2004: 116) explains the lack of /h/-dropping in New Zealand English (/h/-retention was found in the majority of input varieties, including those from Scotland, Ireland and East Anglia). Trudgill (2004: 74–7, 116) makes two other important points which might help us to understand why /h/-dropping did not become established as a feature of MUE. First of all, the /h/-dropping area in England was demonstrably smaller in the nineteenth century than in the twentieth, and if this represents a result of ongoing spread of the feature, then /h/-dropping may have been rather less common in the English input to MUE than might be assumed based on modern dialect evidence. Indeed, it may even be the case that early colonial varieties of English such as MUE and other IrE dialects provide evidence that /h/-dropping was rather less common in England in the seventeenth century than it afterwards became. Secondly, Trudgill makes the point that /h/-dropping is usually variable for speakers that have it, so that the presence of /h/-dropping in a dialect need not mean that there was no /h/-retention there in words which historically had it. To these two points we can of course add the fact that StE in England does not have /h/-dropping, and this may have been true of more standard varieties of the language in previous centuries, if the comments by the orthoepists referred to above are anything to go by. All of these factors together have meant that MUE, like most other extra-territorial varieties of

English that have formed over the last several centuries, retains initial /h/. Whether Irish learners of English could have played any role in this process is another matter, as they would have been happy to learn /h/-less or /h/-full pronunciations, given that Irish has many vowel-initial words, but also allows /h/ in initial position (though only in certain grammatical contexts).

The situation is somewhat different for /h/ in the initial cluster /hw/. This cluster formerly characterised English and Scots as a whole, but has been in sharp decline in recent centuries, preceded by significant variation in the ME period (Minkova 2004, 2014: 109–12; Wells 1982: 229–30). Although /hw/ is not now characteristic of RP English and of most English dialects, it was retained in stand-ard varieties of the language into the eighteenth century, with decline thereafter (Dobson 1957: 974–5; Lass 2000: 123–4; Wyld 1927: 220). Its loss in some non-standard regional dialects was no doubt earlier than this, but the extent to which this was general across England is unknown. Given the existence of /hw/ in MUE and other IrE dialects, it may well be that /hw/ was still usual in many English dialects in the seventeenth century. By the time we get to the nineteenth and twen-tieth centuries, /hw/ was retained only in the far north (Anderson 1987: 140, 145; Maguire 2012c: 97–101). In Scotland, /hw/ was maintained, though it is now disap-pearing in the speech of young urban working-class people in particular (Stuart-Smith *et al.* 2007). Retention of /hw/ was (and is) characteristic of most traditional Scots dialects and of SSE (Johnston 1997b: 507–8), though it has merged with /f/ in traditional dialects in north-east Scotland. Although [ʍ] is the usual pronuncia-tion, [xʍ] is also common in Scots. It is not surprising, then, that MUE traditionally retains /hw/, given that it has been a feature of Scots throughout its history, and was retained in at least some (and perhaps many) varieties of English (including StE) into the eighteenth century (and beyond in some cases). Thus it was likely to have been a majority feature in the British input in the Plantation of Ulster and its associated settlements.

A role for Irish in the retention of /hw/ in MUE is less certain. Irish distinguishes between broad /f/ and slender /f'/, with the former sometimes pronounced as [ɸ] and the latter as [f] (Hickey 2014: 72). This distinction between two labial fricatives in Irish looks similar to the distinction between /hw/ ([ʍ]) and /f/ ([f]) in MUE, but there is less congruence when the realisations and distributions of these and other sounds are taken into account. Firstly, /hw/ in MUE is not pronounced [ɸ], and pronunciations such as [ʍ] and even [χʍ] are more similar to what is found in Scots than in Irish. Secondly, /hw/ only occurs in initial position in MUE, and can do so in contrast with /f/ before front and back vowels (e.g. *fun* [fɔn] vs *whin* [ʍɔn], *feel* [fil] vs *wheel* [ʍil]), whereas both /f/ and /f'/ in Irish can occur in any position in a word. Thirdly, /f/ in MUE occurs after front and back vowels (*stiff* [stɛf], *stuff* [stɔf]), with no patterning of the sort found in Irish, whereby broad /f/ is required after short back vowels and slender /f'/ after short front ones (see Section 4.2.1). Finally, the sequence [fj] can also occur in initial position in MUE as in other varieties of English (e.g. *few*), so that there is a three-way contrast between [ʍ], [f] and [fj] in the dialect, which does not match the two-way contrast in Irish. Given all of this, it is not clear that Irish has impacted the system of labial fricatives in MUE at all, and the more straightforward explanation is that the dialect inherited its contrasts and realisations from English and Scots, and that the predominance of /hw/ in the British input determined its survival in MUE (Trudgill 2004: 146ff.).

MUE also has a voiceless dorsal fricative phoneme, conventionally represented as /x/ (Adams 1981; Barry 1980: 123–4; Braidwood 1964: 75–6; Corrigan 2010: 42; Harris 1985: 59–60; McCafferty 2007: 127), though it covers a range of realisations, and is often uvular [χ] rather than velar [x]. This phoneme is almost never found in words of English origin, though it is usual in traditional MUE in *trough* (Adams 1981: 107–8; Harris 1985: 60), and has been recorded in *tough* in some dialects (see the data for the LAS3 locations Loughinisland, Annalong, Poyntzpass and Mount Norris; Mather and Speitel 1986: 197–8, 205–6). An unusual case is found in *dung-hill*, traditionally [ˈdɔ̃χəl], sometimes with nasalisation and lengthening of the first vowel. Unlike Scots dialects, including USc, /x/ does not otherwise occur for historical English /x/ in MUE, neither word-finally (e.g. *rough*, *thigh*), nor before /t/ (e.g. *daughter*, *light*), and indeed the treatment of /x/ in the dialect is essentially the same as it is in English more generally. In English, historical /x/ in coda position was lost (e.g. *night*, *sigh*, *thought*) or, in some cases after back vowel, became /f/ (e.g. *laugh*). This change began in the ME period, and was nearing completion in the sixteenth and early seventeenth centuries, with StE being more conservative than some other dialects in this respect (Dobson 1957: 985–8; Lass 2000: 116–18; Minkova 2014: 112–14). Given the lack of /x/ in these positions in MUE, other dialects of IrE, and in extra-territorial Englishes more generally, it seems likely that loss of /x/ was well advanced in English by the time of the Plantation of Ulster. Whether survival of /x/ in *tough* and *trough* represent last vestiges of /x/ in English from this period or whether they are the result of Scots influence is unknown.

Unlike English, Scots has retained /x/ in all positions (e.g. in *daughter*, *laugh*, *night* and *sigh*), with loss being a recent development (Johnston 1997b: 505–6). The velar fricative is lost generally in SSE, on the other hand, with it only appearing in borrowings from Scots and Gaelic such as *dreich* 'dreary' and *loch* 'lake' (Johnston 2007: 112; Wells 1982: 408). /x/ is also retained in traditional USc in all positions, and this is one of the key features distinguishing it and MUE (Gregg 1972, 1985). Broad /x/ and slender /x'/ also occur before /t/ and finally in Irish, for example, *bocht* 'poor' and *fliuch* 'wet', as well as in initial position in lenition contexts, for example, *chean-naigh* 'bought'. Not surprisingly, then, /x/ is common in borrowings from Scots (e.g. *pegh* 'pant', *plougher* 'cough', *sheugh* 'drainage channel', *spraughle* 'sprawl') and Irish (*prough* 'hovel', Irish *proch*, *shannagh* 'hearty conversation', Irish *seanchas*), and in personal- and place-names of Irish origin (e.g. *Augher*, *Aughnacloy*, *Clogher*, *Haughey*, *Loughgall*, *Magher*), though /h/ is often found before an unstressed vowel, as noted previously (e.g. in *Monaghan*).

The distribution of /x/ in MUE, a few words (*dung-hill*, *tough*, *trough*) and various borrowings from Scots and Irish aside, is the same as it is in English, and speaks of the importance of Early Modern forms of this input in the development of the dialect. The lack of Scots input (other than in obvious borrowings) in this respect is noteworthy, and points to the essentially English origins of the dialect (as also seen in the lexical distribution of vowels in MUE as described in Section 4.4), despite significant Scots input to various aspects of its phonetics and phonology (as demonstrated in other sections in this and the following chapter). In this respect, MUE is like SSE, which has Scots phonetics but English phonological structure. Since Irish allows /x/ in all positions, it would not have militated against survival of this fricative where it is not (now) found in English, and the fact that it did not survive suggests that the Irish input here was unimportant too (though Irish speakers would just as easily have learned /x/-less pronunciations of English words).

The /x/ phoneme is subject to two significant changes in MUE. In urban varieties and the speech of younger people in particular, it is often replaced by /k/, so that words like *lough* and *trough* may be pronounced [lɒk] and [tɹɒk] (Adams 1981; Corrigan 2010: 42; McCafferty 1999: 250). This is a change which is also occurring in urban Scotland (Stuart-Smith *et al.* 2007) and which matches typical English pronunciations of Scottish and Irish words and names with /x/, and is thus clearly a recent innovation in MUE, involving the levelling of a phoneme which is not typical of most other varieties of English. Another innovation, though one which is rather less recent as it is common in some conservative rural dialects, is the replacement of /x/ by /h/, and sometimes even deletion of the segment altogether, in all positions that it is found, so that words such as *lough* and place-names such as *Clogher* are pronounced as [lɒh] and [ˈtlɒhə˞] (Adams 1981: 107; Corrigan 2010: 42; Harris 1985: 59). Interestingly, weakening of /x/ to [h] (in non-initial position) is also a feature of many dialects of Ulster Irish, especially those of western Donegal and, even more extremely, in the (now extinct) dialects of the central MUE area (Ó Dochartaigh 1987: 122–44). Given that lenition of /x/ to [h] in MUE is most characteristic of west and south Ulster (Adams 1981) and is most characteristic of Irish dialects in the same area, it seems likely that there is a link between this feature in the two languages. But since the feature appears to have developed fairly recently in both languages (i.e. over the last few centuries; see Ó Dochartaigh 1987: 142–3), it is impossible to tell whether this change spread from Ulster Irish to MUE, from MUE to Ulster Irish, or developed in both simultaneously as a result of ongoing contact. Ulster Irish is distinguished from other Irish (and Scottish Gaelic) dialects by this change, whilst MUE is distinguished from Scots by it. Ulster Scots more typically has [x], especially in the east and north-east of Ulster (where some varieties of Ulster Irish also had /x/), though [h] has been commonly recorded in Donegal USc (Gregg 1985: Part II, 1–30).

In summary, then, MUE agrees with Scots and historical varieties of English in retaining /h/ and /hw/, which must have been in the majority in the input British varieties. But it matches only English with respect to its distribution of /x/ (other than in a few relict forms and obvious borrowings from Scots and Irish), which thus has developed in a similar way to the lexical distribution of /l/ (Section 3.9.1) and most vowels (Section 4.4) in the dialect. In this respect (as in various others), MUE is similar to SSE. Other than the presence of /x/ in loanwords and names, Irish appears not to have influenced the distribution or realisation of the dorsal and glottal fricatives in MUE, with the possible exception of weakening of /x/ to [h], though as this feature is shared by both Ulster Irish and MUE and appears to have developed in recent centuries, the direction of influence in this case is unknown.

3.3 Velar Palatalisation

One of the most characteristic features of the phonology of MUE, and one which invites comparison with similar pronunciations in Irish, is the palatalisation of the velar stops and nasal in the neighbourhood of front and low vowels (Corrigan 2010: 46–7; Harris 1984: 130, 1985: 213–16; Hickey 2007a: 115; McCafferty 1999: 249, 2007: 126; Wells 1982: 446). MUE traditionally has palatal [c] and [ɟ] rather than velar [k] and [g] in words such as *keep, kill, kettle, cat, kind, geese, give, gate* and *garden,* and palatalised [k̟], [g̟] and [ŋ] in words such as *seek, stick, ache, neck, back, bike, big, beg, bag, sing, sang, think* and *thank.* This Velar Palatalisation (VP) is not typical of all urban varieties of MUE, nor is it characteristic of more standardised varieties of the dialect (Barry 1981b; Corrigan 2010: 46–7; Harris 1985: 214; McCafferty 1999: 249, 2007: 126), though it is shared with some traditional varieties of SIrE (Henry 1958: 114–18).

Given that this is a feature which distinguishes MUE (and some other traditional forms of IrE) from mainstream varieties of English in Britain, and since Irish has the (phonemic) palatal stops /k'/ ([c]) and /g'/ ([ɟ]) and the palatal nasal /ŋ'/ ([ŋʲ]), it is not surprising that most researchers have suggested that the palatal stops in IrE are the result, in part at least, of language contact (e.g. Adams 1966; Barry 1980, 1982; Bliss 1972; Henry 1957, 1958; Lunny 1981a: 162; Ní Ghallchóir 1981; Ó Baoill 1997; Odlin 1997). However, Harris (1985: 213–16, 1987: 272–5, 1997: 210–11) points out the existence of similar patterns of VP in earlier forms of English and in non-standard dialects of English in England and elsewhere, and suggests that this is a more likely source for the feature in MUE. Given the existence of VP in English, and its presence in some dialects of Scots too (Johnston 1997b: 503), an Irish source for VP in MUE cannot be assumed, and an examination of the patterning of the palatal stops and nasal in the various input languages and dialects is necessary before we can determine the source or sources of the feature in MUE.

3.3.1 *Velar Palatalisation in MUE*

Velar Palatalisation in MUE is described in Adams (1948: 12), Barry (1980: 129) and Harris (1985: 213–14, 1987: 272–5, 1997: 210–11). It is also a consistent feature for all the speakers included in the SwTE corpus. Velar Palatalisation in MUE affects the velar stops /k/ (including in the cluster /sk/ in onset position) and /g/, and the velar nasal /ŋ/. The feature is most obvious in initial position, where the velar stops are often palatalised to [c] and [ɟ] ([k̟] and [g̟] also occur) before phonologically front vowels. The vowels that cause VP in MUE are /ë/ (the typical vowel of the KIT lexical set, usually pronounced [ë], [ə] or even [ɜ], so that it is not necessarily phonetically front), /ɛ/ (the typical DRESS vowel, which in some dialects may be lowered to [æ]), /a/ (the typical TRAP and BATH vowel, which can range from a front [a] to a back [ɑ] vowel, e.g. *cap* [kɑp]), /i/ (the typical FLEECE vowel), /e/ (the typical vowel of the FACE lexical set), /aɪ/ (the diphthong found in a small number of PRICE words, which can be realised as [ɑˑe], e.g. *sky* [scɑˑe]), and /ëi/ (the diphthong found in most PRICE words, e.g. *kite*). Palatalisation also occurs before the typical vowels in the rhotic lexical sets NEAR (/ir/), SQUARE (and the SERVE subset of NURSE, which has the same vowel, /ɛr/, e.g. *kerb* [cɛːɹb]), START (/ar/), and NURSE when the historical vowel was /ɪ/ (equivalent to MUE /ë̇/), as in *girth* and *skirt* (e.g. [ɟɚ·θ], [scɚ·ʈ]), but not when the historical vowel was /ʊ/, as in *curve* (e.g. [kɝ̈ːv]). VP is sometimes not present before the typical vowel in the PALM lexical set in dialects (such as SwTE) which distinguish the vowel in words like *calf* and *calm* (phonemicised here as /ɑ/, e.g. [kɑːm]) from the vowel typical of the TRAP and BATH lexical sets ([a(ː)]~[ä(ː)]~[ɑ(ː)], /a/), though VP can occur before the vowel in these words too for some speakers, suggesting variable phonemic identity with TRAP and BATH.

Palatalisation is most noticeable before low vowels, and may be accompanied by a [j]-like glide (e.g. [cjat] *cat*, [cjɑp] *cap*). This explains why descriptions of VP in MUE most often identify it before low vowels and why symbols such as [kj] and [gj] are often used to represent it. But palatalisation is also present for the higher front vowels, though here [k̟] and [g̟] are not uncommon, and the noticeable [j]-like glide is absent, so that overall VP is less obvious before higher vowels than before low ones. Palatalisation does not occur before /ʉ/ (the typical vowel of the GOOSE lexical set, regardless of how fronted the vowel is), /o/ (typical of the GOAT lexical set), /ɝ̈/ (typical of the STRUT lexical set), /ɔ/ (typical of the THOUGHT lexical set), /ɒ/ (typical of the LOT lexical set in dialects where this is distinguished from THOUGHT, even when it is pronounced as a low, unrounded vowel such as [ɑ] or even front [a]; cf. Harris 1987: 273, 1997: 210–11), /əʉ/ (the typical vowel of the MOUTH lexical set, even when the nucleus is somewhat fronted, e.g. [ë̈ʊ])[2] and /ɔɪ/ (the typical vowel of the CHOICE lexical set), nor before the vowels in the rhotic NORTH (/ɔr/) and FORCE (/or/) lexical sets.

Velar Palatalisation also affects consonants in coda position after phonologically front vowels, especially when they are word-final, and in this environment [k̟] and [g̟] are more typical than [c] and [ɟ], whilst the velar nasal is realised as [ŋ̟]. The same vowels which cause VP in preceding consonants cause it in following consonants. Palatalisation does not occur after the other vowels, including after /ɑ/ in those dialects which have it (e.g. in words like *talk* [tɑːk] and *walk* [wɑːk], which thus contrast with *back* [bäk̟] and *whack* [ʍäk̟]; cf. Adams 1967: 74). After /r/ following a palatalising vowel, VP is not general, though it can occur, at least variably, with /ar/ ([äːɹ]~[ɑːɹ]), as in *dark* [däːɹk̟]. Likewise, VP after vowels word-internally is not usual, though it is not uncommon in cases like *ankle* (e.g. [ˈäŋ̟kəl]) where one of the consonants is in coda position following a palatalising vowel. It does not occur before the phonetically front unstressed vowel in words like *lucky* ([ˈlɔ̈ke]).

Velar Palatalisation of coda consonants is usually accompanied, where possible, by raising of the preceding vowel or, when the vowel is low and especially when it is long, by the insertion of a short upglide after it, symbolised here as [ˈ]. As a result of this process, [ë̇] rather than [ə] occurs for /ë̇/ in words like *big*, [ɛ̇ː] (or even [eː]) rather than [ɛː]~[ɛ·ə] occurs in words like *beg*, [ä(ː)ˈ] or [æ] (or even [ɛ]) occurs for /a/ in words like *back* (e.g. [bæk], [bäˈk̟]) and *bag* (e.g. [bäːˈg̟]), and [eː] rather than [ɪə] occurs for /e/ in words like *bake*. This process is termed 'Pre-Palatal Raising' (PPR) in this book.

Whilst VP is characteristic of MUE, it is rather less typical of USc (for example, Gregg 1958 does not describe it as a feature of the Glenoe dialect). However, VP is also found in SUE and SIrE, and has been recorded in Leinster dialects in particular (Henry 1958: 114–18; see also Harris 1985: 213–14; Nally 1971: 37; Ó Muirithe 1996: 18). Henry recorded VP for onset /k/ (including in /sk/) and /g/ before the typical vowels of the KIT, DRESS, TRAP, FLEECE, FACE, PALM, PRICE and START lexical sets and the 'ir' subset of NURSE. It was occasionally also recorded before [ə] (e.g. in *tinkers*), though this likely depends on the preceding vowel more than the following one. A degree of VP was also recorded word-finally after the TRAP vowel, often with an accompanying [ɪ]-glide. That is, VP in SUE and (eastern) SIrE is essentially the same as it is in MUE, though it appears to be less common and may be inconsistently produced in the non-MUE dialects that have it.

3.3.2 *Broad and slender dorsal stops in Irish*

As was described in Section 3.1, Irish distinguishes between broad (velarised) and slender (palatalised) consonants. In terms of the dorsal stops and nasal, the contrast is between broad [k], [g] and [ŋ] (/k/, /g/ and /ŋ/) and slender [c], [ɟ] and [ɲ] (/k'/, /g'/ and /ŋ'/). Because the difference between broad and slender consonants in Irish originated in allophonic variation in the pronunciation of consonants before front and back vowels (Thurneysen 1946: 97), there is a fairly strong correlation between vowel quality and whether a preceding consonant is palatal or velar in Modern Irish, despite subsequent changes disturbing this pattern. Thus, for example, the diphthong [iə] (orthographically <ia(i)>) can be preceded by /k'/ and /g'/ (e.g. *cian* 'long (adj.)', *giall* 'jaw') but not by /k/ or /g/, whilst conversely the diphthong [uə] (<ua(i)>) can be preceded by /k/ and /g/ (e.g. *cuach* 'cuckoo', *guais* 'danger') but never by /k'/ or /g'/. But there are some cases where slender /k'/ and /g'/ can be followed by a back vowel (e.g. *ceol* 'music' [coːɫ], *ciúin* 'calm, quiet, still' [cuːnʲ], *giolla* 'youth, boy' [ɟʊ̈ɫ:ə]) and where /k/ and /g/ can be followed by a front vowel (e.g. *caor* 'berry' [kiːr], *coill* 'wood, forest' [kɛʎ]~[kɪʎ], *cuí* 'fitting, proper' [kiː], *cuing* 'yoke' [kiŋ], *Gaeilge* 'Irish' [geːʎɟə], *gaol* 'relationship, kinship' [giːɫ], *goile* 'stomach' [gɛlə]~[gɪlə], *guigh* 'to pray' [giː]). Before the vowel /a/, both broad and slender dorsal stops can occur, for example, *cathair* 'city' ([kahərʲ]) vs *ceathair* 'four' ([cahərʲ]), *gal* 'valour' ([gaɫ]) vs *geal* 'white, bright' ([ɟaɫ]). In other words, the distinctions between the broad and slender dorsal consonants are phonemic in Irish and cannot be entirely predicted from the following vowel. Nevertheless, it is a noticeable tendency of Irish phonology that front vowels follow the palatals and back vowels follow the velars (cf. Harris 1997).

A somewhat similar situation pertains after vowels, where broad /k/, /g/ and /ŋ/ are also distinguished from slender /k'/, /g'/ and /ŋ'/. As is discussed in Section 4.2.1, a core rule of Irish phonology is that only phonetically front short vowels can occur before a slender consonant and only phonetically back short vowels can occur before a broad consonant. This is most obvious for the mid and high short vowels, whilst /a/ may also be subject to some front/back allophonic variation. This means that phonetic back and front short vowels in Irish are in complementary distribution, which is why only three short vowel phonemes, unspecified for frontness/backness, may be posited for Irish, as discussed in Section 4.2.1. So while it is essentially true that slender consonants in Irish must be preceded by a phonetically front short vowel and broad consonants by a phonetically back vowel, phonologically either broad or slender consonants can occur after any of the three phonemic short vowels.

Things are more straightforward for the Irish long vowels and diphthongs, though final /k/ and /k'/ in particular are uncommon in Irish after these vowels. All of the relevant stops can be preceded by front or back long vowels and by both diphthongs, and indeed alternation between the two kinds of consonant is used to mark grammatical features such as genitive singular and nominative plural without a change in the preceding vowel. Thus we get /iː/ before /k/ in *íoc* 'payment' but before /k'/ in *íc* 'cure', we get /eː/ before /g/ in *bréag* 'a lie' but before /g'/ in *bréige* 'a lie (gen. sg.)', we get /aː/ before /g/ in *mág* 'paw' but before /g'/ in *máig* 'paw (gen. sg.)', /uː/ before /g/ in *grúg* 'wrinkle' but before /g'/ in *cúig* 'five', /oː/ before /g/ in *óg* 'young' but before /g'/ in *óige* 'young (gen. f. sg.)', /iə/ before /g/ in *fiag* 'rush (plant)' but before /g'/ in *fiaige* 'rush (plant, gen. sg.)', and we get /uə/ before /g/ in *gruag* 'hair' but before /g'/ in *gruaige* 'hair (gen. sg.)'. In cases where a slender consonant follows /aː/, /oː/ or /uː/, an upglide may be heard in some varieties, for example, *cúig* [kuːʲɟ], as a result of the transition from a non-palatal vowel to a palatal consonant.

In summary, then, the situation in Irish is as follows: (1) front vowels (which in the case of short vowels are only phonetically, not phonologically, front) are most common after /k'/ and /g'/ whilst back vowels are most common after /k/ and /g/, though there are not infrequent exceptions; (2) phonetically front short vowels are followed by the slender consonants and phonetically back short vowels are followed by the broad consonants; and (3) long vowels and diphthongs, regardless of whether they are front or back, can be followed by either type of consonant, with an upglide possible between back vowels and a following palatal. This is superficially similar to the situation in MUE, but there are important differences between the two systems. Firstly, there are numerous exceptions to (1), so that it is a tendency of Irish phonology (as a result of its phonological history) rather than a rule. This is not the case for MUE, which has regular rules for when palatalisation can apply to the velar consonants. Secondly, it is not the case that the quality of short vowels dictates the quality of the following consonant in Irish, but rather than the following consonant determines the frontness or backness of the vowel. This is not how VP works in MUE, where the vowel determines whether the following consonant is palatalised. In MUE, phonological front vowels cause VP, even when they are phonetically non-front (e.g. [bɑ'kʲ] for *back*), but phonologically back vowels do not, even when they are phonetically fronted (e.g. [lʉk] for *look*, [läk] for *lock*). Thirdly, VP applies after front vowels in MUE whether they are long or short, with no exceptions of the sort illustrated for Irish above. Fourthly, palatalisation in MUE affects only the velar consonants (though for allophonic variation in /l/ of a superficially similar kind, see Section 3.9.2), but in Irish all consonants follow the same rules. For example, in Irish /t'/ is usually followed by a front vowel, and always preceded by a front vowel if the vowel is short. But in MUE /t/ is never palatalised before or after a front vowel, with the same realisation ([t]) occurring in, for example, *tin*, *ton*, *bit* and *but*. The occurrence of glides between long back vowels and a following slender consonant in Irish looks like PPR in MUE, but these glides in Irish are part of a larger system of transitional glides in the language, including velar/labial glides between broad consonants and front vowel (e.g. *gaol* [gᵚiːˤɫ]/[gʷiːˤɫ]), something which is not a feature of MUE (which can also have them between a short back vowel and a palatal consonant, e.g. [bɑ'ķ] *back*). Given these differences, it is not clear that VP in MUE can be derived directly from the slender/broad distinction in Irish, and an examination of similar phenomena in English and Scots is in order to determine whether closer analogues exist in the other input languages to the dialect.

3.3.3 *Velar Palatalisation in English*

A degree of VP in the neighbourhood of front vowels is characteristic of English generally (see, for example, Butcher and Tabain 2004; Cox 2012: 135–6; Keating and Lahiri 1993; Ladefoged and Johnson 2011: 76–7), and indeed is common cross-linguistically (Keating and Lahiri 1993). Thus in RP English (Collins and Mees 2003: 163; Cruttenden 2001: 167; Jones 1922: 30), the velar stops are pronounced as [ķ] and [ɡ̟] before a following front vowel, contrasting with velar pronunciations [k] and [ɡ] (Keating and Lahiri 1993). This palatalisation of /k/ and /g/ (and /ŋ/) is observable in RP (and other accents of English) after front vowels too (e.g. *week*, *big*, *sing*). So although the degree of palatalisation in RP is typically less than it is in MUE, the pattern is similar in the two varieties, though VP in accents like RP is phonetically motivated, whilst VP in MUE has become phonologised (e.g. it occurs before phonologically front but not necessarily phonetically front vowels). Even in terms of the degree of VP, MUE is not exceptional from a wider linguistic perspective, since palatalisation of velar stops, often resulting in coronal affricates and sibilants, is an extremely common sound change cross-linguistically (Hock 1991: 73–7). Indeed, palatalisation of velar stops before and after front vowels was a significant change in the history of Old English (OE; Ringe and Taylor 2014: 203–14). Given how frequent palatalisation of velar stops in the neighbourhood of front vowels is, it is not unexpected that some accents of English should have more palatalisation than others, and it is possible that MUE just happens to be one such variety. In other words, VP in MUE is hardly unusual, and a contact explanation may not be required to explain this very common kind of change, one which is essentially an extension of a general English pattern.

But in fact, VP in MUE is even less unusual from an English perspective when we consider the pronunciation of the velar stops in England since the Early Modern period. Evidence of significant palatalisation of /k/ and /g/ before front vowels, often indicated in spelling as <ky> and <gy>, appears in the written record from the early seventeenth century (see MacMahon 1999: 471–3 for an overview of the evidence; see also Jespersen 1909: 349–51; Jones 2006: 253–4, 335–6; Wyld 1927: 219). Dobson (1957: 952) argues that this palatalisation may go back to the ME period, but because of its subphonemic status it was not indicated in writing. Thus, for example, the Londoner John Wallis, writing in the 1650s, referred to 'the frequent insertion of /j/ in CAN, GET and BEGIN' (MacMahon 1999: 471), and described this as a Midland English pronunciation (Dobson 1957: 952). Evidence for this form of VP in English extends through the eighteenth and into the nineteenth centuries, especially for the TRAP, START and PRICE vowels, possibly because in these cases the transition from the palatal consonant to the following low vowel was most obvious, as it is in MUE. So in his 'English Spelling and Pronouncing Vocabulary' of 1830, William Angus indicates /gj/ and /kj/ in *guarantee, guaranty, guardian, guidance, guileful, guise, kile* and *kindness* (MacMahon 1999: 472). However, in the eighteenth and, especially, the nineteenth century, the feature was on the wane in standard varieties of English, resulting in it being the subject of often negative comment (ibid.). By the time we get to the second half of the nineteenth century, the feature was becoming obsolete in StE, though some older speakers could still be heard to use it (ibid.). However, the evidence points to significant palatalisation of /k/ and /g/ before front vowels being a common feature of English in the seventeenth, eighteenth and nineteenth centuries. This palatalisation was recorded before /ɪ/ (e.g. *begin*), /ɛ/ (e.g. *get*), /a/ (e.g. *can*), /eː/ > /eɪ/ (e.g. *case*), /ʌɪ/ > /aɪ/ (e.g. *kind*), /ar/ (e.g. *garden*) and /ər/ (e.g. *gird*, i.e. in the 'ir' but not 'ur' NURSE words, just as in MUE). The lack of indication of palatalisation before /iː/ is likely to be the result of this pronunciation not being noteworthy, a degree of palatalisation of /k/ and /g/ before this vowel being a feature of English even today. There is no indication of palatalisation of /k/, /g/ or /ŋ/ in final position after vowels.

Although VP disappeared from StE in the second half of the nineteenth century, it survived in English dialects in England into the mid twentieth century. Ellis (1889) records VP widely across England in words including *again, came, can, candle, cares, carrot, case, gate, get, girl, kettle* and *kind.* The feature was particularly prominent in Lancashire and the Midlands as far south as Oxfordshire and Hertfordshire, and was not uncommon in East Anglia, whilst it was sporadically attested elsewhere in southern England, in Lincolnshire, and in the West Riding of Yorkshire. By the time of the mid-twentieth-century SED, VP had disappeared from many dialects in this area. Nevertheless, remnants of VP were still widely (if sparsely) attested, being recorded across much of the Midlands, and sporadically into south Lancashire, south Yorkshire and East Anglia (see, for example, the responses to the SED questions I.9.3 and I.11.7 *cart*, III.13.8–9 *cat*, V.8.7 *kettle*, VIII.1.3 *girls* and IX.4.10 *care*).

Although VP is not recorded in coda position in England, there is indirect evidence for its existence, or former existence, in some dialects. Certain traditional dialects of English in England had, like MUE, PPR before palato-alveolar fricatives and affricates, especially /ʃ/, most commonly after /a/, but also after /ɛ/ and /ɒ/~/ɔː/, so that words such as *ash(-tree)* were pronounced as [aɪʃ] or the like with an upglide, or as [ɛʃ]~[eːʃ] with raising (see Wright 1905: 24, 312). This was particularly characteristic of dialects in the south-west (e.g. Widén 1949: 32), but was also typical of parts of Lancashire, south-west Yorkshire and Derbyshire (see Hargreaves 1904: 2–3, 19–20; Wright 1905: 24, 312; Shorrocks 1998: 264–6), and raised [ɛ] or [eː]-type pronunciations were recorded in locations across the Midlands and south of England (e.g. Wright 1905: 312). Unfortunately the SED contains very little relevant data for this feature, but instances of upgliding before /ʃ/ were common in south-west England for the words *ash(es)* (Qs. V.4.4–5), *thresh* (Q. II.8.1) and *wash* (Qs. V.9.5, IX.11.1), whilst raising of /a/ to /ɛ/ before /ʃ/ is widely attested. Unfortunately these words may be subject to other changes which obscure or have blocked gliding before /ʃ/ (e.g. *ash(es)* in much of northern and western England traditionally has /s/, not /ʃ/), but the data in Wright (1905) makes clear that this was, until recently, a widespread feature in England (see his entries for *ash (tree), fresh, smash, thresh* and *wash*).

A similar phenomenon is also recorded before final /g/ and, occasionally, before final /k/ in some traditional English dialects, again especially those in the south-west, but also in other dialects. Wright (1905), for example, records upgliding after /a/ in *back, bag, black, drag, rag, wag* in north-west and south-west England (as well as some instances of raising to [ɛ] elsewhere). Some upgliding is also recorded for /ɛ/ in *beg, egg* and *leg*. The SED also recorded upgliding after /a/ (as well as some raised forms) before a final /g/ in *bag* (Q. V.8.5) and *tag* (Q. VI.14.26) in south-west England, Norfolk and Essex. There are also some instances of upgliding in south-west England and Essex after /ɛ/ before /g/ in *eggs* (Q. VII.4.9) and *legs* (Q. IX.8.7). For the Dorset dialect, Widén (1949: 30) tells us that '[b]efore [g, ŋ] a glide [ⁱ] has been recorded (beside a pure long vowel) in [bæˑʲg] bag, n., [bɹæˑʲg] brag, [flæˑʲg] flag (standard), [gæˑʲŋ] gang, n., [twæˑʲŋ] twang, n.'. Shorrocks (1998: 227) recorded raised variants of /a/ ([ɑ̈], [æ]) 'especially before /k, g/ and [ŋ]', but does not record upglides in words of this type, even though these were recorded by Wright (1905) for south Lancashire.

The motivation for an upglide before palato-alveolars is clear: it represents a vowel transition from the low(-mid) position to the (pre-)palatal articulation of /ʃ/. Raising of /a/ to [ɛ] and [eː] before palato-alveolars may have a similar explanation, though increase in the frequency of the second vowel formant is usual before palatal consonants (see Thomas 2011a: 101). The motivation for the upglide before /g/ (and occasionally before /k/ and /ŋ/) is less obvious, though raising before velars is not altogether unexpected (again see Thomas 2011a: 101). There is no reason why a high-front glide should develop between a low(-mid) vowel and a following velar, however. This suggests that these velar consonants were, at some stage in the history of these dialects, palatalised, so that the development of the upglide has the same motivation as it does before /ʃ/. That is, upgliding between /a/ and /ɛ/ and a final velar stop or nasal provides us with evidence of significant palatalisation of these velar consonants after (certain) front vowels in the history of English, even though such a feature is not recorded historically (though a degree of palatalisation of /k/, /g/ and /ŋ/ after front vowels is a feature of many varieties of English in England and elsewhere today). If this is right, then VP in England was even more similar to VP in MUE, since it occurred not only in onset position before front vowels but also in coda position after (at least some of) the same vowels.

Nevertheless, problems remain, especially the fact that pre-velar upgliding in English dialects is most common in south-west England, where VP in onset position is generally not recorded, and is unrecorded in many dialects in the Midlands of England which did have VP in onset position. Some dialects (especially in north-west England) did have both VP in onset position and pre-velar upgliding, but in order to accept a more general connection between the two features, we have to assume that VP in coda position either did not always produce upglides or that these upglides have been lost in many dialects. This may be pushing the evidence too far, but the existence of onset VP and of pre-velar upgliding and raising in many dialects in England is suggestive at least of a more widespread distribution of VP in previous centuries of a type very similar to what is found in MUE. Indeed, VP in English is, as far as can be determined, otherwise almost identical to what is found in MUE.

The existence of VP in England of a very similar kind to what is found in MUE is also the likely explanation for the presence of VP in a number of other extra-territorial Englishes. Velar Palalisation is traditionally found in southern United States (Wells 1982: 552) and in the Caribbean, especially in Jamaica (ibid.: 569; Harris 1987: 272–5). Strikingly, these dialects most obviously have palatalisation before low vowels when they occur in the TRAP and START lexical sets, often accompanied by [j] in initial position and by an upglide [ɪ] in coda position. This is true even when the vowel is no longer front, as in the case of *garden* pronounced as [ˈɟɒːdn̩] in the southern United States (Wells 1982: 552). Furthermore, palatalisation is blocked before [a]-type vowels that derive from an earlier back vowel, so that there is VP in *cat* ([cjat]) in Jamaica but not in *cot* ([kat]). In both respects, these varieties match the patterns of VP found in England and MUE. Whilst a role for MUE or other dialects of IrE in the development of VP in these New World dialects might be possible in some cases, Harris (1987: 274) argues that this cannot be true more generally, as this VP is found in Caribbean varieties of English that have had no input from IrE dialects. Instead, he suggests (ibid.) that '[t]he most likely source of palatalisation in Atlantic contact vernaculars is . . . metropolitan English'.

3.3.4 *Velar Palatalisation in Scots*

Palatalisation of velar /k/ and /g/ is also found in dialects of Scots according to Johnston (1997b: 503), and it is indicated for some locations in LAS3. Johnston describes VP before front vowels as a common feature of Scots dialects 'in Galloway, the mainland far north and the Northern Isles', and as a variable feature in some West-Mid dialects of Scots, 'notably Glaswegian, Clydesmouth and Ayrshire varieties' and 'sporadically in parts of the eastern Border', though outside of the Isle of Bute, LAS3 does not record VP in southern Scotland. Palatalisation may be extreme in northern dialects, going as far as producing palatal affricates such as [tɕ] and [dʑ] (though [c] and [ɟ] are more common). Whilst a source in Ulster for VP could possibly be argued for the Galloway and West-Mid cases referred to by Johnston, it cannot be the source of VP in more easterly or northerly dialects of Scots. Johnston (1997b: 503) also describes palatalisation of the velar stops after front vowels in Scots dialects, particularly in 'east Fife, Morayshire and Northern Northern varieties', and LAS3 also records VP after front vowels in these areas, as well as in Arbroath in Angus on the east coast. Johnston (1997b: 503) notes that although some of the Scots dialects with VP are from areas where we might expect a history of contact with Gaelic or Norse (he notes that 'the phonotactics of these languages both favour palatalisation'), a contact origin for the feature is not necessary given how natural a sound change it is and the close parallels to it found in dialects in England. However, he suggests that 'no doubt the pronunciation habits of bilinguals aided the application and spread of these changes in the far north and south-west'.

Whatever the source of VP in Scots dialects, it occurs before and after a range of front vowels, though palatalisation in the neighbourhood of /a/ (often back [ɑ] in Scots) is less well attested. However, VP in Scots dialects does look similar to the feature in MUE. But since most dialects reported with VP in Scotland are far from Ulster and the areas that supplied the majority of Scottish Plantation settlers, not all of these dialects could have contributed to VP in MUE. There is, however, some evidence for VP in southern and south-west Scotland, as noted in Johnston (1997b), and it may be that the feature was present in some of the input Scots varieties to Ulster in the seventeenth century, though it is unlikely to have been general, something which is perhaps indicated by VP being less characteristic of USc than of MUE.

3.3.5 The origins of Velar Palatalisation in MUE

As was noted in Section 3.3.1, many previous researchers have assumed an Irish origin for VP in MUE and other dialects of IrE, though Harris is a notable exception, suggesting as he does an English origin for the feature. A review of the distribution of velar and palatal stops in MUE, Irish, English and Scots shows that there are similar patterns in all of these varieties, so that determining a single source for this feature may be impossible. Nevertheless, the review has shown that although Irish bears superficial similarities to MUE in terms of its distribution of broad and slender dorsal consonants and their interactions with neighbouring vowels, there are significant differences between the two languages, not least that the palatal/velar distinction in Irish is phonemic whilst it is allophonic in MUE and the fact that the broad/slender distinction operates across the whole consonantal system, not just in the dorsal region. Velar Palatalisation in England is less well attested, being a feature of earlier centuries and, in more recent times, of often poorly recorded traditional dialects. But the evidence we have suggests that VP in England was similar to VP in MUE, especially before vowels, but also possibly after vowels. As Harris (1987: 272–5) points out, this VP in English is or was also found in the Caribbean and the southern United States, and the form it takes in Jamaican Creole is essentially identical to VP in MUE. Harris (1987) suggests that a source in England for this feature in the Caribbean is rather more likely than a source in MUE. VP of a similar sort is also found in some Scots dialects, and although these are mainly in the north of Scotland there is some evidence for VP in southern and south-west Scots dialects too.

So it seems that English in England is the most likely source for VP in MUE (and indeed in other dialects of IrE). It may well be the case that some Scots speakers who came to northern Ireland during the Plantation and associated settlements also had VP, and, if so, this would have been essentially the same as VP in English, and would have added to the number of speakers with the feature. What role is there for Irish, then, if it didn't cause VP in MUE? Harris (1987: 275) suggests that Irish would have been 'at best reinforcing or "preservative"' in the development of VP in MUE. Certainly VP in English was fairly compatible with the distribution of palatal dorsal consonants in Irish, though by no means identical. It is notable, however, that the quality of Irish dorsal stops is unimportant in borrowings in MUE. So, for example, /k/ occurs in Irish *cabhán* 'little hill' and *caorthann* 'rowan', but MUE has [c] in place-names with these elements (e.g. *Cavan* ['cävən], *Rakeeran* [ɹəˈciəɹən]). The pronunciation of dorsal stops in borrowings from Irish is determined by the following vowel in MUE, not by the original pronunciation in Irish. And of course, the slender/broad distinction is not just confined to dorsal consonants in Irish, but operates across the whole system, something which essentially has no analogue in MUE. Why would one part of this slender/broad system become integrated into MUE phonology when the rest of it was ignored?

But with VP (and its associated vocalic effects) present in the English input, with VP of the same sort surviving into twentieth-century English (and Caribbean) dialects which were not reinforced by Irish, and with VP in MUE still essentially identical in various respects to what was found in English, it is not clear that this reinforcement has any explanatory value, especially given that no aspect of VP in MUE specifically requires it. I return to this issue in Section 5.2.1.

3.4 The palato-alveolars and Palatal Velarisation

As a result of changes to the Early Modern English (EModE) diphthong /iu/ (e.g. in *manure, new, pure*) and of sequences of /i/+vowel (e.g. in *Christian, immediate, question*) in many dialects of English, a wide range of consonant+/j/ clusters were created in onset position and across syllable boundaries (for overviews, see Lass 2000: 121–2; Wells 1982: 206–8). A number of these clusters were subject to simplification in most dialects as a result of 'Early Yod Dropping' (Wells 1982: 207), whereby /j/ was deleted after palatal consonants, /r/ and /Cl/ sequences. Further instances of Yod Dropping occur in various dialects, with loss after /θ/ (e.g. *enthusiasm*), /s/ (e.g. *suit*), /z/ (e.g. *resume*) and /l/ (e.g. *lewd*) being particularly common before stressed vowels, including in some forms of RP (ibid.). In dialects of this sort, /j/ is retained after other consonants, though the sequences /tj/ and /dj/ may be subject to 'Yod Coalesence' (Minkova 2014: 143–5; Wells 1982: 207), becoming [ʧ] and [ʤ] and merging with pre-existing /ʧ/ (e.g. *cheese*) and /ʤ/ (e.g. *join*) in the language.

Traditional MUE aligns with RP and similar varieties of English in its development of clusters involving /j/. The Early Modern diphthong /iu/ has become /jʉ/ (i.e. /j/ followed by the usual vowel of the GOOSE lexical set), but /j/ has typically been lost after /θ/, /s/, /z/ and /l/ when before a stressed syllable (/sj/ has become /ʃ/ in *issue*, whilst /j/ remains in words like *million* /mëljən/). Forms such as /ëndjən/ for *Indian* are also common in traditional MUE, as similar forms once were in StE too. Although Yod Coalesence in /tj/ and /dj/ is widespread in MUE, it is not typical of all traditional varieties of the dialect, some of which distinguish these sequences from /ʧ/ and /ʤ/.[3] The clusters /tj/, /dj/, /nj/ and /lj/ are typically realised as palato-alveolar consonants in traditional MUE, [t̪ʲ], [d̪ʲ], [n̪ʲ] and [l̪ʲ] respectively. These are similar in pronunciation to Irish /t′/, /d′/, /n′/ and /l′/, but they are hardly atypical of English and Scots either, especially given the frequency with which they have been affected by Yod Coalesence in Britain, a change which presupposes intermediary pronunciations such as [t̪ʲ] and [d̪ʲ]. Indeed, Ulster Irish, as well as some dialects of Connacht Irish and Scottish Gaelic, has undergone a similar change in its realisation of /t′/ and /d′/, with [ʧ] and [ʤ] (or more accurately [tɕ] and [dʑ]; see further below) being typical of some dialects (see Ó Dochartaigh 1987: 146–55). Whether this change is related to Yod Coalesence in English (a feature which is widespread and not generally connected with areas of potential contact with Gaelic languages) is unknown, this appearing to be a relatively new feature in both languages. It may just be a development which is likely to affect palato-alveolar stops.

Given Yod Coalesence and affrication of the slender coronal stops in Irish, MUE and some varieties of Ulster Irish have ended up with rather similar consonants in the palato-alveolar region. MUE has the palato-alveolar consonants /ʧ/, /ʤ/, /ʃ/ and /ʒ/, whilst Ulster Irish has /t′/ ([ʧ] or [tɕ]), /d′/ ([ʤ] or [dʑ]) and /s′/ ([ʃ] or [ɕ]). Of course, this ignores Ulster Irish dialects which do not have affrication, traditional MUE dialects with /tj/ and /dj/ separate from /ʧ/ and /ʤ/, and the lack of anything corresponding to English /ʒ/ in Irish. However, some previous researchers have also suggested that the palato-alveolar consonants in Ulster Irish and MUE are phonetically very similar, and that MUE diverges from other dialects of English in this respect. Of the palato-alveolar affricates, Adams (1948: 14) states that they

> have not quite the same sound as in English speech where they have a fair degree of lip-rounding and the tip and blade of the tongue are curled up towards the hard palate or teeth-ridge. In Ulster the lips are more spread and the tongue flatter with its blade and front towards the teeth-ridge. This is more like the sound of the Irish slender *s*.

Wells (1982: 446) describes the situation as follows:

> Ulster /ʃ, ʒ, tʃ, dʒ/ have a stronger palatal component in their realization than their counterparts in England, tending towards [ɕ, ʑ, tɕ, dʑ]. This may be attributable to Irish Gaelic influence, [ɕ] being the phonetic quality of the 'slender' /s,/ of Ulster Irish.

This looks like a case of imposition of an Irish feature on MUE, but a couple of notes of caution are in order before we assume that this is the case. We simply don't know how the palato-alveolar consonants are pronounced in most varieties of English or Scots, and as these are relatively subtle differences detailed phonetic analysis is required to determine how typical or atypical the MUE pronunciations of them are from an English perspective. We must also allow for change in the pronunciation of these consonants in English over the last 400 years. Nor do we know the precise phonetics of /s′/ in Ulster Irish, neither today nor in the past. Similarly, we don't know how the palato-alveolar consonants are pronounced in MUE other than from the kinds of indications given by Adams and Wells. The data from the SwTE corpus suggests that they are not dramatically different (auditorily at least) from the general English pronunciations, and they may be subject to a degree of conditioning in their realisation depending upon the preceding vowel (as is the case with a number of other consonants in MUE; see Sections 3.3 and 3.9.2). For example, the /ʃ/ in *McAleesh* (e.g. [ˌmakəˈliʃ]) fits reasonably well with the descriptions in Adams and Wells (though it certainly isn't [ɕ] and the tongue tip and blade are not particularly advanced, as described by Adams), but the /ʃ/ in *rush* (e.g. [ɹɔʃ]) is much more like the /ʃ/ in RP English, with a degree of lip-rounding, whilst the /ʃ/ in *harsh* is prone to (near-)merger with /s/ after /r/ (e.g. [häːɹʂʲ]). So although there may be phonetic similarities between MUE and Ulster Irish in the palato-alveolar region, it is not clear how similar they are or whether this distinguishes MUE from other dialects of English. And of course there are important structural differences too (compare SwTE /tj/, /dj/, /ʧ/, /ʤ/, /ʃ/ and /ʒ/ with Ulster Irish /t′/, /d′/ and /s′/).

There is another change affecting /tj/ and /dj/ in MUE which looks very similar to one affecting /t′/ and /d′/ in some Irish dialects, however. This is a change whereby original /tj/ and /dj/ are retracted to a palatal or even velar position, so that they are pronounced [c] and [ɟ] or in some cases as [k] and [g]. This Palatal Velarisation (PV) results in merger of /tj/ and /dj/ with /kj/ (e.g. in *cure*) and /gj/ (e.g. in *argue*) and with fronted allophones of /k/ and /g/ due to Velar Palatalisation (Section 3.3). This development has been reported not only in MUE (see Harris 1985: 213–14; Todd 1984: 168), but also in some dialects of USc (Evans 1997; Johnston 1997b: 503–4) and in dialects of SIrE in the Irish midlands and south-east (Henry 1958: 127–9; Kallen 2013: 57; Nally 1971: 37; Ó Muirithe 1996: 29; Wells 1982: 434). LAS3 not uncommonly recorded [kj] and [gj] in *dew, tube* and *tune* in Ulster, especially in the MUE dialects of Counties Down and Armagh. In SwTE, PV is a not uncommon feature found in the speech of older Protestants and Catholics,[4] especially in the words *Christian* (['kɹɐscən]/['kɹəskən]), *idiot/eejit* (['iɟət]~['igət]), *Indian-meal* ([ˌëɲɟən'meəl]) and *question* (['kwɛscən]~['kwɛskən]), all of which derive from earlier sequences of /ɪ/ and an unstressed schwa. It also occasionally occurs in other words, e.g. *furniture* (['fɔ̈ˑnëcə˞]), *stupid* (['scʉpət]), *tune* ([cʉn]) and the surname *Virtue* (['väːɹkez] 'Varkies').

A similar change, whereby /t'/ and /d'/ have become [c] and [ɟ] and thus have merged with /k'/ and /g'/, is found in some Irish and Scottish Gaelic dialects. This is reported, for example, in the Irish dialects of Rathlin Island (Holmer 1942: 34), the Glens of Antrim (Holmer 1940: 21), south Armagh (Sommerfelt 1929: 124, 168), north Tyrone (Stockman and Wagner 1965: 49, 145), Galway (Ó Curnáin 2007: 255–6; Ó hUiginn 1994: 553), and 'in a number of other Connacht dialects' (Ó Dochartaigh 1987: 147). Thus, for example, in north Tyrone the pronunciations [ak'ən], [k'e'] and [k'iN:] are recorded for *aiteann* 'whin', *te* 'hot' and *tinn* 'sore'. In Wagner (1958), sporadic examples of this change are recorded in Donegal (pp. 27, 130), Cavan (p. 208), Leitrim (pp. 101, 103, 147, 241), Sligo (p. 147) and Galway (p. 145). In south-west Scotland, Holmer (1962: 18; see also Watson 1994: 665) found that 'the two sounds [d'] and [g'] are constantly interchangeable in Gaelic', whilst Ó Dochartaigh (1994–7) recorded /k'/ and /g'/ for /t'/ and /d'/ consistently in the dialect of St Kilda, and occasionally in Lewis and east Sutherland (see, for example, maps 304 *deas* 'ready', 309 *diallaid* 'saddle', 836 *teanga* 'tongue', 837 *teann* 'tight', 838 *teannaich* 'tighten', 846 *tinn* 'ill' and 847 *tionndaidh* 'turn'). Whilst this is a fairly wide-spread change in Irish and Scottish Gaelic, it is really only characteristic of a few dialects and is sporadic in other dialects which have it.

Other than a few examples of [c] for /tj/ on the Northumberland coast in the early twentieth century (e.g. Rydland 1998: 262), there are no records of PV in English in England. The feature is found in some Scots dialects, however. Johnston (1997b: 503) notes that '[t]his is quite common in both Caithnesian and Ulster Scots, but is also frequent in coastal Moray and Banff Mid-Northern varieties'. He further adds that '[a]ll these dialects have a penchant for palatalising velars and assimilating parts of consonant clusters to each other' (ibid.). LAS3 records sporadic examples of PV in Shetland, Orkney, north-east Aberdeenshire (in *tongs* [kjaŋz]) and in east Perthshire, as well as more common examples in Caithness, Moray and Banff. In addition to the fact that most of these dialects have palatalised /k/ and /g/ before front vowels, none of them are in areas where Gaelic was characterised by the shift of /t'/ and /d'/ to /k'/ and /g'/. This suggests that PV in these dialects has an internal explanation: the proximity of /tj/ and /dj/ to [c] (/k(j)/) and [ɟ] (/g(j)/) has led to some instances of cross-over into the phonetic space of the dorsal pair of stops. Notably, this feature is characteristic of Scots dialects that did not contribute to any significant degree to the formation of MUE and USc, so that its existence in Scotland does not imply a source for it in Ireland.

Are these changes in IrE (including MUE) and Irish connected? The similarity in the changes and their geographical overlap (in part at least) would seem to suggest so. The change depends on close phonetic similarity between palatalised coronal stops (e.g. [t̟ʲ], [d̟ʲ]) and palatal or palatalised velar stops (e.g. [c], [ɟ]). This close similarity is generally characteristic, or was so before affrication, of Irish and Scottish Gaelic, whilst it is also a feature of certain dialects of English and Scots. This can lead to phonetic overlap of the two categories, with (usually sporadic) cross-overs between them. Given that phonetic closeness of the two categories is a general characteristic of the Gaelic languages, and that cross-overs of the palatalised coronal stops into the phonetic space of the palatalised velars is fairly widespread in Irish in particular, influence from Irish on English (and Scots) in Ireland seems like the most straightforward explanation. But there are dialects of English and Scots in Ireland with consistent PV where the change has not been recorded in the local Irish dialect (e.g. in Glinsk, Donegal; see Evans 1997), and there are dialects of Scots with PV in areas where it was not a feature of the local Gaelic dialects (e.g. Moray and Banff), and indeed where contact with Gaelic is unlikely (e.g. Shetland). Furthermore, in MUE there are a number of borrowings from Irish which have /tj/ representing Irish /t'/. Examples from SwTE include the place-name *Gortin* ([ˈgɔːɹt̟ʲən], rhyming with *fortune*, from Irish *Goirtín*), the place-name element *tatty-* (from Irish *táite* 'land division of sixty Irish acres', e.g. in *Tattyreagh* [ˌtät̟ʲəˈɹeː], *Tattysallagh* [ˌtät̟ʲəˈsälə(h)]), and in the words *plawteen* ('round dung desposit' [ˈplä:t̟ʲən], from Irish *pláitín* 'small plate') and *poteen* ([ˈpɔːt̟ʲən],[5] from Irish *poitín*). In none of these cases is PV possible (i.e. they never have [c]), so that the feature is restricted to a small number of words of English origin, especially those with historical /ɪ/ followed by schwa (e.g. *Christian, idiot, Indian, question*), as noted above. If this feature comes from Irish, why is it avoided in words of specifically Irish origin, but present in words of English origin?

Influence in the other direction is perhaps possible, at least in some cases, though given the sporadic nature of PV in most of the English and Scots dialects that have it and the appearance of this change in Irish dialects in areas where PV has not been recorded in Irish English (e.g. Galway), there are problems with this explanation too. But in neither language does the change seem to be deep-rooted (it is usually only sporadic) or of long standing (it is typical of a scattering of dialects only), so a source for the change in one or other language prior to the Plantation of Ulster cannot be definitely determined.

So are other explanations for the existence of these two similar changes in Irish and IrE (including MUE) possible? It is noteworthy that precisely this kind of change is recorded in some other languages in Europe which contrast palatalised coronal stops with palatal or palatalised velar stops. In Common Scandinavian, /tj/, /dj/, /kj/ and /gj/ developed when /t/, /d/, /k/ and /g/ where followed by Germanic *iu and *e, which changed to *jū/jō* and *ja/jǫ* respectively (Haugen 1976: 268). Furthermore, /k/ and /g/ palatalised before front vowels, to [kj] and [gj]. Although these were fronted further to merge with /tj/ and /dj/ in many Scandinavian dialects, they remained as [kj] and [gj] in most Danish varieties, and indeed were depalatalised to /k/ and /g/ in South Jutlandic Danish (Haugen 1976: 268–9). But Haugen (1976: 269) notes that this depalatalisation of [kj] and [gj] 'led to hyperforms by which older *tj* was turned into *k* along with *kj*, e.g. *tjene* serve > *kæne*'. Here we have a situation which is very similar to what happened in MUE: palatalised coronal and palatalised velar stops approximated each other in phonetic space, leading to (near-)merger with some cross-over of the palatalised coronal stops into the phonetic space of the palatalised velar stops, and a reversal of VP resulting in velar stops occurring for original palatalised coronals (cf. pronunciations such as ['igət] and ['kwɛskən] for *idiot*/*eejit* and *question* in SwTE).

A similar situation exists in some Russian dialects (see Orlova 1970: 61–8 for details). Much like in Irish, Russian consonants are either 'hard' (plain) or 'soft' (palatalised), so that it has palatalised coronal stops and palatalised velar stops (though the latter typically occur only before front vowels and are not phonemically distinct from the plain velar stops). In some dialects of Russian (see ibid.: 63), the soft velar stops may be fronted so that they are in a situation of (near-)merger with the soft coronal stops. As a result of contact between dialects which have this (near-)merger and those which do not, reversal of this change can lead to hypercorrect forms with soft velar stops for etymological soft coronal stops, for example, *t'esto* 'dough' as [kʲe]*sto* (ibid.: 68).

Obviously neither of these developments is connected with PV in Ireland, but they do demonstrate that this is a change which can occur when a language contrasts palatalised coronal and palatal or palatalised velar stops, and it may be typical when there is reversal of the (near-)merger. So perhaps this offers an explanation for the existence of PV in IrE alongside a similar change in Irish. For entirely independent reasons, the two languages contrast these two kinds of stops and, just as has happened in some Scottish Gaelic, Scots, Danish and Russian dialects with a similar consonantal system, phonetic overlap of the two categories occurs, leading to some cross-overs between them. In the case of IrE (including MUE), Scots, Danish and Russian, this appears to have been encouraged by the sub-phonemic nature of at least some of the palatalised velars and their 'correction' in contact with dialects that do not have this feature.

Another possibility is that confusion between /t', d'/ and /k', g'/ in Irish is itself motivated by contact with English, though not borrowed from it. It is a well-documented phenomenon that Irish dialects undergoing language death are prone to collapse phonemic distinctions that are maintained in other dialects. Thus, for example, the broad/slender distinction may be lost to an extent, as is reported in Holmer (1942: 18–19) and Stockman and Wagner (1965: 1965). Similarly, lenition, despite being a central aspect of Irish morpho-phonology, may begin to break down (e.g. Holmer 1940: 36, 1942: 60; Stockman and Wagner 1965: 203–5; see also Dorian 1981: 114ff. for a similar situation in Scottish Gaelic). Given that instances of /k'/ and /g'/ are mostly reported for Irish dialects which in the mid twentieth century were at an advanced stage of language death (i.e. those of east Ulster and of north-east Connacht), might this change represent another instance of such phonemic collapse?

It is probably impossible to determine the origins of PV in MUE. It could be that it is the result of contact with Irish, but this explanation is not unproblematic. If this feature of MUE does have its source in Irish, it is unusual, as the present study shows that definite cases of Irish influence on the phonology of MUE, as opposed to rein-forcement of patterns inherited from English and Scots, are otherwise hard to iden-tify. Influence in the other direction is not impossible, but seems unlikely in some cases at least. A general tendency for confusion between palatalised coronal stops and palatal or palatalised velar stops has been identified, and this might suggest that the existence of this similar change in Irish and MUE is coincidental, though such an explanation inevitably feels dissatisfying. It may be that contact was involved in some way, given the preference for the change in Irish dialects which were at an advanced stage of language death, but that no one source or cause of the similar changes in both languages can be identified.

The realisation and development of the palatalised coronal consonants in MUE appears to show some close parallels with Irish, though determining the source of the various patterns is difficult given the recent development of some of them, their imperfect geographical match and the tendency of similar changes to develop in other languages. It is worth pointing out that even in this part of the consonant system, where MUE appears to most closely approximate Irish, contact explanations are not straightforward and indeed may not be sufficient to account for the patterns that exist in the dialect.

3.5 Pre-R Dentalisation

The dental pronunciation of the general English alveolar stops /t/ and /d/ (and sometimes /n/) as [t̪] and [d̪] (and [n̪]) before /r/ and unstressed /ər/ is a well known feature of IrE, including MUE, which has been termed 'Pre-R Dentalisation' (PreRD; see Maguire 2012a, 2016). This feature is typically accompanied by an '/r/-Realisation Effect' (RRE), whereby /r/ is pronounced as a tap after dental consonants, including those which result from PreRD, and by a 'Morpheme Boundary Constraint' (MBC), whereby PreRD operates across 'Class I' morpheme boundaries, but is blocked by 'Class II' morpheme boundaries and word boundaries (see Bermúdez-Otero and McMahon 2006 for an explanation of these terms). The origins of PreRD, the RRE and the MBC are discussed in detail in Maguire (2012a, 2016; see also Harris 1985: 211–18), and the close similarity between this combina-tion of features in IrE and in traditional and historical varieties of English and Scots means that a British origin of the feature in MUE (or indeed in other dialects of IrE) is certain. Rather than reiterate the data and arguments here, I refer the reader to Maguire (2012a, 2016) for detailed discussion. Previous claims of an Irish origin of the feature (see Ellis 1869: 1239; Adams 1967: 72; Lunny 1981a: 166–7; Ó Baoill 1991: 590–1; Ó hUrdail 1997: 146), on the other hand, cannot be supported, relying as they do on superficial similarities between PreRD in IrE and the dental pronunciation of the broad coronal consonants in Irish. Other than the exceptions noted below, Irish has nothing in its phonology equivalent to PreRD, the RRE or the MBC.

Although it is generally the case that there is no equivalent of PreRD in Irish, one dialect, that of Ring in Co. Waterford, has been recorded with a similar feature. Breatnach (1947: 30) notes that a

> variety of **d′** with contact between the tip of the tongue and the backs of the upper front teeth as well as the teeth-ridge, i.e. a dental variety, is heard (i) when **r′** follows immediately, and (ii) when **d′** is followed by a short unstressed vowel + **r′**.

A similar situation pertains to /t′/ (ibid.: 32). This disruption of the core distinction between dental broad coronal stops and slender palatalised ones is isolated within Irish, and given its close similarity with PreRD in IrE, there can be no doubt that it has its origin there. The Ring dialect of Irish had been in contact with English for almost 800 years when Breatnach was writing his description of it, so it is not surprising that features of IrE have made their way into it.

Interestingly, Hickey (2014: 93) finds that '[a]fter dental stops a slightly trilled realisation of /r/ may occur, e.g. in *trom* [t̪rʌm] "heavy"' in some varieties of Irish. This looks like the RRE in IrE, but given the absence of comment on this feature in earlier descriptions of traditional Irish dialects and the fact that modern speakers are all bilingual with (and indeed often dominant in) English, it is clear that this feature of IrE, which has unambiguous parallels in English (and Scots) in Britain, has become established in the speech of some Irish speakers in recent decades too. Neither this nor the presence of dental pronunciations of /t′/ and /d′/ in the Ring dialect are evidence that PreRD and its associated features have a long history in Irish or that PreRD in IrE derives from that.

Maguire (2012a) argues that PreRD was once found across England, including in the ancestor of StE and in the Midland and southern dialects of many of the Plantation settlers in Ulster. This explains why PreRD is found not only in Ulster but across Ireland and how it survived the processes of new dialect formation and language contact that we know to have taken place on the island (see Section 5.3.1) – it was a majority input form. For Ulster there is the additional factor that the feature was also characteristic of the Scots input, so that the survival of the feature in MUE was 'inevitable' (Trudgill 2004).

Although a British origin for PreRD (and its associated effects) cannot be doubted, is there room for a role for Irish in the development of the feature in MUE and other varieties of IrE? Maguire (2012a) raises the possibility that speakers of Irish, having a distinction between broad, dental /t, d/ and slender, lamino-alveolar /t′ d′/, would have been sensitive to the distinction between dental and non-dental coronals in English and, in finding this feature comparatively easy to learn as a result, would have increased the number of speakers in the community with this feature. In so doing, they could have reinforced the feature in the emergent MUE, helping it to survive the process of new dialect formation. The problem with this idea is that it requires us to cherry-pick the data, focusing only on those patterns which most resemble features of Irish whilst ignoring the wider phonological context which doesn't match with Irish. In terms of its coronal stops, Irish had broad [t̪ˠ, d̪ˠ] vs slender [t̠ʲ, d̠ʲ]. Whilst the first pair matches English dentalised [t̪, d̪] quite well, the second pair does not match English [t, d] (/t, d/) particularly well (especially since in Ulster Irish these consonants are prone to affrication to [ʧ, ʤ]; for further discussion, see Section 3.4). When we compare non-sibilant coronal consonants in English and Irish more generally (Figure 3.1, illustrated with the voiceless consonants only), the coincidence of Irish [t̪ˠ, d̪ˠ] and English [t̪, d̪] does

	Irish	**English**	
		θ	*thin*
tá, trá	t̪ˠ	t̪ (/t/)	*tree*
te, trí	t̪ʲ (> t͡ʃ)	t	*tin*
		tj	*tune*
		t͡ʃ	*church*

Fig. 3.1 Correspondences between the voiceless non-sibilant coronal consonants in Irish and English.

not look so convincing, and there is no obvious mapping of Irish consonants on to English ones.

/tr/ and /dr/ are pronounced as [t̪ˠɾˠ] and [d̪ˠɾˠ] in Irish, but the slender counterparts of these clusters (in most cases, consonants in a cluster in Irish are all broad or all slender), /t'r'/ and /d'r'/, are pronounced [t̪ʲɾʲ] and [d̪ʲɾʲ] (or even [t͡ʃɾʲ] and [d͡ʒɾʲ]), which are not similar to /tr/ and /dr/ in IrE. But there is no obvious reason why speakers of Irish would not choose /tr/ and /dr/ over /t'r'/ and /d'r'/ when learning to pronounce English if the English target was, for example, [tɪ] and [dɹ]. Furthermore, there is no feature of Irish phonology which would create PreRD before /ər/ in IrE, the sequences /tər/ (e.g. *uachtar* 'top'), /t'ər'/ (e.g. *leitir* 'hillside'), /tər'/ (e.g. *uachtair* 'top (gen. sg.)') and /t'ər/ (e.g. *itear* 'they eat/it is eaten'), for example, all being possible. Interestingly, the pronunciation of the coronal stop in Irish is unimportant in the MUE pronunciation of place-names with Irish *leitir*, such as *Letterkenny* (Irish *Leitir Ceanain*), since PreRD operates as expected (e.g. [ˌlɛt̪ə·ˈcɛne]).

Regardless of how we look at it, the Irish and English consonants do not match well, and the only coherent explanation for the phonemic distinctions and allophonic variation found in MUE is that it is a continuation of the phonemic distinctions and allophonic variation found in both the English and Scots input dialects of the Plantation of Ulster and associated settlements. The fact that Irish did not impact this system, despite it featuring a range of non-Irish consonants and complex allophonic variation, suggests that with respect to this feature at least, Irish was not an important input to the phonological development of MUE. The importance of these findings for understanding the development of MUE is explored in Chapter 5.

3.6 Intervocalic /t/-Voicing

Voicing of intervocalic /t/ is a well-known feature of certain varieties of English, especially in North America (Wells 1982: 248–52), where /t/ is voiced and tapped, as [ɾ], merging with /d/ in this environment. A similar voicing (often tapping) of /t/, usually leading to positional merger with /d/, is also characteristic of MUE (Harris 1985: 218–19; Wells 1982: 445). /t/-Voicing in MUE affects /t/ in foot-internal, intervocalic position, including across word boundaries. Thus we get pronunciations such as *city* [ˈsəɾe] and *got it* [ˈɡɒɾ ət]/[ˈɡɒd ət] (as well as pronunciations such as *daddy* [ˈdäɾe] and *had it* [ˈhäɾ ət]) in SwTE. Given the phonetic closeness of [d] and [ɾ], the process is much more obvious (and easily analysed) for /t/ than for /d/. It is in competition with PreRD in MUE (see Section 3.5), and indeed in traditional forms of the dialect voicing is not present in PreRD environments, so that *better*, for example, is pronounced [ˈbɛɾɚ] in modern and urban forms of MUE but as [ˈbɛʈɚ] in rural traditional varieties.

An analysis of a subset of the older male speakers in the SwTE corpus reveals interesting patterns of variation for voicing of /t/, which are summarised in Table 3.3. The analysis identified three variants of /t/ in potential tapping environments: unvoiced [t], fully voiced [d] or [ɾ], and uncommon in-between cases, where there is a degree of voicing or tapping (e.g. [ɾ]). Tokens are divided into two main categories, those where the /t/ is morpheme-internal (e.g. *Beattie, city*), and those where the /t/ appears in word-final position followed by a vowel, (e.g. *eat it, got a*). The word-final tokens are further subdivided into those with a preceding historical short vowel and those with a preceding historical long vowel, diphthong or /r/ (see further below). For these speakers, voicing/tapping does not occur in PreRD environments ([ʈ] occurs instead), so these are not included in the analysis. A fully voiced pronunciation was counted as '1', an in-between case as '0.5' and a voiceless pronunciation as '0', so that the numbers to the left of the / in the table represent the total of the voiced and in-between cases and the numbers to the right of the / indicate the total number of tokens.

The analysis summarised in Table 3.3 reveals that although tapping is common (though not general for older speakers) in word-final position in traditional SwTE, it is rather rarer in morpheme-internal position (to which we can add /t/ in PreRD environments, which is never voiced for these speakers).[6] This is in contrast with the speech of young speakers of the dialect, who often have tapping word-internally, as is the case in Belfast for example, including in morpheme-internal and PreRD environments. This suggests that word-internal tapping is spreading in MUE, replacing [t] and, in PreRD environments, [ʈ]. Furthermore, voicing/tapping is more common in word-final position in words which had a preceding historical short vowel, a pattern which has close parallels in dialects of English (see below).[7]

Voicing of /t/ has no analogue in Irish. Nor was voicing traditionally typical of SIrE, though it has become common in the speech of young, urban speakers

Table 3.3 Voicing of /t/ in SwTE.

Speaker	Word-internal	Word-final Preceding short vowel	Word-final Preceding long vowel
PM00	0.5/14	2/19	7/20
PM26	0/9	17/27	2/13
PM42	5/11	16/24	7/11
PM43	0/5	35.5/42	12.5/24
CM32	13/21	32.5/36	17/21
CM36	4.5/14	20/39	18/28
CM39	0/13	22/33	5/12
CM44	11/17	31/31	12/12
Total	34/104	176/251	80.5/141
%	32.3	70.1	57.1

in recent decades (Hickey 2005: 77–8). It is not found in most dialects of Scots in Scotland either, though there is limited evidence for tapping in urban central Scotland, especially in Glasgow (Johnston 1997a: 504). It could be that this feature is ultimately of MUE origin in these dialects of Scots, given the known influence of Ulster varieties on Glaswegian Scots and the lack of this feature in traditional rural Scots dialects in southern Scotland.

Voicing of /t/ in foot-internal intervocalic position, usually symbolised as [d], is a regular feature of traditional southern (especially south-western) English dialects (Wells 1982: 343–4; see, for example, Qs. V.5.4 *butter* and VI.5.18 *pretty* in the SED). This voicing of /t/ is occasionally attested in other southern English dialects too, though voiceless realisations appear to have won out in most of these dialects. For example, Sivertsen (1960: 109–11, 120–1) describes tapping of intervocalic /t/ and, especially, word-final /t/ as common in Cockney (see also Wells 1982: 324–5).

As well as evidence of voicing of foot-internal intervocalic /t/ in southern English dialects, there is also the T-to-R Rule (Buchstaller *et al.* 2013; Wells 1982: 370), which is characteristic of a wide range of British English dialects, especially in the north of England. This rule involves the replacement of [t] with [ɹ] in foot-internal intervocalic position, usually across word boundaries in words with historical short vowels such as *at, bit, but, get, got, hit, let, not, put* and *what*, but occasionally elsewhere (e.g. in words such as *better* ['bɛɹə], *matter* ['maɹə] and *Saturday* ['saɹədə] in north-east England). The T-to-R Rule must have developed via a /t/-Voicing and tapping rule (i.e. via [ɾ]; see Wells 1982: 370), of the sort found in Cockney, and thus was similar to /t/-Voicing in southern England, though it was largely restricted to word bound-aries. This being the case, foot-internal, intervocalic voicing of /t/ was widespread in England in previous centuries.

As such, it is not surprising that this feature also turns up, albeit in a more exten-sive form than in many English dialects, in MUE. Indeed, the patterns identified in the analysis of /t/-Voicing in SwTE, as summarised in Table 3.3, suggest a rela-tionship with word-final voicing and the T-to-R Rule in England. For these older speakers of SwTE, /t/-Voicing is not only most common word-finally, it is also most common in precisely those words which are affected most by the T-to-R Rule in England (i.e. those which had a historical short vowel before the final /t/). This close parallel between /t/-Voicing (including T-to-R) in England and in MUE strongly suggests a historical link between them, with modern MUE innovating in its spread of voiced variants to word-internal position.[8]

The widespread presence of voicing in other extra-territorial varieties of English, especially in North America, but also in Australia and New Zealand (Wells 1982: 603; Gordon *et al.* 2004: 34), is also suggestive of an early presence of the feature in England, though a source, in part at least, in MUE for these varieties cannot be ruled out given the significant numbers of settlers from Ulster in these areas. However, the distribution of voicing in England as well as the close similarity between traditional SwTE /t/-Voicing and word-final voicing and the T-to-R Rule point towards the feature being present in the English Plantation dialects in Ulster, and thus this feature is likely to have had an origin in English in England, though it has undergone further extension in MUE more recently.

3.7 Dental fricatives

3.7.1 /θ/ and /ð/ in IrE

Probably the most well-known feature of the segmental phonology of SIrE is the use of stops where other varieties of English typically have the dental fricatives /θ/ (e.g. *thin*) and /ð/ (e.g. *then*). In SIrE, these consonants are usually realised as [t̪] and [d̪], though affricate pronunciations [t̪θ] and [d̪ð] also occur (Hickey 1984; Kallen 2013: 50–1; Wells 1982: 428–9). In several varieties, especially in the east (including Dublin), alveolar stops [t] and [d] may be used, resulting in merger of historical /θ/ and /ð/ with /t/ and /d/ in words like *tin* and *den*. Fricative realisations [θ] and [ð] are only typical of educated and younger speech in SIrE, and appear to be increasing. The traditional absence of the dental fricatives in SIrE is generally assumed to be the result of contact with Irish, which lacks dental fricatives. Although Old Irish had both /θ(')/ and /ð(')/, these were lost by the thirteenth century (McManus 1994: 351), becoming [h] and [ɣ]/[ɣʲ] respectively. The stopping of historical English /θ/ and /ð/ is thus considered to be one of the more obvious signs of contact-induced change in the phonology of SIrE.

MUE, on the other hand, retains the dental fricatives /θ/ and /ð/ (though there are some complications which I return to in Sections 3.7.2–4), so that *thin* and *then* are pronounced with [θ] and [ð] as opposed to *tin* and *den* with [t] and [d] (Wells 1982: 445). The treatment of the dental fricatives is one of the most striking differences between SIrE and northern IrE varieties, including MUE, and is a key feature used by Barry (1980) to map the boundary between northern and southern varieties of IrE.

3.7.2 Stopping of /θ/ before /r/ in MUE

Although /θ/ and /ð/ are normally retained in MUE, stopping of /θ/ is in fact common in traditional rural forms of MUE before /r/, though not in modern and urban varieties of the dialect. Although it is not recorded in LAS3 for the Ulster Scots locations, most of the MUE locations (Annalong, Glenshesk, Loughinisland, Mount Norris and Poyntzpass) are recorded with this feature, and it is common in SwTE, so that *three* and *through* may be pronounced the same as *tree* and *true*, for example [t̪ɾiː] and [t̪ɾuː] (for the dental pronunciation of /t/ before /r/, see Section 3.5). If the evidence of the SwTE corpus is anything to go by, this is a common but variable change, found in the speech of both Protestants and Catholics, and [θ] is often produced in these words too (but not in words such as *tree* with original /t/). [θ] is used where it is in StE in less traditional forms of the dialect. Whilst it is tempting to link this conditioned change to the more general stopping of /θ/ in SIrE, and thus to suggest contact with Irish as a reason for the change, other explanations are more likely, since there is no obvious reason why contact with Irish would have produced stopping of /θ/ before /r/ only (in addition to the lack of stopping of /ð/). Various forms of /θ/-stopping and/or merger of /θ/ and /t/ before /r/ (but not in other environments) have been recorded in traditional English and south-west Scots dialects in the nineteenth and twentieth centuries, and this change is most common in dialects which had PreRD of /t/, a feature which is also characteristic of MUE (see Section 3.5).

In English dialects south-west of the Thames, a combination of voicing of initial /θ/ and pre-/r/ stopping (as well as retraction of alveolar consonants next to /r/) results in pronunciations such as [dɹiː] for *three* (cf. SED Q. VII.1.3 and Orton *et al.* 1978: maps Ph234 and Ph235). In East Anglia, especially in Norfolk, stopping of /θ/ before /r/ was common traditionally, resulting in at least variable merger with /t/ (cf. pronunciations such as [ʈɹiː] and [tɹi] recorded in SED Q. VII.1.3, and see also Orton *et al.* 1978: maps Ph234 and Ph235; note also a single example of /θ/-stopping before /r/ in West Ilsley, Berkshire). Whether this change in East Anglia is historically related to PreRD (which is not recorded in the area but which was probably typical of many dialects of English at an earlier period) is unknown. Certainly, /θ/-stopping is not uncommon in English dialects which has PreRD, whilst some other dialects with PreRD in northern England had merger of /t/ and /θ/ before /r/ under [θ] or an affricate [ʈθ]. Ellis (1889) records /θ/-stopping as a common change across much of Yorkshire, for example, whilst the SED records /θ/-stopping in variation with [θ] across northern and eastern Yorkshire, and sporadically in southern Yorkshire and Lancashire (see SED Qs. II.8.1 'thresh', V.01.12 'threshold', V.10.2 'thread', VI.6.3 'throat', VII.1.3/VII.5.5 'three' and VIII.7.7 'throwing', for example). In addition, the SED records [θ] (and sometimes [ʈθ]) in variation with [ʈ] for /t/ before /r/ in southern Lancashire, especially at locations La12 (Harwood), showing (variable) merger of /t/ and /θ/ before /r/ in the opposite direction. Indeed in his study of the Bolton dialect (including Harwood), Shorrocks (1998: 351–3) posits a single merged phoneme (which he symbolises as /θ/, but covering a range of realisations such as [θ], [ʈθ] and [ʈ]) for historical /t/ and /θ/ before /r/, noting (p. 351) that 'informants are adamant, that the initial sound in words such as *tram* and *tree* is "not 't'" but "'th'"'.

/θ/-stopping before /r/ was also consistently recorded in most of the Scots dialects of Wigtonshire in south-west Scotland in the mid-twentieth-century LAS3, in contrast to the usual devoiced initial [r̥]/[ɹ̥] of dialects to the north and east. These Wigtonshire dialects also have PreRD. Whether /θ/-stopping in Wigtonshire is evidence of earlier /θ/-stopping in Scots which could have been brought to Ulster during the Plantation and associated settlements, or whether it represents an independent development or a spread of the MUE pattern across the North Channel is unknown (note also the lack of /θ/-stopping before /r/ in Ulster Scots dialects). But given how widespread /θ/-stopping before /r/ is in Britain, its presence in MUE is fairly unremarkable. It may well be that the feature was inherited from English and/ or Scots dialects as part of a larger PreRD package (Section 3.5).

3.7.3 *Debuccalisation of* /θ/

Another change affecting /θ/ in MUE is debuccalisation to [h] (McCafferty 2007: 127; Wells 1982: 447). This change targeted only a small number of words, especially *think* (e.g. [hëŋk]), *thing* (e.g. [hëŋ]) and its derivatives *anything* (e.g. [ˈənəˌhən]), *everything* (e.g. [ˈɛvɹəˌhən]) and *nothing* (e.g. [ˈnɑhən]), *Catholic* (e.g. [ˈcählëk̬]) and *thanks* (e.g. [häˈŋks], especially in the phrases *Thanks* and *No thanks*). Other instances of /θ/ were left unchanged. Although this debuccalisation is reminiscent of the thirteenth-century change of /θ/ to /h/ in Irish referred to above, bridging the 400-year gap between the change in Irish and the development of MUE is impossible unless we assume that the often illiterate Irish speakers knew that <th> in Irish spelling represented [h], and that when they learned English (again remaining for the most part illiterate) they assumed English <th> also represented [h] (but only in a handful of words). And whilst the lack of /θ/ in Irish would have militated against the survival of this consonant in a situation of intense contact (as it appears to have done in SIrE), it is hard to see how this would have resulted in [h] rather than some other more similar consonant (e.g. [ʈ], as in SIrE) and only have affected a few words.

In fact, this unconditioned, lexically specific debuccalisation of /θ/ in MUE is shared by Scots dialects, especially those of the Central Belt, most obviously Glasgow (e.g. Clark and Trousdale 2009: 39–41; Johnston 1997b: 507; Macafee 1983: 33; Stuart-Smith *et al.* 2007: 231–2, 235–6), though the feature is only reported for *think* (especially in the phrase *I think*) and *thing* (and its derivatives *anything, awthing* 'all-thing', *everything, nothing* and *something*).[9] Despite the inclusion of *thing* and *think* in the LAS3 wordlist, [h] was only recorded in *think* at two locations (Auchenleck in Ayrshire and Cellardyke in Fife), whether because the feature was rare, relatively new, or because it typically occurs only 'in spontaneous speech predominantly in word-initial position within an utterance' (Stuart-Smith *et al.* 2007: 247) is unknown. The association of this feature with the Central Belt (and Glasgow in particular) might suggest that it is a fairly new feature in Scotland, indeed perhaps one that has come into Scotland, via Glasgow, from Ulster, in the same way that the second person plural pronoun 'yous' appears to have done (Maguire 2012c). However, Johnston (1997b: 507) states that this feature is in fact found 'in many Scots dialects, including all Southern and Central Belt varieties up to Perthshire' but that it 'is a little rarer in Northern Scots and Galloway', and it is only found in Angus between vowels. Although Johnston does not distinguish debuccalisation of /θ/ in words like *thing* and *think* from the change of initial /θr/ to [ɾ]/[ɹ], and some of the dialects he mentions may only have this latter change, his statements suggest that unconditioned debuccalisation was widespread (as is also suggested by the two records of [h] in *think* in LAS3, from opposite ends of central Scotland). Assuming that Johnston is right in his claim that this feature is widespread in traditional Scots dialects, this suggests that it is of long standing in Scotland, and that a source in Ulster, via Glasgow, is less likely. This being the case, it is probable that debuccalisation of /θ/ was a feature of the Scots dialects brought to Ulster in the seventeenth and early eighteenth centuries.

That may be all there is to it, that this feature became established in MUE like a number of other unambiguously Scots phonological features, though unusually in this case a consonantal feature. But there is some evidence that debuccalisation of /θ/ to [h] is also found in English in Britain. Tollfree (1999: 172) reports that in south-east London English '[i]n broader speech, [h] is also a variant of /θ/ (e.g. *thanks* [hæŋʔks])'. Debuccalisation is also found in RP, in phrases such as *I think* [hɪŋk] *so* and *No thanks* [hæŋks] (see Jones 1909: 29), as is frequently the case in MUE, and Wells (1982: 447) reports that it is also found in RP in *nothing* and *anything*.

So although Scots is a likely source of debuccalisation of /θ/ in MUE, there are close parallels in London and RP English, especially since [h] in *thanks* is not reported from Scotland. The presence of this feature in London and RP suggests that it is (or was) widespread (if perhaps uncommon) in English, and that the feature may have been present in the English input to MUE and other Irish English varieties in the seventeenth century. So despite the lack of evidence for it in many dialects and from the Early Modern period, the feature is likely to have its origin in Britain, with no specific input from Irish.

The survival of /θ/ and /ð/ in MUE is significant, given that they are not found in Irish. Their survival suggests that the impact of Irish on MUE was less than it was on SIrE, and indeed that the native-speaker phonologies of the English and Scottish planters of the seventeenth century were the most significant input to this part of the phonology of MUE. In this respect, at least, MUE groups with other extra-territorial varieties of English, such as those of North America, Australia and New Zealand, where the formation of the new colonial dialects was for the most part the result of contact between speakers of dialects of English (and Scots), rather than the result of language shift or other forms of intense language contact. The additional changes which affected /θ/ (stopping before /r/ and debuccalisation) also appear to have had their source in English and/or Scots in Britain. Although evidence for both changes in English and Scots is patchy, the specific patterning of both (stopping of /θ/ before /r/ and merger with /t/ due to PreRD, and debuccalisation of /θ/ to /h/, especially in the words *thanks*, *thing* (etc.) and *think*) matches patterns in English and Scots exactly.

3.7.4 Changes affecting foot-internal /ð/

Two changes affecting /ð/ in foot-internal position before /ər/ have been reported in MUE. The first of these is deletion of the consonant altogether, so that words such as *brother*, *father* and *mother* are pronounced as ['bɹɔ̃:ə˞], ['fä:ə˞] and ['mɔ̃:ə˞] (Harris 1985: 58, 220–1; McCafferty 1999: 249, 2001: 149–57, 184–95; Milroy 1987: 101–2; Wells 1982: 447). This change is most typically associated with urban varieties of MUE in east Ulster (from which it has probably spread to Glasgow; see Johnston 1997b: 507 and Macafee 1983: 33), but is also reported in Tyrone in Todd (1975) according to Harris (1985: 221), though it is rare in SwTE. In Belfast, the feature is most characteristic of working-class males, a social distribution which suggests to Harris (1985: 221) that it is a conservative feature, though McCafferty (1999: 254, 2001: 151–2) argues instead that it is a twentieth-century innovation in MUE which is spreading, including to (London)Derry, where it is now a common feature of working-class speech. Harris relates the change to loss of /ð/ before /ər/ in English, both historically (see Kökeritz 1953: 321–2 for evidence from Shakespeare) and in traditional English dialects in the nineteenth and twentieth centuries (see Wright 1905: 239, and Qs. VIII.1.1 *father*, *mother*, and VIII.1.3 *mawther* 'girl' in the SED, where the feature is characteristic of Norfolk and parts of Suffolk). Whether Harris is right in making this connection is uncertain, especially if this is an innovation rather than a conservative feature. But in any case an alternative explanation based on contact with Irish is hardly viable, even though Irish does not have intervocalic /ð/, given that /ð/ in other positions (initially, finally, and intervocalically before sequences other than /ər/) is usually maintained in MUE (but see McCafferty 2007: 127). It may just be that this is a change internal to MUE, targeting a sound which is commonly affected by changes in (especially urban) Englishes, such as stopping and fronting to [v] (see, for example, the various studies of urban British dialects in Foulkes and Docherty 1999).

The second change affecting foot-internal /ð/, again usually before /ər/, is to [l] (McCafferty 1999: 249, 254, 260–3, 2001: 149–57, 184–95). McCafferty reports this as another recent innovation in (London)Derry, found at low levels in the speech of middle-aged working-class Catholics and Protestants, but at much higher levels in the speech of the teenagers in his sample. Amongst these younger speakers, [l] is most frequently used by working-class Catholics, it is somewhat less frequent in the speech of middle-class Catholics and working-class Protestants, and it is absent from the speech of middle-class Protestants. This feature is unattested in traditional rural MUE, though one Protestant speaker in the SwTE corpus, born in the 1940s, who has spent much of his time in the local town, Omagh, often has [l] or [l]-like pronunciations of /ð/, suggesting that the change is spreading beyond its (London)Derry heartland. This change is not reported for varieties of English and Scots in Britain, and thus represents a recent, local innovation in MUE, one which again can hardly be connected with the absence of /ð/ in Irish in intervocalic or other positions.

3.7.5 *Summary*

It is not clear that there is any role for Irish in any of the changes affecting the dental fricatives in MUE, despite the absence of /θ/ and /ð/ in the language since the thirteenth century. For example, if Irish learners of English dispreferred /θ/, why would these changes only have affected /θ/ before /r/ and in a couple of words in initial position? An assumption that they preferred, and thus reinforced, English and Scots stopping before /r/ and debuccalisation does not make sense given that they left /θ/ (and /ð/) unaffected more generally. It appears to be the case, then, that Irish had no impact on the development of /θ/ and /ð/ in MUE, and that the existence of these consonants and the changes that affected them are evidence that these patterns already existed in English and Scots at the time of the Plantation of Ulster and associated settlements or, in the case of /ð/, have possibly developed more recently. It is difficult to untangle the contributions of English and Scots to /θ/-stopping before /r/ and debuccalisation to [h] in MUE. /θ/-stopping before /r/ is restricted to Wigtonshire in Scotland and a source in Ulster for this cannot be ruled out, so an English origin, probably connected with PreRD, may be more likely. The sparse attestation of /θ/-debuccalisation in English may point to a more prominent role for Scots in the development of this feature in MUE, though the existence of debuccalisation in a very similar form in London English and in RP and the lack of debuccalisation in *thanks* in Scots suggests that English input was not unimportant here too.

3.8 Rhoticity, /r/ realisation and Post-/r/ Retraction

MUE is usually rhotic (though not entirely, as discussed in Section 3.8.1), and is characterised by post-alveolar or even retroflex pronunciations of /r/, though [ɾ] occurs after dental consonants (see Section 3.5). After /r/, alveolar consonants may be retracted to post-alveolar or retroflex position. In these respects, /r/ in MUE is of a conservative English type, both in its realisation and in terms of (non-)rhoticity. It is not clear that Irish has had any input, and input from Scots, other than reinforcing rhoticity, is not obvious either.

3.8.1 Rhoticity

Irish English, including MUE, is generally described as being rhotic (Corrigan 2010: 45; Harris 1984: 130; Hickey 2007a: 320; Wells 1982: 432), i.e. it retains historical /r/ in coda position, the only (non-Anglified) exception being the working-class English of Dublin, which is often non-rhotic (Hickey 1999: 272). Irish English thus groups with varieties of English and Scots in Scotland and North America, and is conservative in this respect compared to most varieties of English in England (though rhoticity is a well-known feature of south-west and some Lancashire dialects) and to those in the southern hemisphere.

The situation regarding rhoticity in MUE is actually somewhat more complex than general descriptions such as those referred to above suggest. There are in fact three kinds of non-rhoticity in the dialect, all of which have parallels in English in England, but only one of which is traditionally found in Scots. These three kinds of non-rhoticity are:

1. Loss of /r/ before /s/, a change which occurred as early as the ME period (Dobson 1957: 966–7; Lass 2000: 114; Minkova 2014: 121–5; Wyld 1927: 213–14) and which is shared by most traditional dialects of English, including those that have remained rhotic, though it has nowadays been lost through levelling in many cases. Thus we traditionally get forms such as *ass* for 'arse' (e.g. [äːs]), *bust* for 'burst' (e.g. [bɔ̈st]), *cuss* for 'curse' (e.g. [kɔ̈s]), *fust* for 'first' (e.g. [fɔ̈st]) and *hoss* for 'horse' (e.g. [hɔːs]) in MUE dialects (see Braidwood 1964: 70), including SwTE, though most of these forms are now obsolete.[10] This feature does not appear to be found in Scots.
2. Dissimilatory non-rhoticity in the words *cartridge* (e.g. [ˈcäṭr̈ëdʒ]), *partridge* (e.g. [ˈpäṭr̈ëdʒ]) and *quarter* (e.g. [ˈkwäṭɚ]). This change is also apparent in English and Scots dialects (see SED Q. IV.7.8a, the entries for these words in Zai 1942, and Dobson 1957: 992), and was also likely to have been an early change.
3. Variable loss of rhoticity in unstressed syllables (i.e. [ɚ] becomes [ə]), especially in connected speech. This feature has not been previously described for MUE, but it is a feature of some forms of the dialect, including SwTE, where it is not uncommon in the speech of the older, traditional dialect speakers. As is the case in northern England (Maguire 2012a), this variable non-rhoticity in unstressed syllables can accompany PreRD, so that we get pronunciations such as [ˈsäṭəde] for *Saturday* in the dialect.

Whether this third kind of non-rhoticity is connected with the loss of rhoticity in England is uncertain; it could be an independent development of the same feature. But given that general loss of rhoticity in England began in the fifteenth century, though it didn't take off in more standard varieties of the language till the eighteenth century (Lass 2000: 114–16; Minkova 2014: 128), it is possible that this variable non-rhoticity in unstressed syllables that has gone unnoticed in MUE may be of long standing and may reflect an early stage in the loss of rhoticity in the speech of the English settlers of the Plantation of Ulster. The role of the Scots input to (non-) rhoticity is less certain. It could be that as rhotic speakers they ensured that rhoticity was the majority input in the formation of the dialect, just as Trudgill (2004: 116) argues that Scottish and Irish settlers in New Zealand helped to tip the balance in favour of the retention of /h/ in the formation of that new dialect of English. But since English was predominantly rhotic in the seventeenth century, and since there is some non-rhoticity in MUE (assuming that this is not a new feature), it may be that the Scottish input was minimal for this feature. In any case, non-rhoticity in words like *cuss* is of English origin.

It is hard to envisage how speakers of Irish learning English could have played a role in the development of any of these forms of non-rhoticity. Irish allows /r/ in coda position, including before /s/ (e.g. *arsa* 'say(s)', 'said'). There is no reason why the forms of non-rhoticity that do exist in MUE should result from influence from Irish. Nor is there any reason for Irish speakers who encountered non-rhotic English speech to prefer rhotic pronunciations rather than learn the non-rhotic ones. Of course, the majority of English (and Scots) input to MUE was rhotic (at least for the most part), so this hypothetical situation did not arise.

3.8.2 /r/ realisation

The /r/ phoneme in MUE is usually realised as a (post-)alveolar approximant [ɹ], though strongly retracted, retroflex-like pronunciations are also common after stressed vowels in particular (Corrigan 2010: 45; Harris 1985: 57; McCafferty 2007: 125–6; Wells 1982: 446). It is not typically recorded with velarisation, though as is the case with /l/ (see Section 3.9.2) there is likely to be a certain amount of coarticulation with preceding vowels. This contrasts with the pronunciation of /r/ in SIrE, which is typically a velarised post-alveolar approximant [ɹˠ] often with a degree of lip-rounding, though non-velarised, retroflex-like pronunciations are becoming common in younger, urban, female speech in particular (Hickey 2007a: 320–1; Wells 1982: 431–2).

Tapped or trilled allophones of /r/ are not usually recorded unless preceded by a dental consonant (see Section 3.5 for this '/r/-Realisation Effect'). However, tapped [ɾ] occasionally occurs in initial clusters and intervocalically in traditional varieties such as SwTE. Overall the impression given by the realisation of /r/ in MUE is that it is roughly of an English type (on the issue of rhoticity, see Section 3.8.1). That is, the realisation of /r/ is not particularly different from what it is (or was) in the pronunciation of the majority of traditional English dialects in England as recorded over the last century, where [ɹ] was until recently the norm for many dialects, and where retracted and retroflex pronunciations of /r/ in coda position are well recorded for rhotic accents in the south-west and elsewhere (see the descriptions of /r/ in, for example, Hedevind 1967: 72–3 for north-west Yorkshire; Kökeritz 1932: 103–5 for Suffolk; Oxley 1940: 15 for Lincolnshire; Shorrocks 1998: 388–94 for south

Lancashire; and Widén 1949: 27 for Dorset; see also Wakelin 1972: 98–9 for a general description of traditional pronunciations).

That said, the history of the pronunciation of /r/ in English is uncertain. It is likely that in earlier forms of the language taps and trills were common in onset position and intervocalically, contrasting with fricative or approximant pronunciations in coda position (see Dobson 1957: 945–6; Lass 2000: 108; Minkova 2014: 116–18). This is (or was) still the case in some twentieth-century varieties of English (see, for example, Docherty and Foulkes 1999: 51; Hedevind 1967: 72–3; Mathisen 1999: 111; Sivertsen 1960: 135–6; Watt and Milroy 1999: 30), and indeed RP English can have [ɾ] intervocalically and even in onset clusters (Wells 1982: 282). These tapped and trilled pronunciations in onset and intervocalic position were likely to have been even more common in seventeenth-century England, and they must have been present to an extent in the English input to MUE. The same is true of Scots dialects, which are well known for their tapped and trilled pronunciations of /r/, though this has become rather less typical in recent times (see Johnston 1997b: 510–11 for a summary). Traditional descriptions of the realisation of /r/ in Scots suggest that tapped and trilled variants occurred in all positions, though the unpublished phonetic notebooks associated with LAS3 (see Section 1.4) indicate that these were most typical in onsets and intervocalically in many dialects of Scots in the south and west, with fricative or approximant realisations occurring, in some dialects at least, in coda position. In any case, we must expect that the Scottish Plantation settlers mostly brought tapped and trilled realisations of /r/, in onset and intervocalic position at least, to Ulster, and given that these pronunciations must also have been present in the English input to the dialect, it is perhaps surprising that they are not more common in it (or indeed in Ulster Scots) outside of PreRD environments (see Section 3.5), especially as taps and trills also occur in Ulster Irish.

How the realisation of /r/ in MUE might relate to the realisation of R phonemes in Irish is complicated by considerable complexity and recent changes in R pronunciations in the Gaelic languages. Old Irish had four R phonemes, /R/, /R'/, /r/ and /r'/, which were probably pronounced as trilled [r] and [rʲ] and tapped [ɾ] and [ɾʲ] (Stifter 2006: 18). In traditional Ulster Irish dialects, three of these /r/ phonemes may remain distinct (/R/ and /R'/ having merged early in the history of Irish), so that /R/ (e.g. corr), /r/ (e.g. ag cur) and /r'/ (cuir) contrast (Ó Baoill 2009: 166). Details on the pronunciation of these consonants in traditional Ulster Irish dialects are not always given, but typical realisations in Ulster appear to have been [r] for /R/, [ɾ] for /r/, and [ɾʲ] for /r'/ (see Lucas 1979: 2; Ó Baoill 2009: 167; Quiggin 1906: 94–102; Sommerfelt 1929: 134–6). In addition, /r'/ may be subject to frication and even lenition to [j] in Donegal Irish (Ó Dochartaigh 1987: 155–9). Whilst all of these distinctions and pronunciations do survive for some speakers of Ulster Irish today, it is not uncommonly the case that they have, to an extent at least, been replaced by English-like approximant pronunciations such as [ɹ] or [ɹʲ], as has often happened in dialects of Irish in Connacht and Munster (Hickey 2014: 93–7). This change in the pronunciation of R phonemes in Irish is likely to be the result of contact with English. It is not clear, on the other hand, that the pronunciation of /r/ in MUE, including the tapped variant found after dental consonants (Section 3.5), owes anything to the traditional pronunciations of R phonemes in Irish.

Given that tapped and trilled realisations of /r/ were present in the English, Scots and Irish inputs to MUE, it is noteworthy that they are not typical of the dialect. Either English approximant realisations of /r/ won out in the formation of the new dialect, or MUE has undergone the same process that has occurred in other dialects of English: a levelling of tapped and trilled variants and a spread of approximant realisations to all environments (the RRE aside). If there was any input in the form of taps and trills from Scots and Irish, or indeed from English, this has become obscured in the dialect, which is nowadays at least mostly characterised by /r/ realisations which are (or were) typical of varieties of English in England. The low levels of [ɾ] in non-dental initial clusters and in intervocalic position in some traditional forms of MUE may reflect the last traces of these non-approximant pronunciations in the British input dialects.

3.8.3 Post-/r/ retraction

Related to the retracted pronunciation of /r/ in coda position in MUE is the retraction of the alveolar phonemes /t/, /d/, /s/, /z/, /n/ and /l/ after /r/ to post-alveolar [t̠], [d̠], [s̠], [z̠], [n̠] and [l̠], or even to retroflex-like [ʈ], [ɖ], [ʂ], [ʐ], [ɳ] and [ɭ], as found, for example, in *heart, yard, worse, cars, barn* and *world*. This post-/r/ retraction is well attested in the rhotic dialects of the West Midlands and south-west of England (see, for example, the SED responses to Qs. I.1.11 *barn*, I.9.3 *cart*, VII.2.4 *third*, VII.4.3 *Thursday*, VIII.1.3 *girls*, VIII.5.9 *hearse*), but also in other rhotic dialects in England, including in Cumberland (Brilioth 1913: 6–8, 74–6) and north-west Yorkshire (Hedevind 1967: 73–5). It may well have been a widespread effect of post-alveolar retracted /r/ in English in England when rhoticity was the norm, but of course the loss of rhoticity over much of England has removed the necessary conditions of it, as can be seen in west Cumbria, where the post-/r/ retraction recorded by Brilioth is no longer present in the, by the 1950s non-rhotic, dialect recorded at the nearby Brigham (location Cu3) in the SED. A similar phenomenon is reported for some dialects in Scotland (Johnston 1997a: 511), though this is not typical of most dialects of Scots, including those in the south-west. And although a similar effect is present in Scottish Gaelic (Gillies 2009: 247–8), post-/r/ retraction is not a feature of Irish, since /r/ is not usually post-alveolar or retroflex in the language. Thus the only likely source for post-/r/ retraction in MUE is English in England, though it may be more accurate to say that post-alveolar and retroflex-like pronunciations of coda /r/ were inherited from English and that post-/r/ retraction is a common side effect of this pronunciation which can occur in dialects of this kind.

3.9   The distribution and realisation of /l/

3.9.1   The lexical distribution of /l/

English and Scots have been subject to two kinds of /l/-vocalisation since the late medieval period. The first of these, dated to the fifteenth–sixteenth centuries, affected /l/ in coda position after the ME and Older Scots (OSc) back and low short vowels, with various results depending on the dialect and the precise phonological environment of the /l/ (Dobson 1957: 988–91; Johnston 1997a: 107–8; Luick 1940: 1053–6; Molineaux *et al.* 2019). These varied developments have resulted in different lexical distributions of /l/ in dialects of English and Scots. The second kind of /l/-vocalisation is much more recent, being recorded in the twentieth- and twenty-first-century dialects in south-east England and central Scotland in particular, though with the change becoming widespread in young urban speech across Britain towards the end of the twentieth century (Beal 2010: 20, 83; Stuart-Smith *et al.* 2006; Wells 1982: 258–9). This second kind of /l/-vocalisation affects coda /l/ after vowels of any kind and can occur in word-final or pre-consonantal position. The first of these changes antedates the development of MUE, whilst the second post-dates its formation and has not (yet) been reported in MUE.

MUE essentially has the same lexical distribution of /l/ as StE and most other traditional dialects in the south Midlands and south-east of England. In dialects of this kind, /l/ vocalised after ME /a/ and sometimes after ME /ɔ/ before /f/ (e.g. *calf*), /v/ (e.g. *calve*), /m/ (e.g. *palm*) and /k/ (e.g. *folk*, *walk*), but was retained elsewhere, including before /d/ (e.g. *old*) and word-finally (e.g. *all*) (Luick 1940: 1053–6). This differs from dialects in the south-west of England, which may retain /l/ before /m/ (e.g. *palm* [pɔːlm]) and /k/ (e.g. *walk* [wɔːɫk]). It also contrasts with dialects in the north Midlands and northern England (i.e. in Lincolnshire, Nottinghamshire, north-east Leicestershire, Derbyshire, Staffordshire (at least variably), Shropshire, and counties north of these), which are characterised by extensive historical /l/-vocalisation after the ME back and low short vowels before other consonants (e.g. in *old* in pronunciations such as [ɔud] and [ɔːd]) and in final-position (e.g. in *all* in pronunciations such as [ɔː]). For examples of /l/-vocalisation and retention in the traditional English dialects of the mid twentieth century, see the maps in Kolb *et al.* (1979: 246–79) and in Orton *et al.* (1978: Ph8–Ph10, Ph16b, Ph17b, Ph18b, Ph28b, Ph41b, Ph42b, Ph43c, Ph53b, Ph54b, Ph55b, Ph56b, Ph82b, Ph100b, Ph132c, Ph133c, Ph134b, Ph135b, Ph144b, Ph165b, Ph186b). Although MUE may have /l/-vocalisation in *coulter* (e.g. [ˈkʉtə˞]), when this is not replaced by *cutter* ([ˈkɔ̈tə˞]), this pronunciation is widespread in English dialects in the Midlands and south too (see Kolb *et al.* 1979: 262). And as is also very commonly the case in English dialects, MUE traditionally has /l/ in *chimley* 'chimney' (see the returns for SED Q. V.1.3).

Scots dialects are similar to northern English dialects, in that they reflect /l/-vocalisation in the late OSc period after back and low short vowels in word-final position and before most consonants (Johnston 1997a: 107–8; Molineaux *et al.* 2019). Notably, vocalisation did not usually occur before /d/ when the /l/ followed /a/, a feature shared with Cumbrian dialects. Thus we get Scots pronunciations such as [ɔː], [fʉː], [sɔːt], [kʌʉt], [skɔːp], [ˈʃʉðər] and [ɔːld] corresponding to English *all*, *full*, *salt*, *colt*, *scalp*, *shoulder* and *old*. These vocalisations are shared by USc (Gregg 1972: 124–5, 1985: 56).

In terms of its lexical distribution of /l/, then, MUE is obviously of an English south Midland or south-east type, and differs little from StE in this respect. Scots and northern English dialects have not had an impact on this feature of MUE. That is, vocalisation of /l/ has developed like the lexical distribution of vowel phonemes (Section 4.4) and of the consonant phoneme /x/ (Section 3.2) in MUE, reflecting a south Midland, south-east and StE rather than a Scots, northern English or south-west English distribution. It is also not clear that Irish could have had any effect on the distribution of /l/ in the dialect, since Irish learners of English would have been perfectly capable of learning /l/-less pronunciations of English and Scots words, and indeed may have preferred them in some cases, given the lack of certain /l/+consonant clusters in word-final position in their language, including those subject to epenthesis (see Sections 3.10 and 3.11).

3.9.2 The realisation of /l/

Irish English /l/ is well known for being realised as clear [l] in all positions, at least in more conservative varieties (e.g. Barry 1982: 107; Bliss 1984: 138; Hickey 2007a: 321; Kallen 2013: 49; Ó Baoill 1997: 83; Wells 1982: 431), and this is also reported, with some qualification (see below), for Ulster varieties, including MUE (e.g. Adams 1948: 14; Barry 1982: 107; Gregg 1964: 177; Harris 1984: 130; Turton 2017: 22–4; Wells 1982: 446). This characteristic of IrE (including MUE) contrasts with what is found in most mainstream varieties of English in Britain and elsewhere, where there is often allophonic variation between clear [l] in onsets and dark [ɫ] in codas (Wells 1982: 258). It is also rather different from the rich system of lateral consonants found in Irish, and, as a result, demands some sort of explanation. What that explanation might be, and what it may tell us about the phonological origins of MUE, is the subject of this section.

A number of scholars have suggested that this feature of IrE does have its explanation, in part at least, in contact with Irish. Bliss (1984: 137) argues that [l] in IrE results from generalisation of slender Irish /l'/, typically pronounced [l] or [lʲ], as the default realisation of English /l/. Todd (1984: 167) lists clear [l] amongst the features of MUE which characterise Catholic speech, which, she argues, 'owes much to Gaelic' (ibid.: 162), and this contrasts with dark [ɫ], which she considers to be characteristic of Protestant speech. Kingsmore (1995: 18–19) unambiguously attributes clear [l] in Ulster to Irish influence, stating that

> [t]o some degree, Irish Gaelic has influenced all Ulster speech, particularly in outlying areas where there was greater contact between English and Irish. For example, all areas of Ulster tend to use a clear or nonvelarized /l/ in post-vocalic position.

And like Bliss, Hickey (2007b: 148) sees a role for Irish in the development of clear [l] in IrE, suggesting that this results from '[u]se of non-velar, non-palatal [l] from Irish as well as English input'.

As was noted above, an explanation of IrE clear /l/ which involves contact with Irish is complicated by the complex system of laterals which have characterised the language through its history. Old Irish had four lateral phonemes, conventionally transcribed /L/, /L'/, /l/ and /l'/ (McCone 1994), the first two of which were unlenited, the second two of which occurred in lenition environments. These were probably pronounced as [l̪ˠ], [ʎː], [ɫ] and [l(ʲ)] (Ó Baoill 2009; Stifter 2006: 18). The distinction between these four lateral phonemes was maintained in traditional dialects of Ulster and Mayo Irish, but has been collapsed to a three- or two-way distinction in the rest of Connacht and in Munster, for example, between /l/ ([ɫ]) and /l'/ ([l(ʲ)]) (Ó Baoill 2009: 167). Whilst Irish /l'/ is essentially identical phonetically to the clear [l] of IrE, it is not obvious why this Irish phoneme should have been generalised to English /l/ in the way suggested by Bliss (1984), given the well-known clear–dark /l/ allophony in English (see further below), a problem noted in Ó Baoill (1997: 83). Thus an explanation for IrE clear [l] depending (solely) on contact with Irish does not explain the situation, and other factors must be considered.

The clear/dark allophony of the type found in RP is not the only pattern that exists in England, with dialects in the north-east and in Norfolk in particular being well known for having clear [l] in all positions (Wells 1982: 341, 374). In fact, in the traditional dialects of English as recorded by the mid-twentieth-century SED, there was a north–south split between dialects with clear [l] in all positions and those with dark [ł] in coda position and sometimes more generally. Most dialects north of Herefordshire, Worcestershire, Warwickshire, Leicestershire, Northamptonshire, Cambridgeshire and Suffolk had clear [l] in all positions, whilst most dialects in these counties and locations further south had dark [ł] in at least coda position (see Kolb *et al.* 1979: 246–7, 249, 254–8 and 260–79 for illustrative maps). In addition to some variation around the border between these two areas, there are not infrequent examples of clear [l] in coda position in the south (including the south-east) of England in the SED. In other words, clear [l] was widespread in the traditional dialects of England in the mid twentieth century, and it may be the case, given the presence of some coda [l] pronunciations in the south, that dark coda [ł] has been spreading in England. Thus when we consider the seventeenth-century English input to MUE and other IrE varieties, we should not assume that it universally had the clear/dark allophony that we know from English today, and indeed it is possible, even likely, that clear [l] in all positions was common in the input.

Although dark [ł] in all positions is characteristic of well-known Scottish varieties today, including SSE and the Urban Scots dialects of the Central Belt (Aitken 1984a: 102; Johnston 1997b: 510, 2007: 113; Wells 1982: 411–12), this does not necessarily reflect the pronunciation of /l/ in other dialects or in the past. The twentieth-century Scots dialects of the far north and the south-west traditionally had clear [l] in all positions, and although Wells (1982: 412) suggested 'Irish influence' as a source of this feature in the south-west, the peripheral distribution of clear [l] in Scotland points to it being a relic feature, something which is supported by descriptions found in some dialect sources. For example, Mutschmann (1909: 17) describes /l/ as being 'clear' in all positions in north-east Scotland, even though Dieth (1932: 100), a couple of decades later, describes it as dark, 'hollower than in St[andard]E[nglish]'. Similarly, Zai (1942: 20) describes /l/ as being clear in initial position, but dark 'finally and before consonants … as in R[eceived]S[peech]', even though Johnston (1997b: 510) suggests that the Scottish Borders now agree with the Central Belt in having dark [ł] in all positions. Indeed, Johnston (1997a: 107–8) suggests that there has been a substantial change in the realisation of /l/ in Scots. He points out that in OSc /l/ must have been dark after back vowels (and was thus subject to pre-/l/ glide development and vocalisation in some cases), but was probably clear elsewhere, and that the change from clear to dark 'may well have been late rather than early'. He suggests that this change may have begun in working-class speech 'in focal areas by 1700', so that clear [l] may have been characteristic of the majority of Scots dialects in the south and west during the period of the Plantation of Ulster and its associated settlements.

There are, then, British antecedents to IrE clear [l], and these have been considered by some scholars to be the explanation of the IrE realisation of /l/ (see Moylan 2009: 36–7; Ó Baoill 1991: 585). In other words, the reason that clear [l] is so characteristic of MUE and other dialects of IrE may be that this was the usual pronunciation of [l] in the majority of the input varieties, whether English or Scots, and the use of this pronunciation and its occurrence in all positions need have nothing to do with contact with Irish. Given the close match between English [l] and Irish /l'/, however, it is not surprising that speakers of Irish had no difficulty acquiring this pronunciation, though there is no reason why they would have reinforced it over other equally compatible pronunciations (e.g. [ɫ]) in the English/Scots input.

But in fact things are more complicated than the discussion so far indicates. Although clear [l] in all positions is characteristic of most varieties of IrE, this situation is not universal. Dark [ɫ] has been reported in some varieties of SIrE. Wells (1982: 431) reports 'a certain amount of clear vs. dark alternation on the RP pattern' in Dublin English, a pattern which had become characteristic of 'new Dublin English' by the early twenty-first century (Hickey 2005: 77). In addition, a number of researchers have reported increasing levels of dark [ɫ] (in coda position) in the speech of younger speakers of SIrE more generally (e.g. Hickey 2007a: 321; Kallen 2013: 49; Moylan 2009: 36–7; Wells 1982: 431). Furthermore, dark [ɫ] has been reported, in onset and coda positions, 'in areas where Irish is still spoken or was until recently the common vernacular of the place' (Ó Baoill 1997: 83; see also Hickey 1986: 14, 1999: 43, 2007a: 321). That close contact with Irish leads to the production of velar pronunciations of /l/ in IrE is not surprising given the existence of broad, velarised /l/ (and in some cases /L/) in the language (cf. the comments in Ó Baoill 1997: 83).

There is also evidence for dark [ɫ] in MUE, and not only in coda position. Dark realisations of /l/ are usually reported from urban areas, especially Belfast (Adams 1986: 109; Harris 1985: 60; Owens 1977) and (London)Derry (McCafferty 1999: 250).[11] Conversely, Turton (2017) finds only clear [l] in her Belfast data, which covers a range of phonological and morphological environments (though importantly, as we shall see, only next to the /i/ vowel). Some researchers have also noted the existence of [ɫ] in rural areas. As noted above, Todd (1984: 167) claims that in rural east Tyrone, for example, 'Catholics tend to have clear [l] in all positions; Protestants dark [l] [sic]: /lɪlʲi/ = /ɫʌɫi/ – "lily"'. Cunningham (2011: 217–18) also appears to find some evidence of [ɫ] in the neighbourhood of back vowels (regardless of whether they are in onset or coda position) in the speech of younger Catholic female speakers in west Tyrone MUE, though her data is rather limited.

Data from the SwTE corpus helps to clarify some of the patterns that likely lie behind these reports of dark [ɫ] in rural varieties of MUE. In SwTE, /l/ is realised as fairly clear in onset positions, unless it is followed by a back vowel (e.g. law, load, love), in which case it may be pronounced as [ɫ], though this is only a tendency. In coda position, there is more variation. After /r/ (as in world), /l/ is pronounced as a somewhat palatalised, clear, post-alveolar (or even retroflex) [l̠], whilst after /i/ (as in heel) and /ʉ/ (school), and after the diphthongs /ëi/ (e.g. mile), /ɔi/ (e.g. oil) and /əʉ/ (e.g.

owl), it is pronounced as a clear, somewhat palatalised [lʲ]. Clear pronunciations of /l/ can also be heard after /ë/, /e/, /ɛ/ and /o/, though neutral (i.e. non-palatal) or somewhat dark allophones are more common, especially when the /l/ is proceeded by a schwa-type vowel or is syllabic (e.g. *fill* [fəɫ], *fail* [fɪəɫ], *bell* [bɛəɫ], *hole* [họəɫ], *uncle* ['ɔ̃ŋkɫ]). After /ɔ̃/ and /ɔ/, dark [ɫ] is the norm in coda position (e.g. *bull* [bɔ̃ɫ], *all* [ɔːɫ]). These impressionistic observations on the pronunciation of /l/ in SwTE are confirmed by acoustic analysis of /l/ pronunciations (measuring the second formant, f2, at the mid-point of the consonant; see Thomas 2011a: 126–7), though the pattern is more subtle than discrete symbols such as [l] and [ɫ] can represent. Figures 3.2 and 3.3 illustrate variation in the pronunciation of /l/ for two speakers in the SwTE corpus, PM43 (wordlist data) and CM44 (conversational data).

It can be seen from Figures 3.2 and 3.3 that PM43 and CM44 have similar patterns of variation, with very clear pronunciations (i.e with high f2) of /l/ in coda position after /ëi/, /ɔɪ/, /əʉ/, /i/, /ʉ/ and, to an extent, /r/, rather dark pronunciations after /ɔ/, /ɔ̃/ and /o/, and intermediate pronunciations after other vowels. Essentially, the pronunciation of the /l/ is a function of the frontness of the vowel preceding it rather than involving allophonic variation between [l] and [ɫ]. There is also some variation of a similar sort in onset position, but this is less extreme, with non-palatal clear [l] being the norm in most cases. So in summary, SwTE /l/ is often clear, not only in onset position, but also in codas, and the clear or neutral /l/ realisations after certain vowels contrast with the dark [ɫ] realisations found in these positions in most other dialects of English. But at the same time, dark [ɫ] is present in the dialect, most commonly in coda position after back vowels. Whether this situation is long-standing and has gone unnoticed in previous descriptions (dark [ɫ] after back vowels being unremarkable), or whether it is a more recent development (the speakers in

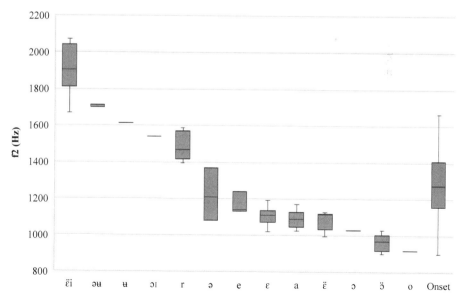

Fig. 3.2 Acoustic analysis of the realisation of /l/ by speaker PM43.

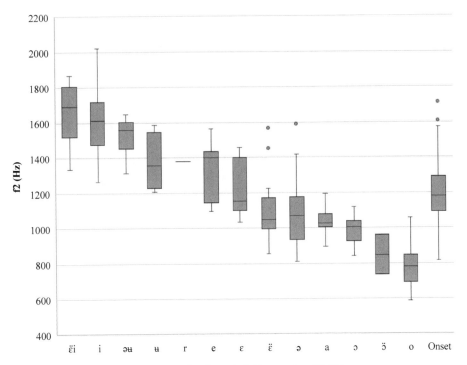

Fig. 3.3 Acoustic analysis of the realisation of /l/ by speaker CM44.

the SwTE corpus being born in the twentieth century) in uncertain, though see further below.

A crucial question is whether this variation in the realisation of /l/ in SwTE is related to influence from Irish. As is discussed in Section 3.3.2, there is a correlation (though with numerous exceptions) between the nature of Irish consonants and the quality of following and preceding vowels, with slender consonants more likely to be followed and preceded by front vowel qualities and broad consonants followed and preceded by back vowel qualities. These correlations also apply to the lateral phonemes in Irish, so that we might expect Irish influence to have the effect of giving preference to clear and palatalised allophones of English /l/ before and after front vowels and to dark allophones of English /l/ before and after back vowels. Although this might seem similar to the situation in SwTE, the fit between what we might expect from Irish influence and the allophony we find in this variety of MUE is far from perfect.

Firstly, although there is a correlation between vowel quality and neighbouring slender/broad consonants, this is far from being a strict rule so that we get both slender and broad laterals following /iː/ (*níl* 'not be' vs *díol* 'sell'), /eː/ (e.g. *géill* 'yield, submit' vs *Gael* 'Irish person'), /aː/ (e.g. *fáil* 'getting' vs *fál* 'hedge, fence'), /oː/ (e.g. *go fóill* 'yet, still' vs *ceol* 'music') and /uː/ (e.g. *siúil* 'walk' vs *ag siúl* 'walking'), for example. Indeed, as *siúil/ag siúl* indicate and as was discussed in Section 3.3.2, alternation between slender and broad consonants after these vowels is a common feature of the language, being used to signal a range of common grammatical functions (e.g. the genitive singulars of *fál* /faːl/ 'fence' and *ceol* /k'oːl/ 'music' are *fáil* /faːl'/ and *ceoil* /k'oːl'/). The result is that whilst there may be some correlation between consonant type and vowel quality, there is no simple rule that can be applied to newly encountered linguistic forms.

Secondly, the Irish distinction is binary, between broad and slender consonants (though with the laterals there is also a tense/lax distinction, e.g. between /L/ and /l/, at least in some dialects). This is not how the coda /l/ allophony in SwTE works. Although it is convenient to symbolise the realisations of /l/ in codas in SwTE as [lʲ], [l] and [ɫ], the realisation of coda /l/ in the dialect is continuous in nature, depending to a large extent on the phonetics of the preceding vowel. In other words, the realisations in SwTE are the result of a phonetic rule, whilst those in Irish depend upon phonemic distinctions. Related to this is the fact that it is the Irish consonant which determines the phonetics of preceding short vowels, whilst in SwTE it is the preceding vowel which determines the realisation of the following lateral, irrespective of its length (which, in any case, is not phonemic, as explained in Section 4.3).

When we add to these issues the lack of a similar allophony in most varieties of SIrE and the somewhat different behaviour of onset /l/ in SwTE, it is not clear that the realisation of /l/ in the dialect is similar to the distribution of the laterals in Irish. So although it might seem reasonable to connect the two, they do not match particularly well when examined in more detail. That Irish has played some role in the development of this /l/ allophony in SwTE is thus uncertain and other explanations may be preferable. I offer two alternative explanations here, though they can only be suggestive without more research on the precise phonetics of /l/ in dialects of English, Scots and Irish.

SwTE has [lʲ] after /i/ (the typical FLEECE vowel), /ʉ/ (the typical GOOSE vowel), /ëi/ (the typical PRICE vowel), /əʉ/ (the typical MOUTH vowel), /ɔɪ/ (the typical CHOICE vowel) and /r/, and this kind of realisation can sometimes occur after /ë/ (the typical KIT vowel), /ɛ/ (the typical DRESS vowel), /e/ (the typical FACE vowel) and unstressed [ə]. An [l] of neutral or intermediate quality is usual after /e/, /ɛ/, /ë/ and [ə], and after /a/ (the typical TRAP vowel). Dark [ɫ] is only typical after /ɔ/ (the typical LOT/THOUGHT vowel), /ö/ (the typical STRUT vowel) and /o/ (the typical GOAT vowel). That means that in most environments where RP and similar varieties of English have dark [ɫ], SwTE has [lʲ] or [l], which is not very different from saying that SwTE typically has clear [l] where RP has dark [ɫ]. Perhaps this is what is meant in descriptions of 'clear' [l] in MUE (and some other 'clear [l]' dialects), so that SwTE is not unusual in this respect. How /l/ was actually pronounced in traditional varieties of English and Scots in Britain, never mind how /l/ was pronounced in earlier stages of the language, may be difficult to determine so that we may never know whether some descriptions of 'clear [l]' dialects really refer to situations like the one found in SwTE.

There is some evidence in SwTE for clear [lʲ] of the type normally associated with the phonetically front vowels after other vowels in the dialect, including /e/, /ɛ/, /ë/ and [ə], as noted above. Furthermore, rather clear or neutral pronunciations of /l/ can be heard after /o/, though this does not come out in the analysis presented in Figures 3.2 and 3.3. It could be that there has been a move away from clear [lʲ] after all or most vowels to neutral [l], and that these instances of [lʲ] after /e/, /ɛ/, /ë/, /o/ and [ə] are remnants of an older situation. Such a change in the pronunciation of /l/ in MUE is perhaps supported by the association of dark [ɫ] with urban areas in the province referred to above. That is, it may be the case that the conditioned /l/ allophony in SwTE is a development from a 'clear [l] only' system. If so, this may be recent, though given that varieties of English (and Scots) have been changing from clear [l] to dark [ɫ] (in codas at least), it may be that SwTE represents a halfway stage in this process, either as an ongoing move towards such a system or as a result of variation of the same kind being present in the Early Modern input to the dialect. If English and Scots dialects in the seventeenth century were in the process of adopting dark [ɫ] (at least in codas), then perhaps the variation we see in SwTE is a continuation of such a pattern, one which has not (yet) led to the generalisation of [ɫ] to all coda positions and beyond. Such variation might have been reinforced by speakers of Irish who were sensitive to the distinction between clear and dark laterals, though this would be difficult to prove if nothing actually changed (see Section 5.2.1).

These explanations are of course tentative, but given that the /l/ allophony we see in SwTE does not seem to be easily derivable from the distributions of laterals in Irish, they are worth considering. In any case, the clear coda [l] which typifies IrE, including MUE and SwTE for the most part, is likely to have a British source rather than an Irish one given the widespread distribution of clear coda [l] in English and Scots and the lack of motivation for a clear [l] only system as a result of contact with Irish.

3.10 Epenthesis

Epenthesis is a well-known feature of IrE, affecting liquid+sonorant clusters, especially /lm/ (as in *film*, e.g. ['fɪləm]), but also /rm/ (as in *farm* ['faɹəm]) and sometimes /rn/ (e.g. *barn* ['baɹən]) and /rl/ (e.g. *girl* ['gɛɹəl]). This feature is found in one form or another in all traditional forms of English in Ireland (Hickey 2007a: 307), including MUE (Maguire 2018), where it particularly applies to /lm/, but also to /rm/ in traditional rural varieties, and occasionally to other clusters as well.

Most previous researchers have assumed that the origins of this feature in IrE lie in Irish (Adams 1948; Barry 1982; Corrigan 2010: 40; Cunningham 2011; Hickey 1986, 2007a; Joyce 1910: 96; Moylan 2009; Ó Baoill 1997; Ó hÚrdail 1997; Pilch 1990: 584), which has a thoroughgoing process of epenthesis affecting liquid+consonant clusters (Ó Siadhail 1989: 20–2). Thus we get epenthesis in Irish in words such as *colm* 'dove' (e.g. ['koləm]), *gorm* 'blue' (e.g. ['gorəm]) and, in some dialects at least, *dorn* 'fist' (e.g. ['dorən]). This looks just like epenthesis in IrE, and it is not therefore surprising that epenthesis in Irish has been assumed to be the source of epenthesis in English in Ireland, as a result of contact between the two languages.

Maguire (2018) analysed epenthesis in MUE in detail, examining the similarities and differences between it and Irish, and exploring patterns of epenthesis in English and Scots in recent times and in previous centuries. The key finding in Maguire (2018) is that epenthesis in MUE (and indeed in other varieties of IrE) is rather less like epenthesis in Irish than examples such as those given above might suggest, and instead the feature bears close similarity to patterns of epenthesis in English and Scots throughout their histories. As a result, Maguire (2018) suggested that the main source of epenthesis in MUE (and perhaps in other varieties of IrE) is epenthesis in English (and Scots), with Irish at most playing a supporting, reinforcing role (though even this is not certain). Rather than reiterate the data and arguments, I refer the reader to the detailed discussion of this feature found in Maguire (2018), and give only a summary of the results of that analysis here.

Epenthesis in MUE and other IrE dialects is just like epenthesis in English and Scots, affecting /lm/, /rm/, /rn/ and /rl/ in (stem-level) coda position, not affecting these clusters morpheme-internally across syllable boundaries, and leaving other clusters for the most part unchanged. As is noted in Iosad and Maguire (2018), this kind of epenthesis is characteristic of (West) Germanic more generally. Epenthesis in MUE (and other varieties of IrE), English and Scots is, however, very different from epenthesis in Irish and Scottish Gaelic, which targets a wide range of liquid/nasal+consonant clusters, occurring across syllable boundaries, and being constrained by the quantity of the preceding vowel and by the number of syllables following the cluster. Whilst epenthesis in IrE (and indeed English and Scots) is for the most part a subset of epenthesis in Irish, the two kinds of epenthesis, Germanic on the one hand and Gaelic on the other, are really very different. Given that epenthesis in MUE (and IrE more generally) is essentially identical to epenthesis in English and Scots and is radically different from epenthesis in Irish, a source in Britain for the feature is much more likely than a source in Irish. Indeed the preference for epenthesis in /lm/, the lower levels of epenthesis in /rm/ and the less common epenthesis in /rn/ and /rl/ is shared by MUE and English in England. The similarities and differences between epenthesis in MUE and the various potential sources for it are summarised in Table 3.4.

Assuming a British origin for epenthesis in MUE (and indeed in other traditional varieties of IrE) explains why there is no epenthesis, of an Irish kind, in other clusters or across syllable boundaries. It also explains why there is epenthesis in some varieties of MUE in /rn/ and /rl/ when these are absent from Irish (in the case of /rn/, absent in Ulster Irish only). Maguire (2018) argues that speakers of Irish learning English at most reinforced existing patterns of epenthesis in the input English and Scots varieties, increasing the number of speakers with epenthesis in

Table 3.4 Epenthesis in MUE, English, Scots and Irish.

Cluster	MUE	English	Scots	Irish
n + other	-	-	-	Y
r + other	rare	sporadic historically	rare	Y
rl	sporadic	sporadic/historical	Y	N
rn	sporadic	sporadic/historical	Y	southern dialects
rm	variably present	variably present in some dialects/historical	Y	Y
lm	Y	Y	Y	Y
l + other	N	N (sporadic in OE)	N	Y

liquid+sonorant clusters. Other kinds of epenthesis would have found no support in the emergent MUE dialect, and as a result did not survive. But since nothing in effect changed (MUE has the same kinds of epenthesis as the input English and Scots dialects), this reinforcement is possible but unprovable. It could just be that speakers of Irish learned the patterns of epenthesis used by native speakers of English, or had no effect on the dialect more widely in this respect regardless of what patterns of Irish origin were found in their speech. For discussion of this issue, see Maguire (2018), and I explore this important issue further in Chapter 5. Crucially though, if Irish did not play an important role in the development of this 'most Irish-like' of phonological features of MUE, this has important consequences for our understanding of the role of language shift and language contact in the origins of MUE phonology. As it stands today, epenthesis in MUE is most similar to epenthesis in traditional English dialects (usual in /lm/, less common in /rm/, uncommon in /rn/ and /rl/). Although epenthesis in MUE looks most like epenthesis in English, it is also likely to have had input from Scots, which had essentially the same system (the sequences /rən/ and /rəl/, whether original or from epenthesis often being removed in traditional forms of MUE by a separate change, as explained in Maguire 2018), and this is another example of a phonotactic constraint in Scots which has contributed towards the phonology of MUE (see Section 5.4).

3.11 Consonant cluster simplification

As well as epenthesis, traditional Mid-Ulster English is characterised by a range of deletions which simplify consonant clusters (Braidwood 1964: 71–4; Corrigan 2010: 45; Harris 1985: 58–9, 223–4; McCafferty 2007: 126), though these are usually restored in more standardised varieties of the dialect. In particular, /t/ may be deleted in the clusters /st/, /ft/, /pt/ and /kt/, /b/ and /g/ are commonly deleted after /m/ and /ŋ/, whilst deletion of /d/ is frequent after /l/ and /n/. All of these consonant cluster simplifications are widely attested in English and Scots in the past and in modern dialects, and thus a British source for these deletions is likely. However, as many of these clusters are absent in Irish (Hickey 2014: 179–82), it is necessary to determine whether language contact played a part.

3.11.1 Deletion of /t/

Dealing first with /t/ deletion, this is attested in MUE in /st/ (e.g. *best*), /ft/ (e.g. *left*), /pt/ (e.g. *kept*) and /kt/ (e.g. *act*). All of these deletions are possible in the conservative rural dialect of south-west Tyrone, for example, though only simplification of /pt/ is at all common. Reduction of /st/ to /s/ is mostly restricted to the words *best* and *next*, especially when a consonant follows, and deletion of /t/ in /ft/ is only usual in *left* (as well as in *often* and *soften*, as in most varieties of English). Simplification of /kt/ to /k/ occurs variably in morpheme-final position in words like *act*, *fact* and *subject*, and with deletion possible before the suffix -*ing* (e.g. *acking* ['akən]), but not before past tense -*ed* (e.g. *acted* ['aktəd]). Deletion of [t] in past tense forms such as *knocked* and *walked* does not occur, whilst no deletion is possible across a syllable boundary (e.g. in *doctor*), though it can occur in word-internal coda position in *actually* (e.g. [ˈɛcəle] /ˈɛkjəlɪ/). The same constraints apply to deletion of /t/ in /pt/, which commonly occurs in final position, especially in the 'semi-weak' past tense forms *crept, dreamt* ([d̪rɛmp]), *kept, leapt, slept, swept* and *wept*, but which does not affect regular past tense [t] in words such as *dropped, nipped, stepped* and *tapped*.[12] Deletion of /t/ after /p/ morpheme-internally is only possible in the sequence /mpt/, (as in *empty* [ˈɛmpe]), and deletion can be retained before words beginning with a vowel (e.g. *tempt it* [ˈtɛmp ət]) and before *-ing* (e.g. *tempting* [ˈtɛmpən]), but not before *-ed* (e.g. *tempted* [ˈtɛm(p)təd]).

All of these deletions of /t/ are well attested from the fourteenth century onwards in the histories of English and Scots (see, for example, Dobson 1957: 961–2; Johnston 1997a: 101; Kökeritz 1953: 302–3; Wyld 1927: 216), though the /t/ has been restored in StE. But there is ample evidence for absence of /t/ in English and Scots dialects in recent centuries, pointing to the continued presence of these deletions across much of England and throughout lowland Scotland. Deletion of /t/ after /p/ is particularly common, especially in Scotland (Murray 1873: 128), the English Midlands and the south, whilst deletion of /t/ in /kt/, /ft/ and /st/ is somewhat less common, though still widespread, especially in the south-west of England, but also elsewhere across England and Scotland. Deletion of /t/ in /kt/ is usual in Scots (Dieth 1932: 131; Johnston 1997b: 509; Murray 1873: 128; Wilson 1915: 22, 1923: 16, 1926: 17; Zai 1942: 193). For examples, see the words *empty* and *kept, facts, left* and *loft*, and *best* and *breast* in the EDG, and *crept* (IX.1.9), *daft* (Qs. VIII.9.3–4) and *breast* (Q. VI.8.5) in the SED. In all cases, deletion of the /t/ occurs in morpheme-final position, or morpheme-internal /mpt/ (as in *empty*). The historical and traditional dialect sources are silent on the issue of whether deletion is possible in regular past tense forms (e.g. *fussed, picked, stepped, stuffed*), but since the examples of deletion they give are all monomorphemic or irregular past tense forms (e.g. *kept*), it seems likely that the same constraint existed in English and Scots in Britain as in MUE in Ireland. The existence of precisely such a constraint in modern accents of English (see Guy 1980: 5–6) supports this hypothesis.

Given that cluster /t/ deletion in MUE is closely homologous with /t/ deletion in English and Scots in Britain, and that the feature must have been common in both the seventeenth-century English and Scots inputs, it hardly seems necessary to seek an alternative explanation for the phenomenon in contact with Irish. However, clusters made up of a sequence of two consonants with the same manner of articulation (plosive+plosive, fricative+fricative and sonorant+sonorant) do not occur in Irish (a few modern borrowings and obscure forms aside). Hickey (2014: 181–2) notes that '[n]one of these are allowed in immediate succession within the boundaries of a non-compounded word'. This means that there are to all intents and purposes no clusters /kt/ or /pt/ (or their slender counterparts) in Irish, either in word-final or morpheme-internal position. The same is essentially true of /ft/ and /fʲtʲ/, but whilst /st/ and /sʲtʲ/ are rare in word-final position (but cf. for example *tost* 'silence'), they are common word-internally. The absence of these clusters in Irish might seem like a not unlikely motivation for their loss in varieties of IrE, but if contact with Irish was responsible for the loss of these clusters in MUE, why were they only lost in some cases, why were they preserved in the inflected past tense *-ed* forms (e.g. *stepped*), and why were they not subject to change in morpheme-internal position (e.g. *doctor*)? Furthermore, if contact with Irish was the cause of these changes, why was deletion favoured when other solutions to the problem could have been selected, for example, deletion of the first consonant, epenthesis, frication of one of the consonants (cf. Irish *dochtúir* 'doctor' with /xt/) or paragoge? Given the presence of these deletions in English and Scots, an Irish source is of course not required, but it is also difficult to see how Irish might have reinforced this feature, considering that the same clusters were accepted in other environments (e.g. *chapter*) where they are not found in Irish, and that other illicit coda clusters in Irish (e.g. /ls/, /ns/, /mp/ and /sp/) were left unaffected. The conclusion must be that deletion of /t/ in consonant clusters in MUE is derived from English and Scots, both of which have long been characterised by this feature.

3.11.2 *Deletion of /d/ after /l/*

As is often the case in English, /t/ deletion is accompanied by /d/ deletion in MUE. Loss of /d/ is frequent in traditional MUE after /l/ in words such as *field* (e.g. [fil]), *wild* (e.g. [wɛil]), *old* (e.g. [əʉl]) and *world* (e.g. [wɔ˞l]), though the /d/ is restored in standardised forms of the dialect (Corrigan 2010: 45; Harris 1985: 59). This only occurs in morpheme-final position, with no loss of /d/ in words such as *childer* 'children' (e.g. ['tʃəl̪d̪ə˞]) and *shoulder* (e.g. ['ʃəʉl̪d̪ə˞]), but it does occur before suffixes except *-ed* (e.g. in *scolding* ['skəʉlən], *older* ['əʉlə˞] and *wildest* ['wɛiləst], but not in *scolded* ['skəʉld̪əd]). In addition, deletion of /d/ is essentially categorical in traditional pronunciations of the irregular plurals *sold* (e.g. [səʉl]) and *told* (e.g. [təʉl]), which contrast with standardised pronunciations such as [so̞:ld] and [to̞:ld]. However, no deletion occurs in regular past tense forms such as *growled* (e.g. [gɹəʉld]), *piled* (e.g. [pëild]) and *wheeled* (e.g. [ʍild]).

An interesting feature of /d/ deletion after /l/ in MUE is that it happens after certain vowels only: after /i/ (*field, yield*), after /ëi/ (*child, wild*) and after /əʉ/ (the usual vowel in the MOUTH lexical set, but also found in traditional MUE in *bold, cold, hold, mould, old, scold, sold* and *told*, which essentially have categorical /d/ deletion when they have this vowel). Deletion also occurs after /r/ (e.g. *world* [wɔ˞l]). Deletion of /d/ does not occur in the few English words with historical short vowels such as *build, held* and *weld*. Nor does it occur after /o/ in words such as *fold* and *gold*, which often have /o/ in traditional MUE, or in the non-traditional pronunciations of words such as *cold* (e.g. [ko̞:ld]). Deletion of /d/ is also not found in the word *bald*, which was bisyllabic in the history of English so that the /d/ was not always immediately after the /l/, and although *scald* is recorded as 'scall' in some sources (cf. Braidwood 1964: 72), this is not found in SwTE, which does not have deletion of /d/ in /ld/ after /ɑ/~/ɔ/ in these two words (traditionally [bɑ:ld], [skɑ:ld], standardised [bɔ:ld], [skɔ:ld]). Whilst the lack of /d/ deletion after /o/ could be attributed to standardisation in the history of the dialect (given that most of the relevant words don't have /o/ in traditional forms of the dialect), the lack of /d/ deletion after the other vowels is a feature of the most traditional forms of the dialect. It is noteworthy that deletion of /d/ occurs after /l/ in those environments where /l/ is most palatalised in coda position in the dialect (see Section 3.9.2).

Deletion of /d/ after final /l/ has a long history in English (see, for example,

Dobson 1957: 962; Lass *et al.* 2013 'Final Coronal Deletion'; Luick 1940: 1036), and was a common feature of traditional English dialects in England in the nineteenth and twentieth centuries (Wright 1905: 234). In the modern period, /d/ deletion after final /l/ is particularly associated with south-west dialects, but it is not uncommon, at least in some words, across much of England, including the Midlands and the south-east. In most northern dialects, /l/ has vocalised after back vowels before /d/, so that deletion is blocked. For examples, see the words *bald, bold, build, child, cold, field, fold, gold, hold, mild, old, sold, told, wild, world* and *yield* in the EDG, and the returns for the following questions in the SED: Q. I.1.1 *field*, Q. III.3.5 *yield*, Q. VI.2.3 *bald*, Q. VI.13.17–18 *cold*, Q. VII.7.10 *gold*, Q. VIII.1.2 *child*, and Q. VIII.1.20–2 *old*. Deletion of /d/ after morpheme-internal /l/ is only rarely attested. Given the nature of traditional dialect data, which typically gives morphologically simple citation forms, it is impossible to tell if the morphological constraints on /d/ deletion after /l/ were present, but as this is attested in modern accents of English (Guy 1980), it seems not unlikely that they were. Interestingly, Widén (1949: 92), in his description of the traditional Dorset dialect, notes that deletion of /d/ after /l/ (and /n/) happens 'especially when these consonants are preceded by stressed long vowels or diphthongs'. The scarcity of words with (historical) short vowels followed by final /ld/ in English means that evidence of this pattern is difficult to find in other studies, but it is noticeable that the words *build* is almost never recorded with /d/ deletion in the EDG unless the vowel has first lengthened. Although the evidence is limited, it suggests that conditioning of /d/ deletion similar to what is found in MUE was characteristic of at least some traditional English dialects in the nineteenth and twentieth centuries, and thus points to a historical connection between them.

Deletion of morpheme-final /d/ after /l/ is also characteristic of many Scots dialects, especially (but not exclusively) those of the south-west and of the north-east (Johnston 1997b: 502; see also Dieth 1932: 126–8; Wilson 1923: 15–16). The change has a long history in the language, going back to the fifteenth century and being well attested across Scotland in the OSc period, including in words such as *wile* 'wild' and *yeel* 'yield' in official documents (Johnston 1997a: 101). In modern dialects in central and southern Scotland, deletion of /d/ in /ld/ is only possible in morpheme-final position, as it is in MUE and most English dialects. Again, the traditional descriptions do not give details of morphological conditioning, and evidence for an effect of preceding vowel is hard to obtain, given that *build* was not typically used in Scots. Perhaps a hint of such a constraint is given by Wilson (1923: 168), who records *held* without /d/ deletion in the Ayrshire dialect even though the feature is common in the dialect more generally.

As with /t/ deletion, then, a source in English and/or Scots for deletion of final /d/ after /l/ in MUE is likely, especially given the evidence for similar phonological constraints on the phenomenon. The widespread dialectal and historical attestation of /d/ deletion after /l/ in Britain suggests that this feature would have been common in the English and Scots inputs to the dialect in the seventeenth and early eighteenth centuries. But as was the case with consonant+/t/ clusters, the cluster /ld/ is not found in Irish, having become /L(')/ between the Old and Middle Irish periods (Hickey 2014: 180; McCone 2005: 177), except in compounds and in words with derivational suffixes beginning with /d/, for example, *-da* (as in *gallda* 'foreign').

Could there be a role for Irish in the deletion of /d/ in /ld/ then? Whilst Irish learn-ers of English may indeed have had an aversion to /ld/ clusters in word-final and non-derived environments, influence from Irish does not account for the lack of /d/ deletion in morpheme-internal position, nor for the constraint against deletion after historical short vowels and in regular past tense forms. Irish speakers would have had to learn where /ld/ could occur and where it could not, which removes the point of a contact explanation for the deletion of /d/ in this cluster. Nor does contact with Irish explain why /ld/ should become /l/ (the change of /ld/ to /L/ in Irish being centuries old) when other solutions, such as epenthesis or /l/ deletion (supported by Scots and northern English dialects) could have been used. As was the case with /t/ deletion, then, the source of /d/ deletion after /l/ in MUE was very likely to have been in Britain, and the lack of a similar cluster in Irish is coincidental.

3.11.3 Deletion of /d/ after /n/

Loss of /d/ after /n/ in morpheme-final position (e.g. in *blind, found, friend, hand* and *wind*) and in morpheme-internal position before [(ə)l] (e.g. *handle* [ˈhan(ə)l]) is also highly characteristic of traditional (but not standardised) MUE (Braidwood 1964: 72; Corrigan 2010: 45; Harris 1985: 59). Unlike /ld/, the preceding vowel does not appear to have an effect, so that /d/ is often lost in words such as *end, friend* and *wind* ([wən]~[wɔ̈n]~[wëin]), and is usual after /a/ in words such as *hand* and *land*. Although deletion of /d/ before [(ə)l] is frequent, deletion of /d/ before [ɚ] is rather less common, not being found, for example, in words such as *cinder, gander, render, thonder* 'yonder', *under* and *wonder*. In fact, deletion before [ɚ] is only common in *hundred* ([ˈhʌɲɚ(d)]), in *thunder*, which did not originally have /d/ in OE (*þunor*), and in the Scots word *dander*.[13] Deletion of /d/ after /n/ in morpheme-internal position does not occur in other cases, such as *Andy, granda* and *window* (e.g. [ˈwɔ̈ndə]~[ˈwɔ̈nde]). It does, however, occur before words beginning with a vowel (e.g. *the end of it* [ðə ˈɛn əv ət]) and before inflectional suffixes (e.g. *blindest* [ˈblëinəst], *handing* [ˈhäːnən]) except *-ed* (i.e. /d/ is retained in words like *handed* [ˈhäːndəd]). As in the other cases, regular past tense forms are not subject to deletion, so that *banned* and *fined*, for example, are always pronounced with final [nd].

Deletion of /d/ in /nd/, especially in word-final position and before [(ə)l], is also common in traditional English dialects, and was a feature of the language in earlier centuries too. Evidence for /d/ deletion in /nd/ goes back to the ME period and is well attested in EModE (see, for example, Dobson 1957: 961–2; Lass *et al.* 2013 'Final Coronal Deletion'; Luick 1940: 1034–5; Wyld 1927: 215–16). Wright (1905: 235) identified deletion of final /d/ in /nd/ as a common feature in traditional English dialects across the country, with the feature being most typical of the south-west (see, for example, the words *blind, bound, end, find, found, friend, grind, ground, hand, hound, kind, land, pound, round, send, spend, stand* and *wind* (n.) in the EDG, and the returns for the SED questions I.8.2 *handles*, IV.4.1 *ground* (n.), VI.3.4 *blind*, VI.7.1 *hand*, VII.6.26 *wind* (n.), VII.8.2–4 *pound* (lb), IX.1.1 *round*, IX.3.2 *find* and IX.3.2 *found*). Although evidence is slim, it appears to be the case that /d/ deletion does not occur before past tense *-ed* (see the responses to the SED Q. VI.7.13 *right-handed*). In addi-tion, Wright (1905: 232) states that '[m]edial **d** seldom occurs in any of the dialects between **n–l** or **n–r**, in words such as *bundle, candle, dwindle, gander, thunder*, &c.'. As was noted above, however, *thunder* does not have etymological /d/, whilst *gander* is only attested without /d/ in the EDG in Scotland and northern England as far south as Derbyshire. A similar picture emerges from the SED, which reveals that, *thunder* aside (Q. VII.6.21), loss of /d/ before /ər/ is uncommon and mostly restricted to the north (see Qs. III.12.9 *render*, IV.6.16 *gander*, V.4.3 *cinders* and VII.1.15 *hundred* in the SED). Compare also the pronunciation of the word *window(s)* in the EDG and the SED (Q. V.1.7), which is never attested with /d/ deletion, even when (as is frequently the case) the second vowel is reduced to [ə].

   Deletion of /d/ in /nd/ was similarly common in the nineteenth- and twentieth-century dialects of Scots and, like the other deletions discussed in this section, had a long history in the language, with examples going back to the fourteenth century (Johnston 1997a: 101–2). The main areas affected by this change were the north-east and the south-west (Dieth 1932: 124–6; Johnston 1997b: 502–3; Murray 1873: 121; Wilson 1923: 15–16), with /d/ being deleted after /n/, but /d/ was also deleted in most Scots dialects (see, for example, Wilson 1915: 23, 1926: 17; Zai 1942: 194–6; and the examples from the EDG referred to above) before /əl/ (e.g. *candle*) and /ər/ (e.g. *hunder* 'hundred'). Although a Gaelic origin for the feature has been suggested (Murray 1873: 28), both Dieth (1932: 125) and Johnston (1997b: 502–3) argue against this hypothesis, pointing out that /d/ is also deleted in dialects of Scots (and English) which have had little or no contact with Gaelic, and that /d/ is retained in final position in some dialects that were in close contact with it.

   As was the case with deletion of /d/ after /l/, deletion of /d/ after /n/ is a feature which has been shared by Scots and English for centuries and one which was common in their dialects into the modern period. As such, it is very likely that /d/ deletion after /n/ was a common feature of the English and Scots input varieties to MUE and it is therefore not surprising that it became established as a feature of the dialect. It is worth pointing out that although deletion of /d/ after /n/, especially in final position and before /əl/, is frequent in MUE, it is not exceptional in this regard, as the feature was equally common in various Scots and English dialects in the nineteenth and twentieth centuries, and no special explanation is needed to account for this situation. Nevertheless, the cluster /nd/ is essentially absent in Irish (compounds and suffixed forms such as *seanda* 'old, aged' aside) as a result of its change to /N/ between the Old and Middle Irish periods (Hickey 2014: 180; McCone 2005: 177), so that a role for Irish in this change (in the same way that Murray suggested Gaelic may have been involved in the change in Scots) cannot be entirely ruled out. Certainly the lack of /nd/ in final position in the English and Scots input was compatible with Irish. But given the essential identity of /d/ deletion after /n/ in MUE and English dialects (i.e. it occurs especially word-finally and before /əl/) and the close similarity with Scots, and the fact that /nd/ is common in morpheme-internal position in MUE (e.g. in *cinders, window*) and in regular past tense forms, the same problem exists for contact reinforcement as exists for /ld/. Irish speakers who were shifting to English would have had to learn where /d/ was deleted and where it was not, and it is not clear that anything changed as a result of this process.

3.11.4 Deletion of /b/ and /g/

The other voiced stops, /b/ and /g/, are also subject to deletion after their homorganic nasals. Morpheme-final /mb/ (e.g. in *comb* and *lamb*) became /m/ in English (and Scots) in the thirteenth and fourteenth centuries (Johnston 1997a: 101; Luick 1940: 1034), and thus is always /m/ in MUE too. Morpheme-internally, /m/ rather than /mb/ may occur in traditional forms of MUE before [(ə)l] in words such as *crumble, ramble, rumble, scramble, thimble, tremble* and *tumble* (Braidwood 1964: 72; note that this is not just an USc feature, as suggested by Harris 1985: 59), but deletion is rare in other environments (though it occurs in *timber* ['təmə·]). Deletion of /b/ in these contexts occurred historically in Scots and is also attested for older forms of English (Johnston 1997a: 101; Luick 1940: 1034) and was still widespread in their dialects in the nineteenth and twentieth century (see *bramble, chamber, cucumber, number, thimble* and *timber* in the EDG, and the SED data for Q. I.9.4 *limbers*, Q. V.7.17 *cucumber* and Q. V.10.9 *thimble*). It is therefore no surprise that the same forms turn up in MUE, though again this may be evidence of substantial Scots input to the dialect, as deletion of /b/ in /mb/ is somewhat more common in Scots than in English (cf. Murray 1873: 120). As a result, an explanation for deletion of /b/ in MUE depending on contact with Irish is not required, even though /mb/ does not occur in Irish, and indeed the continued presence of /b/ in MUE in words such as *cucumber, number, remember* and *sombre* counts against it (note also that deletion of /b/ is almost entirely absent in *remember* in the SED, Q. VIII.3.7, and is also uncommon in *cucumber*, Q. V.7.17).

Deletion of /g/ after [ŋ] is found in all positions, including morpheme-internally (e.g. *finger* ['fɛ̈ŋə·], *single* ['sɛ̈ŋl]), in traditional forms of MUE (Braidwood 1964: 74; Harris 1985: 59). Deletion of morpheme-final /g/ after [ŋ] is found in most dialects of English, a change which occurred in word-final position in the sixteenth century, spreading into pre-suffixal position (e.g. *singer*) in the seventeenth century (Lass 2000: 119–20). Deletion of /g/ after [ŋ] in morpheme-internal position is not so well attested in the history of English, though there is some evidence for it (Dobson 1957: 972–3). It may be that it was more widespread than the written record indicates, the distinction between [ŋg] and [ŋ] not being easily represented in English orthography. The existence of such pronunciations in traditional English dialects in the modern period also points in this direction. Such pronunciations are found in various parts of England in the nineteenth and twentieth centuries, especially in the north, but also in the south-west and south-east and occasionally elsewhere (see *finger, hunger* and *monger* in the EDG, and the answers to the SED questions III.13.5 *mongrel*, VI.7.7 *finger* and VI.13.9 *hungry*). The deletion of /g/ after [ŋ] in all positions is a general characteristic of Scots, where it appears to have a long history (Johnston 1997b: 510; Murray 1873: 124), and this, together with input from English, is the likely source of [ŋ] in all positions in MUE. But deletion of /g(')/ after /ŋ(')/ in all positions is also a feature of many dialects of Irish, including those of Ulster (Hickey 2014: 92; Ó Siadhail 1989: 97; for examples, see the maps for *ceangailte* 'tied', *muing* 'mane', *teanga/teangaidh* 'tongue' and *ding/ging* 'wedge' in Wagner 1958: 14, 54, 70, 162), so a reinforcing role for Irish in this feature of MUE cannot be ruled out. However, in the Irish dialects of the MUE area (see especially Stockman and

Wagner 1965: 202), [ŋ] was lost between vowels (e.g. *teanga* 'tongue' [t'i:]) and at the end of monosyllables (e.g. *muing* 'mane' [mʷi:]). This change is shared by Irish dialects across much of Ulster (see the examples from Wagner 1958 cited above), but has no counterpart in MUE, so we would need to assume that Ulster Irish had [ŋ] for earlier /ng/ during the period when it was most likely to have affected MUE (from the seventeenth to the mid nineteenth century) and that the deletion of [ŋ] between and after vowels happened subsequently and did not affect MUE. So it could be that Irish played some kind of reinforcing role in the entrenchment of [ŋ] (rather than [ŋg]) in MUE, though this is impossible to prove, and a source for the feature in English and, especially, Scots is more straightforward.

3.11.5 Summary

All of the consonant cluster simplifications discussed in this section have close parallels in the histories of English and Scots and were widespread in their dialects in the nineteenth and twentieth centuries. Indeed, the patterns of deletion in Britain and in MUE are essentially identical. In this respect, MUE is a typical, if somewhat conservative, dialect, and there is nothing about the patterns of distribution of deletion in it which cannot straightforwardly be explained by a source in Britain. Pinning down a region of Britain which contributed most to MUE in this respect is difficult given the similarities in consonant cluster simplification in English and Scots, and it is no surprise that a dialect arising in a situation of close contact between these two inputs that were characterised by the same feature should have it too. Deletion of final /t/ could have come from either source. The patterns of /d/ deletion, especially the retention of /d/ in /ld/ after historical short vowels and the lower levels of deletion of /d/ in /nd/ before /ər/, are perhaps more similar to what was recorded in England, though the precise patterning of the feature in most traditional dialects north and south of the border is uncertain. The deletion of /b/ and /g/ after their homorganic nasals is also shared by English and Scots, and although this is most typical of Scots dialects, they are also lost in dialects across England. As is the case with a number of other phonological features of Scots origin in MUE (see Section 4.5), these simplifications of consonant clusters involve continuation of Scots phonotactic constraints in the dialect, and this explains why these particular consonantal features show evidence of influence from Scots when most other consonant features are of an English type (see further Section 3.13). It is also tempting to link all of these consonant cluster simplifications to the absence of the same clusters in Irish. But although reinforcement from Irish in some cases cannot be ruled out, the MUE patterns are essentially identical to the Scots and English ones, including in various particularities (e.g. the preservation of /d/ after /l/ following historical short vowels), and nothing has changed that cannot be predicted from the British input, so it is not clear that Irish did have a role. Why were /t/, /d/ and /b/ retained in /pt/, /kt/, /ft/, /ld/, /nd/ and /mb/ in morpheme-internal position, for example, if contact with Irish played a part in the simplification of these clusters? And why were certain clusters affected when other clusters, also not found in Irish, were left alone? Irish does not have, or only marginally has, the clusters /ks/, /mp/, /ns/, /ls/ and /sp/ in coda position (and in some cases in any position), yet they are common in MUE, as they are in English and Scots more generally. A contact explanation must assume that Irish reinforced compatible patterns but did not affect those which were incompatible with it. In other words, Irish speakers learned where deletion was possible and where it was not, and this did not affect the distribution of deletions. In such a case, reinforcement is invisible and lacks any explanatory power, as is discussed further in Section 5.2.1. Since an adequate explanation for the consonant cluster simplifications in MUE is provided by the English and Scots inputs to the dialect, a role for contact with Irish is at best uncertain.

3.12 Other consonantal features

In this section, I briefly discuss a number of other consonantal features of MUE, the source of most of which present few problems (but which are, as a result, of interest in determining the phonological origins of the dialect).

3.12.1 Aspiration and voicing

Aspiration of voiceless stops in MUE works much like it does in RP English. Voiceless stops are aspirated in onset position before a stressed vowel, but not in foot-internal position or after /s/. In final position, the voiceless stops are not aspirated either, and in some cases may be unreleased (Adams 1948: 11). The degree of aspiration today appears to be roughly the same as it is in RP and similar accents of English, though Adams (1948: 11) suggested that there was less aspiration in MUE, so it may be that there has been a change in this feature. In any case, the heavy aspiration reported for some SIrE accents is not typical of MUE (ibid.). The voiced stops in onset position in MUE are usually voiced or even pre-voiced, though somewhat devoiced variants, as are typical of many English accents, are also possible.

It may well be the case that the situation in MUE is derived from the system which is found in much of England, though details of how the voiced and voiceless stops were pronounced in the Early Modern period are obviously impossible to retrieve. It should be noted, however, that some forms of RP 'have surprisingly little aspiration' (Wells 1982: 282; see also Przedlacka 2012), whilst unaspirated or weakly aspirated voiceless stops were characteristic of some traditional northern, Midland and south-west English dialects even in the mid twentieth century (Wells 1982: 370; see also the phonetic notes in the 'Localities and Informants' sections in the SED). So although the RP-type aspiration system was probably typical of many southern and Midland dialects in the twentieth century, such a pattern was by no means general for English, nor do we know how usual it was in the past. The extent to which the voiced stops in onset position are fully voiced or partially devoiced in traditional English dialects is unknown, though it may be assumed that fully voiced pronunciations are likely in dialects where the voiceless stops are unaspirated. Traditional Scots dialects also typically have unaspirated or only weakly aspirated voiceless stops, whilst the voiced stops are generally fully voiced in onset position (Johnston 1997a: 100, 1997b: 500). USc appears to have a similar situation to MUE.

In Irish, voiceless stops are heavily aspirated, except after /s(')/ and /x/, whilst the voiced stops are either fully voiced or partially devoiced when not between vowels (Ní Chasaide 1985: 60, 1999: 113; see also Hickey 2014: 179; Wagner 1958: xxiv). In this respect, then, Irish and English are very similar, so it is not surprising that varieties of IrE have the same kind of system. However, this close similarity means that determining the origin of the pronunciation of the voiced and voiceless stops in MUE is probably impossible, at least without extensive analysis of aspiration and voicing patterns in a range of dialects in both languages (and even then we cannot be sure what the patterns were in the past, including in the extinct dialects of Irish in the MUE area). It could be that their pronunciation in MUE is inherited from southern and Midland English, that it is a result of contact with Irish, or that the pattern was present in much of the English input and was reinforced by similar pronunciations in Irish. The presence of aspiration for the voiceless stops in MUE, but the lack of heavy aspiration of the Irish kind, perhaps suggest that MUE aligns more closely with English dialects than with Scots or Irish in this respect. The full voicing of the voiced stops in MUE has parallels in Scots, Irish and some dialects of English, and thus could be derived from any or all of these sources.

3.12.2 *Glottalisation and glottal replacement*

Neither glottalisation nor glottal replacement of voiceless stops in foot-internal and final position is typical of traditional MUE, though dialects close to the USc areas can have this feature, and glottal replacement of /t/ before syllabic [l] and [n] is not uncommon, as is the case with English generally (Harris 1984: 131; McCafferty 1999: 249, 2007: 127; Wells 1982: 445–6). Both glottalisation and glottal replacement are common in USc (Gregg 1958: 401, 1964: 178; Milroy 1982b: 25), illustrating the close links between it and the West-Mid dialects of Scots in Scotland, where this feature appears to have been established for some time, though it is unclear whether it is as old as the Plantation of Ulster and associated settlements (see Johnston 1997b: 500–1). Though glottal replacement and glottalisation are now characteristic of many dialects of English in England, this appears to be a recent development (Milroy *et al.* 1994; Wells 1982: 260–1). Glottalisation and glottal replacement of voiceless stops is not a feature of Irish (Hickey 2014: 84). So where glottalisation and glottal replacement (other than before syllabic [l] and [n]) do occur, we can be reasonably sure that Scots is the source, either from the period of Scottish settlement across Ulster following the Plantation, or as the result of subsequent spread of the feature from USc.

3.12.3 *Simplication of /kn/ and /wr/*

Old and Middle English allowed the initial clusters /kn/ (e.g. in *knee*, *knife*) and /wr/ (e.g. in *write*, *wrong*), though these have been simplified to /n/ and /r/ in most modern English and Scots dialects, including StE, and have never been recorded in MUE. It might seem, then, like there is nothing to explain, but since both clusters were still current in dialects of English in the seventeenth century (and indeed in more recent centuries), and were lost rather more recently in Scots, a brief examination of their history is in order so that we may understand their absence in MUE.

The initial cluster /kn/ was retained in StE into the eighteenth century. Loss of the first segment of the cluster, or change of it to [h], began in the seventeenth century in StE, though the usual pronunciation was probably still [kn] at this stage (Dobson 1957: 976; Lass 2000: 123). The loss of /k/ has a longer history in regional dialects of English, however, with evidence of simplification of the cluster from the fifteenth and sixteenth centuries (Minkova 2014: 133). But the cluster also survived much longer in some English dialects, with Ellis (1889), for example, recording [hn] in the dialects of the north-west Pennines and occasionally elsewhere. Loss of /wr/ was somewhat earlier in StE, with the first evidence of the change appearing in the mid fifteenth century and becoming usual in the sixteenth century, though 'educated speech retained the older pronunciation until the seventeenth century' (Dobson 1957: 975; see also Lass 2000: 122; Minkova 2014: 133–4). As was the case with /kn/, Ellis (1889) records distinct reflexes of /wr/ (e.g. [wər-] and [ər-]) in the late nineteenth century in some northern English dialects, especially in the north-west Pennines and Cumberland, though these pronunciations had disappeared by the time of the mid-twentieth-century SED.

Both /kn/ and /wr/ have survived in some Scots dialects to the present day, though they are now highly recessive (Johnston 1997b: 501–2). In the mid twentieth century, /kn/, or some derivative of it, for example, [tn] or [hn], was found across the northern half of Lowland Scotland, as far south as Fife, and it was present in southern Scotland in the mid nineteenth century (Murray 1873: 122). Similarly, /wr/ was characteristic of dialects in northern Scotland in the mid twentieth century, with a wider distribution, including locations as far south as the Borders and the south-west, in the nineteenth century (Ellis 1889: 750, word number 498 *write*, Johnston 1997b: 508; Murray 1873: 130). In some dialects, especially north-east Scotland, but also recorded by Ellis (1889: 750) in Kirkcudbrightshire, /wr/ had become /vr/. Given how widespread /kn/ and /wr/ were as late as the nineteenth century, including in southern Scotland, they must have been present in much of the seventeenth- and early-eighteenth-century Scots input to Ulster.

So /kn/ and /wr/, or reflexes of them, would have been present in at least some, and perhaps a significant part, of the English and Scots input to Ulster during the Plantation and its associated settlements. The failure of either feature to become established in MUE must be the result of variation in the input (especially in English, which by this stage was well on the way to losing /wr/), perhaps with subsequent loss as part of the general English and Scots move away from these clusters.

Notably, the cluster /kn/ is found in Irish (e.g. in *cnámh* 'bone', *cnoc* 'hill'), though in some dialects it has become /kr/ (Ó Siadhail 1989: 95). Irish also has /tn/ (e.g. *tnúth* 'envy') and /xn/ (e.g. *chnámh*, the lenited form of *cnámh*). This means that if /kn/ (or some development of it, e.g. [tn] or [hn]) was present in the English and Scots input to MUE in the seventeenth century, this would not have been a difficult sequence for speakers of Irish to learn, so that a contact explanation cannot help explain the loss of this feature. Instead, the loss of this sequence in English appears to have been the major input, regardless of what was happening in Scots or how Irish speakers may have dealt with it.

Irish does potentially have a sequence like /wr/ (broad /vr/), but broad /v/, normally pronounced as [w] in Ulster Irish, is usually realised as [v] before /r/ (e.g. in *bhrón*, lenited form of *brón* 'sorrow'; see Hickey 2014: 73). Given that initial [wr]~[vr] is not impossible in Irish, and that the first and perhaps the second pronunciation may have been present in the English and Scots input to Ulster, contact with Irish should not have contributed towards the elimination of this cluster. However, such contact has offered no reinforcement leading to survival of this sequence in some form distinct from /r/ in MUE.

3.12.4 *Interchange of /s/ and /ʃ/*

Harris (1985: 222) discusses the interchange of /s/ and /ʃ/ in MUE in two environments: (1) in final position or in final clusters, for example, in *grease* and *mince*, and (2) before /r/ in words such as *shriek* and *shrewd*. He notes that these changes had completely died out in the Belfast Vernacular in the second half of the twentieth century, though there are traces of them in traditional SwTE. Harris suggests, based on patterns in English and Scots dialects, that these interchanges have their origin in Britain. Certainly the change of /s/ to /ʃ/ in final position (and sometimes in other positions) is a common phenomenon in English and Scots dialects in the past and in more recent times (see, for example, the discussions in Dobson 1957: 947; Johnston 1997a: 105, 1997b: 508; Murray 1873: 127; Wright 1905: 241–2, 245, 248). Although this change is most common in the neighbourhood of high front vowels, an environment where /s'/ is favoured over /s/ in Irish (cf. Section 3.3.2), there is no general correlation between /ʃ/ and front vowels or /s/ and back vowels in MUE (cf. *piece* [pis], *push* [pɔʃ], *some* [sɔm] and *seem* [sim]), so a role for Irish is at best tenuous.

The change of initial /ʃr/ to /sr/ is well attested in English and Scots dialects (see Johnston 1997b: 508 and Wright 1905: 248; see also the entries for *shrimp*, *shrink*, *shrivel*, *shroud*, *shrub* and *shrug* in the EDG, and the responses to Q. IV.5.2 *shrew* in the SED), so it is not surprising that this is also a feature of some MUE dialects. But it is notable that the distinction between /s/ and /s'/ is often neutralised before /r/ (which is always broad following a sibilant) in Irish so that *srian* 'reins' and *sráid* 'street' have the same initial in Ulster Irish (Ó Siadhail 1989: 99–100), though there is some variation in how this is realised, including [sr], [ʂr] and [ʂ] (with deletion of the /r/); see Wagner (1958: 128) and Stockman and Wagner (1965: 103) for examples. It is thus possible that speakers of Irish could have reinforced [s] in words with initial *shr-* in English, helping this feature to survive in MUE, though it is not unlikely that it could have done so even without this input.

3.12.5 *Realisation of /kl/ and /gl/ as [tl] and [dl]*

Although it is not usually described as a feature of the dialect, the initial clusters /kl/ and /gl/ are often realised as [tl] and [dl] in MUE (and thus could be phonemicised as /tl/ and /dl/), including traditional SwTE, where these pronunciations are the norm for traditional speakers at least. This is also a feature of many English and Scots dialects, and may thus be of long standing (see Dobson 1957: 951–2; Johnston 1997b: 502; Wright 1905: 246, 251; and see, for example, the words *clay*, *clean*, *clear*, *climb*, *close*, *glass* and *glove* in the EDG, and the responses to Qs. IV.4.2 *clay*, V.9.7 *clothes*, VI.7.14 *clumsy*, VI. 14.7 *gloves*, VII.6.2 *clouds* and VIII.7.4 *climb* in the SED). In

Scotland, this change was particularly characteristic of dialects across the south-west of the country but not the south-east (see the phonetic notes for the words *clay, clean, climb, cloak, clock, close, clothes, cloud, glebe, glour* and *glove* in LAS3), and this pattern continues the distribution of the feature in English dialects, where it is found in a broad swathe of the country from East Anglia to Cumberland, but not in the dialects of the north-east.

Given how widespread this feature is in Britain, especially in dialects from areas which supplied many of the Plantation settlers, it is to be expected that it should also turn up in MUE, and a British source for the feature can hardly be doubted. This is especially the case given that Irish allows initial sequences of broad and slender velar and coronal stops + /l(')/, for example, /kl/ (e.g. *cloch* 'stone'), /k'l'/ (e.g. *cleas* 'trick'), /tl/ (e.g. *tláith* 'weak') and /t'l'/ (e.g. *tslí* 'way' with prefixed /t'/ after the definite article in the nominative singular). Speakers of Irish could have employed any one of four different sequences to represent English and Scots /kl/, and would have had no reason to pick [tl] in particular (even given the clear [l] in onset position in MUE, which might have suggested /k'l'/ or /t'l'/ as an Irish equivalent).

3.12.6 /z/ *and* /ʒ/

Like English, MUE has the two coronal voiced fricatives /z/ and /ʒ/. Both of these sounds are absent from Irish (except in the case of [z] in some recent borrowings or Anglified pronunciations). Their consistent survival in MUE speaks against significant influence from Irish on the phonology of the dialect as a result of contact and language shift. Whilst Scots also has /z/, and usually /ʒ/ in at least some words, many dialects had /z/ instead of /ʒ/ in words like *measure, pleasure* and *treasure* (Dieth 1932: 105; Murray 1873: 127; Wright 1905: 244). This is not a feature of MUE, though traditional forms of the dialect, including SwTE, may have /ʒ/ in *poison* (e.g. ['pɔɪʒn̩]), a feature of some Scots dialects (Murray 1873: 127), which, however, typically have the vowel /ʌ/ in the first syllable.

3.13 Summary

The results of the analysis of the origins of MUE consonantal features in this chapter are summarised in Table 3.5. In this table, the most likely origins of the feature are identified where this can be determined.

Table 3.5 A summary of the origins of consonantal features of MUE.

Feature	Origin
/h/-retention	An English and/or Scots source.
/hw/-retention	An English and/or Scots source.
/hj/ developments	Possibly an English source for loss of /h/ before /j/. The change of /hj/ to [c] is probably an internal development.
/x/ distribution	An English source for the lack of historical /x/, with Scots and Irish contributions via loanwords and place-names.
/x/ realisation	Weakening of /x/ to [h] is shared by MUE and Ulster Irish, but the direction of influence, if any, is uncertain.

Velar Palatalisation	An English source, perhaps with reinforcement from Irish.
/tj/ and /dj/	The distinction between /tj, dj/ and /ʧ, ʤ/ has an English and/or Scots source.
Realisation of /ʧ/, /ʤ/ and /ʃ/	Probably from English and/or Scots, possibly with reinforcement from Irish.
Palatal Velarisation	An Irish source, perhaps also likely in varieties that contrast palatalised alveolars with palatalised velars.
Pre-R Dentalisation	An English and/or Scots source.
Voicing of /t/	An English source.
Dental fricatives	An English and/or Scots source.
TH-Stopping before /r/	An English source, perhaps with some Scots input.
Debuccalisation of /θ/	An English and/or Scots source.
Loss of foot-internal /ð/ before /ər/	Possibly an English source.
[l]-like realisation of /ð/ before /ər/	Probably a recent internal development.
Rhoticity	An English and/or Scots source.
Non-rhoticity	An English source, though loss of /r/ in words like *partridge* is also found in Scots.
/r/-realisation	An English source, perhaps with some Scots input.
Post-/r/-retraction	An English source.
The /r/ Realisation Effect	An English and possibly a Scots source.
Distribution of /l/	An English source.
/l/-realisation	An English and/or Scots source, probably with internal developments and perhaps with reinforcement from Irish.
Epenthesis	An English and/or Scots source, possibly with reinforcement from Irish.
/t/-deletion	An English and/or Scots source, perhaps with reinforcement from Irish.
/d/-deletion after /l/	An English and/or Scots source, perhaps with reinforcement from Irish.
/d/-deletion after /n/	An English and/or Scots source, perhaps with reinforcement from Irish.
/mb/ > /m/	An English and/or Scots source, perhaps with reinforcement from Irish.
/ŋg/ > /ŋ/	An English and/or Scots source, perhaps with reinforcement from Irish.
Aspiration and voicing	An English source, perhaps with some Scots input and reinforcement from Irish.
Glottalisation/Glottal replacement	A Scots source.
Simplication of /kn/	An English source, perhaps with some Scots input.
Simplication of /wr/	An English source, perhaps with some Scots input.
Interchange of /s/ and /ʃ/	An English and/or Scots source, perhaps with reinforcement from Irish.
/kl, gl/ > [tl, dl]	An English and/or Scots source.
/z/ and /ʒ/	An English and/or Scots source.

Table 3.5 indicates that of the thirty-six features analysed, thirteen appear to have an origin exclusively or mainly in England; nineteen are shared by English and Scots and thus have a British origin, whether from English, from Scots or from both is not determinable; one, glottalisation/glottal replacement, appears to have its origin in Scots, though this is peripheral to MUE; one appears to have an origin in Irish; and one (the presence of /x/) largely derives from Scots and Irish via borrowed words and place-names. In addition, eleven of them possibly involve reinforcement from Irish, not because they pattern in a specifically Irish way, but because although they are present in the English and/or Scots input, similar, if not identical, features appear in Irish. But given that they might have developed in MUE due to English and Scots input anyway, Irish reinforcement is uncertain, and I discuss this issue at length in Section 5.2.1.

A number of key patterns are observable from this summary. Firstly, consonantal features of specifically Irish origin are rare in MUE, though Irish may have played a reinforcing role in the development of some others. Features that we might expect to have developed in the dialect if Irish influence was an important factor, such as general stopping of the dental fricatives, are absent. Secondly, the consonant system of MUE is for the most part of a somewhat conservative, non-regional English type, with specific consonantal features associated with the north (e.g. /k/ for /tʃ/ in words like *church*/*kirk* and /l/ vocalisation in words like *old*) and from the south-west (e.g. voicing of initial voiceless fricatives in words like *seven*) being absent. Indeed, the Scots input aside, the MUE consonant system is not very different from what we might expect to have found in the Early Modern ancestor of StE, though many of the features that the two share have disappeared in StE and across much of the south and Midlands of England. The reasons for this non-regional, somewhat conservative character of the MUE consonant system are discussed in Section 5.3.

The Scots input to the MUE consonant system is more subtle. Exclusively Scots contributions are few, though many consonantal features that are or were found in English are also shared by Scots, so it is not possible to determine their source more precisely. It is likely that features which were present in both the English and Scots inputs in seventeenth-century Ulster would survive in the dialect, as is discussed in Sections 5.3 and 5.4, though it is equally apparent from Table 3.5 that although English features survive in the dialect regardless of whether or not they were supported by Scots features, the reverse is not true. In other words, it is not clear that all of these shared features require a Scots input, though it is likely that some of them (e.g. the consonant deletions) would have required it to ensure their survival in the formation of the new dialect (again, see Sections 5.3 and 5.4).

Notes

1. A similar explanation for *Hugh* [cʉ:] can be hypothesised if we assume that original [çʉ:] was interpreted by Irish learners of English as a vocative form (with customary Irish lenition), thus allowing them to 'reconstruct' the basic form [cʉ:], but again this is an ad hoc explanation without any support from other pronunciations in MUE.
2. The symbol [ʊ] is used in this book for a fairly high, rounded, central vowel.

3. There is little published information on the distinction or merger of /tj, dj/ and /ʧ, ʤ/ in MUE. In the unpublished fieldworkers' notebooks which fed into LAS3, the two County Down MUE locations (29.5 Loughinisland and 29.6 Annalong) have Yod Coalesence (as do the other, USc-speaking, locations in the county, though some USc dialects in County Antrim retain /tj/ and /dj/), whilst the two County Armagh MUE locations (31.1 Poyntzpass and 31.2 Mount Norris) do not. The traditional form of SwTE does not have Yod Coalesence either (though its modern form does).

4. In fact, most instances appear in the speech of older Protestant males, but given the small number of tokens and lexical items involved, this is unlikely to be meaningful.

5. This word is also commonly pronounced [ˈpɔːɹʧən] in the dialect, for reasons unknown.

6. The difference between these two environments in Table 3.3 is highly significant, with p < 0.0001 (Fisher's Exact Test).

7. This difference is also significant, with p = 0.0147 (Fisher's Exact Test).

8. Interestingly, the analysis reported in Table 3.3 reveals that voicing is more common (significantly so) in all environments for the Catholic speakers in this sample. As was discussed in Section 2.7, it shouldn't be surprising that there are linguistic differences between Catholic and Protestant speech of subtle kinds like this. Given that /t/-Voicing almost certainly has an English origin and has no parallels in Irish, the reason for this difference between the two ethno-religious groups can have nothing to do with whether the speakers' ancestors spoke Irish. Nor can it have anything to do with Catholic speakers adopting SIrE norms as suggested by Harris (1991: 46; see Section 2.5), since /t/-Voicing is not generally characteristic of the variety.

9. Debuccalisation of /θ/ before /r/, in words such as *three*, is also widespread in Scots (Johnston 1997b: 507), but as this is not a feature of MUE it is not discussed further here.

10. The long vowels in *ass* and *hoss* are not the result of vowel lengthening before /r/ before loss of rhoticity, but rather reflect lengthening of low-mid and low vowels before voiceless fricatives (see Section 4.3).

11. Kingsmore (1995) also records dark [ɫ] in working-class speech in Coleraine, in the USc-speaking area.

12. It is noteworthy that the word *leap* is pronounced [lɛp] in SwTE and other traditional MUE varieties, and that deletion of /t/ is possible in its past tense *leapt* ([lɛp]), revealing it to be a semi-weak form of the same sort as *crept* ([kɹɛp]) and not a regular past tense of the sort found for *step* (*stepped*, always [stɛpt]). The past tense of *kep* 'to head off/herd cattle' is always [kɛpt], whilst the past tense of *keep* can be [kɛp].

13. The well-known MUE word *scunner* 'to feel disgust, to annoy', also of Scots origin, has the same alteration ([ˈskɔ̈ŋə̯]~[ˈskɔ̈ŋdə̯]), even though the /d/ is not etymological, presumably due to hypercorrection on the model of *dander*, *thunder* and *hundred* (Macafee 1996: 293).

4 Vowels

4.1 The MUE vowels

Wells (1982: 72–80) describes a number of ways that varieties of a language can differ from each other, and these are particularly relevant for vowels, which vary considerably between dialects of English. Varieties of English differ from each other in terms of the vowel systems they have (for example, some dialects contrast /ʌ/ and /ʊ/, whilst others only have /ʊ/), in terms of the realisations of these vowels (/ʌ/ may be pronounced as a low, unrounded [ɐ]-like vowel in some dialects, but as a mid centralised rounded vowel [ɵ] in others), in terms of phonotactic constraints on their distribution (e.g. in rhotic varieties of English, some dialects distinguish /ɔ/ and /o/ before /r/ whilst others do not), and in terms of their lexical distribution, that is, even when dialects share the same vowel phonemes and constraints on their distribution, they may occur in different words (for example, /a/ occurs in the words *trap* and *bath* in the north of England but in *trap* only in the south, whilst /ɑː/ occurs in the word *palm* in the north, but in *bath* and *palm* in the south).

These differences between dialects arise from regionally and socially specific phonetic and phonological changes, and over time these changes build up to create substantial systemic, realisational and distributional vocalic differences between dialects. In other words, the vocalic features of a dialect give us a detailed insight into its phonological history. All these different aspects of vowel variation in MUE can be used to investigate the phonological history of the dialect and to assess the impact on its development from the Irish, English and Scots input varieties that have been in contact in Ulster. It will be seen that a reasonably clear picture of the importance of the various input dialects emerges from the investigation of the vowel phonology of MUE in this chapter, with English providing most of the vowel lexical distributions that characterise the dialect and with Scots having a considerable impact on the realisation of these vowels, both in their quality and quantity. Irish, on the other hand, appears to have played at most a minor role in the phonological development of the MUE vowels.

In order to set the scene for the analysis of the phonological origins of MUE vocalic features, the typical vowels found in the dialect, with the lexical set (as defined by Wells 1982) with which they are mostly associated, are summarised in Table 4.1. Note that the phonemic symbols used for these vowels may be slightly different from those used in other sources (e.g. in Harris 1985 and Wells 1982). Vowels in brackets are absent in some varieties of the dialect, and there is a fair

Table 4.1 MUE vowels.

Phoneme	Lexical set
/i/	FLEECE
/e/	FACE
(/e₂/)	'MEAT'[a]
/ë/	KIT
/ɛ/	DRESS
/a/	TRAP
(/aː/)	TRAP, BATH, PALM
(/ɑ/)	PALM, THOUGHT
(/ɒ/)	LOT
/ɔ/	LOT, CLOTH, THOUGHT
/o/	GOAT
/ɵ/	STRUT, FOOT
/ʉ/	FOOT, GOOSE
/ëi/	PRICE
(/aɪ/)	PRICE
/ɔɪ/	CHOICE
/əʉ/	MOUTH

Note:
a See Section 4.4.1.

degree of regional and social variation in their realisation (for further discussion, see Section 4.2).

This chapter is organised as follows. In Section 4.2, I provide an overview of MUE vowel quality and analyse the origins of a number of characteristic realisations in detail. In Section 4.3, I discuss vowel quantity in the dialect, comparing this with other varieties of English and Scots in Ireland and Britain and examining the origins of three key vowel length rules in detail. In Section 4.4, I describe the origins of the lexical distribution of vowel phonemes in MUE, identifying a range of conservative features (from an English perspective) and analysing a number of less straightforward cases that have important consequences for understanding the phonological origins of the dialect. In Section 4.5, I summarise the results of the analyses in this chapter.

4.2 Vowel quality in MUE

The realisation of its vowels is one of the most distinctive features of the phonology of MUE. Part of this distinctiveness lies in the considerable variation in the pronunciation of the vowels that are found in the dialect, much of which correlates with vowel length. Most MUE vowels come in short and long forms, something which is largely determined by the nature of the following consonant (see Section 4.3 for details). There are often significant divergences in quality between the short and long realisations, and there are other contextually determined allophones as well as a fair degree of social and regional variation. This section examines the quality of MUE vowels and explores possible origins for some of the more distinctive patterns in the dialect.

Table 4.2 Vowel quality in BVE and SwTE.[a]

Set	Phoneme	BVE (Harris 1985)		SwTE	
		Short	Long	Short	Long
KIT*	ɛ̈	ɛ̈–ɪ	–	ɛ̈–ə–ɜ	–
DRESS*	ɛ	ɛ–æ–a	ɛː–ɛːᵊ	ɛ–ɛ̧	ɛːᵊ
TRAP, BATH*	a, (aː)	æ–a–ä–ɑ̈	äː–ɑː–ɒː–ɒːᵊ–ɔː–ɔːᵊ	a–ä–ɑ̈–ɑ	ä–äː–ɑː
PALM	a, (aː), (ɑ)	–	äː–ɑː–ɒː–ɒːᵊ–ɔː–ɔːᵊ	–	äː–äː–ɑː
LOT, CLOTH*	(ɒ), ɔ	ɑ–ä–a̠	ɔː–ɔ̈ː–ɔ̈ːᵊ	ɔː–ɔːᵊ > ɑ–ɒ	ɔː–ɔːᵊ
THOUGHT	ɔ	–	ɔː–ɔ̈ː–ɔ̈ːᵊ	–	ɔː–ɔːᵊ
STRUT*	ɔ̈	ʌ–ɔ̈	–	ʌ–ɔ̈–ɔ̧	–
FLEECE	i	i	iː–ᵊiː	i	iː–ɪiː
FACE*	e	eə	ɪˑə, ɛː#	eᵊ–ɛ̧ᵊ	ɛ̧ːᵊ–ɪˑə, ɛ̧ː#
MEAT*	e₂	ɛ̧(ə)	ɛ̧ˑə	eᵊ–ɛ̧ᵊ	ɛ̧ːᵊ; ɛ̧ː#
GOAT	o	ǫ	oː	ǫ	ǫˑu (ǫˑə)
GOOSE	ʉ	ʉ	ʉː–ᵊʉː	ʉ	ʉː–ʊ̈ʉˑ
PRICE	ɛ̈i	ɛ̈i	eˑĭ–æːⁱ	ɛ̈i	ɛ̈iˑ
PRIZE	aɪ	–	–	–	äˑe–äˑe–ɑˑe
CHOICE	ɔɪ	ɔ̈e	ɔ̈e	ɔ̈e	ɔˑe
MOUTH	əʉ	ɔ̈ʉ	əˑʉ–æːʉ	əʊ̈	əʊ̈ˑ

Note:

a For details of length conditioning for each vowel, see Section 4.3.1. Symbols separated by – indicate ranges of pronunciation, sometimes contextually determined but not always. # indicates that the pronunciation is found morpheme-finally. Pronunciations separated by a comma are major positional allophones, whilst those in parentheses are rare or sporadic. The vowels in lexical sets marked by * are subject to PPR, at least in some environments (see Section 3.3.1), and these distinctive allophones are not included in this table.

Table 4.2 summarises the realisation of MUE vowels in two varieties, BVE, as described in Harris (1985), and SwTE, as recorded by the author. The first of these represents an urban vernacular whilst the second represents a conservative rural dialect of MUE. Other accounts of vowel quality in MUE can be found in Corrigan (2010: 32–40), McCafferty (1999: 247–9) and Wells (1982: 440–5). Although there is also variation in the realisation of vowels before coda /r/, this is not covered here. Table 4.2 identifies vowels by the lexical sets laid out in Wells (1982), with the addition of the 'MEAT' and 'PRIZE' lexical subsets (see Sections 4.4 and 4.4.3 for explanations). As is explained in Section 4.4.5, there is no independent vowel in the FOOT lexical set in MUE.

The SwTE vowels given in Table 4.2 are impressionistic values, but they are supported by acoustic analysis of data from the corpus. Thomas (2011b: 19) provides a formant plot for the vowels (stressed monophthongs and diphthongs) of the dialect as produced in conversation by speaker PM43, though allophonic differences between long and short environments are not factored into the analysis. Nevertheless, the relative values of the vowels identified by Thomas match the phonetic symbols given in Table 4.2 quite well.

Whilst MUE quality has things in common with Irish, Scots and English, much of this is the result of them all sharing a historically similar system of short and long vowels distributed in typical ways in the vowel space (e.g. they all have a high front vowel [i(:)] and one or more low vowels in the phonetic range [a(:)] to [ɑ(:)]). It is where the MUE vowel system departs from these kinds of typical qualities that it may be possible to identify the roles of the input varieties. In the rest of this section, I discuss the following divergent aspects of MUE vowel quality: (1) lowered and centralised KIT and STRUT vowels; (2) lowering of the DRESS vowel; (3) backing of the TRAP/BATH vowel; (4) unrounding of the LOT vowel; (5) fronting of the GOOSE vowel and the second part of the MOUTH diphthong; (6) the realisation of the FACE vowel; and (7) quality variation in the PRICE diphthongs. Pre-Palatal Raising (PPR) is discussed in Section 3.3 in connection with Velar Palatalisation.

It will be seen that while there has probably been some specifically English input, Scots in particular has played an important role in the development of MUE vowel quality. A role of Irish in the development of MUE vowel quality, on the other hand, is uncertain and at most amounts to a degree of reinforcement of patterns in the English and Scots input, though even this is uncertain.

4.2.1 Lowering and centralisation of the KIT and STRUT vowels

The main sources for the KIT and STRUT lexical sets are ME /ɪ/ and /ʊ/, with some additional input from ME /oː/ to STRUT (Wells 1982: 127, 132). The vowels characteristic of both the KIT and STRUT lexical sets in MUE show a considerable degree of lowering and some centralisation. The typical values recorded in working-class and traditional varieties are [ɛ̈]–[ə]–[ɜ] for KIT and [ʌ]–[ʌ̈]–[ö̞]–[ɔ̈] for STRUT. As is discussed in Section 4.4.5, most FOOT words have the same vowel as STRUT in conservative varieties of MUE. Lowering and centralisation of the KIT vowel is not found in other varieties of IrE (USc aside), whilst lowering and centralisation of the typical STRUT vowel, to [ɔ̈] or the like, is (Hickey 2007a: 316–17; Kallen 2013: 61–2; Wells 1982: 422–3). However, many varieties of SIrE maintain a distinction between the vowel in STRUT and the vowel in FOOT ([ʊ]), and for those that do not (e.g. traditional Dublin English), the usual value of the unsplit vowel is [ʊ].

Lowering and centralisation of /ɪ/ (the typical KIT vowel) is not characteristic of most English dialects in Britain, though there was a degree of lowering to [e]/[ɛ] in some south-west dialects (Luick 1940: 678–9; Widén 1949: 45–6; Wright 1905: 69–70). Lowering (and a degree of centralisation) of the STRUT vowel (to [ʌ] or the like) is a well-known feature of southern English dialects (including RP), however, being found south of a line from the Wash to the Severn Estuary, as well as along the Welsh Border in the mid twentieth century (see Anderson 1987: 34–5, 37; Kolb *et al.* 1979: 227). The split in original /ʊ/ to [ʊ] and [ʌ], which gave rise to the FOOT and STRUT lexical sets, probably occurred in the middle and second half of the seventeenth century (Dobson 1957: 585–8; Lass 2000: 89–91), though this may have been preceded, as early as the second half of the sixteenth century, by some allophonic unrounding and lowering of the vowel (Kökeritz 1953: 240–4; Lass 2000: 89). Precisely what the value of this lowered STRUT vowel was in the seventeenth century is uncertain, especially given that '[ʌ]' is typically used as a cover symbol for it without necessarily implying a definite phonetic value (Lass 2000: 90). Assuming a straightforward lowering of [ʊ], it might be assumed that it passed through the stages [ʊ] > [ɤ] > [ʌ], perhaps with some centralisation, even as far as [ə] (Kökeritz 1953: 240). The realisations of this vowel in the transition zone between southern [ʌ] and northern [ʊ] in the traditional dialects of the mid twentieth century is illustrative, with variants across the range [ɤ]–[ɤ]–[ɤ]–[ɤ]–[ʌ]–[ʌ]–[ʌ] being recorded (Chambers and Trudgill 1980: 132). Whether this lowering of the STRUT vowel was early enough or geographically widespread enough to have had a significant impact in the development of MUE is another matter, given that much of the English settlement in the province occurred in the early and mid seventeenth century and was mostly from areas across both the south and Midlands of England. It may be that there were some settlers with the split, or with allophonic lowering of /ʊ/ at least, though they are unlikely to have been in the majority at the time. The fact that STRUT and FOOT have not split in traditional MUE and that the single vowel in both sets is lowered [ɔ] further complicates an English explanation for the value of this vowel in Ulster.

Lowering and centralisation of OSc /ʊ/ and /ɪ/ is a widespread feature of modern Scots, being recorded in almost all the traditional dialects recorded in Scotland in the mid-twentieth-century LAS3 (Johnston 1997b: 468–70, 476–8). Typical values, especially in the southern half of Scotland, include [ë]–[ë]–[ə] for OSc /ɪ/ and [ö]–[ɤ]–[ʌ]–[ɐ] for OSc /ʊ/, and these ranges probably indicate the likely trajectory of development of the vowels (cf. Aitken and Macafee 2002: 150–1; Johnston 1997a: 79, 83). The date that this lowering of the OSc high short vowels began is uncertain, though Aitken and Macafee (2002: 155–6) suggest the values 'ɪ (ë)' for the front vowel and 'ö' for the back vowel by 1600, so it is likely that the lowering had begun by the time of the Scottish Plantation settlements in Ulster. Given that the values for these two vowels in Scotland and in MUE are very similar, and that these are shared with USc (which has [æ]/[ë] for the front vowel and [ʌ]/[ɔ] for the back vowel, as documented in Gregg 1985, for example), a source in Scotland for this feature seems likely. It is noteworthy that in some peripheral, conservative Scots dialects, the back vowel is [ö] or [ɤ] rather than [ʌ] (Johnston 1997b: 476–8), which matches the vowel in MUE more closely than the low-mid or even low unrounded vowel (e.g. [ʌ]/ [ɐ]) of many Scots dialects. It is also important to note that OSc /ʊ/ lowered in all cases in southern Scotland at least (e.g. in FOOT words such as *bull* and *bush* as well as in STRUT words such as *cut* and *dull*), so that no distinction between [ʊ] and [ʌ] developed, as it did in England. This again matches the situation in MUE, which has a single vowel corresponding to the STRUT and (for the most part) the FOOT lexical sets, which lowered across the board (i.e. [ɔ] is found in *bull* and *dull*).

Interestingly, Aitken and Macafee (2002: 150–1) suggest that the lowering and unrounding of OSc /ʊ/ might have been inspired by contact with southern English, where a similar change took place (as discussed above). However, it is not clear that such an explanation is necessary, especially given the parallel lowering of /ɪ/ in Scots (something that did not typically happen in England) and the early date for this change in Scotland, which does not lag behind the English change, and indeed may have preceded it. In any case, if both Scots and southern English dialects were already possessed of somewhat lowered STRUT vowels in the early seventeenth century, it is not surprising that this has also become a feature of MUE, though in its wider context (the lowering of the vowel in both STRUT and FOOT words and the

$$[\text{ɪ}] \longleftarrow /\text{ɯ}/ \longrightarrow [\text{ʊ}]$$

$$[\text{ɛ}] \longleftarrow /\text{ə}/ \longrightarrow [\text{ɔ}]$$

$$[\text{æ}] \longleftarrow /\text{a}/ \longrightarrow [\text{ɑ}]$$

Fig. 4.1 Short vowel phonemes and realisations in Irish.

lowering of /ɪ/), the change in MUE is more similar to what occurred in Scotland than in southern England.

The evidence for lowering of /ɪ/ and /ʊ/ in English and, especially, Scots strongly suggests a British origin for this feature of MUE. But it is also worth considering the development of the high short vowel(s) in Irish, as there are parallels to these changes there too. In order to understand the phonetics of the short vowels in Irish, it is first necessary to understand their phonology. Although Irish dialects typically (and historically) have five short vowel phones in stressed syllables (Hickey 2014: 139–40; Ó Baoill 2009: 174; Ó Siadhail 1989: 35–7), roughly [ɪ], [ʊ], [ɛ], [ɔ] and [a] (the last often used as a cover symbol for both [æ]/[a] and [ɑ]), at a more abstract level only three phonemes can be posited (/ɯ/, /ə/ and /a/), distinguished by height but not on the front/back dimension. This is because of the Irish rule (some complications aside) whereby short front vowels only occur before a slender consonant and short back vowels only occur before a broad consonant, so that the pairs [ɪ] and [ʊ], [ɛ] and [ɔ], and [æ] and [ɑ] are in complementary distribution (Ó Siadhail 1989: 36–7; see also Ó Maolalaigh 1997: 88–99, 108–9 for an extended discussion of this issue). This situation is illustrated in Figure 4.1.

This scheme is phonologised in various ways by analysts, and may also be disrupted by a number of changes in Irish dialects. The Irish vowel [ɔ], which is typically somewhat centralised and unrounded in non-Ulster dialects (Hickey 2014 uses the symbol [ʌ] for it), is often equated with the similar vowel in the STRUT lexical set ([ɔ̈]) in SIrE, and influence from Irish is usually suggested. However, Harris (1990) argues that IrE [ɔ̈] in STRUT is not unusual given the trajectory of the change in this vowel in English and the existence of [ɔ̈]-type vowels in other, non-Irish varieties of English (see also Lass 1990a: 141–2). Hickey (2014: 150–1) concurs, suggesting that the phonetic similarity between the Irish and Irish English vowels may be coincidental.

The usual values for the six short vowels in Figure 4.1 in Ulster Irish are '[ï]', '[ọ]', [ɛ], [ɔ], [æ]/[a] and [ɑ] (see Ó Maolalaigh 1997: 109–20 for an extended analysis of their phonemic status in Donegal Irish). The symbols '[ï]' and '[ọ]' are used in transcriptions of Irish for vowels in the phonetic area of [ï] and [ọ] respectively (see Wagner 1958–64: xxiii), and these values are also typical for these vowels in the mid-twentieth-century Irish of north Tyrone in the middle of the MUE area, as recorded in Stockman and Wagner (1965: 176–7). It is noteworthy that both Ulster Irish and other dialects of Irish have a vowel in the area [ọ]/[ɔ̈], but that this vowel is a reflex of [ʊ] in Ulster, but a reflex of [ɔ] elsewhere (see above). The lowering and centralisation of [ɪ] and [ʊ] to [ï] and [ọ] in Ulster Irish looks very similar to what we find in MUE, and the obvious question arises as to whether they are connected.

Both Hickey (2014: 140; see also 146, 150–1) and Ó Maolalaigh (1997: 394–5) suggest that they are, though they don't claim that Irish has influenced MUE in this respect. Hickey (2014: 140) describes the shared lowering as an 'areal feature', though this is an observation rather than an explanation. Ó Maolalaigh (1997: 394) notes in this context that '[o]ne possible avenue for further research would be to assess the effects which varieties of Ulster and Scottish English have had on Donegal Irish', suggesting that he believes this aspect of Ulster Irish to have its origin in English and Scots in Ulster. Given that the lowering and centralisation of [ɪ] and [ʊ] is specific to Ulster Irish, precisely the area of Ireland where lowering and centralisation is characteristic of English (and Scots), this seems quite possible, so that the values of these vowels in MUE are not attributable to Irish influence (as their close parallels in Scots would indicate in any case). Furthermore, the development of [ɔ̈] for two different vowels in Irish, for historical [ɔ] in non-Ulster dialects and for historical [ʊ] in Ulster, also suggests that English and/or Scots influence on Irish may have been at play.

In summary, then, lowering of the typical KIT and STRUT/FOOT vowels in MUE closely parallels Early Modern developments in Scots and is shared with USc, whilst a supportive role for English in the latter is also possible. Although similar changes are also found in Ulster Irish, these may well have their origin in MUE and USc influence on the language.

4.2.2 Lowering of the DRESS vowel

A degree of lowering of the DRESS vowel in short environments is a characteristic of many varieties of MUE. Whilst lowering to [æ] or even [a] is especially characteristic of BVE (Harris 1985: 50–1), similar lowering is recorded in County Armagh in LAS3 (Mather and Speitel 1986: 204–6), and a degree of lowering (e.g. [ɛ̞]) also occurs in traditional SwTE.[1] Such a lowering of the front mid historical short vowel is not characteristic of Irish, which typically has [ɛ] or [e] in this part of the vowel space, nor is it usual in English, although there is some evidence for lowering to [æ] in English dialects in the south-west, Kent and East Anglia (Wright 1905: 51), so English input to the change is not impossible. But the most obvious parallel to lowering of this vowel in MUE is found in Scots. In southern Scots dialects, from Berwickshire in the east to Dumfriesshire in the west, and occasionally further west in Kirkcudbrightshire and Wigtonshire, lowered realisations of the DRESS vowel are typical, ranging from [ɛ̞] through [æ] to [a], though these are not restricted to short environments (see the locations for these counties in LAS3; see also Johnston 1997b: 472). This lowering was being replaced in southern Scotland by mid and even raised realisations of this vowel ([ɛ] and [ɛ̝]), typical of the Central Belt, and it may be that lowered realisations were once more widespread in southern Scotland than they were in the mid twentieth century. Johnston (1997b: 472) suggests that USc has combined this lowered [æ] (in short environments) with raised [ɛ̝:(ə)] (in long environments) as a result of it being a 'koinéised' form of Scots, but it is possible that such a system also once existed in dialects of Scots in Scotland. Assuming that lowering of /ɛ/ in MUE is not an internal development, it is likely that this feature of MUE derives from the Scots input to the dialect, perhaps with some support from regional seventeenth-century English dialects.

4.2.3 Backing of the TRAP/BATH vowel

In addition to variation in length dependent upon the nature of the following consonant (see Section 4.3), there is considerable variation in the quality of the typical
TRAP/BATH vowel in non-standard forms of MUE, as described in Harris (1985:
177–97) and Milroy (1982a). As Harris (1985: 177) notes, '[t]he range of variation
in B[elfast]V[ernacular] /a/ is quite extensive, occurring on a phonetic continuum
from front [ɛ], through low [ä] to back round [ɔ]'. Although this extreme variation
may not be typical of all varieties of MUE, a degree of variation in the quality of
the typical TRAP/BATH vowel is evident in most dialects, even when we set aside [ɛ]
forms that represent a phonemic change in the context of certain velar or coronal
consonants. For example, the quality of the low vowel in SwTE ranges from [a]
through [ä] to [ɑ], with this variation depending on the nature of the following consonant and (often connected with this) the length of the vowel.

Harris (1985) argues that the backing of the TRAP/BATH vowel is of unambiguous Scots origin, being most characteristic of varieties that are closest to the USc
dialect area, being shared by USc, and being found in Lowland Scots dialects too.
Johnston (1997b: 484–8) describes the realisation of the vowel derived from OSc /a/
in modern Scots dialects, and it is clear that there are close parallels with the variation found in MUE. Although some Scots dialects have back [ɑ] in all environments,
others have variation between [a] and [ɑ], with back variants preferred before labials
and 'in high sonority environments' (ibid.: 486). One change identified by Johnston
(1997b) as typical of Mid-Scots dialects is '*hand*-Darkening', whereby particularly
retracted realisations, even as far as [ɔ], are found before /r/, /l/ and /n/, especially
when a (voiced) consonant follows. These Scottish developments are very similar to
the pattern reported in Belfast by Harris (1985) and Milroy (1982a).

One point that is implied in Harris's and Milroy's descriptions and which is
apparent in the LAS3 MUE data and in SwTE is that back realisations are most
typical of long realisations of the low vowel (though they are also common for short
variants before labials). As is described in Section 4.3, these are most typical before
final voiced consonants and voiceless fricatives. Whilst this pattern may well derive
from Scots (back variants of the low vowel being most common in 'high sonority'
environments, which are also the most likely to trigger lengthening of preceding
vowels, as is described in Section 4.3), it also opens up the possibility that backing
of the TRAP/BATH vowel in MUE may have been influenced by realisations of low
vowels in English and Irish.

The short low vowel in English typically found in the TRAP lexical set is usually
front in quality (and indeed may be raised to [æ] in all environments in southern
dialects, including RP) – see Anderson (1987: 12–15). Dobson (1957: 545) argues
that this vowel was also front in the Early Modern period, with the late ME value [a]
raising to [æ] in (some) southern dialects in the sixteenth and seventeenth centuries,
though with [a] being the 'usual pronunciation' amongst 'careful speakers' till about
1650 (ibid.: 548). The [a] realisation is close to the MUE realisation of the TRAP
vowel in MUE, at least in non-backing environments. Before /r/, /a/ lengthened
in most dialects of English in the Early Modern period, whilst it also lengthened
before voiceless fricatives in the south and south Midlands (see Section 4.3.5). These

lengthened variants were at first [aː] (or perhaps [æː]), but are now represented in RP and many other southern English dialects by [ɑː], representing a backing of this long vowel. Although this appears to be similar to the development of the long low vowel in MUE, which is typically retracted in pronunciation when lengthened, it is difficult to connect these two developments, since backing of long [aː] in southern England is a relatively recent change, becoming established in the eighteenth century or even the nineteenth century (MacMahon 1999: 455–6), long after the Plantation of Ulster. Even in the mid twentieth century, back [ɑː] was only typical of traditional south-east English dialects (Anderson 1987: 18), so an English source for backed realisation of the TRAP/BATH vowel in MUE is unlikely.

Irish has two low vowel phonemes, /a/ and /aː/. As is discussed in Section 4.2.1, the first of these varies allophonically depending upon the nature of the following consonant, with front [æ]/[a] pronunciations being typical before slender consonants and back [ɑ] pronunciations being typical before broad consonants. It is not clear how this situation might map on to the variation we see in low vowel realisation in MUE given the lack of a palatal/non-palatal distinction for most consonants in English and the existence of pronunciations such as *back* [bäⁱk] and *fashion* ['fäʃn̩] in traditional MUE dialects such as SwTE, and it is not compatible with an alternative equation of Irish [ɑ] with the LOT vowel (Section 4.2.4). There may be closer parallels between the pronunciation of long /aː/ in Irish and lengthened variants of the low vowel in MUE, however. Although some dialects of Donegal Irish front /aː/ to [æː], this is not found in other areas of Ulster, nor is it typical of Irish more generally (Ó Dochartaigh 1987: 64–75; Ó Siadhail 1989: 60). In the Irish dialect of north Tyrone, for example, /aː/ was typically pronounced [ɑː] (Stockman and Wagner 1965: 178–9), a realisation it shared with many other Irish dialects. That the low long vowel in Irish has a similar pronunciation to the low long vowel in MUE may be accidental, but it is tempting to see a reinforcing influence of Irish on the realisation of this vowel (cf. the pronunciation of the Irish borrowings *plawteen* ['plɑːtʲən] and *prawkus* ['pɹɑːkəs] referred to in Section 4.4.6). But given the obvious parallels between MUE and Scots in retraction of the TRAP/BATH vowel, a more significant role is unlikely, and indeed the situation in MUE could well have developed without any Irish input.

4.2.4 Unrounding of the LOT vowel

The typical LOT vowel, specifically in short environments (see Section 4.3), has a tendency to be unrounded in MUE, especially in Belfast and the Lagan Valley area. The result is roughly [ɑ], whilst more fronted pronunciations such as [ä] or even [a] are also attested (Harris 1985: 46, 53–5, 1997: 210–11; Wells 1982: 442–3). That said, unrounding is not universal, and [ɒ] is also possible in LOT in short environments (a raised, definitely round [ɔː(°)] is typical in long environments, the off-glide being most common before tautomorphemic alveolar consonants), whilst traditional rural varieties of MUE may have [ɔː(°)] in LOT in all environments, thus merging it with THOUGHT (see Section 4.4.6 for details).[2] Unrounded [ɑː]/[äː] in THOUGHT words which had ME /au/ (e.g. *jaw*, *walk*) is a separate development, discussed in Section 4.4.6, as is unrounding of the LOT/CLOTH vowel before, and sometimes after, labial consonants (see Section 4.4.2).

Unconditioned unrounding of LOT (especially in short environments) is also a well-known feature of SIrE (Wells 1982: 419), and it is likely that unrounded LOT in Ulster is an extension of this pattern. The origins of this unrounding are unclear. It has been suggested (e.g. Bliss 1984: 135; Lunny 1981b: 124; Wells 1982: 419) that it results from an attempt to match the English short vowel system (/ɪ/, /ɛ/, /æ/, /ɒ/, /ʌ/ and /ʊ/) to the nearest equivalents in the Irish short vowel system. Although they are probably best viewed as allophones rather than phonemes (see Section 4.2.1), the qualities of these vowels in Irish are [ɪ], [ɛ], [æ]/[a], [ɑ], [ʌ] and [ʊ] (see Figure 4.1), resulting in [ɪ] in KIT, [ɛ] in DRESS, [æ]/[a] in TRAP, [ɑ] in LOT, [ʌ] in STRUT and [ʊ] in FOOT in SIrE. That is, the unrounding may be the result of contact with Irish, and if this is right it is possible that the same explanation applies to Ulster. There is a difficulty in this though, in that Ulster Irish had the short vowel values [ï], [ɛ], [æ], [ɑ], [ɔ] and [ọ̈], whilst MUE has the values [ë]/[ə] (KIT), [ɛ] (DRESS), [a]/[ä]/[ä̤] (TRAP), [ä̤]/[ɑ]/[ɒ] (LOT) and [ʌ]-[ö̈]-[ö̤] (STRUT/FOOT). That is, MUE has one fewer vowel corresponding to the historical short vowels, and it is not clear why short Irish [ɔ] should not have been equated with the English LOT vowel. Furthermore, unrounding of LOT is not a feature of some traditional rural MUE dialects (e.g. SwTE), where we might expect to see most influence from Irish, and it is also worth pointing out that [æ]/[a] and [ɑ] are allophones of the same phoneme in Irish, whilst they are realisations of two different phonemes in MUE.

A source for [ɑ] in LOT in Scotland is difficult to find. Seventeenth-century Scots probably had [ɔ] in this set, with raising to [o], characteristic of many modern Scots dialects, perhaps already apparent (Aitken and Macafee 2002: 156). Scots dialects contrast [ä]/[ɑ] in TRAP/BATH with this vowel, and may have another low back vowel in the range [ɑ:]–[ɒ:]–[ɔ:] (from OSc /au/), but this is typically long and may merge with either the TRAP/BATH or LOT vowel (Johnston 1997b: 481, 484, 488). Lowering and unrounding of LOT beyond [ɔ] does not seem to have ever been a feature of Scots in southern Scotland, and is also not a typical feature of USc.

There is, however, evidence for unrounding of the typical LOT vowel in English. This feature is most well known from North America and the Caribbean (Wells 1982: 131, 245–7), where [ɑ] (or even [a]) is the usual realisation of the vowel. It is unlikely that this quality derives from IrE given the otherwise English origin of most vocalic features of these New World varieties. Whether it derives from unrounding of LOT in England is another matter.

There is some evidence for unrounded LOT in EModE. Although rounded [ɒ] was probably the usual value, this was not only lowered from its earlier value ([ɔ]), but also had rather less rounding (Dobson 1957: 578). Some analysts have gone as far as suggesting that the vowel unrounded to [ɑ] generally in EModE (see, especially, Luick 1940: 666–7). That this was general in English is, however, refuted by Dobson (1957: 578) and Lass (1976: 139), and the presence of unrounded vowels in certain LOT words may be the result of specific transfers to the typical TRAP vowel at various points in the history of English and of developments in non-standard dialects, some of which appear to have had unrounding of this vowel in the Early Modern period (Dobson 1957: 578–80; Lass 2000: 87; Wells 1982: 245–6). Nevertheless, unrounded pronunciations of LOT more generally appear to have been current in some forms of standard EModE speech, being 'a fashionable affectation for some time during the 17th century' (Kökeritz 1953: 223; see also Wyld 1927: 181). The common equivalence of the LOT vowel with French <â> ([ɑ]) by orthoepists, especially in the eighteenth century (Kökeritz 1953: 223), at least suggests that the vowel may have been unrounded for some speakers, despite the rather circular arguments in Dobson (1957: 576–80) that it was not. In any case, the phonetic distance between somewhat unrounded [ɒ] and unrounded [ɑ] is slight (as noted in Wells 1982: 347), so it should not be surprising if there was some variation in the quality of the vowel in EModE.

As well as it being a feature of various English dialects in the Early Modern period, unrounded LOT was also a feature of some traditional dialects in England in more recent times, especially in Norfolk and the south-west (Wells 1982: 339–40, 347). This feature is rather poorly recorded in the SED, though there is good evidence for it in Norfolk, Northamptonshire, north Oxfordshire, the south-west Midlands and the south-west more generally (Anderson 1987: 21–2). Wells (1982: 347) specifically compares this pronunciation to that of LOT in Ireland and North America. The presence of unrounded LOT in England in the Early Modern period (and later) may be enough to explain the presence of similar pronunciations in North America and the Caribbean, though Wells (1982: 245) notes that there is some disagreement on this issue and suggests that unrounding of LOT in the North America could be an independent development.

Nevertheless, the presence of unrounded LOT in extra-territorial varieties of English that began to form in the seventeenth century suggests that an English source for the feature is possible, and if this is true, then it is equally possible for IrE (and indeed IrE adds to the number of extra-territorial varieties formed in the seventeenth century with unrounded LOT). Harris (1985: 202) concurs, suggesting that unrounding of the LOT vowel in MUE when not in the neighbourhood of labial consonants 'appears to have an exclusively English background'. It is likely, then, that [ɑ] in LOT in MUE has its origin in the seventeenth-century English input to Ulster, perhaps reinforced by the equivalence of this vowel with Irish [ɑ].

4.2.5 Fronting of the GOOSE vowel and the second component of the MOUTH diphthong

The GOOSE vowel is fronted to [ʉ(ː)] in MUE, with a similar fronting apparent in USc, which has [ʏ]~[ʉː] in words such as *mouth* and *now* (Harris 1985: 24–5, 47; see also the data for the Ulster locations in LAS3). In some cases, especially after /j/, this is fronted as far as [y], but it never merges with /i/ (the typical FLEECE vowel) or with /ɛ̈/ (the typical KIT vowel, usually lowered and centralised [ɛ̈]/[ə]). Probably as part of the same development, the second component of the MOUTH diphthong has also been fronted (e.g. to [əʉ] or [əʊ̈]).

The nearest equivalents to MUE /ʉ/ in Irish are the vowels represented by <ú> and <ao>, originally /uː/ ([uː]) and /ɯː/ ([ɯː]) (Ó Siadhail 1989: 35, 57–9). In most dialects of Irish, /uː/ has remained as [uː], whilst /ɯː/ has disappeared, merging with either /iː/ or /eː/ (ibid.). In some varieties of Ulster Irish /ɯː/ has remained distinct, as [ɯː], whilst /uː/ may be fronted to [ʉ] (Ó Dochartaigh 1987: 105–21). Given that this fronting is isolated within Irish, and occurs in exactly those areas where Irish has been in contact with MUE and USc, both of which have fronted [ʉ(ː)], it is likely that this represents a recent contact-induced change in Irish rather than a source for this feature in MUE (and USc).

Given the presence of similar pronunciations, not only in MUE and USc, but also across the North Channel in many Scots dialects and in SSE, it seems likely that this fronting of the GOOSE and MOUTH vowels instead has a Scottish source. The OSc high back vowel /uː/ has fronted in Mid Scots dialects to [ʉ(ː)] or [üː)], and this fronting is evident throughout most of southern Scotland and as far north as Angus in LAS3, as well as in Caithness (see also Johnston 1997b: 474–6). Original [u(ː)] is retained in most of the north of Scotland and in peripheral areas in the south-east of the country. Johnston (1997a: 82) hypothesises that certain OSc spellings indicate that fronting to [ʉ(ː)] has a long history in Scots, and thus it is not only a likely source of the fronting of this vowel in USc (which is essentially identical to other Mid Scots dialects in this respect), but also that the Scottish input to Ulster was the most likely source of fronting of the GOOSE vowel in MUE, the English vowel [uː] in GOOSE being equated phonologically with the vowel in the MOUTH lexical set in Scots (just as it was in SSE). The fronting of the second part of the MOUTH diphthong can be explained in a similar way. The OSc diphthong /ɔu/ (in, for example, *colt*, *ewe* and *grow*) has become [ʌü]–[ʌʉ] in the same Scots dialects that have fronting of the MOUTH vowel, including USc (see Johnston 1997b: 497–9). The equivalence of this Scots diphthong with the MOUTH vowel in MUE (as was also the case in the development of SSE) explains the presence of the near identical pronunciation of this vowel in Ulster.

Although there is a considerable amount of fronting in the GOOSE vowel in modern accents of English in England, including in mainstream RP (Wells 1982: 294; see also the various descriptions of late-twentieth-century urban varieties in Britain in Foulkes and Docherty 1999), this is for the most part recent. However, the SED reveals that fronted realisations of /uː/ (e.g. [ʏː], [ʉː], [üː]) were character-istic of traditional dialects in Devon, East Anglia and a narrow strip of the country from London in the south-east to Lancashire in the north-west (Anderson 1987: 93). Whilst the usual value assumed for EModE was [uː] (Dobson 1957: 681; Kökeritz 1953: 235–6), as it still was in old-fashioned RP in the twentieth century (Wells 1982: 281), it is possible that fronted pronunciations of this vowel are of long standing in some regions, so that these may have been present in some of the seventeenth-century English inputs to MUE. If so, they would have supported the patterns found in Scots, contributing to the general fronting of the GOOSE vowel in MUE.

4.2.6 The FACE vowel

In most descriptions of traditional MUE, the FACE vowel (Wells 1982: 141–2) is tran-scribed as [e(ː)] (e.g. Adams 1948: 20; Harris 1985: 44, 48; Staples 1896; Wells 1982: 440; see also the MUE data in LAS3 for Loughinisland and Annalong in County Down and Poyntzpass and Mount Norris in County Armagh), a pronunciation it shares with traditional varieties of SIrE and with USc. This pronunciation is hardly exceptional from an English or Scots point of view, given that [eː] was widespread in the traditional dialects of English and Scots in the mid twentieth century and underlies the modern RP diphthong [eɪ] (Dobson 1957: 594; Lass 2000: 95–6).

The FACE vowel has two main sources, ME and OSc /aː/ ('MATE') and /ai/ ('BAIT'). In the seventeenth century, these two vowels merged (under [ɛː], soon rising to [eː]) in the ancestor of StE (Dobson 1957: 594–603, 765–80; Lass 2000: 95–6), though they remained distinct in many English dialects, especially in the north, East Anglia and the south-west, right up to the twentieth century (Anderson 1987: 68–9). Early Modern StE was rather slower than other varieties in its development of [eː] (see Dobson 1957: 594), and indeed in Scots the value for MATE was [e(ː)] by 1600 (Aitken and Macafee 2002: 152). But Scots maintained the distinction between MATE and BAIT, with the latter having [ei] in non-final position around 1600 (ibid.: 154), and having a split development in final position (ibid.: 153–4), with [ɛi] in some words (e.g. *hay, stay*) and [ẹː] in others (e.g. *day*). Other than the [ɛi] variant in final position, which merged with the PRICE vowel, the rest of these MATE and BAIT vowels merged under [e(ː)] in most Mid Scots dialects (Johnston 1997b: 459, 461–3, 465). However, in peripheral dialects in southern Scotland (as well as in various northern Scots dialects), the two sets remained distinct. In Southern Scots dialects (in Roxburghshire and Dumfriesshire), the distinction is between [iə]/[ɪə] in MATE and [eː]/[eə] in BAIT, whilst in South-Mid Scots (in Kirkcudbrightshire and Wigtonshire), the distinction is between [ẹ(ː)] and [ę(ː)] (Johnston 1997b: 462–3, 465; see also LAS3).

Traditional MUE matches EModE and most varieties of Mid Scots not only in the realisation of the FACE vowel, but in the merger of ME /aː/ and /ai/. But the FACE vowel has been subject to a change in quality in MUE, with an [ɪ(ˑ)ə] diphthong (probably via [e(ˑ)ə]) developing in non-final position, and with [eː] being retained (sometimes lowered to [ɛː]) in final position (Harris 1985: 48–9; Wells 1982: 440–1). This change has given rise to the pronunciation of, for example, *daze* ([dɪˑəz]) contrasting with that of *days* ([deːz]/[dɛːz]). The diphthongisation of the non-final FACE vowel may be a fairly recent development, starting in Belfast, but spreading from there (Harris 1985: 48–9; McCafferty 2001: 145–9, 176–84). But even in traditional SwTE, the FACE vowel is [e(ˑ)ə] or even [ɪˑə] in non-final environments (it is typically [ẹː] in morpheme-final position), especially in lengthening environments (see Section 4.3), so this change is becoming entrenched in MUE. If the [eˑə]–[ɪˑə] realisations have a recent, urban origin, it is probably unnecessary to seek a source for them in the similar developments of the MATE vowel seen in many English dialects (see Anderson 1987: 58–9) and in Southern Scots, nor are they likely to be connected to the diphthong /iə/ in Irish (Hickey 2014: 156), which in any case contrasts with /eː/ in the language. However, Gregg (1958: 400) records [eə]/[ɪə] as an uncommon variant of the FACE vowel in the traditional USc dialect of Glenoe in the mid twentieth century, and links this to the occurrence of similar diphthongs in southern Scotland. Whether this is indicative of the feature having a longer history in Ulster (and thus potentially being connected with the similar diphthongisation in southern Scotland), or whether it is evidence of the first spread of [ɪə] from Belfast into other Ulster dialects (Glenoe lying less than twenty miles from the centre of Belfast) is unknown, but certainly [ɪə]-type pronunciations of the FACE vowel were more widespread in the past in England, including the south and Midlands, than they were in more recent decades (see Anderson 1987: 56, 58–9). If these were present in the English and Scots input to Ulster in the seventeenth century, this would provide an explanation for their presence in MUE. But it could also be that this diphthongisation is part of the wider process of diphthongisation of long mid vowels in Ulster, as also seen in the DRESS and LOT/CLOTH/THOUGHT lexical sets (see Table 4.2), so that an internal explanation is possible.

4.2.7 *Variation in the* PRICE *vowel*

Wells (1982: 443–4) and Harris (1985: 48, 147–9) describe only a single PRICE vowel in MUE, with some allophonic variation such that an allophone with an open nucleus (e.g. [aː^ɪ]/[æː^ɪ]/[æ·ɪ]) occurs in word-final position, whilst an allophone with a raised nucleus (e.g. [ɛi]/[ei]) occurs elsewhere. Whilst this may be true of BVE in the second half of the twentieth century, this was not (and is not) the situation for more conservative forms of MUE. In mid-nineteenth-century Belfast English (Patterson 1860; see also Harris 1985: 147–9), in the traditional mid-twentieth-century MUE dialects of Counties Down and Armagh in LAS3, and in (London) Derry English (McCafferty 1999) and SwTE, there are two PRICE phonemes, which may be symbolised as /aɪ/ and /ëi/. The first of these occurs only in Scottish Vowel Length Rule (SVLR) long environments, whilst the second occurs in SVLR short environments and also, in some words only, in SVLR long environments (see Sections 4.3.4 and 4.4.3 for details of length conditioning and lexical distribution). Thus we get /aɪ/ (e.g. [ä·ɪ], [ä·e], [ɑ·e]) in *fire, five* and *cry*, but /ëi/ (e.g. [ëi], [əi]) in *wire, rise* and *why*. The same situation is found in USc and in 'Urban Ulster Scots' (Gregg 1964, 1975; Harris 1985: 27–30), and is also characteristic of Scots dialects in Scotland. This is true not only of the SVLR patterning of these vowels, but also of their realisations. In Scots, the PRICE diphthong found in SVLR short environments is typically in the range [əi]–[ëi]–[ɛi], whilst the vowel restricted to SVLR long environments is in the range [aɪ]–[äɪ]–[ɑɪ], with first element of the diphthong often lengthened (e.g. [ä·ɪ]) and the second element not infrequently lowered to [e]. There can be no doubt that the variation we see in the PRICE vowel in conservative MUE has its origins (at least for the most part) in the near identical situation found in Scots. As Harris (1985: 147–9) acknowledges, the BVE situation likely represents a simplification of this more Scots-like pattern.

The likely value of the PRICE vowel in Early Modern StE was [əi], the lowering of the nucleus of the diphthong to [a] having not yet taken place (Dobson 1957: 659–64; Kökeritz 1953: 216–17; Lass 2000: 102). Whether this lowering had begun in other dialects is unknown. The traditional English dialects of the late nineteenth and early-to-mid twentieth centuries by and large had this lowered nucleus, or reflexes of it (see Anderson 1987: 42–9), with [ɛi]/[ëi]-type pronunciations only typical of the far north-east of England. However, dialects with a somewhat raised PRICE nucleus (e.g. [æɪ]), especially before voiceless consonants, were recorded in east Yorkshire and parts of the south-west in particular, and in these dialects this alternated with a more open diphthong (e.g. [aɪ]) before voiced consonants and word-finally (Anderson 1987: 48–9). Other dialects, especially in the south-west Midlands and the central south-west, were recorded with a centralised nucleus (e.g. [əi]) in all environments (ibid.: 46–7). Thus it is likely that English variants of the PRICE vowel with mid or centralised nucleus existed in regional dialects of English in the seventeenth century. In any case, EModE [əi] in PRICE is close to the value of the

MUE vowel in SVLR short environments (and sometimes in long environments). It may be, then, that the English input played a supporting role in establishing the quality of this vowel in the dialect.

It is not clear that Irish played any role in the development of the quality of the PRICE vowels in MUE. Although Irish does have phonetic diphthongs [aɪ] and [ɛɪ], derived from sequences of /a/ and /ɛ/ plus [j] (/ɣ'/; Hickey 2014: 157; Ó Siadhail 1989: 75), there is nothing equivalent to the semi-conditioned patterning of /ëi/ and /äɪ/ in MUE, and indeed Irish [aɪ] and [ɛɪ] tend to be monophthongised to [ɛː] or [eː] in Ulster Irish (Hickey 2014: 157; Ó Siadhail 1989: 75–6).

4.3 Vowel quantity in MUE

One of the most distinctive features of MUE is its treatment of vowel quantity, since this aspect of the dialect departs substantially from the etymological distinction between long and short vowels in English, and is subject to complex rules of distribution. In this respect, MUE differs significantly from USc, on the one hand, and from SUE and SIrE (and indeed English English), on the other, leading Harris (1985: 14) to claim that 'a more satisfactory classification' of Irish English dialects 'is one based on vowel quantity differences, since this enables us to discern more clearly the competing influences of English and Scots source dialects'. In this section, I give an outline of vowel quantity in MUE, based on Wells (1982: 439–40), Harris (1985: 42–3, 52–5), and on my own observations of vowel length in SwTE. The situation in MUE is then compared with vowel quantity patterns in Irish, USc and in SUE and SIrE, and to conditioning of vowel length in English and Scots in Britain. It will be seen that vowel quantity in MUE contains elements present in both the Scots and English inputs, with the former being the more important in the formation of this aspect of MUE phonology. Contact with Irish, on the other hand, appears to have had no effect on the development of vowel quantity in the dialect.

4.3.1 The MUE patterns

In contrast to the historical situation in English (and Scots, at least before the Early Modern period), whereby vowels are phonemically short or long and are not conditioned by phonological environment, length in MUE is largely determined by the nature of the consonant(s) following the vowel. Although some vowel phonemes are always short or long, most of them alternate between short and long allophones according to complex, overlapping rules that apply to different sets of vowels. Both Wells (1982: 439–40) and Harris (1985: 42–3) describe this variation in outline, and I summarise these here, adding further details based on observation of the patterning of vowel length in SwTE.

Two MUE vowels are (with an exception noted below) always short, regardless of the nature of the following consonant. These are the typical vowels of the KIT and STRUT lexical sets, symbolised in this book as /ë/ (often a lowered and centralised vowel such as [ë], [ə] or even [ɜ]) and /ɔ̈/ (usually realised with some lip-rounded and centralisation). Thus we get [ë] in *bit*, *bid* and *fizz* and [ɔ̈] in *but*, *bud* and *buzz*. Before coda /r/, these two vowels are subject to merger under [ə˞] in less traditional forms of MUE, but are usually distinguished as [ɚ] and [ɝ] in traditional rural dialects, and in both cases the length of the vowel may be determined by the consonant following the /r/, with long allophones (e.g. [ɚː], [ɝː]) occurring finally and before (non-alveolar) voiced consonants, and short allophones before voiceless consonants and sometimes before alveolar voiced consonants (e.g. *burn* [bɝn̩]).

Several vowels are always long in MUE, though this is complicated by the potential for merger of some of these with lengthened versions of other vowels in the dialect in certain environments. The vowel in words like *father* and *banana* is often long [äː] (/aː/), contrasting with short [ä] (/a/) in *gather* and *Anna*. This long vowel is restricted to a small number of words (see Harris 1985: 45), and may be absent in them in traditional forms of MUE. However, traditional dialects of MUE such as SwTE have an inherently long /ɑ/ vowel (e.g. [ɑː]) in words like *talk* and *walk*, contrasting with short /a/ ([ä]) in words like *back* and *whack*. The typical vowel in the THOUGHT lexical set is also usually long (e.g. [ɔː]) in all positions in MUE, and is often phonetically identical to the LOT/CLOTH vowel when that vowel is subject to lengthening (see below). In some traditional rural dialects such as SwTE, the LOT vowel can also be [ɔː] across the board or in certain words, even before voiceless stops (e.g. *bottom* ['bɔːtəm]; see Section 4.4.6). Finally, in dialects of MUE which distinguish the vowel in words such as *price* and *die* (/ëi/) from the vowel in words such as *prize* and *dye* (/aɪ/; see Section 4.4.3 and Harris 1985: 147–9), the /aɪ/ diphthong is always long (e.g. [äˑɪ]), except when it is followed by monomorphemic [ɚ] (as in *fire* [fäɪɚ]).

The other vowel phonemes of MUE vary in length according to the nature of the following consonant and their position within the word. Harris (1985: 42–3) distinguishes three groups of vowels within this larger set, though Wells (1982: 439–40) only distinguishes two of these. A more satisfactory account of these variable vowels depends upon recognising that there are a number of different vowel length rules in the dialect, and that some vowels are subject to more than one of these. The vowel length rules in MUE, with some simplification, are:

1. 'Pre-Fricative Lengthening' (PFL), before final voiceless fricatives and clusters beginning with a voiceless fricative. Harris (1985: 43) indicates that /ɛ/ (the typical DRESS vowel), /a/ (the typical TRAP and BATH vowel) and /ɒ/ (the typical LOT and CLOTH vowel, for which he uses the symbol /ɑ/) are affected by this rule. Wells (1982: 439) adds /e/ (the typical FACE vowel) to this group, and SwTE agrees in this respect. However, '/e₂/' in MEAT (see Section 4.4.1) is not affected by PFL in SwTE (note the contrast between *pace* [pe̞ˑəs] vs *peace* [pe̞ˑs]). Harris (1985: 53) notes that lengthening before voiceless fricatives is usual before /f/, /θ/ and /s/, but may be absent before /ʃ/ and /x/ in 'conservative MUE'. Whilst this is true for /x/ in SwTE (e.g. *trough* [ʈɹɒχ]), it is not for [ʃ], which causes lengthening in the dialect (e.g. *ash* [äːʃ] and *mesh* [mɛːʃ]).
2. The 'Voicing Effect' (VE), whereby vowels are long before final voiced consonants and clusters (except when the voiced consonant is followed by a voiceless obstruent, e.g. *pint*). Harris (1985: 43) indicates that /a/ (the typical TRAP/BATH vowel), /ɛ/ (the typical DRESS vowel), /ɒ/ (the typical LOT/CLOTH vowel), /e/ (the typical FACE vowel), /o/ (the typical GOAT vowel), /ɔɪ/ (the typical CHOICE

vowel), /ëi/ (the typical PRICE vowel) and /əʉ/ (the typical MOUTH vowel) are affected by this rule, though Wells (1982: 439) excludes /o/. In SwTE, /a/, /ɛ/, /ɒ/, /e/ (and '/e₂/' in MEAT), /o/, /ɔɪ/, /ëi/ and /əʉ/ are all subject to the VE.

3. A version of the 'Scottish Vowel Length Rule' (SVLR; Aitken 1981), whereby vowels are long in any syllable before voiced fricatives, /r/ and morpheme boundaries, and short elsewhere. In MUE, the SVLR conditions the length of the vowels typical of the FLEECE (/i/) and the GOOSE (/ʉ/) lexical sets, which are not affected by the VE. But vowels which are affected by the VE can also be subject to the SVLR, though this is only visible in non-final syllables, where the VE does not operate. The typical GOAT vowel /o/ is subject to both the VE and SVLR, at least in some varieties of MUE (see Wells 1982: 439; this is also true of SwTE), as indicated by *clover* (e.g. ['tlo·ʊvɚ-]) vs *noble* ['nǫbl̩]), though Harris (1985: 50) suggests that it does not usually act in this way in Belfast. The same is true for /e/ (and '/e₂/' in MEAT) in SwTE.

A number of other lengthening rules may interact with these in some dialects of MUE, including lengthening of /e/ (but not '/e₂/' in MEAT) before velar and palatal consonants in all positions (cf. *bake* [be̞:ḵ] vs *beak* [be̞ḵ] in SwTE), lengthening before coda /r/ for all vowels, and lengthening of /a/ before non-final coda voiced consonants and voiceless fricatives. The result is a set of complex and interacting vowel length constraints in the dialect, with each vowel being affected in particular ways. But in general terms, vowels in MUE fall into one of the following groups:

1. Those that are always short (/ë/ and /ɔ̆/);
2. Those that are always long (/aː/, /ɑː/, /ɔː/ and /aɪ/);
3. Those that are variable in length:
   a. Those affected only by the SVLR (/i/ and /ʉ/);
   b. Those affected by the VE only (/ëi/, /əʉ/ and /ɔɪ/);
   c. Those affected by the SVLR and the VE (/e₂/ and /o/);
   d. Those affected by the VE and PFL (/a/, /ɛ/ and /ɒ/);
   e. Those affected by the SVLR, VE and PFL (/e/).

4.3.2 Vowel quantity in USc, SUE and SIrE

Vowels in USc similarly fall into three groups according to how their quantity is determined. This overview is based on Harris (1985: 20–3), which itself builds on the work of Robert Gregg on the conservative USc dialects of the mid twentieth century (e.g. Gregg 1958, 1964). These groups are:

1. Vowels which are short in all environments: /ǽ/ (the typical KIT vowel) and /ʌ/ (the typical STRUT vowel); to these can be added the diphthong /əi/ (typical of the PRICE lexical set), which is, with few exceptions, restricted to SVLR short environments and to word-final position (where we might perhaps expect it to be longer, though Harris does not note this);
2. Vowels which are long in all environments: /ɛː/ (the typical DRESS vowel), /aː/ (the typical TRAP/BATH vowel), /ɔː/ (the typical LOT/CLOTH vowel), /eː/ (the

typical FACE vowel), /oː/ (the typical GOAT vowel) and /ɔe/ (the typical CHOICE vowel); to these we can add the diphthong /ɑe/, typical of the PRICE lexical set in SVLR long environments;

3. Vowels which vary in length according to the nature of the following consonant; again similar to MUE, there are sub-groups:

    a. Vowels which are subject to the SVLR: /i/ (the typical FLEECE vowel), /ʉ/ (the typical MOUTH vowel) and /ï/ (the vowel derived from OSc /øː/ in words such as *boot* and *blood*, and which is not found in SVLR long environments, except before /r/, where it is long);

    b. /əʉ/, which is subject to VE conditioning.

Not surprisingly, the conditioning of vowel quantity in USc is closely similar to patterns found in West-Mid Scots dialects in Scotland (see Johnston 1997a: 76 and 1997b for details), especially in the phonemic length of the mid and low vowels. In general terms, the USc system is like the MUE one, with some vowels being phonemically short or long, and others having their quantity determined by the phonological environment. Indeed, some of the specifics are very similar between the two dialects. But there are important differences, not least the minimal role of the VE in the USc system, and the phonemic length of all the mid and low vowels in USc. That said, the patterns described by Harris may be most typical of Antrim USc dialects and they may represent something of a simplification of the facts, especially given that the precise details of how vowel quantity is conditioned across the USc area are largely unexplored (the scattered references to vowel quantity in USc given in Johnston 1997b suggest that the neat picture provided by Gregg and Harris may not be general in USc, and that some dialects of it may be more similar to MUE in their distribution of vowel quantity).

The conditioned vowel length found in MUE and USc contrasts sharply with the situation found in SUE and SIrE (Harris 1985: 34–5; Hickey 2007a: 316–17; Kallen 2013: 59–63; Wells 1982: 418–27). In these dialects of Irish English, vowel length is phonemic, and reflects the distinction between short and long vowels that was historically characteristic of English in Britain. Thus the typical vowels of the KIT, DRESS, TRAP, LOT, STRUT and FOOT (where this is distinguished from STRUT) lexical sets are short, and the typical vowels of the FLEECE, FACE, PALM, THOUGHT, GOAT and GOOSE sets are long. Nevertheless, there is a degree of phonological conditioning of vowel quantity in SUE and SIrE, at least in some varieties. SUE shares with MUE the lengthening of historical short /a/ and /ɒ/ before voiceless fricatives in the BATH and CLOTH lexical sets (Harris 1985: 35), and this change is also evidenced in some SIrE dialects, if not always regularly, whilst some dialects also lengthen these vowels before voiced consonants (see Wells 1982: 423–4 for a summary). So, for example, in the Roscommon dialect Henry (1957: 214ff.) records lengthening of historical /a/ in *after*, *ask*, *bad*, *cast*, *daft*, *fast*, *grass*, *last*, *laughing*, *mass*, *master*, *pass* and *staff*, and of historical /ɒ/ in *broth*, *cloth*, *cost*, *frost*, *loft*, *loss*, *lost*, *off* and *soft*. Similarly, Nally (1971) records /aː/ in the Westmeath dialect in *basket*, *blast*, *elastic*, *fasting*, *plaster*, *rascal* and *task*, but /a/ in *castle*, *scatter* and *slap*, which, as far as the small amount of data can indicate, is exactly the pattern found in MUE. He also records long /ɑː/ in *cost*, but short /ɑ/ in *bottom*, *scallop* and *wander*. Although the data is limited, the quantity of these vowels also appears to pattern as it does in MUE. Likewise, Bertz (1975: 157–8) records lengthening of historical /a/ in Dublin before voiced consonants and clusters (e.g. in *bag, bad, badge, band, man, pal, tram* and *twang*) and before /f/, /s/ and, sometimes, /θ/ (e.g. in *after, ask(ed), craft, daft, gas, glass, last, pass, path* and *staff*). A similar lengthening of historical /ɒ/ is recorded in Bertz's Dublin data in words such as *boss, costs, cross, dogs, God, job, lost, off, often, on* and *was* (ibid.: 172–4). Although these lengthenings may be a tendency rather than a regular rule in Dublin, they closely resemble the conditioning of quantity for /a/ and /ɒ/ in MUE. Thus, there is ample evidence for lengthening of /a/ and /ɒ/ before voiceless fricatives, and sometimes before voiced consonants, in SUE and some forms of SIrE, so that MUE is not exceptional in Ireland in this respect, even if it is more regular in its treatment of vowel quantity than some more southerly dialects.

4.3.3 The origins of MUE vowel quantity

As was noted in the introduction to this section, vowel quantity in MUE appears to show no influence from Irish. Irish is characterised by a phonemic distinction between short and long vowels which is largely independent of the following conso-nant, though see Ó Siadhail (1989: 48–56) for details of the interaction between tense consonants and vowel lengthening in the language. None of the vowel lengthenings in Irish particularly resemble the conditioning of quantity in MUE, and thus the search for the origins of this conditioning must lie in Britain, in internal develop-ments within MUE itself, or in both. In what follows, I examine patterns of vowel quantity in Scots and English to determine what, if any, sources can be determined for the patterns observed in MUE. In particular, I concentrate on the origins of two features: (1) SVLR conditioning of the high vowels; and (2) lengthening of the historical mid and low short vowels before voiced consonants and the voiceless fricatives.

However, a major difficulty in trying to determine the origins of the distinctive MUE patterns is that details of quantity conditioning have been poorly recorded in English and Scots in Britain. This is true not only of historical varieties, which for the most part lie beyond close phonetic analysis, but also for most modern dialects. Traditional dialectologists in the late nineteenth and twentieth centuries gathered large amounts of phonetic data, giving us detailed insights into the historical phonol-ogy of the language. But they were usually poor at recording vowel length. English and Scots dialects were (and are) extremely variable in this respect and have often replaced the historical distinction between short and long vowels with conditioned, allophonic quantity rules. But in the SED, for example, most fieldworkers followed the tradition of transcribing historical short vowels as short and historical long vowels as long, unless a phonemic merger resulted. See, for example, the near exclu-sive use of [ɛ] (or the like) in the word *red* (Q. V.10.7), and of [iː] (or the like) in *feet* (Q. VI.10.1).[3]

This is also a problem in LAS3, despite the survey being specifically designed to determine vowel realisation in particular phonological contexts (see Maguire 2020a for discussion). The word-list for LAS3 was divided according to the nature of the following consonant, with, for example, 'Section 0' containing words with a

/t/ following the stressed vowel and 'Section 9' containing words with a following non-velar voiceless fricative. This should have meant that a detailed record of vowel length conditioning in Scots dialects was made, as Aitken (1981) hoped and predicted in his important overview of vowel quantity in Scotland. But this was not the case. South of the Forth–Clyde isthmus, for example, there were three main field-workers for LAS3, one of whom (JSW) recorded data for all the south-west counties, the other two (CMacG and JYM) sharing the south-east counties of Scotland. Of these, only JYM recorded vowel length consistently, paying close attention to quantity conditioning and distinctions across all environments.[4] CMacG only sporadically recorded vowel length, very often leaving this feature untranscribed, even in obviously lengthening environments such as word-final position, unless it was phonemically distinctive. The transcriptions made by JSW were essentially phonemic. That is, he was careful to indicate where phonemic distinctions were made but gave very little phonetic information and showed almost no variation in his transcriptions of phones. He appears to have adopted one of three strategies in his transcriptions as regard vowel quantity: (1) he didn't indicate vowel length at all unless it was required to show a phonemic distinction between two sounds which would otherwise have been the same (e.g. in location 27.7, Monreith, Wigtonshire); (2) he gave a default phonetic transcription, indicating for at least some vowels long allophones in SVLR long environments and short allophones in SVLR short environments (e.g. in location 18.5 Auchinleck, Ayrshire); (3) he assumed phonemic length for some vowels and transcribed them as long in all environments, without regard as to how long the vowels actually were per environment (e.g. location 18.1 Beith, Ayrshire). That these were conventional representations rather than real indications of vowel quantity in the dialects is clear not just from their suspicious regularity (compared, for example, to JYM's transcriptions), but also from a preliminary comparison of some of his transcriptions with their associated audio recordings (see Maguire 2020a) and from unpublished comments (in one of the data notebooks) by JSW himself, who in one case refers to his transcriptions as being 'systematic' rather than 'narrow'.

This means that CMacG's and JSW's transcriptions, which cover the majority of southern Scotland (including the south-west, which was the area most of the Ulster settlers came from), cannot be relied upon to indicate vowel quantity conditioning in the traditional Scots dialects of the mid twentieth century. When we add to this the sometimes severe systematisation of the data that were included in LAS3, so that some of the useful information on vowel quantity that was gathered was obscured (for examples, see below), this can only be considered a major failing of the LAS. For my present purposes, this, together with the rather conventional marking of vowel length in the SED, means that tracing the origins of vowel length conditioning in MUE is rather more difficult than it might otherwise have been.

4.3.4 SVLR conditioning

As its name implies, SVLR-conditioning of vowel quantity is characteristic of Scots and SSE in Scotland (see Aitken 1981 for details), and there can be no doubt that the SVLR conditioning found in MUE has its source there. The SVLR developed in

Scotland from at least the late sixteenth century (Aitken and Macafee 2002: 129–30), which means that the feature would have been present, in some form at least, in the Scots dialects that were brought to Ireland in the Plantation of Ulster and its associated settlements. Almost all Scots dialects (as well as SSE) agree in their SVLR conditioning of the high vowels /i/ and /ʉ/ and the PRICE diphthong, and in the lack of lengthening of /ɛ̈/ (the typical KIT vowel, however it is realised) and /ʌ/ (Aitken 1981), and this is apparent in LAS3, despite the problems with the transcriptions discussed above. Other vowels may also be affected by the SVLR, especially in central areas of Scotland, though the low-mid and low vowels in particular may not be subject to it, and may lengthen in other environments or across the board. The modern reflexes of OSc /ai/ (typically [eː]) and /au/ (typically [ɔː] or [ɑː]) may retain their historical length in all environments. It thus seems likely that the SVLR firstly and most consistently affected /i/, /ʉ/, the PRICE vowel and to an extent the high-mid vowels (see Aitken 1981: 153–5), and this is the situation which has been inherited by MUE (and USc).

Both MUE and USc are characterised by consistent SVLR conditioning of the length of the high vowels /i/ and /ʉ/, and of the quality of the PRICE diphthong (discussed in Section 4.2.7), and of the associated invariant short quantity of /ɛ̈/ and /ʌ/~/ɔ̈/. The SVLR may also, in conjunction with the VE (and in the case of /e/ with PFL), affect the high-mid vowels /e/ (including /e₂/) and /o/. That the SVLR does not affect the low-mid and low vowels in MUE is not surprising given that SVLR conditioning of these vowels is by no means general in Scots dialects either (see further below).

The fact that the SVLR has survived in MUE is noteworthy, given that we might expect the process of NDF that must have occurred in Ulster (see Section 5.3.1) to have militated against the survival of such a complex pattern that was characteristic of only one input variety. That the SVLR did become part of MUE speaks of the importance of the Scottish input in its development, as is discussed further in Chapter 5. It is not surprising, given the obvious Scots origin of the feature in MUE and the lack of it in most dialects of English, that the SVLR is not found in IrE dialects further south, which received little or no input from Scotland.

4.3.5 The VE and PFL

Cruttenden (2001: 95) says of (Standard British) English that '[i]n accented syllables the so-called long vowels are fully long when they are final or in a syllable closed by a voiced consonant, but they are considerably shortened when they occur in a syllable closed by a voiceless consonant' and that '[t]he same considerable shortening before voiceless consonants applies also to the diphthongs'. Conversely, the historical short vowels are subject to a degree of lengthening before voiced consonants. Although the short vowels, all other things being equal, are not as long as the historical long vowels, the short allophones of the 'long' vowels are shorter than the long allophones of the 'short' vowels, indicating the importance of phonological context in English in determining vowel quantity. This 'Voicing Effect' (VE) is a well-known feature of many varieties of English around the world (see Tanner *et al.* 2019 for an overview), and thus the presence of the VE in MUE is not remarkable. In RP, the typical TRAP vowel, /æ/, falls somewhere between the historical short and long vowels, being subject to considerable lengthening before voiced consonants, and not being quite as short as the other 'short' vowels in voiceless contexts (Cruttenden 2001: 96). In fact, the behaviour of /æ/ in RP shows some similarities with that of /a/ in MUE, with lengthening of /æ/ being particularly noticeable before voiced consonants in word-final position in, for example, *cab, bad, bag, badge* and *man* (Cruttenden 2001: 111).

Although lengthening of the historical short vowels before voiceless fricatives is not apparent in Cruttenden's account, this is not because there never was any such change. Southern and south Midland English dialects are characterised by length-ening of historical /a/ and /ɒ/ (but not /ɛ/) before the voiceless fricatives /f/, /θ/ and /s/ in particular, this lengthening often leading to phonemic merger with pre-existing /ɑː/ (e.g. in *father* and *palm*) and /ɔː/ (e.g. in *thought*). This 'Pre-Fricative Lengthening' (PFL; Wells 1982: 203–5) is one of the most obvious features separat-ing northern and southern dialects in England, with varieties south of a line from the Wash to the Welsh Marches characterised by the change (see Wakelin 1972: 87; Chambers and Trudgill 1980: 127–9, 137–42; Kolb *et al.* 1979: 182–3, 213–14; Anderson 1987: 12, 16–17, 21, 24–5). The lengthening occurred in the seventeenth century (Dobson 1957: 525–8; Lass 2000: 103–8), giving rise to what Wells (1982: 133–5, 136–7) called the BATH and CLOTH lexical sets. It was also characteristic of the ancestor of RP English, though it has largely been reversed in the CLOTH set, with old-fashioned pronunciations such as [ɔːf] *off* and [kɹɔːs] *cross* attesting to its former presence (Wells 1982: 281–2).

It may well be that PFL in south Midland and southern England is the source of PFL in MUE, given the near identical effects of the change in both areas. This would represent good evidence of the importance of specifically southern English varieties in the formation of the dialect, as might be expected, in part at least, given the Plantation settlement patterns described in Chapter 2. There are some points which complicate this explanation, however. Firstly, lengthening also affected /ɛ/ and, in some cases at least, /e/ in MUE, whereas these vowels were unaffected in England. Notably, SUE and SIrE are only reported to have lengthening of /a/ and /ɒ/ (see above), just as in England. If English in the south Midlands and southern England is the source for this feature of MUE, then it must be the case that the rule was generalised in Ulster to affect all of the non-high short vowels, as well as /e/. This kind of generalisation would also explain why lengthening of /a/ and /ɒ/ in MUE is entirely regular, unlike in southern England (see Harris 1985: 45). Secondly, the timing of the change in England is potentially problematic for its appearance in MUE. Dobson (1957: 525) notes that the change is only evidenced from 'towards the end of the seventeenth century' in England and that, especially in the case of CLOTH, there was considerable variation, with unlengthened pronunciations being attested throughout the eighteenth and nineteenth centuries (and indeed these ultimately won out for the most part in the CLOTH set). If the change did develop in England in the late seventeenth century, this is too late for it to have been present in the early-seventeenth-century English input to Ulster during the Plantation. This problem could possibly be overcome by assuming that the written evidence for the change (discussed in Dobson 1957) did not appear till some time after the change had devel-oped (it perhaps first being a low-level, unnoticed phonetic rule), or the change was first characteristic of certain regional and social dialects (through which it was introduced to Ulster) and not of others. In fact, Kökeritz (1953: 167–8) argues for an earlier, late-sixteenth-century, date for the change, and this possibility is supported by the existence of forms of PFL in SUE and SIrE (described above) which are very similar to what is found in southern England, and thus likely have their source in seventeenth-century English too.

So an English explanation for PFL in MUE is possible, perhaps even likely, though it is not perfect. Harris (1985, ch. 2; cf. especially pp. 120–5) offers a possible alternative, arguing that lengthening of non-high short vowels before voiceless fricatives is a phonetically natural change and as a result could have an internal explanation in MUE. He thus side-steps the issue of whether the feature has a source in southern England. There is, however, another possible source of these patterns which Harris does not consider. Although evidence is limited (especially due to the fieldworker transcription practices described above), it appears to be the case that lengthening of the non-high historical short vowels (including /ɛ/) in exactly the same environments as in MUE was a feature of some traditional Scots dialects in southern Scotland in the twentieth century. In addition, VE conditioning of these and other vowels is a noticeable feature of many of the dialects in southern Scotland (at least in those where vowel length was consistently recorded), adding to the parallels between Scots and Ulster dialects.

4.3.6 The VE and PFL in Scots

Dealing first with historical /a/, there is widespread evidence for variations in quantity depending on the nature of the following consonant in twentieth-century dialects of Scots in southern Scotland. Both Wettstein (1942: 7) and Zai (1942: 16) record allophonic variation in length for this vowel in Berwickshire and Roxburghshire respectively, with short allophones found before voiceless consonants and long allophones most common before voiced consonants, but also before voiceless fricatives and sometimes /k/.

These patterns are confirmed by JYM's original transcriptions for dialects in East Lothian, Berwickshire and Roxburghshire for LAS3. Although there is variation between dialects and some of these patterns are obscured by the systematisation in the published atlas, there is a clear conditioning whereby short allophones are found before voiceless stops and long allophones are found elsewhere, including in some locations before voiceless fricatives. The data in Table 4.3, from locations 23.3 (Cockburn, Berwickshire) and 24.9 (Newcastleton, Roxburghshire) illustrate.

A probably related pattern is also recorded in the LAS3 data in south-west Scotland, though in these cases there appears to be a quality rather than a quantity difference (though as was discussed previously the fieldworker for this part of Scotland did not record vowel length consistently). In dialects of southern Ayrshire, Wigtonshire and western Kirkcudbrightshire (see Mather and Speitel 1986: 125–8, 176–8 and 181–90), there is variation between [ɐ], which is typically found before voiceless alveolar stops and velar stops (voiced or voiceless), and [ɑ], which is typically found before voiced consonants (other than /g/), before labial consonants of any kind, and before voiceless fricatives. All of these patterns across southern

Table 4.3 Quantity variation in /a/ at LAS3 locations 23.3 and 24.9.

23.3 (Cockburn)		24.9 (Newcastleton)	
Allophone	Words	Allophone	Words
ɒ	*fat, sat*	ɑˑ	*sat, fat*
ä	*strap, tap*	ɑ	*back, bank, drank, sank, tack, tap*
ä	*back, bank, drank, sank, tack, wasp*	ɑ	*ash(es), band, daft, hand, grand, sand, want, wander, wasp*
ä·	*bad, drab, had, ham, mad*	ɑ·	*bad, bag, bang, drab, ham, mad, was*
ä·	*ash(es), bag, ban, band, bang, bass, bath, daft, fan, grand, hand, man, path, sand, splash, want, wander, wash*	ɑ·	*ban, bass, bath, fan, man, pal, wash*
ɒ·	*pal*		

Scotland resemble the conditioning of /a/ in MUE as described in Section 4.3.1, some of them very closely indeed, and suggest that the allophonic variation we see in Ulster may well have its source, in part at least, in a similar allophonic variation in /a/ in Scotland.

A similar situation holds for /ɛ/, but in this case most Scots dialects have carried through the lengthening of the vowel to all environments (Johnston 1997b: 472) so that evidence for this pattern in Scotland is sparse. Nevertheless, Wettstein (1942: 7) describes VE conditioning of the vowel (lowered to [a(:)] in this dialect) in Berwickshire, and his data show that half-long and fully long allophones also occurred before voiceless fricatives (see, for example, the transcriptions of *heft, mess, pest* and *press* in his glossary). Zai (1942: 17) describes a similar pattern in Roxburghshire.

Similar conditioning is also recorded by JYM at Newcastleton in Roxburghshire (location 24.9) in the unpublished LAS3 data, though the length distinctions he records are not reproduced in the published atlas's systematisation of the data. Short [ɛ] is recorded before voiceless stops and affricates, whilst long [ɛ·] is recorded before voiced consonants. Before the voiceless fricatives there is variation, with [ɛ] recorded in *grass, left, path* and *west*, and [ɛ·] recorded in *aneath* 'beneath', *ash* (tree), *best, mess* and *wash*. The variation in quantity before voiceless fricatives aside, this is identical to the conditioning found in MUE. Although this kind of pattern was restricted to only a few dialects in southern Scotland in the mid twentieth century (as far as we can tell due to the lack of reliable information on vowel length in many dialects, especially in the south-west of the country), it may well have been more widespread at one time, given that similar patterns occur in central Berwickshire and west Roxburghshire, and may represent a stage in the general lengthening of /ɛ/ that characterises the region. Certainly, these patterns, especially in Newcastleton (including the lower realisation of /ɛ/ that is also typical of some MUE dialects; see Section 4.2.2), look more similar to what we find in Ulster than what we might expect by chance.

Evidence for allophonic lengthening of the LOT/CLOTH vowel in Scotland is complicated by the raising of this vowel to [o] and its merger in many dialects, in

Table 4.4 Vowel quantity in the LOT, CLOTH and GOAT lexical sets in Cockburn, Berwickshire.

Vowel	Words
o	*bogle, box, broken, cloak, clock, close, croak, folk, frost, ghost, hoast, hope, oak, pope, post, roast, rock, slope, soak, sock, stroke, toast, tossed, yoke*
ǫ	*pot*
ǫ·	*cot, knot, lot, note, rot, throat*
o·	*bog, coal, dog, drone, foal, fond, hole, job, John, on, roam, rob, robe, rogue, Rome, thole*
ǫ·	*cod, code, load, road, rod*
o·ᵊ	*boat, coat*
o:	*drove, frozen, nose, rose*

some environments at least, with the typical GOAT vowel (Johnston 1997b: 481). This raising of the LOT/CLOTH vowel means that it is no longer in the low-mid part of the vowel space and is not, perhaps as a result, recorded with lengthening before voiceless fricatives in these dialects. Unfortunately, dialects where this raising (and merger) did not happen (mostly those of south-west Scotland) were transcribed by fieldworkers who did not record vowel length accurately (if at all), so that it is not possible to determine vowel quantity conditioning for [ɒ]- and [ɔ]-type variants of LOT/CLOTH in southern Scotland. From the evidence available, all from dialects with raising and sometimes merger with the GOAT vowel, the [o]-type vowel is subject to VE conditioning in at least some dialects (cf. Wettstein 1942: 7; Zai 1942: 17). Data from the unpublished LAS3 fieldworkers' notebooks for Cockburn (location 23.3, Berwickshire) illustrate this kind of pattern (Table 4.4), which is again obscured in the published atlas.

This conditioning of an [o]-type vowel is very similar to what we find in MUE for the GOAT vowel, as described in Section 4.3.1, though the sparsity of bisyllabic tokens means that we cannot determine whether the vowel was affected by *both* the VE and the SVLR in Scots. Whether a similar conditioning of an [ɒ]- or [ɔ]-type LOT/CLOTH vowel once existed in southern Scotland remains unknown.

Length conditioning of the FACE vowel in Scotland is also complicated by the existence of two [e]-type vowels in some dialects, derived from OSc /aː/ and /ai/ respectively. In many Scots dialects, these have merged under a single vowel, as they have done in StE, and this may be subject to VE conditioning, just as the GOAT vowel is (see Wettstein 1942: 7; Zai 1942: 17). Whether the vowel is affected by both the VE and the SVLR cannot be determined from the data, which largely consists of monosyllabic tokens. Earlston in Berwickshire (LAS3 Location 23.6) provides a good example of a dialect with VE conditioning of /e/ (it does not distinguish between reflexes of OSc /aː/ and /ai/), with short [e] recorded before voiceless consonants (including voiceless fricatives), and long [e·] recorded before voiced consonants and morpheme-finally.[5] Newcastleton has a more complex situation, since it distinguishes two FACE vowels, a higher /e̞ⁱ/ vowel derived from OSc /aː/, and a lower /e̞ᵊ/ vowel from OSc /ai/. The first of these is long in all environments except before /t/, whilst the second is short before voiceless consonants, /l/ and /n/, and is long elsewhere.

4.3.7 *The origins of the VE and PFL in MUE*

Whilst the SVLR length allophony in the high vowels (and quality allophony in the PRICE diphthong) in MUE can only have one source (Scotland), the VE may be a general feature of English and Scots, being found, for example, in southern English dialects (including in RP) and in the dialects of southern Scotland. Although records of vowel quantity in Scotland are badly obscured by fieldworker and editorial practices, the patterns which were recorded there are sometimes very similar to what is found in MUE, and a Scots source is thus not unlikely, especially if the observed patterns once had a wider distribution and/or were typical of those dialects for which data on vowel quantity is lacking. The same is probably true of English dialects too, which likely had more VE conditioning of vowel quantity than the transcriptions of the traditional dialects suggest. If the VE was a feature of both the English and Scots dialects brought to Ulster in the seventeenth and early eighteenth centuries, it is not surprising that this has become established as a feature of MUE too.

Pre-Fricative Lengthening was also present in the traditional English and Scots dialects of the mid twentieth century, and so may also have more than one source in MUE. The feature has a long recorded history in English, but as it was first reported in the late seventeenth century and did not affect /ɛ/, connecting this with PFL in MUE is not straightforward. Nevertheless, the existence of PFL in other IrE dialects in a form which is similar to what is found in southern England suggests that the feature was brought to Ireland in the seventeenth century. If it was brought to Ulster during the Plantation, it may well have been reinforced by similar patterns in Scots, given the existence of PFL of /a/ and /ɛ/ at least in some modern dialects. Indeed, the similarity of some of the Scots patterns to what is found in MUE is suggestive of a close relationship between them, so that the reinforcement may have gone the other way, and it is probably unnecessary to assume an independent development of PFL in MUE along the lines suggested by Harris (1985), though of course existing patterns could have been entrenched by natural phonetic and phonological tendencies of this sort. When the unambiguous Scots origin of the SVLR conditioning of the high vowels and the PRICE diphthong is factored in, it is clear that the MUE conditioning of vowel quantity is not only typologically similar to what is found in Scots, but is also similar in many of its details, suggesting an important role for Scots in the development of this defining characteristic of MUE phonology.

4.4 Lexical distribution

4.4.1 *The lexical distribution of the MUE vowels*

The lexical distribution of vowel phonemes (i.e. which vowels occur in which words) is one of the most obvious ways that dialects differ from each other (see Wells 1982: 78–80). Regardless of their realisation, if the vowel phonemes of two varieties are distributed similarly, then the two varieties are likely to be closely related, whilst dialects that have been separated for some time will have been affected by various independent phonological splits and mergers, leading to rather different lexical distributions. Classic examples of the importance of different lexical distributions for indicating dialect differences including the FOOT/STRUT and TRAP/BATH isoglosses which separate southern and non-southern dialects in England (Chambers and Trudgill 1980: 127–42; Wells 1982: 196–9, 203–6), the isoglosses of the Ribble–Humber Line, which separate traditional Scots and far northern English varieties from other English dialects (Wakelin 1972: 102–3), and the substantial bundle of isoglosses separating USc from MUE (Gregg 1972, 1985). In his survey of phonological differences between USc and MUE, Gregg found that although the phonetics of vowels in both might be similar, their distribution was often radically different. For example, the USc and MUE dialects he surveyed both had the vowels [e], [o], [ï], [ʉ] and [əʉ], but the words each occurred in was often different. So, for example, USc had [e] in *home* and *stone*, [ï] in *foot* and *goose*, [ʉ] in *house* and *out*, and [əʉ] in *ewe* and *grow*, whilst MUE had [o], [ʉ], [əʉ] and [o] respectively in these groups of words. It is differences like these that not only allowed Gregg to draw a sharp boundary between USc and MUE, but which also allow us to categorise USc as a dialect (or dialects) of Scots and MUE as a dialect of English of a Midland/southern English type (see further below).

So the lexical distribution of vowel phonemes is important for understanding the history of a variety and, as a result, its relationships with other dialects. This section examines the lexical distribution of vowel phonemes in MUE and shows that the dialect is closely related to Midland and southern English dialects and, in particular, to the ancestor of modern StE. But it also shows evidence of influence from Scots, and these patterns are of a particular type, something which has important consequences for understanding how MUE developed phonologically.

A role for Irish in the development of the lexical distribution of vowel phonemes in MUE is less clear, other than the obvious additions to the lexicon of the dialect in the forms of borrowed words and, especially, place-names. Effects of Irish through language shift on the lexical distribution of vowel phonemes in MUE might be expected to include:

1. loss or confusion of an English/Scots phonemic distinction where there is no corresponding distinction in Irish;
2. phonemicisation of a distinction that exists in Irish but which did not exist in the English/Scots input;
3. restriction of phonemes to particular phonological environments, reflecting phonotactic properties of Irish.

An examination of the lexical distribution of vowel phonemes in MUE provides little or no evidence for the first two of these changes, and only ambiguous evidence for the third (see Section 4.4.4), so it appears that contact with Irish has had a minimal impact on this aspect of the phonology of MUE. This lack of contact-induced change is important for understanding the history of the dialect and the nature of the shift from Irish to English that occurred in the MUE area, a topic which I return to in Chapter 5.

The lexical distribution of vowel phonemes in MUE is summarised in Table 4.5, using the lexical set labels from Wells (1982) in addition to new labels for a number of important subsets. A table of this sort necessarily leaves out various minor patterns

Table 4.5 Lexical distribution of vowel phonemes in MUE.

Lexical set	Phoneme(s)	Lexical set	Phoneme(s)
FLEECE	/i/	FOOT	/ɔ̈/ > /ʉ/
'MEAT'	/e$_{(2)}$/ > /i/[a]	'BOOK'	/ʉ/
FACE	/e/	GOOSE	/ʉ/
KIT	/ë/	PRICE	/ëi/
		'PRIZE'	/aɪ/ (> /ëi/)
DRESS	/ɛ/	CHOICE	/ɔɪ/
TRAP	/a/	MOUTH	/əʉ/
BATH	/a/	NORTH	/ɔr/ (> /or/)
PALM	/ɑ/ > /a/, /aː/	FORCE	/or/
		'DOOR'	/ʉr/ > /or/
LOT	(/ɔ/ >)[b] /ɒ/~/ɔ/	START	/ar/
CLOTH	/ɔ/	NEAR	/ir/
THOUGHT	/ɔ/	SQUARE	/ɛr/ (> [ɚː])
'WALK'	/ɑ/ > /ɔ/		
GOAT	/o/	CURE	/ʉr/
'OLD'	/əʉ/ > /o/		
STRUT	/ɔ̈/	NURSE	/ër/ vs. /ɔ̈r/ > [ɚː]
		'SERVE'	/ar/ > /ɛr/ (> [ɚː])

Note:
a The symbol > indicates that the traditional phoneme to the left is being replaced by the general MUE phoneme to the right. Examples in parentheses are only typical of certain varieties of MUE, e.g. certain urban or standardised forms of the dialect.
b /ɔ/ in LOT is typical of some traditional forms of MUE including SwTE but is/was not typical of all areas.

in the dialect restricted to small sets of words, or even to one or two lexical items. Just as examples, the words *deaf, ladder, none, one, quit, red, shed, stubble, wind* (n.) and *wrestle* have the phonemes /i/, /ɛ/, /o/, /a/, /ɛ/, /ë/, /e/, /ë/, /ëi/ and /a/ in traditional SwTE (and other traditional MUE dialects), but these patterns cannot be generalised to larger groups of words.

Some of the more distinctive patterns of lexical distribution in MUE are the following:

• As is the case in other conservative forms of IrE, words which had ME /ɛː/ (the 'MEAT' subset) have an [e]-type vowel in traditional MUE, which is the same as or very similar to the vowel in FACE (Harris 1985: 149–50, 231–96). The symbol '/e$_{(2)}$/' is used to indicate this possible phonemic identity/distinction. This is modified to /i/ in more standardised forms of the dialect.

• After /w/, /ë/ in KIT may be replaced by /ɔ̈/ in traditional MUE, for example, *whip, window, winter* (see Section 4.4.4). /i/ also occurs instead of /ë/ in a few words (e.g. *idiot, kick, king, religious, swim*) in traditional forms of the dialect (Harris 1985: 161).

• /ɛ/ in DRESS is replaced by /ë/ in certain words, for example, *any, bless, ever(y), many, never, next, vet, yes* (Harris 1985: 155–7), a feature which is widespread in traditional English and Scots dialects, and by /a/ in a few others (e.g. *wreck, wren, wrestle, yellow*) in traditional MUE (Harris 1985: 171–2).

- The status of the vowel(s) in TRAP, BATH and PALM is complicated in MUE. Simplifying somewhat (see Section 4.3.1), /a/ is short [ä] before voiceless stops and in non-final syllables and long [ä:] elsewhere. In some, but not all, forms of MUE, there is a minimal contrast between [ä] and [ä:], so that [ä:] occurs in a small number of words where we would expect [ä], for example, *banana, father* and *tomato*, which contrast with [ä] in *Anna, gather* and *shadow*. In these kinds of MUE, a distinction between /a/ and /a:/ is required. In some traditional forms of MUE (such as SwTE), which do not distinguish /a/ and /a:/ in this way, there is a separate /ɑ/ ([ɑ:]) phoneme in some PALM words (e.g. *calf, calm*) which, unlike /a/, does not cause palatalisation of neighbouring velars (see Section 3.3). This vowel is also found in words in the THOUGHT lexical set which had ME /aʊ/ (the 'WALK' subset, e.g. *raw, walk*), and is replaced in these words by /ɔ/ in less traditional forms of the dialect (see Harris 1985: 205–7). See Section 4.4.6 for further discussion.
- Some TRAP and BATH words have /ɛ/, especially before alveolar and velar consonants and in non-final syllables, in traditional MUE, for example, *after, grass, ladder* (see Harris 1985: 182–5, 191–7). This feature is widespread in traditional English and Scots dialects.
- The relationship between the LOT, CLOTH and THOUGHT lexical sets is similar to that between the TRAP, BATH and PALM sets. In many varieties of MUE, LOT has (simplifying somewhat; see Section 4.3.1) [ɒ] before voiceless stops and in non-final syllables and [ɔ:] elsewhere, and [ɔ:] is also found in CLOTH and THOUGHT (though as noted above, WALK words may have /ɑ/ in traditional MUE). This gives rise to minimal pairs such as *cot–caught*, so that [ɒ] is phonologised as /ɒ/ and [ɔ:] as /ɔ/. Some traditional forms of MUE (including traditional SwTE) have no distinction between [ɒ] and [ɔ:] in any environment (e.g. *cot = caught*, both with [ɔ:(ᵊ)]), and thus have a single phoneme /ɔ/ in LOT, CLOTH and THOUGHT (see Section 4.4.6).
- /ɒ/ and /ɔ/ are replaced by /a/ in the neighbourhood of labial consonants (especially before /p/ and /f/). This feature is discussed in Section 4.4.2.
- Traditional MUE retains /a/ after /w/ in words such as *quality, swan, swarm, what, war, warm, wash, wasp, watch* and *water* (Harris 1985: 190–1). This feature is widespread in traditional English and Scots dialects.
- Like other forms of IrE, traditional MUE has /əʉ/ (the typical MOUTH vowel) instead of /o/ in words in the GOAT lexical set which had /ɔʊl/ in ME, for example, *bold, bowl, bolt, cold, hold, old, roll, shoulder, sold, soul* and *told* (Harris 1985: 159–60; Maguire 2020b). This is replaced by /o/, except in a few lexicalised cases (e.g. 'oul' in pejorative uses of *old*) in more standardised varieties of the dialect.
- In MUE, FOOT words can have either /ɔ̈/ or /ʉ/. The relationship between the STRUT, FOOT, BOOK and GOOSE sets in MUE is discussed in Section 4.4.5.
- STRUT words typically have /ɔ̈/ in traditional MUE. But a few words may have /ɛ̈/ (e.g. *just, stubble*) in traditional forms of the dialect, and a small set of STRUT words often has /ɒ/~/ɔ/ (including in more standard forms), for example, *oven, under, understand* and words with the prefix *un-* (e.g. *uncertain*).

- There are two PRICE vowels in most traditional forms of MUE, though these are merged under a single phoneme in Belfast and in some (though not all) more standardised forms of the dialect (Harris 1985: 147–9). The distribution of these two phonemes is discussed in Section 4.4.3.
- MUE traditionally distinguished NORTH (with /ɔr/) from FORCE (with /or/), though the two sets are merged for many speakers in Belfast, and this merger is spreading. A small set of FORCE words (*board, coarse, course, court, discourse, door, floor, whore*) have /ʉr/ in traditional MUE, a widespread feature of traditional English and Scots dialects, though this is being replaced by /or/ (*moor, poor* and *tour* retain /ʉr/, however, as they do in some English accents).
- NEAR (/ir/) and SQUARE (/ɛr/) remain distinct, though a small set of NEAR words with ME /ɛː/ have /ɛr/ in traditional MUE, for example, *interfere, quare* 'great, excellent, strange, very' (from *queer*) and *rear* 'to raise' (as do ME /ɛːr/ words which belong to SQUARE, e.g. *bear* 'carry', *mare, pear, wear*). In Belfast and Lagan Valley MUE, SQUARE may have [ɚː], thus merging with NURSE (e.g. *hair = her*), but this feature is not generally typical of MUE, though it may be spreading (see McCafferty 2001: 139–44).
- In non-traditional and standardised forms of MUE, NURSE has [ɚː], representing a neutralisation of the contrast between /ɛ̈/ and /ɔ̈/. As noted above, this vowel may be merged with SQUARE in Belfast and the Lagan Valley. However, many speakers of MUE distinguish the vowel in the 'SERVE' lexical set from other NURSE words, having /ɛr/ (= SQUARE) in words spelt with <e(a)r>, for example, *certain, early, earth, heard, learn, mercy, nervous, person, prefer, search, serve* and *term*. Traditional forms of MUE (including SwTE) also have (or had) /ar/ in some SERVE words (e.g. *certain, clergy, learn, mercy, nervous, search, serve*), but this feature, once general in dialects of English, is now obsolescent, being retained if at all in a couple of words but remembered in others. In addition, traditional forms of MUE often distinguish /ɛ̈r/ and /ɔ̈r/ in NURSE, the latter being found in words with <ir> spellings such as *birch, circle, circus, dirt, fir, firm, girth, third, thirty* and *virgin*, whilst /ɔ̈r/ is found in NURSE words with <(o)ur> and <or> spellings, and in some <ir> words, for example, *bird*. In less traditional forms of the dialect, /ɛ̈r/ and /ɔ̈r/ are merged under [ɚː].

MUE lacks the key lexical distributions that distinguish far northern English (and Scots) from dialects in the Midlands and south (Wakelin 1972: 102–3). Thus MUE has /əʉ/, not /ʉ/, in *house*; /ɛ̈i/ and /əʉ/, not /ɛ̈/ and /ɔ̈/, in *blind* and *found*; /ʉ/ in both *goose* and *room*; /o/, not /e/, in *stone*; /o/, not /a/ or /ɔ/, in *know*; and /ɛ/, not /i/ or /e/, in *dead*. Other northern features that extend somewhat further south, such as the vowel in words like *night* and *eight* being different than the vowel in the PRICE and FACE sets more generally, are also absent in MUE. One 'northern' feature shared by traditional MUE is the lack of a split between FOOT and STRUT (the BOOK subset aside), but this feature was also characteristic of dialects as far south as south Lincolnshire, Northamptonshire, Oxfordshire and Gloucestershire in the mid twentieth century (see Anderson 1987: 34–5) and may have had a wider distribution in the south in earlier centuries, so it is as much a Midland feature as a northern one (see Section 4.4.5). On the other hand, MUE shares with south Midland and southern English dialects the lengthening of ME short /a/ and /ɔ/ before voice-less fricatives (assuming this feature of MUE does not have a Scots source; see Section 4.3.6), leading to merger of these vowels with long [aː] and [ɔː] from other sources. In the mid twentieth century, this feature extended as far north as south Lincolnshire, Northamptonshire, parts of Leicestershire, most of Warwickshire and all of Herefordshire.

The lexical distribution of vowel phonemes in MUE is also rather similar to that of Early Modern StE, as described in Dobson (1957), Kökeritz (1953) and Lass (2000), and it is not radically different from modern StE either, ignoring a number of recent mergers (e.g. of NORTH and FORCE) and the retention of rhoticity in MUE. For example, MUE shares with StE the 'FACE merger' of ME /aː/ and /ai/ and the 'GOAT merger' of ME /ɔː/ and /ɔʊ/ (Wells 1982: 192–4; see also Lass 2000: 91–4), such developments not being typical of the majority of southern and Midland tradi-tional English dialects (see Anderson 1987: 60–1, 68–9, 122, 130). The main differ-ences that exist in lexical distribution between MUE and varieties in England are mostly the result of a range of innovations, especially in StE and other southern and Midland English dialects, with MUE retaining a number of distributions that were once found in StE and across much of England. Several of these are also found in Scots. These conservative features of MUE lexical distribution include the retention of a FACE or FACE-like vowel in the MEAT subset (Harris 1985: 149–50, 231–96; Lass 2000: 95–8), the appearance of the typical MOUTH vowel in the OLD subset (Dobson 1957: 691–2, 809; Kökeritz 1953: 245; Maguire 2020b), the retention of the typical GOOSE vowel in the BOOK subset (Anderson 1987: 31, 94; Dobson 1957: 510–12), the retention of the distinction between NORTH and FORCE and the retention of the typical CURE vowel in the DOOR subset (Anderson 1987: 103, 116–18; Dobson 1957: 735–45; Lass 2000: 111–12), the retention of the distinction between /ɛ̈r/ and /ɔ̈r/ in NURSE (Dobson 1957: 750–9; Lass 2000: 112–13), the retention of a distinct vowel in the SERVE subset as well as the survival of the typical START vowel in some SERVE words (Dobson 1957: 558–64, 746–50; Lass 2000: 109), the use of /ɛ̈/ in some DRESS words (Dobson 1957: 567–9), and the retention of /a/ and /ar/ after /w/ (Lass 2000: 86).

In these respects, MUE is of a conservative Midland/southern English type, and given that these features were present in English dialects, including Early Modern StE, at the time of the Plantation of Ulster, and also occurred to an extent in Scots, it is not surprising that they became characteristic of the dialect. Why MUE should be rather more conservative in terms of its lexical distribution of vowel phonemes than the Midland and southern English dialects from which it largely derived is a question I return to in Section 5.3.2. In the rest of this discussion of the lexical dis-tribution of vowel phonemes in MUE, I examine a number of cases which are rather less straightforward and which appear to have involved input from Scots of particu-lar kinds. These features are: (1) the appearance of a low unrounded vowel in the neighbourhood of labials in LOT and CLOTH words; (2) the development of two PRICE diphthongs; (3) the change of /ɛ̈/ to /ɔ̈/ after /w/; (4) the lack of a FOOT–STRUT split (other than in BOOK words); and (5) the divergent development of the WALK subset of the THOUGHT lexical set.

4.4.2 top and off

The unrounding and lowering of the LOT and CLOTH vowels before (and occasionally after) labial consonants, resulting in merger with the TRAP/BATH vowel (in /a/), is typical of traditional forms of the dialect across the MUE area, including in Belfast (Harris 1985: 198–204), in Counties Down and Armagh (LAS3) and in SwTE. It occurs, almost regularly, before /p/ and /f/ in all varieties, and before /b/ in some (e.g. in some or all of *job*, *rob* and *stob* in the LAS3 MUE locations), before /m/ (in *Tommy*), and after /f/ (in the word *fond*) in SwTE at least. This unrounding and lowering of LOT and CLOTH must be distinguished from general unrounding of the LOT vowel found in some varieties of MUE (see Section 4.2.4), since it occurs in traditional varieties such as SwTE and the LAS3 locations which retain a rounded vowel in LOT. Even in those varieties which have unrounded LOT, it essentially remains distinct ([ɑ]) from TRAP ([a]), and words like *top* and *off* have the TRAP (or BATH) vowel – see Harris (1985: 198–204).

Unrounding and lowering of the LOT/CLOTH vowel in the neighbourhood of labials is also found in USc (Gregg 1985: 18–19, 55; Harris 1985: 26), and has a wide distribution there, not only being found before /b/ in some words, but also before /m/ (e.g. in *Tom*) and sometimes after /f/ (e.g. *fond*), /p/ (e.g. *porridge*) and /b/ (e.g. *bottle*), though this is never as regular as before /p/ and /f/. This is not surprising given that this pattern is also found in most Scots dialects in Scotland (Johnston 1997b: 481, 483), where it first developed in the fifteenth century (Aitken and Macafee 2002: 100; Johnston 1997a: 87). Although there are a few exceptions, the feature in Scots is essentially regular before /p/ and /f/, and rather less so in other environments. It was thus a feature of the Scots dialects brought to Ulster in the seventeenth and early eighteenth centuries, and it is likely, then, that this feature of MUE has its origins in Scots.

However, there may have been another contribution to the establishment of this pattern in MUE. Although there is nothing analogous in Irish (there is no merger of '/ɔ/' and /a/ in the neighbourhood of labials in the language), there was a similar development in the history of English, in some dialects at least. In EModE, in addition to possible general unrounding of the LOT vowel (see Section 4.2.4), there is evidence of merger of the LOT and CLOTH vowels with the TRAP and BATH vowels in some words, especially (though not exclusively) in the neighbourhood of labial consonants (Dobson 1957: 578–81; Kökeritz 1953: 222–7; see also Braidwood 1964: 55–6). Examples include *chap* 'chop', *Gad* 'God', *plat* 'plot' and *strap* 'strop', and rhymes and jingles in Shakespeare including *abject–object*, *bob–crab*, *doffed–craft*, *follow–hallow*, *folly–dally*, *foppish–appish*, *hop–pap*, *Tom–am* and *trap–tropically*. Whilst some of these may have other explanations, they attest to the merger of the LOT/CLOTH and TRAP/BATH vowels in some words, especially in the neighbourhood of labials, in at least some forms of EModE. It may be, as Kökeritz (1953: 223) suggests, that this feature in Shakespeare's works reflects his Warwickshire background, but in any case this looks like an English version of the feature that is found in MUE and Scots. Although this feature is poorly attested in twentieth-century dialect sources such as the SED, it was recorded in the EDG (Wright 1905: 73–4) for a range of Midland and southern English dialects, again especially (though not consistently or exclusively) in the neighbourhood of labial consonants, and Anderson (1987: 21) claims that it occurred 'sporadically in many dialects of southern and western England'. Examples given by Wright include *bottom* (in Kent and Devon), *crop, hop, shop, stop, strop* and *top* (in at least some of these words in Berkshire, Cheshire, Devon, Dorset, Lancashire, Leicestershire, Northamptonshire, Oxfordshire, Somerset, Staffordshire, Sussex, Wiltshire and Worcestershire), and *croft* and *loft* (in Cheshire, Gloucestershire, Northamptonshire, Somerset and Staffordshire). It is noteworthy that the main environments for this change in England are before /p/ and /f/, just as they are in MUE.

So although a Scots source for the unrounding and lowering of the LOT/CLOTH vowel in the neighbourhood of labials in MUE is undeniable, it may also have received support from patterns in some dialects of English (cf. Braidwood 1964: 56). However, the lack of this pattern in SIrE suggests that it is a specifically Ulster development, pointing towards the Scots input as the most important source for the feature. Whether the existence of 'crap' for *crop* in some traditional SIrE dialects (i.e. Roscommon, as recorded in Henry 1957: 218, and Kilkenny, as recorded in Moylan 1996: 296) is indicative of this English input is uncertain, given that it is the only such example recorded (Henry also records the typical BATH vowel in *cross*). In any case, Scots was key in the development of this aspect of the lexical distribution of vowels in MUE, and why this should be when the dialect for the most part follows the lexical distribution of Early Modern Standard and southern/Midland English (Section 4.5.3) is a crucial question for understanding the phonological origins of MUE. Unlike most other Scots lexical distributions (e.g. /ʉ/ in the MOUTH lexical set), which are the result of historical accident and thus are not predictable, /a/ before /p/ and /f/ in the LOT and CLOTH sets is a conditioned change. It is (and was) thus an essentially regular rule, one which was transferred into MUE. How this might have happened, and what consequences that has for understanding language and dialect contact in post-Plantation Ulster is an issue I return to in Section 5.4.

4.4.3 The PRICE diphthongs

As was described in Section 4.2.7, there are two PRICE vowels in traditional and some modern forms of MUE, /ëi/ and /aɪ/. The single PRICE vowel phoneme in BVE represents a collapse of this phonemic distinction, with 'dephonologisation' of it to the allophonic level (Harris 1985: 149). The diphthong /aɪ/ occurs only in SVLR long environments (see Section 4.3.4 for an explanation), whilst /ëi/ occurs in SVLR short environments and also, in specific words, in SVLR long environments. There is almost no variation between /aɪ/ and /ëi/; other than a small number of cases, words either have one phoneme or the other. Table 4.6 lists a selection of words with /aɪ/ and /ëi/ in SVLR long environments in SwTE (which mostly matches the description of mid-nineteenth-century Belfast English in Patterson 1860: 20–2 in this respect) by way of illustration.

A small number of words vary between /aɪ/ and /ëi/, in particular the *-igh* words *high, nigh, sigh* and *thigh*, which usually have /ëi/ for older speakers, and a few words with a following /r/, for example, *entire* and *hire*. Inflectional suffixes do not change the vowel in a word, so that *knives, lives* and *wives* have /ëi/, and *cried, fried, tied* and *tried* have /aɪ/ (cf. /ëi/ in *died*, and also before monomorphemic /d/ in *bide*,

Table 4.6 The lexical distribution of /aɪ/ and /ëi/ in SVLR long environments.

Environment	/aɪ/	/ëi/
Before voiced fricatives	*advertise(ment), disguise, five, prize, scythe, size, surprise*	*advise, (a)live, apologise, arrive, conniving, demise, deprive, dive, drive, hive, ivy, miser, realise, recognise, revise, rise, rival, skive, strive, thrive, wise*
Before /r/	*byre, entire, fire, retire, tire* (v.), *tyre*	*choir, desire, iron, Maguire, shire, spire, squire, wire*
Before [ə]	*bias, dandelion, dial, Goliath, liable, lion, riot*	*Brian, O'Brien, quiet, Ryan, Sion Mills*
Morpheme-finally	*aye* 'yes', *buy, by, bye, cry, defy, deny, dry, dye, fry, Guy, I, lie* 'recline', *magnify* (and other words ending in *-ify), my, pie, ply, pry, rely, reply, rye, sky, spy, sty, tie, try*	*die, eye, fly* (n.), *fly* (v.), *lie* 'fib', *shy, sly, why, Y*

bride, guide, hide, pride, ride, side, slide, stride, tide and *wide*). The phonemic distinction between /aɪ/ and /ëi/ is most obvious in morpheme-final position in the minimal pairs *dye–die, I–eye* and *lie–lie*.

The SVLR-type distribution, especially the restriction of /aɪ/ to SVLR long environments, unambiguously points towards a role for Scots in the development of the distribution of /aɪ/ and /ëi/ in MUE, and this is supported by the existence of similar patterns in USc and in 'Urban Ulster Scots' (see in particular Gregg 1964: 173–4, 179–80, 182; Gregg 1975; Harris 1985: 27–30, 32). It is a well-known feature of almost every Scots dialect that in the PRICE lexical set [aɪ] (or the like) occurs in SVLR long environments and [ëi] (or the like) occurs in SVLR short environments (Aitken 1981; Johnston 1997b: 493–5). The distinction between [aɪ] and [ëi] in Scotland would only be allophonic (as it usually is in SSE) were it not for a number of complications in Scots (including USc). Firstly, and most importantly, OSc /ai/ became [ëi] in some words (e.g. *clay, May, pay, stay*) in morpheme-final position (Aitken and Macafee 2002: 146–50), giving rise to minimal pairs such as *pie* [paɪ] and *pay* [pëi], resulting in phonemicisation of the contrast (i.e. /aɪ/ vs /ëi/). Secondly, inflected forms such as *knives* and *wives* retain /ëi/ in some Scots dialects (Aitken 1981: 142). Lastly, /ëi/ is common after /w/ and /r/ in some Scots dialects, in words such as *drive, rise, why* and *wire*, and can sometimes occur more widely in SVLR long environments, in words such as *dive* and *hive* (Aitken 1981). Notably all but the first of these complications is shared by MUE, again highlighting the importance of the Scots input to this feature of MUE.

Furthermore, the distinction between /aɪ/ and /ëi/ in morpheme-final position in Scots (*pie* vs *pay*) has also been instrumental in the development of the distinction between these vowels in morpheme-final position (*dye–die*) in MUE. Ignoring cases with preceding /w/ (*why, Y*), which favours /ëi/, word with morpheme-final /ëi/ in MUE fall into two groups: those like *eye* and *die* which had early ME and pre-OSc /ei/, and those like *shy* and *thigh* which had ME and OSc /ix/, sometimes also becoming /ei/ in pre-OSc (Aitken and Macafee 2002: 24–5; Johnston 1997b: 455).

Table 4.7 Correspondences between the *dye*, *die*, *thigh* and *pay* groups.

Group	Source	MUE	USc	ModSc	StE
cry, *dye*, *pie*	iː	aɪ	aɪ	aɪ	aɪ
die, *eye*, *fly*	eɪ	ëi	i	i	aɪ
shy, *sigh*, *thigh*	ɪx (> eɪ)	ëi	æx, iː	ëx, i	aɪ
clay, *pay*, *stay*	aɪ	e	ëi	ëi	eɪ

In English dialects south of a line from the Humber to the Mersey (Kolb *et al.* 1979: 9–10; Orton *et al.* 1978: Ph113–Ph116), including the ancestor of StE, both groups of words developed /iː/, merging with the PRICE vowel, so that *die* and *thigh* have /aɪ/, just like *dye*. But in Scots, pre-OSc /ei/ became /eː/ instead, merging with the FLEECE vowel and raising in the Great Vowel Shift to /iː/ (becoming /i/ in Modern Scots (ModSc); Aitken and Macafee 2002: 25), whilst /ɪx/ either merged early with /eɪ/, becoming /i/ (*high*, *skeich* 'shy' and *thigh*), or remained distinct (ModSc /ëx/ in *sigh*). This means that in morpheme-final position traditional Scots dialects distinguish between words with OSc /iː/ > ModSc /aɪ/ (e.g. *cry*, *dye*, *pie*), /eː/ > ModSc /i/ (e.g. *die*, *eye*, *fly*), /ɪx/ > ModSc /ëx/ or /i/ (e.g. *sigh*, *thigh*), and /aɪ/ > ModSc /ëi/ (e.g. *clay*, *pay*, *stay*). The correspondences between the sources and their developments in MUE, USc, ModSc and StE are set out in Table 4.7.

From these correspondences, it can be seen that MUE essentially has the same lexical distribution as StE, but its PRICE vowel has been split between /aɪ/ and /ëi/ following exactly the same split in distribution found in Scots between /aɪ/ on the one hand and /i/~/ëx/ on the other. Both the distinction between /aɪ/ and /ëi/ in MUE and the lexical distribution of /ëi/ in morpheme-final position have their source in Scots, with Scots /ëi/ appearing to have undergone a kind of 'reallocation' to that part of the StE PRICE set which does not have /aɪ/ in Scots. MUE has thus compromised between conflicting input from English and Scots by developing a similar lexical distribution to StE but keeping phonemic and lexical distinctions characteristic of Scots. But this is not reallocation of the sort discussed in Trudgill (2004: 87–8), whereby learners who are confronted with competing variants for some feature assign some of them to one phonological environment and some to another. Instead, this reallocation was done by following an *already known* lexical distribution. That is, the reallocation was done by speakers who knew which words 'belonged together' in Scots, and this important difference has significant consequences for understanding how MUE developed.

Why and how such an apparent reallocation occurred is discussed further in Section 5.4, but it is clear that the Scots input played an important role in this development, as it did in the distribution of /aɪ/ and /ëi/ in the PRICE lexical set in MUE more generally. It is unlikely that input from England was important in the development of this phonemic contrast given that SVLR patterning of the PRICE vowel is only found in Northumberland, north Durham and north Cumberland (Glauser 1988), and the distinction between the subsets of PRICE in morpheme-final position is only characteristic of dialects north of the Humber–Mersey line (Kolb *et al.* 1979: 9–10; Orton *et al.* 1978: Ph113–Ph116), an area that was not a major contributor of Plantation settlers in Ulster. Similarly, it is not clear that Irish could have played any role in the development of the distribution of these vowels in MUE, since it has nothing equivalent to the conditioned patterning of /ëi/ and /aɪ/ in MUE.

4.4.4 /wë-/ > /wɔ̈-/

Although it is not a feature of BVE and is absent from more standardised varieties, the change of /ë/ to /ɔ̈/ after /w/ (including /hw/) is characteristic of some traditional forms of MUE, including the dialect of Annalong in County Down, as recorded in LAS3 (Mather and Speitel 1986: 197–8), and SwTE.[6] And although Gregg (1985: 54–5) considers this to be a feature which distinguishes USc and MUE, his data shows that /ɔ̈/ forms are common in the MUE dialects he recorded in the southern parts of his survey areas in Counties Down, Antrim and Donegal (Gregg 1985: 107–36 and maps #266 'twister' and #267 'whin'). In addition, Patterson (1860) records the form 'whup' for *whip*, providing evidence for the former presence of the feature in Belfast.

In dialects with this feature, /ë/ becomes /ɔ̈/ after /w/ when the vowel is not followed by a velar consonant (e.g. *quick, twig, wing*), and the change is also blocked by various other minor patterns (e.g. *quit* is /kwɛt/ in SwTE, whilst *swim, wish* and *women* traditionally have /i/ across the MUE area). Thus we get /ɔ̈/ in words and names such as *Quinn, twist, which, whin* 'gorse', *whip, whisper, whistle, will, Willie, win, window* and *winter*. As Gregg's inclusion of this feature as a dialect marker indicates, the change of /ë/ to /ɔ̈/ after /w/ is also shared by USc, where it is consistently present and has the same patterning (i.e. it is absent before velar consonants). This is part of a wider distribution, with the change attested in most dialects of Scots in Scotland (Johnston 1997b: 468), including those of the southern half of the country (as indicated in LAS3). Johnston (1997a: 79) points to spellings of words of this type with <u> and <o> in Scots from the fifteenth century, indicating that the change was in place before the Plantation of Ulster and its associated settlements, thus explaining its presence in USc. But how and why did this Scots feature also become a feature of MUE?

Before briefly examining this issue, it is worth considering whether this change has parallels in English in England and in Irish. The change is present in some English dialects, but only those of the far north, especially in Northumberland, in what is clearly an extension across the border of the Scottish pattern (see SED questions I.5.12 *whip*, V.1.7 *windows* and VII.6.26 *wind*). That said, pronunciations of *will* with [ʊ]/[ʌ] have been recorded sporadically across England (see Wright 1905: 70, 680–1), a change which is probably connected to the frequent unstressed pronunciation of this word.

In Ulster Irish, [w] is the usual realisation of broad /v/, which in initial position takes the place of /b/ and /m/ in lenition contexts and of /f/ in eclipsis contexts. As was discussed in Section 4.2.1, Irish has (at a certain level of abstraction) only one short high vowel phoneme, /ɯ/, which is, some minor complications aside, realised as [ɪ] ([ï] in Ulster) before slender consonants and as [ʊ] ([ÿ] in Ulster) before broad consonants (Ó Siadhail 1989: 36–7). This means that [ʊ]/[ÿ] occurs after a broad consonant, including [w], if the vowel is followed by a broad consonant, but [ɪ]/[ï] cannot occur in this environment. However, [ɪ]/[ï] can occur after

[w] in Irish when the vowel is followed by a slender consonant in forms such as *bhuidéal* 'bottle', *bhfuil* 'be' and *mhuinéal* 'neck'. Whilst [ʊ]/[ọ̈] pronunciations can sometimes occur in words of this type, this is not specifically because of the [w] but instead is a result of the unstable nature of the realisation of /ɯ/ after broad consonants. For example, in the Ros Goill dialect of Donegal Irish the local variants of general Irish [ɪ] and [ʊ] are [ə] and '[ọ̈]' (i.e. [ọ̈]), with 'with ə usually occurring between two slender consonants and ọ̈ between two broad consonants' (Lucas 1979: 1). However, '[b]etween a broad and slender consonant, or between a slender and a broad consonant, the vowel is intermediate between ə and ọ̈' (ibid.). Whether these patterns in Irish can be connected to the change from /ɛ̈/ to /ɔ̈/ after /w/ in MUE is uncertain, but given that [ɪ]/[ɪ̈] is impossible after [w] before a broad consonant in Irish, and is sometimes in variation with [ọ̈] even before a slender consonant, it is just about possible that Irish has reinforced the pattern. However, this would require us to ignore other consonant plus vowel sequences in MUE which do not match the Irish patterns (e.g. in words like *bit* and *tin*, which never show the change in MUE). Furthermore, this feature is absent from varieties of SIrE that show obvious signs of contact with Irish, including the dialects of Roscommon (Henry 1957), Kilkenny (Moylan 1996) and Ballyvourney in Cork (Lunny 1981a). If Irish played a role in the development of this feature in Ulster, why did it not do so elsewhere, given that the same constraints existed in Irish dialects in those areas and the important role Irish played in the development of these dialects? So although a role for Irish in the origin of this feature in MUE is not impossible, it requires a fair amount of cherry-picking of the data. Even if there was some Irish reinforcement, in its specific patterning this feature of MUE follows the change that occurred in Scots, and its chief source must lie there.

Returning briefly to the issue of how and why this feature of Scots became part of MUE, especially when most other characteristic Scots vowel distributions did not, it is likely that the answer lies in the rule-like form of this change. Most other Scots vowel distributions are essentially randomly distributed from a phonological point of view. For example, the fact that Scots has /ʉ/ in *house* and /e/ in *stone* is just an accident of history and cannot be predicted from any phonological factors. But the change from OSc /ɪ/ to /ʌ/ after /w/ is essentially regular, being blocked only before velar consonants, and obviously not occurring in words which have other vowel developments (e.g. *swim*). It is this rule which has been transferred to MUE, just as the Scots rule whereby /a/ rather than /ɒ/ or /ɔ/ appears before /p/ and /f/ has become part of the dialect. But this explanation assumes that learners of English in Ulster knew the Scots rule and applied it to their new language, and this has important consequences for understanding the phonological origins of MUE. I return to this issue in Section 5.4.

4.4.5 *The* FOOT *lexical set*

Whilst the lexical distribution of vowels in the STRUT and GOOSE lexical sets is similar in MUE and RP, the same is not true of FOOT. Like RP, MUE distinguishes the vowel in STRUT (usually /ɔ̈/) from that in GOOSE (usually /ʉ/), but MUE has no separate vowel equivalent to RP /ʊ/ for the FOOT lexical set. Instead FOOT words in

MUE have /ɔ̃/ or /ʉ/. Standardised varieties of MUE typically have /ʉ/ in all FOOT words (except *woman*), and thus follow the pattern found in SSE (Wells 1982: 401–2). But this is a newer system which is in the process of replacing traditional vowel distributions in the FOOT lexical set.

In traditional MUE, taking SwTE as an example, most FOOT words have /ɔ̃/, just like STRUT, but some only have /ʉ/, especially *book, brook, cook, crook, good, hood, hook, nook, rook* and *soot* (though *look* and *shook* typically have /ɔ̃/).[7] These words are called the 'BOOK' subset in this analysis. A few words vary between /ɔ̃/ and /ʉ/, even for the most traditional speakers, particularly *could, took*, which are most often produced with /ʉ/ but which can also have /ɔ̃/. In less traditional forms of MUE, including BVE, FOOT words which have /ɔ̃/ in the most traditional forms of the dialect vary between /ɔ̃/ and /ʉ/, with some words more likely to have one vowel or the other, and with the choice depending on a range of sociolinguistic factors (Harris 1985: 150–5).

The origins of the traditional distributions of these vowels evidently lie in England, since the MUE patterns closely match those of EModE and of non-southern English dialects in more recent times (Lass 2000: 87–91; Wells 1982: 196–9). Scots dialects, on the other hand, have a radically different distribution of phonemes in these words as a result of the development of early ME /oː/ to OSc /øː/ (which has various reflexes in ModSc dialects), and transfers of early ME /ʊ/ to that vowel (Aitken and Macafee 2002: 39–42, 98–9). Three main processes contributed towards the establishment of the STRUT, FOOT (including BOOK) and GOOSE lexical sets after the raising of ME /oː/ to /uː/ in Midland and southern England (see Lass 2000 and Wells 1982 for further details). These were:

1. Early Shortening of /uː/ (from ME /oː/) to /ʊ/ in a few words (e.g. *blood, flood*), a change found in almost all Midland and southern English dialects. This change occurred before the seventeenth century;

2. Lowering of /ʊ/ in some words to /ʌ/, causing the 'FOOT–STRUT Split' (Wells 1982: 196–8), since this was not a regular change. Words with early shortening of /uː/ already had /ʊ/ so were susceptible to this change (e.g. *blood, flood*). This change only happened in southern English dialects, and even in the twentieth century was only characteristic of dialects south of a line from the Wash to the Severn Estuary, as well as dialects along the Welsh border (see Anderson 1987: 34–5 and Kolb *et al.* 1979: 227 for illustrative maps). The FOOT–STRUT split is first solidly evidenced from the 1640s (Dobson 1957: 585–9; Lass 2000: 87–91), and thus was likely an early-seventeenth-century change (see Section 4.2.1).

3. Late Shortening of /uː/ to /ʊ/, which was thus not affected by the FOOT–STRUT split (though it is possible that the vowel in some of these words shortened earlier but did not lower). This group includes various words with final /d/ such as *could, good, should, stood, wood* and *would*, words with final /t/ such as *foot* and *soot*, and words with -*ook* (e.g. *book, cook, hook, look, shook, took*). Shortening of the words with final /d/ and /t/ was usual across the English Midlands and in the south, but retention of /uː/ before /k/ was not uncommon in north Midland dialects and sporadically elsewhere (especially the south-west), as indicated by the widespread presence of these forms in the mid twentieth century (see Anderson 1987:

94). Late shortening of /uː/ was also a seventeenth-century change, and must have followed the date of the FOOT–STRUT split for most words.

Traditional MUE shows evidence of Early Shortening (*blood, flood*), but not of the FOOT–STRUT split, whilst it has some forms indicating Late Shortening (e.g. *foot, look, should, shook*) and others that do not (the BOOK subset, e.g. *book, cook, good*). Since Late Shortening must have followed, or at the earliest have been concurrent with the FOOT–STRUT split, MUE should also show evidence of the split if its lexical distribution of vowel phonemes derives from southern English dialects. It may be, then, that MUE derives, in the main, from dialects of English which did not have the split but at the same time had some Late Shortening. This need not mean dialects north of the current Wash–Severn line, as the geographical distribution of the FOOT–STRUT split may well have been different in the early seventeenth century given that the change was new at this time. It is entirely possible that it was absent in most of the Midlands and perhaps even the south-west, so that it was not characteristic of the majority of the input English dialects to Ulster. What [ʌ] there was in the input may have been generalised across the whole of STRUT and FOOT, in an instance of simplification (Trudgill 2004: 86), explaining the lowering of the single vowel that we see in MUE.

There may also have been another factor at play, however. It could be argued that the five main short vowel phones of Irish, [ɪ], [ɛ], [a], [ɔ] and [ʊ], realised as [ɪ̈], [ɛ], [a]~[ɑ], [ɔ] and [ǫ̈] in Ulster (see Section 4.2.1), match an unsplit English system (with five short vowels) better than a split one (with six short vowels), so that the FOOT–STRUT split did not survive language contact. But this ignores the fact that [ɪ]–[ʊ] and [ɛ]–[ɔ] are allophonic pairs and conveniently leaves out the low-vowel back allophone [ɑ] (i.e. Irish has six short vowel phones, not five).

An alternative solution is influence from Scots in Ulster. Seventeenth-century Scots had [ɔ] for OSc /ɔ/, corresponding to the LOT set, and [ö] (later becoming [ʌ]) for OSc /ʊ/, roughly corresponding to the STRUT lexical set. But it had no equivalent to the [ʊ] vowel, which means that Scots speakers learning a mixed English input of [ʌ]~[ʊ] in STRUT and [ʊ] in FOOT would have been likely to resolve the situation by collapsing the distinction in some way. One obvious solution is to merge [ʌ] and [ʊ] under a single vowel, the nearest equivalent being Scots [ö], especially since English /ʌ/ was probably somewhat higher at this time (see Section 4.2.1). Even if the majority English input was an unsplit set with [ʊ], Scots speakers may have equated this with their [ö] vowel (the only other alternative, [u]/[ʉ], being needed for the GOOSE set). In either case, the Scots input helps to explain why MUE has [ɔ̈] in both STRUT and FOOT, and may have played a role in the establishment of unsplit FOOT–STRUT in MUE if it can't simply be explained by the English input. Once again, it is possible that a characteristic feature of MUE phonology has its origins in the efforts of Scots speakers to adapt their speech to English patterns, an issue I return to in Section 5.4.

4.4.6 *The* THOUGHT *vowels*

In MUE, the distinction between the LOT and THOUGHT vowels is usually neutralised before voiced consonants and voiceless fricatives, at least in final stressed syllables, but the two vowels (/ɒ/ and /ɔ/) are kept distinct in other environments (see Table 4.2). But in some traditional, rural varieties of MUE, including SwTE and the dialects of Annalong in Co. Down and Kilrea in Co. (London)Derry as recorded in LAS3, a somewhat different set-up exists. In dialects of this sort, LOT words typically have /ɔ/, even when this is followed by a voiceless stop, whilst THOUGHT words are divided into two groups reflecting the historical origins of the set (see Lass 2000: 94–5): words that had ME /ɔx/ (e.g. *caught*, *daughter*, *thought*; the 'CAUGHT' subset), which also have /ɔ/ in MUE, and words which had ME /aʊ/ (e.g. *hawk*, *jaw*, *raw*, *talk*, *walk*; the 'WALK' subset), which have a distinct /ɑ/ phoneme in MUE, contrasting both with /a/ in TRAP/BATH and /ɔ/ in LOT and the rest of THOUGHT. The same vowel is found in a small number of PALM words such as *calm* and *calf*. This /ɑ/ phoneme, typically pronounced as long [ɑː] or [äː], may overlap in realisation with lengthened forms of the TRAP/BATH vowel, but it is distinguished from them not only in its consistent backness but also in its failure to trigger Velar Palatalisation (Section 3.3), such that words like and *calm* and *calves* start with [kɑː], not [cäː] (as in *can*), and words like *talk* and *walk* end in [ɑːk], not [äᶦk̟] (as in *back*).

This means that there is a partial merger of LOT and THOUGHT in dialects of this type, not conditioned by phonological environment as it is in BVE, for example, but by etymological set. Thus traditional SwTE has /ɔ/ in *lock*, *lot* and *thought*, but /ɑ/ in *jaw* and *talk*. The merger of ME /ɔx/ and /aʊ/ in England occurred in the mid seventeenth century and into the eighteenth century (Lass 2000: 95), so the English brought to Ulster during the Plantation would have had this distinction, at least variably. The Early Modern StE values for the vowels in these two sets of words were probably ([aʊ] >) [ɒʊ] > [ɒː] (WALK) and ([ɔʊx] >) [ɔː(ʊ)] > [ɒː] (CAUGHT), both of which contrasted with the LOT vowel ([ɔ]/[ɒ]). The EModE patterns explain, in part at least, why traditional MUE has a distinction between the vowels in WALK and CAUGHT, though they do not explain why CAUGHT has merged with LOT in dialects of this type, nor do they explain the low, unrounded vowel in WALK.

One obvious parallel with MUE dialects of this type is USc. In USc, OSc /ɔ/ (equivalent to LOT) had become [ɔː] (/ɔ/) via [ɔ] by about 1600, OSc /aʊ/ (equivalent to WALK) had become [ɑː] (/ɑ/) via [ɑː] or [ɒː] by about 1600, and OSc /ɔx/ (equivalent to CAUGHT) had become [ɔːx] (/ɔx/) via [ɔx] by about 1600 (see Aitken and Macafee 2002: 161–2 for Early Modern values). There is nothing equivalent to the distinction between [ɒ] and [ɔː] in LOT and CAUGHT found in English or those forms of MUE that have it. That is, USc has two vowels in this part of the vowel space, just like these conservative varieties of MUE, /ɑ/ and /ɔ/, and both varieties pronounce them [ɑː] and [ɔː]. If we assume the correspondences between English and Scots in the early seventeenth century in Table 4.8, an explanation of these similarities between MUE and USc presents itself.

Scots-speaking settlers in Ulster only had two vowel phonemes available, [ɔ] and [ɑː]/[ɒː], and in applying this system to English would have collapsed the distinction between [ɒ]/[ɔ] and [ɔː(ʊ)] (Early Modern Scots [ɔʊ] > [ʌʊ] being needed for the English diphthong in the MOUTH lexical set). A similar merger of the LOT and THOUGHT vowels occurred in Urban USc (Gregg 1964) and in SSE (Wells 1982: 402–3) for precisely this reason. The retention of a different vowel in WALK was no doubt encouraged by Scots speakers who also had a distinct vowel in this set, and

Table 4.8 The LOT and THOUGHT lexical sets in seventeenth-century English and Scots and in USc and MUE.

	English	Scots	USc	MUE
LOT	[ɒ]/[ɔ]	[ɔ]	[ɔ:]	[ɔ:]
CAUGHT	[ɔ:(ʊ)]	[ɔx]	[ɔ:x]	[ɔ:]
WALK	[ɒ:]	[ɑ:]/[ɒ:]	[ɑ:]	[ɑ:]

the low unround pronunciation of it either represents a continuation of the Early Modern Scots value, or a slight change in its pronunciation shared by MUE and USc.

The development of the THOUGHT vowel in MUE, then, appears to represent another example of a compromise between the EModE and Scots systems, and I return to exactly how and why Scots speakers had this effect on these vowels in Section 5.4. But there may also have been a role for Irish in their development. In the low back part of the vowel space, Irish distinguishes (and this reflects historical distinctions in the language) short [ɔ] (technically interpretable as an allophone of /ə/; see Section 4.2.1), short [ɑ] (an allophone of /a/) and long [ɑ:] (/a:/). The lowering of /o:/ to [ɔ:] characteristic of modern Ulster Irish (Hickey 2014: 126) probably had not yet occurred in the Early Modern period (place-names of Irish origin in the MUE area with Irish /o:/, such as *Omagh*, have /o/ in MUE). The lack of a distinction between short [ɔ] and long [ɔ:] in Irish together with the presence of long [ɑ:] means that the main phones of Irish in this part of the vowel space were similar to what we find in Scots, USc and MUE, though the equivalence is complicated by the presence of short [ɑ] in Irish and by the sub-phonemic status of [ɔ]. The mapping of Irish [ɑ:] on to MUE /ɑ/ ([ɑ:]) is supported by the existence of this sound in MUE in a number of borrowings from Irish (e.g. SwTE *plawteen* 'round dung' ['plɑ:t̠ʲən] < Ir. *pláitín*, *prawkus* 'mixed up mess' ['pɹɑ:kəs] < Ir. *prácás*). The rather different mapping of Irish sounds on to English vowels in southern Ireland (where [ɑ] in LOT and [ɑ:] in THOUGHT appear to be equivalent to Irish [ɑ] and [ɑ:]; see Wells 1982: 419) suggests that Irish would have had a reinforcing rather than a causal role in the development of these vowels in MUE, assuming that it did play a part in these changes at all.

4.5 Summary

This section summarises the results of the analysis in sections 4.2 to 4.4, drawing particular attention to the different roles played by English, Scots and Irish in the development of aspects of the vocalic phonology of MUE.

4.5.1 Vowel quality

The results of the analysis of the origins of the quality of a range of vowels in MUE, as discussed in Section 4.2, are summarised in Table 4.9. Input from Scots is an obvious characteristic of vowel quality in MUE. Of the ten features listed in Table 4.9, seven have close parallels in Scots and likely derive from that source. Conversely, input from English is rather more limited, with a main source in English only being likely

Table 4.9 Origins of MUE vowel qualities.

Feature	Origin
Lowering and centralisation of KIT	A Scots source. A similar lowering and centralisation of [ɪ] is found in Ulster Irish, but this is not typical of other Irish dialects, and the complex underlying phonology of the Irish short vowels complicates any equation. Influence from MUE on Ulster Irish is possible, though some reinforcement from Irish cannot be entirely ruled out.
Lowering and centralisation of STRUT	An English and/or Scots source. A similar lowering and centralisation of [ʊ] is found in Ulster Irish, but this is not typical of other Irish dialects, and the complex underlying phonology of the Irish short vowels complicates any equation. Influence from MUE on Ulster Irish is possible, though some reinforcement from Irish cannot be entirely ruled out.
Lowering of the DRESS vowel	A Scots source, perhaps with some English input.
Backing of the TRAP/BATH vowel	A Scots source, perhaps with some English input and some reinforcement from Irish.
Unrounding of LOT	An English source (perhaps with some reinforcement from Irish?).
Fronting of GOOSE	A Scots source, possibly with some input from English.
Diphthongisation of the FACE vowel	Parallels in both English and Scots, but possibly an internal development and likely no connection with Irish.
The PRICE vowel	A Scots source, the [ëi] variant possibly also supported by EModE [əɪ].
The MOUTH vowel	A Scots source, [əʉ] possibly also supported by EModE [ʌu].
Pre-Palatal Raising	An English source, possibly with some Scots input and reinforcement from Irish.

for two features (one of which, Pre-Palatal Raising, having as much to do with the realisation of consonants as it does with the realisation of vowels). However, there may have been some input from English for a further five vowel quality features.

The role of Irish in the development of MUE vowel quality was even more limited, with none of the features in Table 4.9 having its primary source in the language. However, it is possible that Irish has played a reinforcing role in the development of five of the listed features, though this is complicated by the fact that the lowering and centralisation of [ɪ] and [ʊ] in Ulster Irish is not found in other dialects of the language, and it may be that this is a case of MUE (and/or USc) influence on Irish instead. Overall, the quality of vowels in MUE has a distinctly Scottish character, and this is reflected in the similarities between the vowels of MUE and USc. However, input from English, possibly from Irish, and some internal developments within the dialect mean that vowel quality in MUE has a character all of its own.

4.5.2 *Vowel quantity*

The results of the analysis of the origins of the quantity of a range of vowels in MUE, as discussed in Section 4.3, are summarised in Table 4.10. It is noticeable that Irish,

Table 4.10 Origins of MUE vowel quantity rules.

Feature	Origin
SVLR	A Scots source.
VE	An Scots and/or English source.
PFL	An Scots and/or English source.

which has phonemic vowel length, appears to have played no role in the development of MUE vowel quantity, whilst two of the three main effects on vowel quantity in MUE are shared by English and Scots and are likely to derive from both. But the SVLR conditioning of the FLEECE, GOOSE and PRICE vowels in the dialect can only have come from Scots. The unusual combination of SVLR, VE and PFL found in MUE is shared by some southern Scots dialects, suggesting that in this case English may in fact have played a supporting role to a substantial Scots contribution to the phonology of the dialect.

4.5.3 Vowel lexical distribution

In general terms, the lexical distribution of vowel phonemes in MUE is of a southern or south Midland English type, but is otherwise non-regional from an English perspective. The dialect is lacking the various regionally restricted features characteristic of dialects in East Anglia, the south-west and the north of England, and indeed is close to the seventeenth-century ancestor of StE in this respect.

But MUE is also characterised by a range of vowel distributions that have been lost in StE but which were widespread in the Early Modern period and which were still current in some traditional dialects of English in the twentieth century. A number of these conservative features are also shared by Scots. These features include the lack of a FOOT–STRUT split, the retention of the typical GOOSE vowel in a number of FOOT words, a FACE or FACE-like vowel in the MEAT set, /ë/ (the typical KIT vowel in MUE) in various words in the DRESS lexical set, the retention of an unrounded low vowel after /w/ in words like *quality*, *watch* and *war*, the presence of typical MOUTH diphthong in the OLD set, a distinction between the vowels in the NORTH and FORCE lexical sets, a vowel typical of the CURE lexical set in a number of FORCE words such as *board*, *court* and *door*, the survival of a low vowel (typical of the START lexical set) in SERVE words, and the retention of the distinction between ME /ɪr/ and /ʊr/ in the NURSE lexical set. Again none of these features was tied to a particular region in the Early Modern period, and all were characteristic of a wide range of dialects.

In addition to contributing to or reinforcing some of the conservative features of MUE, Scots played an important role in the development of a number of vowel lexical distributions in the dialect. All of these cases have particular characteristics which distinguish them from other Scots lexical distributions, such as /ʉ/ in MOUTH words, which did not become part of MUE. Both the change of /ɔ/ to /a/ in the neighbourhood of labial consonants and the change of /ë/ to /ɔ̈/ after /w/ are, to a large extent, conditioned changes, depending on rules of distribution in Scots, rather than being assemblages of 'random facts'. That is, MUE has these distributions not just because they were found in Scots but because they were rules of Scots vowel distribution that appear to have been transferred to the dialect. Distributions of vowels in Scots that were not in some way rule-governed were usually not, isolated examples aside, transferred to MUE. The lack of a distinction between the typical vowels in the LOT and THOUGHT and STRUT and FOOT lexical sets in MUE is of a similar sort, reflecting the lack of these distinctions in varieties of Scots and resulting in mergers of these vowels of the same kind as is found in SSE. The distribution of the two PRICE diphthongs is a somewhat different case, but it too reflects an attempt to map Scots vowel distinctions on to English lexical distributions. The distribution of /ëi/ and /aɪ/ in non-final position reflects SVLR conditioning, along with some of the irregularities in distribution that are still current in Scots dialects. The assignment of /ëi/ in morpheme-final position to words with Scots /i/ and /ëx/ and of /aɪ/ to words with Scots /aɪ/ is a case of reallocation, but of an unusual kind in that it follows *already known* lexical distributions. In other words, this case also involves the application of phonological knowledge to the distribution of vowel phonemes rather than constituting an assemblage of essentially random facts. The reasons for the rather specific kinds of Scots input to the lexical distribution of vowel phonemes in MUE are discussed further in Section 5.4.

Evidence of input from Irish to the lexical distribution of vowel phonemes of MUE is, other than contributions in the form of borrowed words and place-names, limited. The case for an Irish role in the change of /wë/ to /wɔ/ and in the development of the vowels in the LOT and THOUGHT lexical sets is weak, and at most amounts to a degree of reinforcement, though even this is uncertain.

Notes

1. In addition, there is merger of original /ɛ/ and /a/ (under /a/) in the neighbourhood of (historical) /w/ in a number of words (e.g. *wreck, wren, wrestle, yellow*) in traditional MUE (as noted in Section 4.4.1), a feature which is shared with various traditional dialects of English and Scots. See the entries for these words in Wright (1905).
2. Cf. Harris (1985: 53) and Wells (1982: 443).
3. There are numerous records of '[ɪ]' (i.e. [ɪ]) for *feet* in the SED, but these are cases where historical /iː/ has merged with /ɪ/. Transcriptions such as [iˑ] or [i] for shortened, but still phonemically distinct /iː/ are rare, even though such pronunciations must have been common, being the norm in many accents and dialects of English today.
4. JYM's close attention to vowel quantity is also demonstrated by the close similarity of his transcriptions of vowel length in the Down and Armagh MUE data underlying LAS3 to descriptions of vowel length in MUE in other sources.
5. These patterns are still mostly apparent in the published atlas, though it conflates long and short allophones under '/e/' before labial and velar consonants; see Mather and Speitel (1986: 148–9).
6. The feature is also found in the dialect of Kilrea in County (London)Derry in LAS3, which is on the edge of the USc area, though the dialect recorded in LAS3 was phonologically a MUE dialect. However, the dialect of the same location

recorded by Robert Gregg in the mid twentieth century (Gregg 1985) falls inside the USc phonological area.

7. GOOSE words which vary between preferred /uː/ and less common /ʊ/ in RP, such as *hoof, roof, room* and *tooth*, also only have /ʉ/ in MUE. The word *hood* may once have had /ɔ/ in some forms of traditional MUE too, as indicated in Patterson (1860: 8).

5 Discussion

5.1 Preliminaries

The origins of a wide range of phonological features of MUE, covering consonant realisation and distribution, vowel quality, vowel quantity and vowel lexical distribution, were analysed in Chapters 3 and 4. This is the most extensive analysis of the origins of phonological features of the dialect, or any dialect of IrE, that has ever been undertaken. Summaries of the findings are given in Sections 3.13 and 4.5. A number of key patterns emerge from the data which, given the wide scope of the analysis, reveal the extent and nature of the input to the dialect's phonology from English, Scots and Irish. These key patterns are:

1. There is a distinct lack of evidence for direct influence on the phonological development of the dialect from Irish, with only one phonological feature (Palatal Velarisation) being likely to be derived in its entirety from the language, in addition to the contribution Irish has made, through borrowed words and place-names, to the distribution of the /x/ phoneme in the dialect. In addition, there are a number of cases where reinforcement of patterns present in the English and/or Scots input to the dialect from Irish is possible, though in all of these cases the precise nature and patterning of the feature in MUE is more similar to what is or was found in English and/or Scots.
2. In terms of its consonant realisations and distributions and its lexical distribution of vowel phonemes, MUE is of a non-regional Midland and southern English type, close to the Early Modern ancestor of StE. There are few features in these aspects of MUE phonology that do not have close antecedents and analogues in England. However, MUE appears to be somewhat conservative in many of these respects, retaining a range of phonological patterns characteristic of Early Modern English and peripheral modern English dialects but which are not now found in many dialects of English in the Midlands and south of England. At the same time, MUE is not characterised by various innovations that have affected dialects in England.
3. There has been obvious Scots input to the development of vowel quality and vowel quantity in MUE, as well as to some aspects of the lexical distributions of vowels in the dialect. The cases where there has been Scots input to the lexical distribution of vowels in MUE are of a specific kind, involving loss of phonemic distinctions and phonological conditioning or reallocation in reference to

145

existing Scots lexical distributions. In addition, Scots input to consonant realisation and distribution is likely, given that many of these feature were shared by Early Modern English and Scots varieties. However, unlike the English input to the consonants, specifically Scots patterns are absent other than contributions to the distribution of the /x/ phoneme in borrowed words.

The purpose of the rest of this chapter is to offer explanations for these patterns. MUE formed as a result of contact between different languages (Irish and English/ Scots) and different dialects of the same language (a range of English dialects, as well as a range of Scots dialects), and indeed between two closely related languages or sharply divergent dialect groups (English and Scots) in situations of settlement colonisation and language shift. Thus an explanation of these patterns must lie in contact-induced changes as a result of language shift, koinéisation and new dialect formation. I discuss all of these processes, as well as examining the notions of 'reinforcement' and 'colonial lag' in this chapter.

The rest of this chapter is organised as follows. In Section 5.2, I address the lack of obvious input to the development of MUE phonology from Irish in the context of a substantial language shift from that language to English. In doing so, I discuss the issue of reinforcement and problems with it, and note that phonology may have acted differently than syntax and lexis, offering tentative explanations as to why this might be. Key points in this discussion are that MUE was established by a very sizable native-speaker population who, for the most part, did not learn Irish, and that the language shift from Irish to English in Ulster happened over a long period, often in more peripheral areas, so that the shifting speakers were never in the majority, especially in the populous lowland areas of the province, and had time to accommodate fully to more prestigious supraregional phonological patterns that derived from English and Scots. As such, they were never in a demographic position to substantially alter the speech of the native English speaker community. In Section 5.3, I discuss why the English input to the dialect has the character it has, explaining its non-regional character in terms of koinéisation and new dialect formation. The English input to the province came from various parts of the Midlands and south of England, but no one dialect was dominant, and the non-regional nature of the English input to MUE reflects this. In addition, I discuss the nature of conservatism in MUE phonology, examining the problematic idea of colonial lag and how we might explain, through 'peripheralisation' and 'polarisation', this aspect of MUE phonology. In Section 5.4, I discuss the Scots input to MUE and why it had the form it did. In particular, I explore the differences in behaviour of consonants and vowels, the character of the phonetic and phonological input from Scots, and what these tell us about the nature of contact between English and Scots, two closely related languages or divergent dialect groups, in Ulster. It appears to be the case that the Scots input to MUE was partly a result of 'language' shift, with adult speakers of Scots learning English in Ulster and carrying through aspects of their Scots phonology to create a new, Scots-influenced, dialect of English.

5.2 Contact with Irish

The analyses in Chapters 3 and 4 reveals that direct input from Irish to the phonology of MUE has been limited. Through borrowed lexical items and, especially, place-names, Irish has contributed to the lexical distribution of vowel and consonant phonemes in the dialect, most noticeably in helping to establish /x/ as a characteristic of the dialect (Section 3.2). But as this was also a feature of the Scots input to the dialect and may have had a limited presence in the seventeenth-century English input to the dialect (cf. /x/ in *trough*), this feature did not originate solely in Irish. In fact, only one of the phonological features surveyed in Chapters 3 and 4 appears to be likely to derive primarily or wholly from Irish. This feature, Palatal Velarisation (Section 3.4), is found in both MUE (and some other varieties of IrE) and in some dialects of Irish, including in Ulster, but is not found in English and is characteristic of only a few dialects of Scots in north-east Scotland. In Section 3.4, a number of reasons why we might consider alternative origins for PV in MUE were considered, and this search for an alternative explanation is called for given the isolated nature of this apparent case of Irish influence on the phonology of the dialect. Nevertheless, an Irish origin of the feature remains the most likely explanation.

In addition to these two contributions, it is possible that Irish has 'reinforced' a range of phonological features which were present in the English and/or Scots input to MUE. The notion of reinforcement is, however, problematic, and it is examined in detail below. But essentially it amounts to saying that these features were compatible with Irish phonology so that Irish learners of English found them (relatively) easy to acquire (and thus preferred them to various alternatives in the input), and that without this added input from Irish learners of English these features would not, or would not all, have survived in MUE. If this is the case, then Irish has played an important role in shaping the phonological development of the dialect, though only in conjunction with the necessary inputs from English and/or Scots. However, given the discussion of the problems with diagnosing reinforcement in Section 5.2.1, it is by no means certain that this did in fact happen.

That Irish could have influenced the phonological development of MUE is not at all unexpected given the situation of language contact that has existed in Ulster since the seventeenth century. As was discussed in Chapter 2, this largely took the form of 'language shift', with speakers of Irish learning English and with Irish consequently dying out across most of Ulster as bilingualism gave way to monolingualism in English. What effects might this language shift from Irish have had on English in Ulster?

Siegel (1999: 2) explains that 'in the early stages of language contact, individuals attempt to speak a common second language (L2) . . . and doing so, transfer features from their first languages (L1), the substrate languages, onto forms of the L2'. That is, when Irish speakers learned English in Ulster, the English that they spoke would inevitably have contained features carried over from Irish, a situation that is familiar to anyone who has ever tried to learn another language. Thomason and Kaufman (1988: 39) note that in such situations, it may be the case that '[t]he errors made by members of the shifting group in speaking the T[arget]L[anguage] then spread to the TL as a whole when they are imitated by original speakers of that language'. This process is known as '(substratum) interference' (e.g. Thomason and Kaufman 1988: 119–46), or 'imposition' (Winford 2005), the latter term preferred here. The nature and extent of imposition depends on the circumstances of the language shift. If the language that speakers are shifting from belongs to a powerful group in society (i.e. it is a superstratum), it will have different effects than if the language that speakers are shifting from belongs to those who are not in power. In the former case, shift is only likely if the shifting speakers are a small minority of the population (as was the case for the Norman aristocracy in medieval England), since a powerful majority or even substantial minority is unlikely to shift at all, and those with less power in the society are the ones who shift in such cases. Language shift of a small powerful minority may not produce much in the way of imposition, though it may be accompanied (or more likely preceded) by substantial lexical borrowing reflecting the cultural dominance of the shifting speakers (Thomason and Kaufman 1988: 123–4).

In other cases of language shift it is the substratum language that is abandoned. The precise effects this will have on the target language depend upon a range of factors, and vary from little or no imposition to heavy imposition. Little or no imposition is likely in two circumstances: when it involves 'a small shifting group relative to the number of TL speakers, and a slow shift, i.e. one that takes at least several generations to complete' (Thomason and Kaufman 1988: 119). The reasons that there may be no imposition in such a situation are that the shifting speakers are not demographically important enough to affect the linguistic behaviour of the wider target language community, and the long period of language shift means that the L1 population adopts the L2 gradually, so that they both learn it more thoroughly and do so in smaller numbers at any one time relative to the number of native speakers (see Thomason and Kaufman 1988: 47). At the opposite extreme are situations in which 'an entire population shifts to the language of a much smaller group of conquering invaders over one or two generations' (Thomason and Kaufman 1988: 119), in which case 'the shifting speakers are unlikely to be fully bilingual in the TL before they abandon their native language, so we expect to find extensive substratum interference in the TL' (ibid.: 119–20). This is most likely to be evident in the phonology, syntax and, depending upon how extensive the imposition is, in the morphology of the target language. Effects can include simplification (e.g. phonemic mergers and loss of morphological complexity) and changes which replace features of the target language with features similar to those in the L1 (Thomason and Kaufman 1988: 130 give as an example the dental stops [t̪] and [d̪] in IrE for the English dental fricatives [θ] and [ð]). Lexis may also be affected, but this may be rather more limited in cases of language shift than in other forms of language contact that result in substantial borrowing between languages. Thomason and Kaufman (1988: 117) note that

> if the language of a shifting population did *not* contribute lexicon to the target language, other than a few words for local natural and cultural items, then we can conclude that the shifting population did not enjoy much social or political prestige.

As such socio-political relations are often the case in language shift from a substratum language, it is typical of such situations that lexical interference is slight and of a particular kind.

A key point about imposition as a result of language shift is that it is variable in extent depending on the precise conditions of the shift, and it is not the case that language shift inevitably causes significant imposition in the target language. Given the right circumstances, imposition may be slight and hard to identify, or it may indeed be absent. Where it does occur, it is likely to affect phonology and syntax in particular, but to have rather less impact on lexis.

In Ireland, including Ulster, there has been a shift amongst speakers who 'did not enjoy much social or political prestige' (Thomason and Kaufman 1988: 117) from a substrate language (Irish) to a prestigious and powerful superstrate language (English). It is usually claimed that IrE represents an example of noticeable, even heavy imposition as a result of this language shift (examples amongst many include: Bliss 1984; Filppula 1999; Hickey 2007a; McColl Millar 2016: 97–105; Odlin 1997; Thomason 2001: 79; Thomason and Kaufman 1988: 43; Winford 2005), and this is considered to be most obvious in phonology and, especially, syntax, whilst lexical interference has been peripheral (Thomason and Kaufman 1988: 129). Although these descriptions usually apply to 'IrE' generally, often referring by default to the linguistic history of southern Ireland, we have also seen, throughout this book, that similar claims have been made for MUE. Why, then, if IrE, including MUE, is assumed to show significant signs of imposition as a result of language shift, is evidence for Irish influence on the phonology of MUE so slight, as demonstrated in Chapters 3 and 4? We know that language shift can cause phonological imposition in the target language. We know that there has been a large-scale language shift from Irish to English in Ulster over the last 400 years. We know that there has been some syntactic imposition in the development of Irish English, including in MUE (see Section 5.2.2), though lexical interference has indeed been peripheral, as demonstrated by the lack of core vocabulary in the dialect deriving from Irish and the culturally specific nature of most such lexical borrowings (also see Section 5.2.2).

A number of factors appear to have played a role in producing this result in Ulster, which represents a rather different case than much of the rest of Ireland. Firstly, the size of the native English/Scots speaker population was, as a result of the Plantation of Ulster and its associated settlements throughout the seventeenth century and into the early eighteenth century, considerable. As was discussed in Chapter 2, the Plantation of Ulster was an example of settlement colonisation, involving the movement of large numbers of settlers into the province. By 1659, around 37 per cent of the population of Ulster was British, and this was unevenly distributed, so that between 43 and 45 per cent of the population of the most densely populated counties (Antrim, Down and (London)Derry) were English or Scottish. By 1732, the population of the province had been transformed to an even greater degree. By that time, 62 per cent of the population was Protestant. Assuming a fairly high degree of continuity between the mostly Protestant settlers on the one hand, and the ethno-religious groups of the early eighteenth century on the other (see Section 2.4), this represents a large increase in the non-Irish population of the province, fuelled for the most part by continued immigration from Britain, rather than by large-scale conversions (again see Section 2.4). By the first half of the eighteenth century, well over half of the population was probably of settler origin, and in some counties (Antrim, Down and (London)Derry) this was at levels of over 70 per cent. Even Armagh, Donegal,

Fermanagh and Tyrone had Protestant populations of between 48 and 65 per cent by this time. In other words, the settler population was massive, probably outnumbering the native Irish population by the early eighteenth century, certainly so in the lowland, populous, economically powerful areas of Ulster. As such, they represent a very significant 'founder population', as is discussed further in Section 5.3.1. Given that the settlers did not speak Irish, that there is little evidence that they learned the language in significant numbers, and that speakers of Irish were already beginning to shift from Irish in and around the main population centres, most of lowland Ulster was predominantly English/Scots speaking in this period, and indeed Irish very quickly became a minority language in large swathes of territory in the province from which it was soon to disappear altogether. This is very different from the situation across much of the rest of Ireland, especially in the west and south, as described by Filppula (1999: 6–10, 30–2), where the major shift from Irish to English occurred rapidly in the nineteenth century, leading to a very large proportion of the population being made up of bilingual and recently monolingual English speakers.

Secondly, we must at the same time take into account the potentially negative attitudes of the settlers to the Irish and their language. The Plantation of Ulster was a process of settlement colonisation with the transformation of the province ethnically, religiously and politically as some of its chief goals. The settlers had different identities, religion, politics and language than the native Irish. Colonial attitudes as a result of these differences, which would contrast the settlers with the 'other' (Schneider 2007: 33–4), must inevitably have spilt over into linguistic domains, as was discussed in Section 2.4. The settlers, who were almost all British Protestants who spoke English or Scots, would mostly have had little reason to abandon their language, especially given their numbers and social status. Indeed, it is not clear that they would have had much motivation to learn Irish, given this and the attitudes that they are likely to have had towards the native population and their language. This is typical in situations of settlement colonisation, where it is usually the case that 'most members of immigrating, invading, and occupying groups, who tend to be dominant in political, military, and economic terms, do not bother to learn indigenous languages (the notable exception typically being missionaries)' (Schneider 2007: 34). Instead, '[f]or whatever inter-group communication is required, the task of acquiring the necessary linguistic skills tends to be left to individual members of the indigenous population' (ibid.). In this way, then, bilingualism was mostly unidirectional: native Irish speakers, through conversion to Protestantism and for reasons of utility but also through lack of choice and through internalising negative attitudes towards their language, became bilingual, but the settlers rarely did. Thus a process of language shift with unidirectional bilingualism began, so that any influence on English/Scots from Irish would be via bilingual Irish speakers who, as long as they remained Catholic, poor and/or rural, would still 'not enjoy much social or political prestige' (Thomason and Kaufman 1988: 117) and thus would have been less likely to influence the language of the socially and politically dominant majority.

Thirdly, the shift from Irish to English in Ulster did not happen quickly. The massive intrusion of English and Scots meant that Irish became a minority language in the province, especially in lowland areas. But it was still widely spoken in the late eighteenth and early nineteenth centuries in many areas (see Section 2.6), and it wasn't until the late nineteenth century, and indeed into the early and mid twentieth century, that Irish disappeared from counties other than Donegal. In other words, the shift from Irish to English/Scots occurred over a 300-year period across most of Ulster. This means that Irish learners of English were only ever a small minority of the population of Ulster at any one time, even though they may have been common locally. This follows from the fact that Irish speakers were probably already in a minority in the early 1700s as a result of the settlements of the previous century and from the fact that they did not all abandon the language at once, but did so gradually through the course of the seventeenth, eighteenth and nineteenth centuries (and into the twentieth century in some places). This is unlike much of the rest of Ireland, where the shift was often late (i.e. in the nineteenth century), where shifting speakers were a majority of the population, and where the shift from Irish to English occurred over the space of a few generations, leading to a predominance of bilingual and recently monolingual speakers in those parts of the island (Filppula 1999). As a result of Irish-speaking communities more gradually shifting to English in Ulster, not only were such speakers very much in the minority, they would have been increasingly characteristic only of peripheral and upland areas and would have had longer to accommodate to supraregional varieties of Ulster English that had developed in the lowlands of the province. This gradual shift to English and retraction of Irish away from the lowlands meant that these relatively small numbers of speakers would have had little chance of significantly impacting the development of English in the province more generally, especially in terms of its phonology, as is discussed in Section 5.2.2.

These factors together, that is the size of the settler population, their attitudes towards the Irish and their language and the consequences this had for bilingualism, and the drawn-out shift from Irish to English, conspired to mean that this language shift had little effect on the development of the phonology of MUE. Thomason and Kaufman (1988: 43) note of (southern) Ireland that 'the English settlers presumably had no positive motive for imitating Irish-influenced English, but the more numerous shifting Gaelic speakers' speech habits prevailed anyway'. In Ulster the first part of this statement applies, but the second part does not. This contrasts with other parts of Ireland, especially in the west and south, and is not unexpected, given that slight or even no interference is characteristic of such situations (as is discussed in Thomason and Kaufman 1988: 119–29). In fact, it is likely, given that bilingualism has characterised Irish-speaking communities in Ulster for four centuries, that Ulster Irish should show signs of influence from English, and several such cases have been suggested in Chapters 3 and 4. This influence in the other direction is, given everything that we know about language contact, more likely to explain some of these phonological commonalities between Irish and English, in Ulster and elsewhere in Ireland.

5.2.1 Reinforcement

A range of features of MUE have been identified in Chapters 3 and 4 as possibly involving reinforcement from Irish. This notion has not been explained in detail so far, but has been appealed to in cases where Irish has features which are similar to ones that were in the English and/or Scots input to the dialect so that a possible 'supporting role' may have been played by Irish. In this section I explore what is meant by reinforcement, and identify some problems with the notion which cast doubt on a role for Irish in the development of these features.

What exactly is reinforcement? Following Filppula (1999), Siegel (1999), Thomason and Kaufman (1988; see especially pp. 58 and 242), and also the role of determinism in dialect contact described in Trudgill (2004), I take reinforcement to mean 'strengthening or preservation of a feature in the target language which might otherwise be expected to disappear due to it being a variable or recessive feature' (Maguire 2018: 20). This strengthening or preservation comes about because those who are learning the target language have the feature, or something very similar to it, in their speech due to imposition from their L1, which is also characterised by a similar or identical feature to the one being reinforced. This means that they add to the number of speakers of the target language who have the feature, helping to maintain it, or at the very least not adding to the numbers of speakers who do not have the feature. Reinforcement, rather than a direct causal role, is assumed when the feature is present in the language anyway in the same form, and when a similar, 'compatible' feature is found in the L1 of shifting speakers, so that imposition is not needed to explain its existence in the target language, merely its persistence. Thus, for example, epenthesis in coda liquid+sonorant clusters in MUE (and other varieties of IrE), especially in /lm/ and /rm/, was present in an identical form in the English and Scots input to what is found in MUE (Maguire 2018), whilst a similar kind of epenthesis, but much more extensive in terms of the clusters and environments affected, is also characteristic of Irish. Irish cannot have caused epenthesis in MUE, since MUE epenthesis patterns just like epenthesis in English and Scots and not like epenthesis in Irish, but as epenthesis in these varieties is a subset of epenthesis in Irish, Irish learners of English may have reinforced the feature in MUE and elsewhere in Ireland.

This all seems reasonable, but there are problems which make diagnosis of reinforcement difficult, perhaps even impossible. Thomason (2001: 93–4) states that in identifying cases of imposition due to language shift

> we must prove that the shared features – the proposed interference features – were not present in the receiving language before it came into close contact with the source language. That is, we have to prove that the receiving language has changed by innovating these features.

Similar criteria are laid out in Poplack *et al.* (2012: 204), who argue that

> [a] conclusion in favor of contact-induced change should rest on the demonstrations that the candidate feature
> (i)   is in fact a change,
> (ii) was not present in the pre-contact variety,
> (iii) is not present in a contemporaneous non-contact variety,
> (iv) behaves in the same way as its putatively borrowed counterpart in the source variety, and
> (v)   differs in non-trivial ways from superficially similar constructions in the host language, if any.

But it is precisely the nature of reinforced features that they were already present in the receiving language and may still be present in other dialects of the language, so our main heuristics for determining whether the L1 has played a role are not available to us. As Maguire (2018: 20–1) points out, and as the criteria in Poplack *et al.* (2012) make clear, if reinforcement did not change anything about a feature that was already present in the target language, we cannot know whether it ever occurred, whilst if interference from the L1 has led to obvious changes in the target language which are not identical to what was present in it already, then this is no longer reinforcement, but rather more substantial contact-induced language change.

So how might we diagnose reinforcement? Given that reinforcement is essentially invisible, no individual cases of it can easily be identified. But perhaps when enough features that are present in the L1 end up also being found in the target language, we might begin to suspect that something other than chance is at play. That is, if a new variety of the target language just happens to have retained feature after feature, often lost elsewhere in the target language, that are also found in the contact L1, then it is more likely that this is the result of reinforcement than chance. The problem then becomes one of quantifying such apparent reinforcement, a task made difficult and perhaps even impossible by the need to quantify cases where reinforcement does not seem to have occurred, even though it might have done.

In order to even begin getting a handle on this, we have to know what could count as a case of reinforcement and what should not. It is not enough for the L1 to be neutral with respect to features in the target language. For example, Hickey (2007a: 282) suggests that retention of rhoticity and distinctions between different vowels before /r/ in the NURSE lexical set in IrE involve '[c]onvergence of English input and Irish'. But this cannot be right. Irish learners of English, exposed to varieties of English which were rhotic and others which were not, had no reason to choose one over the other just because their native language allows /r/ in coda position. It does not require it, so there is no rule 'Have /r/ in coda position'. They could just as easily have learned English pronunciations such as [pɑːt] for 'part', the sequence /paːt/ (e.g. [pɑːt̪ʲ]) being perfectly licit in Irish. The same goes for short vowel distinctions before /r/. Irish learners of English could just as easily not learn these distinctions as learn them (indeed, given Herzog's Principle, as discussed in Labov 1994: 313, it would have been easier for them to learn the merged vowel in the NURSE lexical set). These are not, then, cases of reinforcement or 'convergence', but instead represent at most cases where Irish did not conflict with English phonology so that Irish learners of the language had no particular difficulty with them. Reinforcement can only involve cases where learners of the target language are likely, given phonological characteristics of their L1, to favour a particular variant in the target language over others.

We also have to consider what might count as negative evidence of reinforcement. Is it possible to identify features that were present in the target language input and should have characterised the new variety of it due to reinforcement but which do not? This question is difficult to answer, as we cannot be certain that features which do not exist in the new variety were present in the target language input to it. But one obvious example, in the case of MUE, is vowel length. Both English and Irish are characterised by phonemic vowel length, each having a set of phonemically short and phonemically long vowels. The essentially conditioned, sub-phonemic vowel length characteristic of Scots is alien to Irish and, to an extent at least, English. We would expect, then, that Irish speakers, used to having a phonemic distinction between short and long vowels, would find the English system rather than the Scots system much more compatible. But as was shown in Section 4.3, MUE vowel quantity is essentially of a Scots type, for the most part conditioned by the nature of the following consonant. Why, then, if Irish played a reinforcing role in the development of MUE phonology, did it not reinforce this important feature of the English input? Reinforcement can't be a case of cherry-picking only those features which seem to suggest it and ignoring those that don't.

Returning to the issue of the number of apparently reinforced features of a new dialect not being the result of chance, it is clear, then, that this only makes sense if we know what was affected by reinforcement and what was not, something which it is probably impossible to determine. Is the number of features that are compatible between MUE and Ulster Irish so great that we can only assume that reinforcement has played a role? For example, is the combination of Velar Palatalisation, epenthesis, clear [l] in all positions, deletion of /t/ and /d/ in clusters, lack of aspiration after initial /s/ and interchange of /s/ and /ʃ/ so unlikely in English and/or Scots that we are forced to assume a reinforcing role for Irish in their preservation in MUE? The answer to this must be 'no', given that precisely this combination of features was characteristic of various English dialects and, Velar Palatalisation aside, Scots dialects that were brought to Ulster during the Plantation and its associated settlements. There is nothing unique or unusual about this combination from a British perspective (all of them were widespread in England in the nineteenth century), even if few modern dialects in the twentieth century retained all of these features. And given that all of these features survived in English and/or Scots dialects that have not been subject to possible reinforcement from Irish (or Gaelic), there is no reason to assume that they can't have survived in MUE in precisely the same way, especially given the peripheral position of the dialect (as discussed in Section 5.3.2 below). These problems with reinforcement are similar to the ones that characterise claims of colonial lag, also discussed in Section 5.3.2.

There are other problems with the notion of reinforcement too. If, as Maguire (2018: 20) suggests, reinforcement involves 'strengthening or preservation of a feature in the target language which might otherwise be expected to disappear due to it being a variable or recessive feature', the obvious point for this influence to manifest itself is in the formation of the new dialect which comes to be characterised by the feature (see also Knooihuizen 2009). During this period of new dialect formation (see further Section 5.3.1 below), a crucial factor in survival of features of the input varieties is how common they are in the pool of variants that the first couple of generations of children are exposed to. If a feature is in the majority, it is likely to become established in the new dialect, but not if it isn't. This means that Irish learners of English could have tipped the balance for particular features surviving if their speech was characterised by the same feature as was found in the speech of large numbers of native speakers of the target language. But given that the shift from Irish to English occurred over a 300–400-year period, it is not the case that in the initial stages of development of MUE large numbers of Irish learners of English were part of the new dialect-formation process. Some no doubt were, and it is not impossible that they had such an effect (though as noted above, it is impossible to tell whether or not this was the case), but if they did the features involved must already have been common in the English and Scots input and would have stood a very good chance of surviving anyway. Once this initial period of new dialect formation, lasting only a couple of generations (see Section 5.3.1), was over, new Irish learners of English would not have been in a position to tip the balance in favour of one feature or another, since the dialect would have become focused and been characterised not by a mix of competing input variants but by an established suite of features.

Once MUE had become established and stabilised with a particular set of features, i.e. as soon as the initial period of new dialect formation was over, it is not clear that reinforcement from Irish could have easily affected the dialect. The Irish learners of MUE were no longer faced with a pool of competing variants, some of which were more compatible with Irish phonology than others, but by a focused set of variants that they would learn as best they could. The only way they could reinforce particular features of MUE thereafter is if there was variation in the dialect, as a result for example of a feature being lost from it as part of a general trend in English. In such cases, the Irish learners of English would have to find the recessive feature more compatible with their Irish phonology than the new one and thus easier to learn than it, leading to more speakers of MUE having the recessive feature in their speech and so halting or at least slowing its decline. For example, if epenthesis became established in MUE in the seventeenth century due to English and Scots input, but then began to decline in the dialect, Irish learners of the language would, given that epenthesis is compatible with Irish phonology and non-epenthesis is not, have added to the numbers of speakers of MUE with epenthesis, helping to preserve it in the dialect. Whilst this is possible, we again can't just rely on positive evidence. Are there features of MUE that have disappeared or changed despite the recessive form being more compatible with Irish? And have these features survived in varieties of English and Scots that have not been in contact with Irish (or Gaelic)? The answer to the second of these questions is a definite 'yes' (e.g. Velar Palatalisation and epenthesis, especially in /lm/, were common until recently in English dialects), whilst the answer to the first question may be impossible to give, though the lack of tapped realisations of /r/ outside of dental environments and the recessive nature of TH-stopping before /r/ in MUE ([θ] now being common in the dialect in words such as *three*, see Section 3.7) suggest that reinforcement has not retarded development of features of MUE that are not compatible with Irish phonology. When we set all of this in the context of the wider population of Ulster, of which the Irish learners were only ever a minority who 'did not enjoy much social or political prestige' (Thomason and Kaufman 1988: 117), it is no surprise that we can't easily identify cases of reinforcement of this kind, as they were unlikely to have been in a position, demographically or sociolinguistically, to have affected the further phonological development of the dialect.

Whilst reinforcement is an attractive idea, it is, as Maguire (2018: 20) points out, essentially 'impossible to prove that it happened if the reinforcement did not lead to some change, however minor, in the feature, distinguishing it from what might well have been inherited in any case' (see further Siegel 1999). The number of features of the phonology of MUE which have been identified in Chapters 3 and 4 as possibly involving reinforcement from Irish is not overwhelming, an assumption of reinforcement in these cases involves a degree of cherry-picking since only positive evidence is available, these features and combinations of them were characteristic of English and Scots dialects into the twentieth century at least, and in almost all cases the patterns in MUE are more similar to those in English and/or Scots than to those in Irish. In other words, it is entirely plausible that the combination of phonological features with suspected reinforcement would have existed in the dialect anyway had there been no input from Irish, especially given the peripheral status of the dialect and the somewhat conservative nature of aspects of its phonology discussed further in Section 5.3.2.

If these cases of reinforcement are in doubt, then the contribution of Irish to the phonological development of MUE was peripheral, and the role of the language in the development of Palatal Velarisation (Section 3.4) may thus need to be reappraised too, given that it is the only apparently clear-cut example of Irish interference that has been identified in the non-loanword phonology of the dialect.

5.2.2 Lexis and syntax

This book is about the phonological origins of MUE, and the analysis in it shows that contact with Irish has had minimal impact, especially once the notion of reinforcement is interrogated. But it is worth briefly comparing these findings to evidence that Irish has contributed to the lexis and syntax of MUE (as well as other IrE dialects) and suggesting explanations as to why phonology might be acting differently in this respect.

Turning first to lexis, it is obvious that varieties of IrE, including MUE, have adopted large numbers of place-names from Irish. A glance at a map of any part of Ulster shows that place-names of Irish origin predominate. In addition, dialects of IrE, including MUE, contain some borrowed lexical items from Irish. But neither of these things is unexpected in a situation of language shift, and indeed both are characteristic of varieties of English in North America and the southern hemisphere which show no phonological or syntactic influence from indigenous languages. The adoption of local place-names and some lexical items occurs even when the L1 and shifting populations are small relative to the target language population. Typically loanwords are in semantic fields associated with native technologies, practices and local knowledge (Thomason and Kaufman 1988: 77). An examination of Macafee (1996) shows that although Irish loanwords are not uncommon in Ulster dialects, they are not an over-riding characteristic of them either, and they are largely restricted to exactly the kinds of semantic fields just referred to. There has been little impact on core, basic vocabulary. And given that Macafee (1996) is a collection of 'unusual' words that have been noted in Ulster dialects, not just MUE but also contact varieties in former and current Gaeltacht areas, the appearance of substantial numbers of words of Irish origin in the dictionary is not surprising. A more objective picture of the lexical impact of contact with Irish on MUE can be gained by examining the origins of words in a fixed meaning list. As part of my survey of the traditional MUE dialect of south-west Tyrone, I have elicited answers to the SED questionnaire (Orton 1962) from two traditional male speakers of the dialect born in the late 1930s and early 1940s, one Protestant (who answered the whole questionnaire) and one Catholic (who answers Books I–IV of the questionnaire). The dialects of both speakers was characterised by a rich use of traditional phonological, morphosyntactic and lexical features, and their answers to the first four books of the SED questionnaire are very similar. The questions in these books (i.e. a fixed meaning list), which cover semantic fields related to agriculture and the natural environment, provide an excellent opportunity for assessing the impact of Irish on the lexis of this MUE dialect. The Protestant speaker answered 422 questions from SED books I–IV, and of the responses he gave five contained items unambiguously derived from Irish, with a further one item which could have had an origin in either English/Scots or Irish. The Catholic speaker answered 330 question from SED books I–IV, and of his responses only one contained an item of unambiguous Irish origin, whilst another answer could have had an origin in either English/Scots or Irish. That is, of the answers these speakers gave to this part of the SED questionnaire, only 1.30 per cent and 0.45 per cent respectively were from Irish (the Protestant speaker in fact giving significantly more answers containing words of Irish origin than the Catholic speaker). This cannot be the result of dialect levelling, since the answers these speakers gave are replete with non-standard lexical items found in English and Scots dialects. The evidence suggests that even in semantic areas where we might expect Irish influence on the lexis of the dialect, it was minimal. If this is typical (and the dialect is a typical traditional MUE dialect in other respects), this suggests that lexical interference from Irish on MUE has been slight, other than in the adoption of place-names. This is not surprising given the situation of language shift that characterised the area.

Assessing the impact of contact with Irish on the syntax of MUE is rather more difficult. There does appear to have been some impact, given the well-known presence of syntactic features in the dialect that are hypothesised to be of Irish origin (in part at least). Characteristic IrE syntactic features such as 'habitual *be*' (Filppula 1999: 135–50; Harris 1993: 162–3; Hickey 2007a: 213–32), the '*after* perfect' (Filppula 1999: 99–107; Harris 1993: 141, 160–1; Hickey 2007a: 197–208; Ó Corráin 2006), 'subordinating *and*' (Filppula 1999: 196–208; Harris 1993: 165–6; Hickey 2007a: 261–5), as well as patterns of word order typically attributed to Irish in indirect questions (Filppula 1999: 167–79; Harris 1993: 167–8; Henry 1995: 105–23; Hickey 2007a: 273–6) and specific uses of prepositions (Filppula 1999: 218–41; Harris 1993: 171–3; Hickey 2007a: 246–51), are all features of MUE, for example. Although Filppula (1999) has identified some EModE and dialectal English parallels to these and other syntactic features, in most cases a role for Irish is likely, and usually of more than a reinforcing kind. That said, many of the syntactic features identified as being of Irish contact origin by Filppula in IrE are rather less typical of MUE or are absent from the dialect entirely, so that MUE is probably the least Irish-like dialect in terms of its syntax. Furthermore, the syntactic input to MUE from Scots, though touched upon by Filppula and others, is not explored in detail, and it is possible that further parallels exist between Scots and MUE in these respects. It should also be noted that we are dealing here with a relatively small number of constructions, some of which are relatively common, others less so, and that the syntax of MUE is for the most part transparently English (and/or Scots) in origin and character, as indicated in the passage given in Section 5.3.1.

Regardless of this, the Irish origin of various syntactic features of MUE seems clear, and this thus contrasts with the lack of definite Irish input to the phonology of the dialect. Thomason and Kaufman (1988: 60) suggest that '[i]n interference through shift, if there is phonological interference there is sure to be some syntactic interference as well, and vice versa'. We know that there has been some syntactic interference from Irish in the development of MUE, and this suggests, if Thomason and Kaufman are right, that there ought to be some phonological interference too. But the analysis in this book suggests that such phonological interference has been limited, and an explanation of why this contrast exists is required. A detailed exploration of this question is beyond the scope of this book, but a few tentative suggestions are offered here as avenues for further research.

Phonology and syntax are typically conceived of as rather different things by linguists, both in their synchronic status and patterning and in their diachronic development (see Bermúdez-Otero and Honeybone 2006; Matras 2009, esp. pp. 193–233). Phonology is a closed, integrated system of frequently repeated, rule-governed patterns, whilst syntax is a rather more open-ended system of constructions, many of which are related to lexical properties of the constituents involved (including, for example, the '*after* perfect'), and although they too are repeated, this may, in the manner of lexis, be infrequent. It should be no surprise, then, that they act differently synchronically and diachronically. The regular changes we see in phonology that have formed such an important part of historical linguistic study are not found in syntax, for example, and specific syntactic constructions such as the '*after* perfect' can be borrowed like lexical items without significant disruption of the wider linguistic system.

A further, and related, difference between phonology and syntax is highlighted in Eckert and Labov (2017). Eckert and Labov (2017) state that '[p]honological variables are most readily adapted to convey social meaning by their frequency, flexibility and freedom from referential functions' (p. 467) and that the 'social meaning in variation' has 'its locus in the phonological system' (p. 468). Conversely, they argue (p. 470) that 'socially meaningful variation is not equally distributed over all phases of language structure, and that the more abstract categories and processes may not be socially evaluated by users of the language'. This is true not only of abstract phonological phenomena such as splits and mergers, but also to an extent of syntactic patterns which, although they vary between different speakers and communities, are not as commonly put to the same social work as surface phonological patterns.

An important consequence of this is that phonological patterns are not just, in the language of Labov (1972), sociolinguistic 'indicators' (patterns which are 'differentiated only in their relative degrees of advancement among the initiating social groups'; Labov 1994: 78); they also frequently become 'markers' (which 'show consistent stylistic and social stratification'; ibid.) and 'stereotypes' (variables which 'are overt topics of social comment and show both correction and hypercorrection'; ibid.). Or, in terms of the concept of 'indexical order' (Silverstein 2003), phonological patterns 'can progress from indexing a social position (e.g. with a region, a class position, an ethnic group) to indexing some quality apparently associated with the people occupying that social position' (Eckert and Labov 2017: 470), something which is rather less commonly true of syntactic constructions, at least in spoken language.

An outcome of this, in the context of language contact in Plantation and post-Plantation Ulster, is that phonological variables which showed influence from Irish would be likely to index particular meanings such as 'Irish', 'Catholic', 'rural' and 'poor', and thus would be evaluated in the same way as those meanings. In as much as these associations were viewed negatively, they would be unlikely to be imitated by native speakers (cf. Thomason and Kaufman 1988: 43), and would have been subject to levelling, especially given the long-term language shift and the demographic insignificance of the shifting population compared to the native-speaker population across the province at any given time. This would result in phonological features of Irish origin failing to become established in the wider MUE speech community, even though they would have been common in the speech of shifting speakers.

What is true of phonological features need not, however, be true of syntactic features. Although syntactic features of Irish origin would have been present in the speech of shifting speakers, production of these would have been relatively infrequent, at least in comparison with phonological features, and they would not in most cases have developed meaning beyond the level of the sociolinguistic indicator. As such, they would not have been subject to the same sociolinguistic pressures as phonological features of Irish origin, and some would have persisted in the speech community, ultimately becoming divorced from their language-shift origins. They would thus be more likely to become part of MUE more generally, especially since native speakers would not have assigned negative meanings to them. So although both syntactic and phonological patterns of Irish origin would have been present in the speech of shifting speakers, some of the former would have escaped notice and would not have been edited out, especially in cases where there were parallels in English and Scots, whereas the latter were more likely to have been recognised as different and socially marked, and would thus have been subject to rejection by native speakers and levelling amongst post-language-shift speakers.

These suggestions are of course only tentative, and much further research is needed in order to determine why phonological and syntactic features of Irish origin have behaved differently. That syntax and phonology might be subject to divergent developments is not surprising given their contrasting natures, and it is likely that the particular circumstances of language contact and shift in Ulster explain their differing contributions to MUE.

5.2.3 Summary

The limited evidence for phonological influence from Irish on MUE follows from what we know of the linguistic history of Ulster. MUE had a very substantial native-speaker founding population, within a century probably in the majority in the province. These speakers of English and Scots would have had little reason or inclination to learn Irish, whilst speakers of Irish, initially in the towns and lowlands, but increasingly elsewhere, became bilingual as part of a long process of language shift. Over the next three to four centuries, Irish-speaking communities shifted to English in Ulster and, given the size of the English-speaking population and the length of the shift, these speakers can only have been a relatively small minority at any given time, in contrast to other parts of Ireland where there was a rapid language shift in the nineteenth century. Throughout much of the period they were most characteristic of peripheral, less populous areas, and at all times they lacked prestige and power. These factors together meant that their impact on the phonological development of MUE was negligible, though the evidence from lexical and syntactic interference suggests that they did nevertheless contribute to the development of the dialect more generally, though in the terms of Thomason and Kaufman (1988: 121–9), this only amounted to 'slight interference'. Indeed, MUE shares more in common with other extra-territorial dialects of English that developed in situations of settlement colonisation in North America and the southern hemisphere, which evidence only superficial signs of contact with indigenous languages, than with languages and dialects that have been subject to moderate to heavy interference (Thomason and Kaufman 1988: 129–46), including at least some forms of English in southern Ireland.

Whilst reinforcement of various phonological developments in MUE from Irish is possible, this notion has been shown to be problematic. As Maguire (2018: 20) asks, 'unless the process of reinforcement changed something, how do we know it happened at all?'. An overwhelming preponderance of phonological features that just happen to be shared by Irish and MUE would be a sign that reinforcement has been in play, but it is not clear that the number of features for which reinforcement is suspected is anything other than the product of chance, and we must avoid cherry-picking of the data to highlight these cases whilst ignoring other cases where reinforcement has not occurred.

A crucial point in this analysis is this. None of the English or Scots explanations for phonological features of MUE involves special pleading. In almost every case they are obvious and a British origin of the features can hardly be doubted. The same is not true of Irish explanations. In almost every case, an Irish explanation is less good than a British one, the similarities being superficial or rather poor. In other words, this is not just a hypothesis, but is demonstrated by the evidence presented in Chapters 3 and 4. The tragic loss of the Irish language in Ulster is not mitigated by an effort to find traces of Irish influence in MUE phonology, and indeed the lack of significant input to the dialect from Irish speaks of the massive linguistic inequalities that the Plantation of Ulster and its associated settlements helped to create.

The lack of Irish input to the phonological development of MUE has another consequence. Since phonological features of Irish origin are mostly lacking in the dialect, it is impossible that differences between Protestant and Catholic pronunciation can be explained through an appeal to the differing linguistic backgrounds of these speakers (as argued in Todd 1984, 1989). If features of Irish origin are essentially absent in the phonology of MUE, then they cannot be more characteristic of Catholic speech. If such differences did once exist (e.g. in Gaeltacht and post-Gaeltacht areas of Ulster, which often have a higher Catholic proportion of the population), they have failed to become established in MUE more generally. Any differences that exist in the phonologies of Catholics and Protestants today, such as those identified in (London)Derry by McCafferty, are a result of differences in residence, political and social identity and attitudes towards local and non-local forms of speech. That is, they are the kinds of differences we would expect to develop between any two ethno-religious groups, and in most cases their history is unlikely to be very deep.

5.3 The English input to MUE

5.3.1 *The English input and New Dialect Formation*

Whatever else it is, MUE is a dialect of English. Its English character is obvious in its morphology, syntax and lexis, which for the most part are shared with other varieties of English of a southern and Midland type, though many of these features are also found in English and Scots throughout Britain and beyond. The following excerpt from a conversation with the traditional speaker PM43 in the SwTE corpus, given in StE orthography but with no standardisation of morphology, syntax and lexis, illustrates this point.

> **Interviewer**: And did you ever have any pet lambs or pet pigs or anything?
> **PM43**: Aye, we'd pet pigs.
> **Interviewer**: Right.
> **PM43**: We used to have pet pigs in a tea chest in the house up beside the fire and they used to be fed with, just with milk in a bottle, you know, and a tit on it and
> **Interviewer**: What size of pigs were they?
> **PM43**: Och, they were wee pigs and then they'd have been maybe six or seven weeks before they'd have went outside.
> **Interviewer**: Right.
> **PM43**: Maybe up to ten weeks. And I mind[1] when people used to be in on their cailey,[2] there'd have been two pigs maybe in a box and they'd have sit up in the box, sit up with their two front feet out over the box listening to the whole conversation.
> **Interviewer**: I'd love to have seen that.
> **PM43**: And then whenever they were took out then to be fed, then they skipped round the floor and said 'wugh, wugh', you know the way they do there,
> **Interviewer**: Uh-huh.
> **PM43**: and run under the table and all.
> **Interviewer**: Uh-huh.
> **PM43**: But they used to, when people come in at night they just, they never done nothing or they, they made no noise or nothing. They just sit there with their two front feet out over the edge of the box, watching from one to the other and listening to every word.

Despite the existence of various non-standard morphological, syntactic and lexical features, the core English character of the dialect is clear. This is also true of many aspects of the phonology of MUE. In terms of its lexical distribution of vowel phonemes, MUE is of a non-regional Midland or southern English type closely related to the Early Modern ancestor of StE, though one that retains various patterns long lost in StE and in many English dialects. The realisation of consonant phonemes in the dialect also has close similarities with English, though again many of the features which characterise the consonants of MUE are no longer found in StE and many English dialects, though they were once (and in some cases fairly recently) widespread.

How do we explain the non-regional Midland/southern/StE character of the phonology of MUE? The key to this is the origin of the seventeenth-century English settlers in the province. As was outlined in Chapter 2, the English settlers in Ulster came from across the Midlands and south of England, but rarely from the north of the country. For example, settlers came from counties such as Devon, Bedfordshire, Norfolk and Staffordshire, and it does not appear to be the case that settlers from any one of these areas predominated. The English settlers mostly came to Ulster in the early and mid seventeenth century, i.e. over a relatively short period of time, and, together with the seventeenth- and eighteenth-century Scots settlers, they massively outnumbered any previous English presence in the province, which was only ever tenuous and which thus could not have constituted a founding population (see below).

The coming together in Ulster of English settlers from different parts of the Midlands and south of England provides the perfect circumstances for koinéisation (Siegel 1985) and New Dialect Formation (NDF; Trudgill 2004), well-known outcomes in other cases of settlement colonisation involving a mix of dialects of English (or of other languages), as was the case, for example, in the settlement of New Zealand. Koinéisation, leading to NDF, has a number of stages involving various processes (see in particular Siegel 1985: 372–6; Trudgill 2004: 83–128). The first of these stages occurs as a result of contact between the first adult settlers in (or even en route to) the new colony. As a result of differences between their speech, speakers of different dialects in the new colony accommodate to each other, leading to 'rudimentary levelling' of features, i.e. the suppression of extremely local variants that are not shared by their interlocutors. Even though speakers have not lost knowledge of these features, the new dialect has already started to take shape, since these features are being edited out of the mix and the result is that speakers use, where possible, forms that are shared between their dialects. In the context of Plantation Ulster, we can envisage the suppression of the most marked phonological features of dialects from places like the south-west, East Anglia and the West Midlands in this stage of the formation of the new dialect.

The next stage in the formation of a new dialect occurs when the children of the first settlers in a new colony learn the language. These children find themselves in a rather different situation than their parents. There is no one fixed model for the local dialect, and they have an extremely heterogeneous linguistic input, with parents and neighbours potentially having rather different dialects, even taking into account the effects of rudimentary levelling. Trudgill (2004: 100–8) finds that this gives rise to a situation of 'extreme variability', that is, a situation in which there is considerable inter- and intra-speaker variation, with many unusual combinations that are not present in the input dialects themselves. But despite this, the speech of this first generation of children born in the colony already shows significant signs of levelling of localised and minority features of the input dialects. Trudgill (2004: 110–12) adds a 'Threshold Rider' to this period of extreme variability, whereby forms which are insufficiently common in the speech of the original settlers (say at levels of below 10 per cent), even after the rudimentary levelling in the first stage of the formation of the dialect, are unlikely to make it into the second-stage mix, simply because they are not prominent enough in the new speech community to be noticed by child learners. Thus in seventeenth-century Ulster, it was likely that there was initially a profusion of variants and unique combinations of features from dialects across the Midlands and south of England, but a loss already at this stage of the most localised phonological patterns.

The final stage in NDF is 'stabilisation' or 'focusing', and according to Trudgill (2004: 113–28) this takes place in the next generation of speakers (i.e. amongst the grandchildren of the original adult settlers). It is this generation which completes the formation of the new dialect, converging on a set of shared features which predominate in the speech of their parents. Trudgill makes the point that this process, and indeed each stage of NDF, is essentially 'deterministic': those features which are in the majority in the heterogeneous speech of the second generation will be the ones inherited by the third generation, whilst minority variants will not survive. That is, the new dialect is a koiné or 'compromise subsystem' (Siegel 1985: 373). This is a crucial feature of the NDF process, and results in the new dialect being characterised by features which were shared by the input dialects and lacking features that were regionally restricted in the home country. The result in seventeenth-century Ulster must have been an English dialect which was characterised by phonological features found in a wide range of Midland and southern English dialects but which lacked patterns specific to particular regions of England.

A further aspect of koinéisation and NDF is that it is typically characterised by a degree of simplification and unmarking (Siegel 1985: 376; Trudgill 2004: 85–6). In essence, in the formation of new dialects, simple linguistic features will be preferred to complex, marked ones, even in cases where the complex, marked feature is in the majority. This is a result of the rapidity of formation of the dialect and the heterogeneity of the input that the second and third generations are faced with, such that it is easier for them to learn and generalise more regular and less complex features that are present in the input. It is no surprise, then, that MUE lacks a number of phonological distinctions found in some southern and Midland English dialects, for example, the contrasts between the vowel which derived from ME /ai/ (in words like *bait*) and the vowel which derived from ME /a:/ (in words like *mate*), given that learning a merger is easier than learning a distinction (Labov 1994: 313–21). It may also explain the failure of the FOOT–STRUT split to survive in the dialect, even though lowered forms of the vowel were generalised to words of both kinds (Sections 4.2.1 and 4.4.5). It suggests, on the other hand, that PreRD and its associated features, which involve complex morphological conditioning, must have been very much in the majority in the input to have survived in an essentially identical form in MUE (and other IrE dialects) to what is found in Britain.

Trudgill (2004) identifies a number of other factors that determine the outcome of NDF. One important factor is that his model of NDF assumes a '*tabula rasa*' situation in order for it to work (Trudgill 2004: 26). By this, Trudgill means that 'there is no prior existing population speaking the language in question, either in the location in question or nearby' (ibid.). Why this should be so is connected with the idea of the 'Founder Effect' or 'Founder Principle' (Mufwene 1996; Trudgill 2004: 163–4). The idea behind the Founder Effect is that the first population to bring their speech to a new territory is the most important for establishing the linguistic character of the new dialect that will be spoken there. As Trudgill (2004: 163) puts it, 'the lin-guistic founding population of an area has a built-in advantage when it comes to the continuing influence and survival of their speech forms, as opposed to those of later arrivals'. This effect can be the result of the founding population being big enough that subsequent arrivals do not have a significant impact on the development of the dialect, and even with a smaller founding population it results from the fact that the speech community already has established sociolinguistic norms so that the children of new immigrants aren't in a situation of having to pick features at random from the initial settler population. In other words, an essential component of Trudgill's NDF model and the determinism that accompanies it is absent in such situations.

In fact, the Founder Effect requires a certain amount of qualification, since Trudgill (2004: 164) notes that small numbers of early English-speaking settlers in New Zealand in 1800, for example, were 'swamped out' by a much larger group of settlers forty years later, and it was the dialects of these later speakers that gave rise to New Zealand English. This is of course not surprising, since the language of any founding population can be overwhelmed by later immigrants to the area (as has frequently happened to the languages of indigenous populations). This means that *tabula rasa* does not mean that there were no speakers of the language prior to the main settlement in a new territory, but rather that the previous population was linguistically unimportant for the future development of the new dialect. As Trudgill (2004: 164) puts it in reference to Mufwene (2001), 'the founder principle works unless it doesn't'. But the general point remains that if a founding popula-tion has already established a dialect in a new territory, this is likely to underlie the further development of the language in the area regardless of future immigration, unless the speakers of this established variety are overwhelmed demographically. It seems likely that the English settlements in Ulster prior to the Plantation were so demographically insignificant compared to the massive population changes of the following century that they played no role in the development of MUE, just as the original small founding population in New Zealand had no input to the later devel-opment of the dialect. Certainly, there is no evidence that phonological features of MUE (as discussed in Chapters 3 and 4) require input from this source rather than from seventeenth-century English.

Trudgill (2004) also claims that deterministic NDF operates free of the socio-linguistic constraints that were present in the home country. That is, indexing of linguistic features in the colony with factors such as prestige, stigma and identity is absent, since this depends on pre-existing social conventions which simply don't exist in the new speech community (Trudgill 2004: 151–7). If children have no linguistic model to follow, they can hardly be expected to follow the original sociolinguistic conventions and associations of the input dialects either. This aspect of Trudgill's NDF model has been challenged, however. For example, Kerswill (2007: 660) argues that Trudgill's hypothesis may be theoretically true in 'a single, completely isolated settlement of transported, unsocialized children ... until a new social order emerges'. But Kerswill points out that the settlers in New Zealand, for example, 'came with cultural baggage, even if ... much of it was discarded' (ibid.: 659). As a result, the kinds of social stratification that were found in Britain were replicated in the colony, so that there was never a social disconnect between the

pre-settlement and post-settlement social order, and children growing up in New
Zealand would have had to operate within existing social structures. As a result,
they, like children in Britain, would have had similar experiences in terms of prestige, stigma and identity. A similar point is made by Schneider (2007, 2008), who
develops a 'Dynamic Model' of the development of colonial varieties in which identity plays a role throughout the formation and development of English in colonial
settings. Schneider's Dynamic Model and Kerswill's arguments suggest that social
factors such as prestige, stigma and identity do play a role in the development of
new dialects, but at the same time they fit well with models of koinéisation and with
Trudgill's stages of NDF. Indeed, Kerswill (2007: 659) notes that Trudgill's 'thesis is
plausible, not only because the data does not contradict it, but also because it often
gives support for it' and that 'for virtually every variable the force of T[rudgill]'s
numerical argument holds'. The role of social factors in directing change is particularly important in contact with the indigenous language(s), something that Trudgill
does not touch upon, but which must have been crucial in Plantation Ulster, as is
discussed in Section 2.4. Social factors must also have an effect in the initial rudimentary levelling of a dialect, since the adult speakers involved in contact are aware
of the issues of prestige, stigma and identity that characterise their original speech
community, and this may lead to the levelling going in a particular direction (for
example, the suppression of not only highly localised but also of non-standard and/
or stigmatised forms). Although Kerswill and especially Schneider argue for an
ongoing role for social factors in the development of post-colonial varieties, this
need not affect the kind of deterministic, child-learner koinéisation process that
Trudgill models, though it may well have consequences for directions of change
(for example, alignment with or away from the home country variety, as is discussed
further in Section 5.3.2) once the new dialect has stabilised. But in as much as the
seventeenth-century English settlers considered certain forms to be prestigious or
stigmatised, this may have influenced which variants survived the initial rudimentary levelling, and may be one explanation for the similarity between the phonology
of MUE and Early Modern StE discussed further below.

Applying Siegel's and Trudgill's models of koinéisation to the formation of MUE
makes sense given the geographical heterogeneity of the English settlers, and a
scenario of NDF indeed appears to predict much of what we find in the phonology
(and in other aspects) of the dialect. For example, the consonant features and the
lexical distribution of vowels in MUE phonology do not match the phonology of
any one area of England and are of a fairly generic, though somewhat conservative,
English type. As has been noted, MUE shares much in common with Early Modern
StE, and this is also not surprising in the context of the process of NDF. Standard
English itself developed as a result of koinéisation when dialects from across the
Midlands and south of England found themselves in contact in London, leading to a
compromise variety that is not quite like any of the surrounding dialects and which
shares features that have a wide geographic distribution (Thomason and Kaufman
1988: 304–6). Furthermore, StE would, even in the seventeenth century, have been
known and used in various forms across the Midlands and south of England and
would already have had an impact on the phonologies of these dialects (by, for
example, adding to the range of variants of particular phonological features). Indeed,

it is possible that regiolect koinés close to StE, such as characterise large swathes of England today (Trudgill 1999a: 80–4; Williams and Kerswill 1999), were already forming in the Midlands and south in the Early Modern period (see Anderson 1987: 3–4 for discussion of this idea). This means that the Midland and southern dialects of English that were brought to Ulster in the seventeenth century would have shared even more in common than they might have otherwise, and many of these features would also have been shared by StE. In the resulting dialect mix, these features shared by StE would have escaped rudimentary levelling, especially if they were considered to prestigious, or at least not stigmatised, and would have been prominent in the extreme variation found in the second generation, leading to a greater likelihood of survival in the new dialect. It should not be surprising, then, that MUE shares many phonological characteristics with varieties of seventeenth-century StE.

5.3.2 Conservatism

At least in terms of its consonantal features and its lexical distribution of vowel phonemes, MUE appears to be rather conservative even compared to the traditional dialects of English found across the Midlands and south of England in the twentieth century. For example, it retains features such as PreRD, VP, rhoticity, onset /h/ (including in /hw/), deletion of /d/ after /n/ and /l/, the MOUTH vowel in the OLD subset, and the TRAP/BATH vowel in words like *wash* and *watch*, and lacks mergers of MEET and MEAT, of NORTH and FORCE, of BOOK and FOOT, and of the various NURSE subsets (including some retention of /ar/ in SERVE), all of which were once widespread in England.

This apparent conservatism of MUE has been noticed by previous commentators (see, for example, Harris 1993: 140–2; Milroy 1981: 2–3), and indeed there is a tradition of claiming that English in Ulster has a special relationship with Elizabethan English and the language of Shakespeare. In the early years of the twentieth century, Sir John William Byers published a short treatise called 'Shakespeare and the Ulster Dialect' (Byers 1916), which compares features of Ulster English (by which he means MUE) with the language used by the Bard. Byers (1916: 6) claimed that although

> a glossary of more than 2,000 words would be required to enable a modern Englishman to read his Shakespeare, probably about 200 words (one in ten) or less, would be all that an intelligent North of Ireland person would need to understand the works of the greatest of poets and dramatists.

Similarly, the author St. John Greer Ervine, born in Belfast in the late nineteenth century, 'advised his readers to go to Ulster if they wanted to hear English spoken as it was in Shakespeare's day' (Braidwood 1964: 46). And the 'Bard of Tyrone', the Rev. W. F. Marshall, strikingly claimed that 'you can hear Elizabethan English in every county in the North of Ireland' (Braidwood 1964: 46). This connection has entered public consciousness, as exemplified by the recording made in Omagh in Co. Tyrone in 2004 for the BBC 'Voices' project, in which the participants connect features of the local dialect with the language of Shakespeare and Elizabethan English more generally.[3]

Mid-Ulster English is not of course the only modern dialect of English to be compared to the language of Shakespeare. Joyce (1910: 6) states that in the seventeenth century 'the native Irish people learned to speak Elizabethan English – the very language used by Shakespeare', and that 'the remnants of the Elizabethan English are spread all over Ireland' (ibid.: 7; see further Hickey 2007a: 297–8). And in North America, '[t]he idea that in isolated places somewhere in the country people still use "Elizabethan" or "Shakespearean" speech is widely held' (Montgomery 1998: 66), with a particular association with the isolated dialects of mountainous areas such as Appalachia and the Ozarks, though this 'ignores many things that linguists know to be true' (ibid.: 72).

Whilst this enduring identification of out-of-the-way dialects of English with the language of Shakespeare may seem fanciful (indeed, Montgomery's aim is to debunk this 'myth'), it is not surprising that Ulster English has been amongst those varieties most frequently connected in the public (and, in the past, the linguistic) imagination with Elizabethan English and the language of Shakespeare. The Plantation of Ulster overlapped the life of Shakespeare and was preceded by the Elizabethan conquest of the province, whilst the first Plantation settlers spoke forms of Jacobean English, often from the English Midlands (including from counties in the West Midlands, as discussed in Chapter 2). And of course some well-known features of MUE that are not found in StE today do have close parallels in the language of Shakespeare, for example, the forms *ax* for 'ask' and *hit* for 'it', though this is true for all dialects of English and requires us to ignore the many other dissimilarities that are evident. But there are more serious questions here. Can MUE be considered to be conservative phonologically, as it appears to be, retaining more of the phonological character of its Early Modern input than dialects of English in the Midlands of Britain, for example, and, if it does, why should this be so?

The idea that MUE might be conservative, indeed might be more similar to Elizabethan English and the language of Shakespeare than it 'ought' to be, ties in with the notion of 'colonial lag'. Ellis (1869: 20) claimed that

> there is a kind of arrest of development, the language of the emigrants remains for a long time at the stage in which it was at when emigration took place, and alters more slowly than the mother tongue, and in a different direction.

Ellis points towards Icelandic, North American English and, indeed, Irish English as examples of such a phenomenon. This idea is set out in Marckwardt (1958: 80), in his discussion of the apparent archaism of American English, as follows:

> These post-colonial survivals of earlier phases of mother-country culture, taken in conjunction with the retention of earlier linguistic features, have made what I should like to call a colonial lag. I mean to suggest by this term nothing more than that in a transplanted civilization, as ours undeniably is, certain features which it possessed remain static over a period of time. Transplanting usually results in a time lag before the organism, be it a geranium or a brook trout, becomes adapted to its new environment. There is no reason why the same principle should not apply to a people, their language, and their culture.

Marckwardt suggests that the very act of transplanting a language to a new territory stalls linguistic change, leading to features of the language at the point of separation being more likely to be retained in the new variety. Certainly this idea of colonial lag, if it is right, might account for why MUE appears to be conservative in many respects, even if it does not explain the mechanism by which this situation has developed.

But the notion of colonial lag has been criticised by later researchers (for example, Görlach 1987; see Hundt 2009 for a useful overview). Indeed in the revision of Marckwardt's work, J. L. Dillard interpreted the apparent archaism of North American English rather differently. He comments (Marckwardt and Dillard 1980: 69–70) that

> [w]hen speakers from the mother country comment upon their language as spoken in a colony, they are almost always struck by two things: the unprecedented innovations and the unbelievable archaisms of the colonists. This seeming paradox is fairly easily resolved: The visitors are typically struck by whatever is different from their own usage, whether it is old-fashioned or new-fangled.

These differences are explicable by the fact that 'languages change with time, but not always in the same way among various groups who speak the language' (Marckwardt and Dillard 1980: 69). In other words, dialects may be conservative in some features and innovative in others, and it is only by cherry-picking the data that a dialect can be considered to be archaic. Lass (1990b: 268) notes that

> it is possible for E[xtra]T[erritorial]E[nglishe]s (especially the older ones) to show both archaic and advanced features, often stemming from quite different layers of the Mainland evolutionary sequence; ETEs do not result from simple differential change in a monolithic input.

Indeed, Hundt (2009) suggests that the situation may be even more complicated than a simple balance of archaising and innovative tendencies, with, for example, seemingly archaic features actually representing 'resurrection' or 'revival' of certain features in one or other dialect, alongside true cases of archaism and innovation as well as parallel changes in both varieties.

Whilst rejecting the notion of colonial lag as a general stalling of change in a new environment, Trudgill (1999b, 2004) suggests that a limited version of colonial lag operates in the context of NDF. In such a scenario, he suggests that there is

> a lag or delay, which lasts for about one generation, in the normal progression and development of linguistic change, and which arises solely as an automatic consequence of the fact that there is often no common peer-group dialect for children to acquire in first-generation colonial situations involving dialect mixture. (Trudgill 2004: 34)

The result of such lag is not a general, long-lasting archaising tendency in a new dialect, but rather a brief stalling in linguistic change which will be noticeable in recently formed dialects but which will have long since disappeared in 'new' dialects with a longer history (such as MUE).

So it may be the case, if Trudgill is right, that there was a short period of lag during the formation of MUE. But this is not enough to explain the apparent archaism of aspects of the phonology of the dialect. It is quite likely, then, that the apparent archaism of MUE is only illusory and is a result of highlighting precisely those patterns which have been retained in traditional forms of the dialect and lost in StE in England, and ignoring the numerous changes that have occurred subsequently in the dialect as a result of internal evolution or contact with Scots and Irish. In this way, the apparent conservatism of dialects like MUE may be like reinforcement (Section 5.2.1); it may be a product of selective analysis and can only be proved, if at all, by showing that a wide range of features, more than could be produced by chance, are conservative.

But before we dismiss the idea of conservatism in MUE altogether, there *are* reasons why the dialect might appear to be conservative phonologically, at least in some respects, which connect with the wider notion of colonial lag. Firstly, the dialect has been 'peripheralised' geographically. The input English dialects in particular came from the Midlands and south of England, from areas in or near to the geographical and linguistic centre of gravity of the language. But when these dialects were brought to Ulster during the Plantation and its associated settlements, they were taken out of this central zone and were transplanted to a geographically peripheral area, far from the main population centres in England and from the linguistic heartland of the language. Once English had been brought to Ulster, it was partly removed and cut off from the currents of change that continued to affect English in Britain. Any changes in English which began in the linguistic centre (e.g. loss of rhoticity, /h/-dropping, merger of MEET and MEAT) will have been slower to reach peripheral areas such as Ulster, and indeed may have failed to enter the dialect. Thus we have a mechanism whereby MUE might retain certain features found in EModE that have been lost in other dialects of English. The Midland and southern origins of the English input to MUE combined with the peripheralisation of the dialect and continuing change in the linguistic heartland of the language mean that the dialect has a character that we don't find elsewhere: it is in origin (in part at least) a dialect of a central type that has been removed from the trends of change which have continued to affect these central dialects, leading to phonological conservatism in certain respects. In this sense, conservatism is not some mysterious force acting on a new dialect of a language, but rather is a not unexpected consequence of the geographical relocation of the variety affecting certain aspects of the phonology of a dialect.

Another factor that could help to explain the apparent conservatism of MUE is linguistic 'polarisation' (Hinskens *et al.* 2000: 4, 2005: 9) or 'dissociation' (Hickey 2013). Polarisation is a reaction against (or at least a disinterest towards) changes encountered in contact with another linguistic variety. Hock (1991: 428) states of polarisation that '[t]his force can act defensively, by retarding structural borrowing, but also offensively, by engendering developments diametrically opposed to what is found in other dialects or by bringing about something like hypercorrections in reverse'. As Hinskens *et al.* (2005: 9) put it, this leads at least to 'resistence to convergence', and may even involve the introduction of changes which lead to divergence (see also the discussion of dissociation in Hickey 2013). The key point in polarisation is that the speakers of a dialect do not identify with, and indeed may have antipathy to, some other dialect(s) of the language and, as a result, resist the changes that characterise them. The plantation of speakers of English from the Midlands and south of England in Ulster must have resulted in political and psychological as well as geographical peripheralisation of them and their descendants. That is, the English settlers in Ireland had a new identity (see Schneider 2007: 33–56 for an outline of this process and its linguistic effects), no longer English but British-Irish (as distinct from the Irish-Irish). Just as England was no longer their home, new features of speech in England were no longer markers of their linguistic identity. In as much, then, as the Plantation settlers had a new British-Irish identity, it would not be surprising if they rejected some incoming phonological changes from England that reached this peripheral area. This polarisation may well have resulted in a certain character of conservatism in aspects of the dialect. A modern example of this is found in the minimal inroads that RP-type English has made into the MUE dialect area, even amongst Protestant middle-class members of the community (Barry 1981b; Milroy 1981: 98–103). This can be contrasted with England where RP-type speech is not uncommon amongst middle-class speakers even in the more remote south-western and northern counties. The reason for the failure of RP to impact MUE is that the accent is viewed negatively, as the variety of another place and social class (Douglas-Cowie 1984: 541–2). This even extends to a feature such as loss of rhoticity, which characterises most English dialects, not just RP, but which is largely absent in MUE. It is likely that MUE has remained (mostly) rhotic not just because of its peripheral position but also because of a certain level of resistance to incoming English features which might threaten the linguistic identity of speakers (cf. the resistance to certain standard linguistic features in working-class Glaswegian as described in Stuart-Smith *et al.* 2007).

So it is probably the case that MUE is phonologically somewhat conservative compared to Midland and southern English dialects (including StE) *in certain respects*, and there are good reasons for this connected to peripheralisation and the formation of a new British-Irish identity. But of course the idea that MUE is phonologically conservative does involve a fair amount of cherry-picking and ignoring aspects of its phonology which show evidence of innovation and influence from the other, non-English, input varieties, and this is the major weakness with theories of colonial lag. As was discussed in Chapter 4, MUE vowel quality and quantity is not really of an English type, nor are various aspects of its lexical distribution of vowel phonemes. Indeed, conditioning of vowel quantity is one example in the dialect of considerable complexity of a sort that we would not expect to survive the process of NDF. This leads us on to the elephant in the room which has not thus far featured in the discussion of NDF in Ulster: the Scots input. The English settlers in Ulster did not operate in isolation and often lived alongside settlers from Lowland Scotland. Given that MUE looks, in substantial parts of its phonology, like the outcome of contact between different dialects of English from England, what role did these speakers from Scotland play in the process? Did their Scots speech feed into the NDF process that gave rise to MUE and, if it did, how were the radical differences between Scots and English dialects resolved? Given the very substantial settlement in the province from Scotland, why is MUE essentially of a Midland and southern English type phonologically (if not always phonetically)? And why did the Scots input to its phonological development, especially in terms of its influence on vowel quality and quantity, and on certain lexical distributions of vowel phonemes, take the form it did? It is to these issues that I turn in the next section.

5.4 The Scots input to MUE

As was discussed in the previous section, MUE is in various ways of a conservative Midland/southern English type phonologically, and this reflects the origins of the English settlers in seventeenth-century Ulster, the linguistic, social and political peripheralisation of the dialect and its speakers, and the process of NDF that must have occurred in the colony. These factors together account for much of the phonological character of the dialect. But of course the English were not the only settlers and, as was discussed in Chapter 2, Scottish settlers came to the province in large numbers too, predominating in northern and eastern parts of Ulster (as reflected by the survival of Scots in these areas), but being common throughout the MUE area. Indeed the continued Scottish settlement throughout Ulster into the early eighteenth century meant that even beyond the Scottish heartlands in Antrim, Down and Donegal they contributed significantly to the population (see Section 2.3.4). This major Scottish contribution to the population of these areas is reflected in the obvious input from Scots to MUE, as discussed in Chapters 3 and 4.

But how did this substantial Scottish settlement and the Scots dialects of these settlers interact with the process of NDF described in the previous section? It might be hypothesised that their dialects would contribute to the process in the same way as the English dialects, but there are a number of issues with this idea that suggest that things were not so straightforward as this. Firstly, there were (and are) radical linguistic differences between Midland and southern English dialects on the one hand and Scots dialects on the other, requiring a considerable degree of levelling before a compromise dialect could develop. Secondly, it is not clear whether we should conceive of this as contact between two groups of divergent dialects of the same language, or between two closely related languages. Up until 1603, Scotland and England were entirely separate kingdoms, and indeed it wasn't until 1707 that they were joined under a single parliament as 'Great Britain'. Prior to the seventeenth century, English and Scots were considered to be separate (if similar) languages, though written Scots was showing signs of a degree of convergence with English in the sixteenth century (Corbett *et al.* 2003; Maguire 2012b). And although Scots disappeared as a standard written language through the seventeenth century, being replaced by English, this really only affected the upper echelons of society. The Scottish settlers of Ulster would have spoken varieties of Scots that were as different from English as they had ever been and would almost certainly have been aware that Scots, whatever it was, was something rather different from English. In as much as we are dealing with two languages rather than two groups of dialects of the same language, it may be the case that we have to consider language shift as well as NDF in the interaction of Scots and English in Ulster (see further McColl Millar 2016). Thirdly, the kinds of input that Scots had to the phonology of MUE are of specific sorts and do not all fit well with the processes of rudimentary levelling, unmarking and focusing that play such important roles in NDF.

In a process of NDF, we would expect initial rudimentary levelling of phonological variants that were highly localised. How this might have affected the often extremely divergent Scots input in the MUE area in the first phase of the Plantation is uncertain, but if it did happen, as would seem likely given that Scottish settlers did not predominate over much of Ulster in this period, we should expect the levelling of many or indeed most of the vowel distributions that distinguish Scots from Midland and southern English dialects. In the next stage of NDF, the period of extreme variability, we would expect a complex mix of features of Scots origin in unusual combinations with English features, though already the dialect would be showing signs of having edited out the most localised input patterns. Furthermore, we would expect a breakdown in complex, marked phonological features that did not predominate in the input, an obvious candidate being the complex vowel length conditioning of the SVLR and associated patterns. Thirdly, we would expect focusing on variants that predominated in the input and which were not highly marked in terms of their complexity. Assuming that by the middle of the seventeenth century speakers of English origin and descent outnumbered those of Scottish origin and descent over most of Ulster, we would expect the phonology of the dialect to have an essentially English character, and for those features which were shared by many Scots and English dialects (e.g. in the consonantal system, where Scots and English are not so divergent) to have survived. Conversely, we would expect most specifically Scots features to have been eliminated and for complex patterns such as the SVLR not to have survived.

This scenario seems to work reasonably well for the consonants of MUE, which are essentially of an English type but which have much in common with Scots dialects too. Specifically English features such as VP, /t/-Voicing and loss of rhoticity before /s/ survived because they were common in the majority English input, whilst features such as /h/-retention (including in /hw/), PreRD, consonant cluster simplification, epenthesis and rhoticity generally were shared by English and Scots and were thus very likely to survive in the new dialect. But it doesn't seem to work when we consider the character of vowel quality and quantity in MUE, nor does it explain the existence of a number of conditioned lexical distributions of vowel phonemes in the dialect.

For example, how would NDF involving contact between a majority of English dialects and a substantial Scots input have produced [ʉ], [ë], [æ], [ɑː], [əʉ] and [ëi]~[aɪ] as the typical values of the vowels in the GOOSE, KIT, DRESS (short environments), TRAP (long environments), MOUTH and PRICE lexical sets, considering that none of these values were particularly typical of the English input and that all of them replicate patterns in the input Scots dialects? How would the NDF process, which typically involves simplification of complex, marked patterns, have resulted in the establishment in MUE of the SVLR (including idiosyncratic patterning of the PRICE vowels also found in Scotland), in a unique combination with the VE and PFL found otherwise only in Scots dialects? And why would /ö/ rather than /ë/ appear after /w/, /a/ rather than /ɒ/~/ɔ/ appear in the neighbourhood of labials, and /ëi/ rather than /aɪ/ occur in final position in the dialect in words which had Scots /i/ if other Scots-specific vowel lexical distributions were eliminated? None of these developments can be accommodated within an essentially deterministic process of NDF of the type that Trudgill (2004) describes.

Instead I suggest an alternative scenario which *can* explain these patterns based on what we know from other contact situations, one which may come into play when the contact is between two closely related languages (or two divergent dialect groups) rather than between a range of more and less similar dialects of the same language. This scenario follows from the fact that the Scots features in MUE resemble, to an extent at least, the results of imposition through language shift rather than of new dialect formation as modelled by Trudgill (2004). However, some parts of the phonological system that were shared in large part by the two varieties in contact, especially consonantal features, may have acted as predicted by Trudgill's NDF model. These developments are a consequence of the two varieties lying somewhere between being two different languages and two dialects of the same language.

The scenario that could have led to these effects is as follows. The Scottish settlers who came to Ulster in the seventeenth century were mostly adult Scots speakers. In the areas where English settlement predominated, these Scottish speakers learned English as a second language (or second dialect). Initially at least they may have retained their Scots L1 (or 'D1'), in the same way that speakers across Scotland have often learned English whilst maintaining their local Scots dialects (Johnston 1997b: 438–40). These adult Scottish learners of English would have carried forward Scots features into the English they were learning in the usual manner, leading to phonological (and doubtless other forms of) imposition. What kinds of phonological imposition might we expect in such a scenario? In learning English phonology, one of the most immediate tasks for Scots speakers was to learn the lexical distribution of English phonemes, especially the vowels, this being one of the defining structural differences between the two closely related languages. But in so doing, they would have carried over the realisations of their Scots phonemes. For example, the word *boot* was traditionally /bøt/ ([bøt] or the like, perhaps already unrounded to [bït]) in seventeenth-century Scots (see Section 4.4.5). In learning English /buːt/, the Scots speakers would have substituted their nearest Scots phoneme for English /uː/, and the vowel in MOUTH words in Scots ([u], probably already fronted to [ü] or even [ʉ] in the seventeenth century, as discussed in Section 4.2.5) was an obvious equivalent, resulting in a new pronunciation such as [büt] or even [bʉt] (i.e. what we find in MUE today). This is exactly what we see in the development of SSE in the seventeenth and eighteenth centuries: the variety more or less has the lexical incidence of English, but is heavily influenced by the phonetics of Scots (Aitken 1984b: 523–4; Johnston 2007: 108–9). 'More or less' is an important aspect of this process though. Where Scots did not have phonological distinctions found in English (e.g. [ʌ] vs [ʊ]), we are likely to see mergers in the new variety (as is indeed the case in SSE, which has [ʉ] as the typical vowel of both the GOOSE and FOOT lexical sets, as opposed to [ʌ] in STRUT). In MUE, this took a different route, with the FOOT and STRUT lexical sets ending up with an [ʌ]-type vowel ([ɜ]), as opposed to [ʉ] in GOOSE. This was likely the result of many of the input English dialects having no distinction between the vowels in FOOT and STRUT, so that a straightforward mapping of English [ʊ] to Scots [ʌ] was possible, doubtless encouraged by those English input varieties which already had [ʌ] in STRUT words. The collapse of the distinction between the vowel in the LOT and THOUGHT lexical sets in some traditional varieties of MUE (see Section 4.4.6) is likely to have the same explanation.

The imposition of vowel quality is expected, but so too is the imposition of vowel quantity. Vowel quantity in Scots was (and is) largely rule-governed, so that Scots speakers learning English in seventeenth-century Ulster would have imposed their vowel length rules on the English phonological system they were learning, resulting in a variety with an English-type lexical distribution of vowel phonemes but a Scots-type conditioning of vowel quantity, i.e. precisely what we find in MUE (and, not coincidentally, in SSE). Furthermore, the conditioned vowel lexical distributions of Scots origin found in MUE can also be explained by imposition as a result of language shift from Scots to English. The appearance in Scots of /ʉ/ in *mouth*, /ø/ in *boot*, /i/ in *head* and /e/ in *stone* is a set of arbitrary facts, determined by phonological history and not rule-governed in the synchronic phonology of the language. In learning English in Ulster (or indeed SSE in Scotland), Scots speakers just had to learn that *mouth* had /əʉ/, *boot* had /ʉ/, *head* had /ɛ/ and *stone* had /o/. But the appearance of /a/ rather than /ɔ/ in the neighbourhood of labials and of /ɔ̈/ rather than /ɛ̈/ after /w/ were essentially phonotactic constraints in Scots, i.e. rule-governed lexical distributions of vowel phonemes. /ɔ/ and /ɛ̈/ could not appear in these environments unless some other sub-rule was at play (e.g. /wɛ̈/ occurred before velars, as in *wig*). Phonological imposition is the imposition of rules (realisational or phonotactic) of the L1 on the TL. When Scots speakers learned English in Ulster, they imposed these constraints of Scots phonology on the TL, producing a variety of English which had a number of conditioned Scots vowel distributions, i.e. exactly what we find in MUE. The other Scots lexical distributions which were not rule-governed were replaced with English distributions, again as we see in the phonology of MUE.

This explanation for the appearance of conditioned Scots vowel lexical distributions in MUE also helps to account for the distribution of the two PRICE diphthongs, /ɛ̈i/ and /aɪ/, in the dialect. In this case, adult speakers of Scots had an extra vowel phoneme that did not correspond to anything in English. Rather than failing to produce the two diphthongs (which indeed we might expect to have merged, i.e. simplified, in a situation of NDF), the Scots speakers assigned them to separate parts of the PRICE lexical set, reflecting pre-existing lexical distinctions involving other vowels in their Scots speech. The Scots speakers learning English in Ulster knew that PRICE words could have /ɛ̈i/ or /aɪ/, but they also had a distinct DIE subset (see Section 4.4.3) in their Scots speech, so they reallocated /ɛ̈i/ to this subset and retained /aɪ/ where they had it in morpheme-final position in PRICE words in Scots already. The retention of the two diphthongs was doubtless helped by the mostly rule-governed distribution of these diphthongs in SVLR short and long PRICE environments respectively, which they also carried over into English from Scots.

All of these changes depend upon adult speaker knowledge. Adults already have grammars in place, including phonological rules and constraints (Honeybone 2019). This is what causes imposition when we learn other languages as adults. Children on the other hand do not have these rules and constraints. A child learning English does not have a set of realisational or distributional rules to overcome, and so we would not expect these kinds of changes in phonological development if the dialect derived from a child-led selection of variants in a process of NDF. Adult speakers of Scots thus played a crucial role in the development of the phonology of MUE. That this role should have been so important for the phonological development of

MUE not only stems from the initial settlement of Scots speakers in the MUE area, but also from the continued migration to this area from Scotland throughout the seventeenth century and into the early eighteenth century. As a result of this, the process outlined above was repeated again and again over the space of a century-and-a-quarter, constantly reinforcing the imposition of Scots features on English as a result of adult language shift. Given that Scottish immigrants made up at least half of the settler population in much of Ulster, and close to half throughout the rest of the majority English areas of the province, it is not surprising, then, that they should have had such a significant input to the dialect. If it is assumed that a minority of the population engaged in language shift can affect the phonological development of a language, as it often has been for Irish speakers in Ulster, then it should follow that a very substantial population of settlers engaged in a shift from Scots to English should have a much more significant effect, and this is what we find in the phonological development of MUE. Indeed, the Scots-influenced variety of English that would have developed as a result of this language shift is remarkably close to MUE as we know it in more recent times, so that it appears that the Scots input to the dialect was instrumental in giving it the phonological character that it has.

So far I have only discussed the Scottish input to vowels, to which we can add the lexical distribution of certain consonants which interacted with them, such as /x/ in words like *night* (Scots [nïxt] was replaced by MUE /nëit/) and /l/ in words like *full* (Scots [fü:] was replaced by MUE /fɔl/). But what about the realisation of consonants? The scenario outlined above would predict that Scots consonant realisations and constraints on their distribution would also have been imposed on MUE. Of course, the Scots and English consonant systems were rather similar in the first place, much more so than the vowels which had radically different lexical distributions in the two languages/dialect groups. This meant that there were far fewer differences that would result from imposition of Scots consonantal features on English in Ulster. In addition to sharing the same phonemes (with perhaps the exception of /x/, though see Section 3.2), dialects of the two varieties shared many of the same realisational and distributional rules. For example, PreRD, the change of /kl/ and /gl/ to [tl] and [dl], /h/-retention (including in /hw/), deletion of /t/ and /d/ in clusters, deletion of /b/ and /g/ after their homorganic nasals, rhoticity, clear [l] in all positions, epenthesis in liquid+sonorant clusters, and the change of /θ/ to [h] in certain words were (and are) all shared by dialects of English and Scots. It is not surprising then that these should also have become features of MUE, an issue I return to below. But the differences in consonantal features between English and Scots mean that we might expect some of these features to have developed differently in MUE if we assume a straightforward imposition of Scots consonantal realisations on English in Ulster. For example, most Scots dialects have tapped [ɾ] or trilled [r] for /r/ in onset position and in clusters, but this is not what we find in MUE. Scots dialects also typically have little aspiration of the voiceless stops, but MUE has aspiration patterns similar to what is found in RP (see Section 3.12.1). In addition, MUE is characterised by a number of consonantal features typical of English but not of Scots, including Velar Palatalisation and /t/-Voicing. How do these fit with the idea that MUE phonology developed in large part as a result of imposition of Scots features as Scottish settlers shifted to English in seventeenth- and early-eighteenth-century Ulster?

One solution to this problem is that imposition need not affect everything in the phonology of the target language. Although learners will inevitably carry through some of the phonological rules of their L1 into the target language, the learning process is more complex than that, and when faced with phonological rules in the target language, learners may well attempt to learn those too, creating an 'interlanguage' that does not quite match the phonological rules of either the L1 or the TL, but combines elements of both or compromises between them (Archibald 1998). So if the Scots settlers in Ulster were exposed to a majority of English speakers with Velar Palatalisation, as well as Irish learners of English who potentially reinforced the feature, then they could have learned this relatively straightforward phonological rule rather than imposing their Scots velar realisations in all environments. Alternatively, they may not have learned it, but given that VP is a regular realisational rule, it would have been easy for child learners, exposed to both English VP and Scots L2/D2 lack of VP, to learn it. The same goes for the realisation of /r/. If children were exposed to Scots-influenced English with [r]/[r] in onsets and varieties with English [ɹ] in all positions, it would not be difficult for them to generalise the English pattern. This is quite different from the complexities involved in, for example, vowel quantity in the dialect.

It is also possible that consonants act somewhat differently from vowels in these circumstances. Indeed, in his study of dialect-levelling changes in modern British English, Kerswill (2003: 231) describes consonants as 'torchbearers of geographical diffusion', contrasting them with vowels, changes in which do not appear to be spreading across the country in the same way. In Plantation Ulster, Scots learners of English would have noticed that although their vowels were radically different (in distribution), their consonants were really rather similar. This would make it much easier for them to implement simple realisational changes to the consonants of the sort identified by Kerswill in recent studies of British English. Exactly this situation is evident in Scotland today, for example. The Urban Scots of Glasgow is characterised by vowel distributions and realisations which are rather different from those found in English (Stuart-Smith 2003). Whilst there is evidence of redistribution of some vowel phonemes to closer match English, there is little sign of change in vowel quality and quantity towards external models. However, the consonants of Glaswegian Scots are acting in a different way altogether. Here we see substantial evidence of exogenous, English influence on realisations and distributions, with changes of English origin such as TH-Fronting (i.e. /θ/, /ð/ > /f/, /v/), increased glottal replacement of /t/ (though this is also a traditional feature of Glaswegian Scots), replacement of /x/ with /k/, coda /l/-vocalisation after all vowels, loss of the distinction between /ʍ/ (i.e. /hw/) and /w/, and loss of rhoticity becoming characteristic of the dialect (Maguire 2012b; Stuart-Smith 2003; Stuart-Smith et al. 2007). In other words, contact between Glasgow Scots and English has led to changes in the consonants, but little change in vowel realisation. Consonants can and do act differently in situations of contact between closely related varieties which share many consonantal features but which are more divergent with respect to their vowels. So the changes in the realisation of the Scottish settlers' consonants and the lack of substantial changes to their vowel qualities and quantities, which they imposed on English in Ulster, are not unexpected. This is even before we factor in the possibility that certain changes have occurred in MUE in subsequent centuries, potentially obscuring instances of imposition from Scots (e.g. on the realisation of /r/, as is discussed in Section 3.8.2).

There is a further point to be made, which arises from the close similarity between the consonant systems of seventeenth- and early-eighteenth-century Scots and English, as opposed to the sharp differences that existed in vowel realisation and distribution. This close similarity meant that the Scots consonantal values could have fed into the NDF process outlined in Section 5.3.1 in a way that the Scots vowels could not. Faced with radical differences in vowel distribution and realisation, Scots settlers learned English, imposing their vowel realisations on the target language. But since their consonantal systems were already very similar to the English ones, they would have added to the proportions of various phonological patterns present in the dialect mix, tipping the balance in favour of particular features surviving in the process of NDF. For example, the Scots settlers were rhotic, and their dialects did not have /h/-dropping (including in /hw/). This meant that they would have added to the number of speakers with these features in their speech in Plantation Ulster, so that any /h/-dropping or loss of rhoticity present in the English input would have been even more in the minority than they otherwise would have been, and thus would have failed to become established in the new dialect. This means that the other consonantal features shared by English and Scots referred to above would also have been more likely to survive in the new dialect than they might otherwise have been. This process helps to explain the presence of features such as loss of /g/ after [ŋ] and /t/-deletion in clusters in MUE, which were present in some English dialects and general in Scots. The fact that these deletions were essentially phonotactic constraints in Scots would have meant that they would also have been particularly likely to have been imposed on the English learned by the Scottish settlers.

The Scots input to the phonological development of MUE is clear, impacting as it did the quality and quantity of vowels and the distributions of some vowel phonemes. These changes were the result of adult Scottish settlers learning English and imposing Scots phonological rules on the target language. In many ways *this* was the crucial language shift in the development of the phonology of MUE, not the shift from Irish to English. But at the same time the close similarity between English and Scots consonants meant that not only did the Scots realisations and distributions of these feed into the NDF process, but also that Scots speakers were more likely to adopt some of the straightforward English realisations of them as they shifted to that language. Despite this, the large numbers of Scots settlers who came to Ulster, not only to the Ulster Scots areas of Down, Antrim, (London)Derry and Donegal but also across much of the Mid-Ulster area, meant that their speech had a considerable and lasting impact on the development of MUE.

Notes

1. 'remember'.
2. 'social visit', from Irish *céilí*.
3. https://sounds.bl.uk/Accents-and-dialects/BBC-Voices/021M-C1190X0044X X-1201V0#.

6 Conclusions

In this book, I set out to investigate the phonological origins of MUE, seeking to assess the extent to which the three main input varieties (English, Scots and Irish) contributed to its phonology and to explain why the phonology of MUE has the shape that it does. As one of the oldest 'new' extra-territorial varieties of English, one which developed in a context of language and dialect contact, MUE provides an excellent opportunity to study how new dialects develop in situations of settlement colonisation.

Chapter 2 of this book reviewed the history of Ulster in order to determine what this can tell us about the origins of the dialect and to put its development in a wider linguistic context. Although English was spoken in Ulster before the seventeenth-century Plantation, its speakers were likely to have been few in number and restricted to specific parts of the province. It is unlikely that they constituted a big enough population, especially after the tumultuous years of the second half of the sixteenth century, to have contributed to the development of MUE. It was the Plantation of Ulster and its associated settlements in the seventeenth and early eighteenth centuries that gave rise to MUE. The very large numbers of English and Scottish settlers, swamping any pre-existing British presence, brought an array of Early Modern English and Scots dialects to the province. The English settlers in Ulster came from across the Midlands and south of England, as well as from the north-west. As such, no one dialect of English was predominant amongst them, though supra-regional and Early Modern varieties of StE must have been common. The Scottish settlers mostly came from the south-western and southern fringes of Scotland, and would have spoken a variety of Early Modern West-Mid, South-Mid and Southern Scots dialects. The extent to which these Scottish settlers spoke Gaelic is uncertain; some of them must have done, but given the date of settlement and the origins of most of the settlers, this can only have been a minority.

The Plantation and its associated settlements, a classic case of settlement colonisation, rapidly transformed the demography of Ulster. By the mid seventeenth century, almost 40 per cent of the population of Ulster was of British origin. By the early eighteenth century, over 60 per cent of the population was Protestant. A large part of this was the result of continued migration of English and Scottish Protestants to the province, though conversions of some of the Irish must also have contributed towards this figure. The result of this massive demographic change over the course of little more than 100 years was that varieties of English and of Scots were thrown together in a relatively small geographical area, leading to intense linguistic contact and creating ideal conditions for the formation of a new dialect.

Despite early plans, the Plantation did not remove the Irish population from the Plantation estates, though there must have been countless cases of local displacement. The Irish often stayed on as tenants on the estates, becoming socially and, increasingly through time, geographically marginalised in the province. This meant that in the centuries since the Plantation, English has been in contact with Irish in Ulster. But the very large numbers of settlers, especially in lowland parts of Ulster, meant that the Plantation and its associated settlements very quickly led to the replacement of Irish over much of the province. There is little evidence of substantial, prolonged bilingualism amongst the settler population, and it is likely that speakers of Irish, both those who remained Catholic and those who converted to Protestantism, quickly shifted to English in the areas of densest settlement, though the language continued to be spoken by much of the population in upland and remote western areas into the late eighteenth and early nineteenth centuries (and beyond in some areas). After the initial swamping of the province by the English and Scottish settlers, the use of Irish gradually declined over the next 300 years, probably falling to below 40 per cent by the early eighteenth century, to below 20 per cent by the late eighteenth century, and to below 5 per cent by the late nineteenth century (see Figure 2.2). This gradual decline of Irish means that at no point did Irish learners of English predominate in the population. Indeed, for most of the period and in most areas it is likely that Irish learners of English were only a small minority, socially disadvantaged and increasingly restricted to remote rural and upland areas. The consequences of this are that although English and Irish have been in contact in Ulster over the last 400 years, this has been demographically, socially and geographically limited so that we should not necessarily expect Irish to have had the same influence on English in Ulster as it has had elsewhere in Ireland.

The Plantation of Ulster and its associated settlements gave rise to the ethno-religious division between Catholics and Protestants that has characterised Ulster ever since. That is not to say that Protestants are the direct genetic descendants of the settlers and Catholics the direct genetic descendants of the native Irish. A combination of Catholic settlers (including before the seventeenth century), intermarriage and conversions, often accompanied by name changes, puts paid to any such straightforward equation. But that is not the same as denying political, religious, cultural and even a degree of ethnic continuity in the two communities. It should not be surprising that two distinct ethno-religious groups, no matter what their genetic origins, might differ linguistically, as indeed they have been shown to do in recent sociolinguistic analyses (see Section 2.7). Whether these present-day linguistic differences reflect past correlations between Catholicism and Irish and between Protestantism and English/Scots is another question. It is not unreasonable to suggest, as Todd (1984, 1989) has, that in some rural parts of Ulster Catholics are more likely than Protestants to have had Irish-speaking ancestors in the not too distant past (see Robinson 1982). This being the case, it may be possible that features of Irish origin in MUE are more likely to occur in the speech of Catholics than in the speech of Protestants, at least in certain rural areas, and this may also help us to understand the phonological origins of the dialect. There is much about the history of Ulster that we cannot be sure of, and an investigation of the phonological origins of MUE may in fact help to clarify this and other points of interest.

The linguistic history of Ulster set out in Chapter 2 provides the context for understanding the phonological origins of MUE, but what does the phonology of the dialect tell us itself? Chapters 3 and 4 set out a detailed analysis of a large number of phonological aspects of MUE, comparing them to patterns in historical and modern varieties of English, Scots and Irish. Chapter 3 deals with the MUE consonants, analysing the origins of thirty-six features of the dialect, covering phonological distinctions, distributions and realisations. The analyses in this chapter go beyond superficial comparisons between the contact varieties, examining the status of and constraints on the various features under analysis. For example, it is not enough to note that deletion of /d/ in the cluster /ld/ occurs in MUE (see Section 3.11.2). It is also important that it occurs only in morpheme-final position, it occurs after certain vowels but not others, and is blocked by particular suffixes. Even though /d/-deletion after /l/ occurred in English, Scots and Irish, understanding the exact nature of it in MUE points towards a close connection with the phenomenon in English and Scots rather than in Irish, in which none of the constraints just given were a factor. The overall result from the analysis of consonantal features is that MUE is most similar to English of a somewhat conservative non-regional Midland and southern type, and many of these features are also shared by Scots. Although there are some parallels between consonantal developments in MUE and in Irish, most of these consist of superficial similarities and it is probable that Irish at most played a reinforcing role in the development of some consonantal features of the dialect, though even this is uncertain. In only one case, outside of additions to lexical distributions of consonants in borrowed words and place-names, is direct Irish influence on the consonantal phonology of MUE likely: the development of Palatal Velarisation, which is found in MUE and some other varieties of IrE (and USc) and in Irish, but which is absent from English in Britain and marginal in Scots (Section 3.4). But even here other factors may have been at play.

The analysis of the MUE vowels in Chapter 4 examined realisation (quality and quantity) and lexical distribution, and again scrutinised the features in detail in order to determine the likely input to the dialect from English, Scots and Irish. Perhaps most obviously, the lexical distribution of the MUE vowel phonemes is for the most part of a conservative, non-regional Midland and southern English type, close in fact to the Early Modern ancestor of StE and sharing much in common with SIrE dialects. For example, the use of the typical MOUTH vowel in words which had ME /ɔl/ (but not /ɔːl/), i.e. in the OLD subset, is found across Ireland and was typical of varieties of English in the seventeenth century, including versions of Early Modern StE (see Section 4.4.1 and Maguire 2020b). It is not clear that Irish has had any role to play in the development of the dialect's vowel distributions (e.g. through influence on the phonotactic distributions of distinctions), other than additions to the lexicon in the form of loanwords and place-names. A similar kind of contribution was made by Scots, but there is also evidence for a more substantial Scots input to the lexical distribution of MUE vowel phonemes. Crucially, these Scots distributions are of a particular type: they involve phonotactic restrictions and pre-existing Scots phonemic distinctions that have been applied to what is otherwise an English system. These are the kinds of patterns we might have expected had Irish influenced the lexical distribution of the dialect's vowels, and they are suggestive of language shift by adult speakers with established phonotactic patterns and lexical distributions, but in this case from Scots to English. Some of this influence is extremely specific, for example in the distribution of /ëi/ and /aɪ/ in the PRICE lexical set in MUE, which maps on to the distribution of /ëi/, /i/ and /aɪ/ in the 'PRICE' lexical set in Mid Scots dialects, including various apparent exceptions to the SVLR such as *drive* and *hive* (Section 4.4.3).

Scots influence is even more apparent in vowel realisation, to the point where both the quality and, especially, the quantity of the MUE vowels are decidedly Scottish in character. Although English influence is likely in the unrounding of the typical LOT vowel (in as much as it remains distinct from the THOUGHT vowel in the dialect), Scots influence is evident in the quality of the typical GOOSE, KIT, STRUT, DRESS, TRAP/BATH, PRICE and MOUTH vowels, with the MUE values being close to what is found in modern western and southern Scots dialects and to the Early Modern progenitors of these. The degree of Irish influence on the quality of the MUE vowels is uncertain; there are similarities between the development of the short high vowels in Irish and MUE in particular, which have undergone lowering and centralisation in both languages. But any equation is complicated by the rather different underlying phonologies involved (Irish has one underlying short 'high' vowel, MUE has two phonemes, /ë/ in KIT and /ɔ/ in STRUT and FOOT), and by the Ulster-specific nature of these changes within Irish, which suggests possible influence from MUE and Scots on Ulster Irish rather than Ulster Irish influence on MUE and Scots (see Section 4.2.1). In terms of vowel quantity, MUE and Irish are even less similar. Irish has a system of phonemic vowel length, whilst vowel length in MUE is largely allophonic, conditioned for the most part by the nature of the following consonant. MUE also contrasts with English in this respect, though it does share some similarities with it too, especially in terms of the Voicing Effect and the lengthening of low-mid and low vowels before voiceless fricatives. However, a close examination of the data underlying the third volume of the *Linguistic Atlas of Scotland* (Mather and Speitel 1986) reveals that both of these lengthening effects are also found in certain Scots dialects and, what's more, they pattern in a very similar way to how they pattern in MUE (with, for example, lengthening of the typical DRESS vowel, /ɛ/ before voiceless fricatives, something which has not been recorded in English dialects). When we add to this the existence of the SVLR in both Scots and MUE, it is clear that the conditioning of vowel length in the dialect has had considerable input from Scotland.

Chapter 5 considers what the patterns identified in Chapters 3 and 4 mean for the phonological origins of MUE given what we know about the linguistic history of Ulster. Three key findings were identified: (1) the distinct lack of direct influence on the phonology of the dialect from Irish; (2) the non-regional, conservative Midland and southern English nature of much of the phonology of the dialect, especially of its consonantal features and vowel lexical distributions; and (3) obvious Scots influence on vowel quality and quantity and on certain kinds of lexical distributions of vowels in the dialect. The first of these findings runs contra the claims of various scholars in the past and to general assumptions that IrE is a variety of English which shows evidence of considerable contact influence from Irish (see Section 5.2). But it also makes sense from a historical point of view. The English and Scots settlers quickly outnumbered the Irish in Ulster as a result of the Plantation and its associated settlements, they would have had little reason to learn Irish (and indeed may well have had negative attitudes towards it), and Irish speakers shifted to English in the province over the space of 300 years (and indeed longer in some areas), so that the number of Irish learners of English at anyone time was only ever a small proportion of the population, one without the demographic power or social prestige to significantly affect the language of the wider population. It is more likely, in fact, that linguistic influence would go in the other direction, as some of the analyses in Chapters 3 and 4 suggest. The possibility that Irish influence has supported certain features in MUE that were already present in the English and/or Scots input was also considered, and the notion of 'reinforcement' was interrogated. The discussion in Chapter 5 suggests that defining reinforcement is problematic and there is a danger of cherry-picking the data if we have no means of determining what counts as an instance of non-reinforcement. At most we can suggest that Irish may have reinforced certain English and Scots features, but that this is unproven and perhaps unprovable given that nothing need actually change linguistically. It would seem, then, from the discussion in Chapter 5 that Irish has played a fairly minimal role in the phonological development of MUE. This finding in no way diminishes the importance of Irish in Ulster, including in Northern Ireland, historically or in the present day, in the same way that the lack of phonological influence on North American, Australian or New Zealand English from indigenous languages is of no importance in our estimation of the value and importance of these languages. A further consequence of this finding is that the hypothesis that there are linguistic differences between Protestants and Catholics that have arisen as a result of their different linguistic histories cannot be supported. If there is little evidence of influence from Irish on the phonology of MUE, then we cannot expect it to be particularly characteristic of one social group or another. But there is evidence of limited influence from the language on the lexis and syntax of MUE, and the reasons for the different behaviour of these compared with phonology was considered. Although no definitive answer was given, a number of reasons why we might expect phonology and syntax in particular to act differently were suggested, with the characteristic social indexing of phonological variation perhaps being key to understanding this difference. This is an area where further research is required.

The non-regional Midland and southern nature of the English input to MUE was explained in reference to the geographical origins of the settlers from England. As was outlined in Chapter 2, these mostly came from across the Midlands and south of the country, with no one area predominating as a source for English migrants to the province. This meant that no one dialect of English predominated in seventeenth-century Ulster. Appealing to the principles of koinéisation and NDF set out in Siegel (1985) and Trudgill (2004), the lack of regional specificity in MUE is a result of contact between these different English dialects and the development of a compromise variety which retained features shared between them and which failed, as a consequence of levelling, to retain minority dialect features. The heterogeneous but essentially southern and Midland nature of the English input meant the English component in MUE would be of a non-regional southern and Midland type, as the analyses in Chapters 3 and 4 indicate that it is. In fact, the English component of MUE phonology is very similar to that of Early Modern varieties of StE. This similarity is likely to have a number of causes, including Early Modern StE input to Ulster, StE features already being shared by regional English dialects in the seventeenth century (so that they were the most likely ones to survive the koinéisation process), and StE itself having a koiné origin as a result of contact between southern and Midland English dialects. But compared to modern StE, MUE is somewhat conservative in certain respects, retaining phonological patterns (e.g. a FACE-like vowel in the MEAT lexical subset, the retention of the typical START vowel in words in the SERVE subset, and rhoticity) which were once a feature of StE but which have long since disappeared from the variety. The conservative character of the English input to MUE was considered in Chapter 5 in light of connections that previous commentators have made between the dialect, the language of Shakespeare, and Elizabethan and Jacobean English. Although MUE has no special relationship with the language of Shakespeare and the notion of 'colonial lag' as some mysterious force arresting the development of extra-territorial dialects is not supportable (though Trudgill 2004 argues for a limited form of lag in the formation of new dialects), it is not unreasonable to suggest that the geographical and social peripheralisation of MUE cut it off from currents of change that continued to affect other Midland and southern English dialects, leading to some aspects of its phonology having a conservative character. But this must be considered in the context of other innovations in order to avoid cherry-picking the data, and it is evident from the analyses in Chapters 3 and 4 that there have been many of these in MUE, not least as a result of Scottish input to the dialect.

The Scottish input to MUE is for the most part of a specific kind. Rather than contributing essentially random features to the phonology of the dialect, it appears to be the case that Scots has imposed various phonological patterns and rules on the dialect. In addition to the Scots-like realisation of various vowel qualities, Scots rules of vowel length conditioning (most notably the SVLR) have been inherited by MUE. Other kinds of patterns and rules inherited from Scots affect the lexical distribution of vowel phonemes. For example, the appearance of /a/, the typical TRAP/BATH vowel, in MUE in the neighbourhood of labial consonants (especially a following /p/ or /f/) and the occurrence of the typical STRUT vowel /ɔ/ after /w/ instead of the typical KIT vowel /ë/ in words such as *whip* and *winter* are reflexes of Scots phonotactic constraints on the distributions of these phonemes. To these can be added the imposition of Scots lexical categories on to the phonology of MUE in the PRICE lexical set, with the distinction between words with Scots /i/ (e.g. *die, eye*) and those with Scots /aɪ/ (e.g. *buy, cry*) being maintained by redistribution of the Scots distinction between /ëi/ and /aɪ/, such that the first occurs in MUE *die* and *eye*, the second in MUE *buy* and *cry*. The lack of certain phonological contrast in MUE, i.e. those between the vowels in the STRUT and FOOT and LOT and THOUGHT lexical sets, also speaks of the transfer of Scots phonological patterns to English in Ulster. All of these changes of Scots origin depend upon native-speaker phonological knowledge, and point towards the Scots input to MUE arising as a result of adult speakers of Scots learning English in Ulster and imposing Scots phonological rules on their new

'L2' as we might expect in a situation of language shift. As was suggested in Chapter 5, it is this language shift rather than the shift from Irish to English that was the important one in the formation of MUE. But of course this was complicated by the fact that English and Scots were closely related languages or, alternatively, divergent dialect groups, and shared much in common. This was especially true of their consonant systems, and it was noted in Chapter 5 that consonants may act differently than vowels in any case. It is not surprising, then, that the Scots consonants, perhaps already influenced by English, fed into the NDF process in the way modelled by Trudgill (2004).

The study detailed in this book has explained how the phonology of MUE has developed and why it has many of the characteristics that it does. It has confirmed that the dialect developed as a result of the Plantation of Ulster and its associated settlements and the subsequent history of the province. It has also clarified the roles of the three input varieties, English, Scots and Irish, and has demonstrated that the dialect's phonology formed as a result of new dialect formation and contact between two closely related languages (or divergent dialect groups). The phonology of MUE is not for the most part the result of contact with Irish. Determining these facts about the historical development of MUE has only become possible through analysing a very wide range of features of its phonology and a detailed understanding of the phonological patterns in the input languages.

The analysis of the historical phonology of MUE also informs us about aspects of the history of the province. The pre-Plantation settlements in Ulster must have been insignificant compared to later settlements, given the lack of any evidence of pre-seventeenth-century English input to the dialect. The character of the English input to the dialect suggests that the seventeenth-century English settlers predominantly came from the Midlands and south of England, with no one geographical origin predominating. A similar situation pertains to the Scottish settlers, who mostly came from the south-western fringes of Scotland but without one specific sub-dialect predominating in the input to MUE. There is no evidence in the phonology of MUE that the Scottish settlers spoke Gaelic, and it is likely that those who did were very much in the minority. The distinct lack of Irish input to the phonology of MUE, in most cases consisting, if at all, of reinforcement of features already present in the English and Scots inputs, indicates a number of things about the history of the language. Firstly, speakers of Irish were outnumbered by speakers of English and Scots in the province, especially in lowland areas. Secondly, the language shift from Irish, however it happened, had limited effect on the language of the wider English-speaking population. It appears to have been a gradual process, with shifting speakers only ever being a small minority of the population, thus helping to explain the limited impact on MUE. Thirdly, it appears to be the case that bilingualism was for the most part unidirectional, with native Irish speakers shifting to English but with most native English speakers failing to learn the language. Fourthly, it is likely that there were negative attitudes towards Irish and Irish-influenced forms of English, so that phonological features of Irish origin that characterised the speech of the shifting population mostly did not spread in MUE. The lack of similar social evaluation of Irish syntactic patterns in the speech of the shifting population may explain the persistence of some of these patterns in MUE.

This analysis of the historical phonology of MUE also has consequences for understanding the development of IrE more generally. Many of the features discussed in Chapters 3 and 4 are also shared by varieties of SIrE, especially by its more traditional, long-established eastern forms. These features include clear realisation of /l/ in all positions, Pre-R Dentalisation, Velar Palatalisation, retention of /h/, including in initial /hw/, epenthesis in liquid+sonorant coda clusters, lengthening of low-mid and low vowels before voiceless fricatives, unrounding of the typical LOT vowel, the retention of a FACE or FACE-like vowel in the MEAT lexical subset, the presence of the typical MOUTH vowel in the OLD lexical subset, identity of the vowels in the STRUT and FOOT lexical sets, and a distinct vowel in the SERVE subset of the NURSE lexical set, with some survival of /ar/ (typical of START) in this set. None of these has its source in contact with Irish, and the extent of Irish influence on these varieties of SIrE is thus not as great as it might appear. All of these features are, in fact, reflexes of widespread Early Modern English patterns and thus it is likely that traditional forms of SIrE have developed in a similar way to MUE, through NDF, from the same kinds of English input varieties. SIrE is of course missing the obvious Scots input that is present in MUE, so that features such as the lowering and centralisation of the KIT vowel, the presence of the typical STRUT vowel after /w/ in KIT words, the split reflexes of the PRICE vowel, and the SVLR are all absent from it (something which further supports the Scottish origin of these features in MUE). And of course some varieties of SIrE, especially those spoken in areas where there has been a recent shift from Irish to English (e.g. in Ballyvourney in Cork, as documented in Lunny 1981a, 1981b), have been subject to considerable influence from Irish as a result of the rapid nature of the language shift, which involved a large proportion of the local population. But there is more than a little truth to the claim in Lass (1990a: 148) that, in terms of its phonology, SIrE developed 'not as a "contact English" in any important sense . . . but as a perfectly normal first-language, internally evolved variety, with only marginal contact effects', though this of course ignores contact between different dialects of English in Ireland. In any case, the analysis of the phonological origins of MUE in this book is of considerable relevance for understanding the phonological origins of IrE more generally.

The phonological development of MUE also has much to tell us about the phonological history of English and Scots, as exemplified by two features of the dialect, PreRD and the SVLR. PreRD was also found in traditional northern English dialects in the mid twentieth century, but not in dialects in the Midlands and south of England (Maguire 2012a). The existence of PreRD in MUE in an essentially identical form to what is found in northern England indicates that the feature was once more widespread in English, given that the main input dialects were from the Midlands and south of England. Scots input on its own to this complex feature (see Maguire 2016) is unlikely to have been sufficient to ensure its survival in the process of NDF. Thus MUE provides evidence for the existence of a widespread sub-phonemic feature of Early Modern English which was not otherwise recorded, and this is supported by both the pan-English distribution of the (probably) related lenition of /d/ to /ð/ before /ər/ (Maguire 2012a) and the presence of PreRD across Ireland, not just in Ulster (where Scottish input may have been a factor). The SVLR, which is found in most dialects of Scots in Scotland, is characteristic not only of USc but also of traditional dialects of MUE in places far from the USc heartlands such as south-west Tyrone. The rule not only affects the length of the high and high-mid vowels in MUE, but has also fed into the distribution of its two PRICE diphthongs, including a number of 'exceptions' (e.g. *drive*, *hive*) which are shared by some southern Scots dialects. The existence of these SVLR-associated patterns points not only towards an early date for the development of the rule in Scotland (see Aitken and Macafee 2002: 129–30), but also towards a seventeenth-century or earlier date for the development of the exceptions to the rule in the PRICE lexical set. Thus MUE becomes an important source of evidence for the historical phonology of the English and Scottish varieties that contributed most towards its development.

This study of the phonological origins of MUE also has much to tell us about koinéisation and NDF, especially in the context of contact between closely related languages or, alternatively, sharply divergent dialect groups of the same language. In some ways the formation of MUE is unremarkable. Different dialects from across Midland and southern England were brought to Ulster in the seventeenth century and the result is, in part at least, a new variety of the language which, from an English phonological perspective, is non-regional in character. This is exactly what we'd expect in a situation where no one English input dialect predominated, and it speaks of the usefulness of Trudgill's model of NDF that it can help us understand the development of old 'new' Englishes such as MUE as well as more recent ones such as New Zealand English. In some cases, especially with respect to consonantal features, Scots interacted with this NDF process in the expected way too: consonantal features shared by English and Scots (e.g. /h/ retention, including in initial /hw/, and rhoticity) survived in MUE because they were in the majority in both the English and Scots input dialects. The disappearance of most Scots vowel lexical distributions in MUE is the result of English speakers initially outnumbering Scots speakers in the MUE dialect area, and this too can be understood in terms of a deterministic NDF process and the founder effect. But in other cases, especially those involving vowel realisation, the result was rather different. How is it that Scots speakers had such an effect on vowel quality and, especially, quantity, if their dialects fed into a process of NDF which removed other minority Scots features? The inheritance of complex, specifically Scottish vowel length conditioning in MUE is unexpected given that speakers with such systems were not, initially at least, in the majority in many areas. It is especially surprising given that, according to Trudgill (2004), complex, marked features such as the SVLR should not survive NDF unless they are very much in the majority in the input. But the SVLR, including idiosyncratic patterning of the PRICE diphthongs, was inherited by MUE. This suggests that something else went on in the development of the dialect and that contact between closely related languages (or divergent dialect groups) may give different results than contact between rather more similar dialects of the same language. The hypothesis offered in this book is that the Scots speakers in Ulster contributed to the NDF process where their phonological systems coincided with those of the English settlers, but that in some ways they acted like non-native learners of English. It is likely that many of them retained their Scots speech for some time after settling in Ulster, adapting English realisations of the consonants in some cases, and learning English as a second 'language', imposing Scots features such as the SVLR on it. This process would have been ongoing throughout the seventeenth and early eighteenth centuries, especially given the continued rise in the numbers of Scottish settlers across the province, so that the presence of features like the SVLR was continually reinforced and ultimately became established in English in Ulster, not as part of the NDF process but as a result of intense 'language' contact.

This study also has considerable relevance for understanding the outcoming of contact between very different languages in situations of settlement colonisation. From the early seventeenth century to the present day, English and Irish have been in contact in Ulster, though in most areas this ceased to be the case in the nineteenth century. During this period, large numbers of Irish speakers have learned English, inevitably imposing phonological features of their L1 on their L2 (as is evidenced by, for example, Ní Ghallchóir's 1981 study of Donegal Gaeltacht English). Yet MUE is, outside of current and recent Gaeltacht areas, largely devoid of obvious phonological influence from Irish. That is, even in the face of a substantial language shift and prolonged language contact, contact-induced phonological change has not, for the most part, spread beyond the speech of the shifting population. There are various reasons why this has failed to happen. Firstly, the founding English (and Scots) population was so large that it soon outnumbered the Irish-speaking population. Secondly, the English-speaking population would have had little inclination to learn Irish, for social, political and utilitarian reasons, whilst speakers of Irish had much greater motivation to learn English, the language of the economically, socially and politically more powerful majority, so that bilingualism must have been unidirectional for the most part. Thirdly, the shift from Irish to English occurred in much of Ulster over a 300-year period, so that the number of shifting speakers was low compared to the number of native speakers of English. Given their relatively small numbers, and their socially and geographically marginal status, they would not have been in a position to substantially influence the development of English in Ulster. This is especially true of phonological features, which typically index a great deal of social meaning. The small number of Irish syntactic features which have become established in MUE (see Section 5.2.2) suggest that Irish learners of English did have some impact on the development of MUE and that these features were less likely to be edited out in the speech community given that they were relatively infrequent and less likely to be endowed with social significance.

The upshot is that situations of apparently intense language contact need not lead to significant change, at least not on all linguistic levels. The degree and nature of contact-influenced change depends on the demography, social conditions and timescale of the language shift. It is not necessarily true, as Thomason and Kaufman (1988: 60) suggest, that '[i]n interference through shift, if there is phonological interference there is sure to be some syntactic interference as well, and vice versa'. Nor is it true that all forms of IrE exhibit signs of heavy imposition, as is usually assumed to be the case (Bliss 1984; Filppula 1999; Hickey 2007a; McColl Millar 2016: 97–105; Odlin 1997; Thomason 2001: 79; Thomason and Kaufman 1988: 43; Winford 2005). English in Ulster, at least, has more in common with English in North America, Australia and New Zealand, being primarily the product of contact between varieties of English (including, in its widest sense, Scots) rather than of shift from an indigenous language. Indeed, in contributing to these varieties itself, the phonological origins of MUE are also part of the story of the phonological history of English across the globe.

Whilst the analysis in this book has been extensive, there is much that we still do not know about MUE and the history of Ulster that would allow us to better understand the development of the dialect. Most descriptions of MUE are brief and detailed data of the sort available for many traditional English and Scots dialects have not been published. Ongoing documentation and analysis of SwTE will considerably deepen our knowledge but publication of data collected in earlier surveys such as those described in Henry (1958) and Barry (1981a), as well as further research on other traditional forms of MUE, will also be required to gain a fuller understanding of the interaction of English, Scots and Irish in the formation of the dialect. Further analysis of the origins of the English and Scots Plantation settlers, of the dialects they spoke, of the degree to which Irish was used by Protestants as well as Catholics in the eighteenth and nineteenth centuries, and of the wider impact of Irish on MUE would also be instructive. So whilst this book offers the most extensive investigation of the phonological origins of a dialect of Irish English, it is far from being the last word on the subject.

Bibliography

Adams, G. Brendan (1948), 'An introduction to the study of Ulster dialects', *Proceedings of the Royal Irish Academy* 52C, 1–26.

Adams, G. Brendan (1950), 'Phonological notes on the English of south Donegal', *Proceedings of the Royal Irish Academy* 53C, 299–310.

Adams, G. Brendan (ed.) (1964a), *Ulster Dialects: An Introductory Symposium*, Holywood, Co. Down: Ulster Folk Museum.

Adams, G. Brendan (1964b), 'The last language census in Northern Ireland', in G. Brendan Adams (ed.), pp. 111–45.

Adams, G. Brendan (1966), 'Phonemic systems in collision in Ulster English', in Sever Pop (ed.), *Verhandlungen des zweiten Internationalen Dialektologenkongresses*, Marburg, Wiesbaden: Franz Steiner, pp. 1–6.

Adams, G. Brendan (1967), 'Northern England as a source of Ulster dialects', *Ulster Folklife* 13, 69–74.

Adams, G. Brendan (1973), 'Language in Ulster, 1820–1850', *Ulster Folklife* 19, 50–5.

Adams, G. Brendan (1974), 'The 1851 language census in the north of Ireland', *Ulster Folklife* 20, 65–70.

Adams, G. Brendan (1975), 'Language census problems, 1851–1911', *Ulster Folklife* 21, 68–72.

Adams, G. Brendan (1976), 'Aspects of monoglottism in Ulster', *Ulster Folklife* 22, 76–87.

Adams, G. Brendan (1979), 'The validity of language census figures in Ulster 1851–1911', *Ulster Folklife* 25, 113–22.

Adams, G. Brendan (1981), 'The voiceless velar fricative in northern Hiberno-English', in Michael Barry (ed.), pp. 106–17.

Adams, G. Brendan (1986), 'Common [consonantal] features in Ulster Irish and Ulster English', in Michael Barry and Philip Tilling (eds), *The English Dialects of Ulster: An Anthology of Articles on Ulster Speech by G. B. Adams*, Holywood, Co. Down: Ulster Folk and Transport Museum.

Aitken, A. J. (1981), 'The Scottish vowel-length rule', in Michael Benskins and Michael Samuels (eds), *So Meny People, Longages and Tonges: Philological Essays in Scots and Medieval English Presented to Angus McIntosh*, Edinburgh: Edinburgh University Press, pp. 131–57.

Aitken, A. J. (1984a), 'Scottish accents and dialects', in Peter Trudgill (ed.), pp. 94–118.

Aitken, A. J. (1984b), 'Scots and English in Scotland', in Peter Trudgill (ed.), pp. 517–32.

Aitken, A. J. and Caroline Macafee (2002), *The Older Scots Vowels*, Edinburgh: Scottish Text Society.

Anderson, Peter (1987), *A Structural Atlas of the English Dialects*, North Ryde, New South Wales: Croom Helm.

Archibald, John (1998), *Second Language Acquisition*, Amsterdam and Philadelphia, PA: John Benjamins.

Ball, Martin and Nicole Müller (eds) (2009), *The Celtic Languages* (2nd edition), London and New York: Routledge.

Bardon, Jonathan (1992), *A History of Ulster*, Belfast: The Blackstaff Press Ltd.

Bardon, Jonathan (2011), *The Plantation of Ulster*, Dublin: Gill & Macmillan.

Barry, Michael (1980), 'The southern boundaries of northern Hiberno-English speech', in Robin Thelwall (ed.), *Linguistic Studies in Honour of Paul Christophersen: Occasional Papers in Linguistics and Language Learning*, Coleraine: New University of Ulster, pp. 105–52.

Barry, Michael (ed.) (1981a), *Aspects of English Dialects in Ireland*, Belfast: Queen's University.

Barry, Michael (1981b), 'Towards a description of a regional standard pronunciation of English in Ulster', in Michael Barry (ed.), pp. 47–51.

Barry, Michael (1982), 'The English language in Ireland', in Richard Bailey and Manfred Görlach (eds), *English as a World Language*, Ann Arbor: University of Michigan Press, pp. 84–133.

Beal, Joan (2010), *An Introduction to Regional Englishes*, Edinburgh: Edinburgh University Press.

Bermúdez-Otero, Ricardo and Patrick Honeybone (2006), 'Phonology and syntax: a shifting relationship', *Lingua* 116, 543–61.

Bermúdez-Otero, Ricardo and April McMahon (2006), 'English phonology and morphology', in Bas Aarts and April McMahon (eds), *The Handbook of English Linguistics*, Oxford: Blackwell, pp. 382–410.

Bertz, Siegfried (1975), *Der Dubliner Stadtdialekt, Teil I: Phonologie*, PhD thesis, University of Freiburg.

Blaney, Roger (1996), *Presbyterians and the Irish Language*, Belfast: Ulster Historical Foundation and the Ultach Trust.

Bliss, Alan (1972), 'Languages in contact: some problems of Hiberno-English', *Proceedings of the Royal Irish Academy* 72, 63–82.

Bliss, Alan (1977), *A Dialogue in Hybernian Stile, by Jonathan Swift*, Dublin: Cadenus Press.

Bliss, Alan (1984), 'English in the south of Ireland', in Peter Trudgill (ed.), pp. 135–51.

Boldorf, Marcel (2015), 'The Ulster Linen Triangle: an industrial cluster emerging from a proto-industrial region', in Juliane Czierpka, Kathrin Oerters and Nora Thorade (eds), *Regions, Industries, and Heritage Perspectives on Economy, Society, and Culture in Modern Western Europe*, London: Palgrave Macmillan, pp. 25–41.

Braidwood, John (1964), 'Ulster and Elizabethan English' in G. Brendan Adams (ed.), pp. 5–109.

Breatnach, Risteard (1947), *The Irish of Ring Co. Waterford: A Phonetic Study*, Dublin: Dublin Institute for Advanced Studies.

Brilioth, Börje (1913), *A Grammar of the Dialect of Lorton (Cumberland)*, London: Publications of the Philological Society.

Britain, David (ed.) (2007), *Language in the British Isles*, Cambridge: Cambridge University Press.

Buchstaller, Isabelle, Karen Corrigan, Anders Holmberg, Patrick Honeybone and Warren Maguire (2013), 'T-to-R and the Northern Subject Rule: questionnaire-based structural, geo- and sociolinguistics', *English Language and Linguistics* 17(1), 85–128.

Butcher, Andrew and Marija Tabain (2004), 'On the back of the tongue: dorsal sounds in Australian languages', *Phonetica* 61: 22–52.

Byers, Sir John William (1916), *Shakespeare and the Ulster Dialect*, Belfast: Northern Whig.

Chambers, J. K. and Peter Trudgill (1980), *Dialectology*, Cambridge: Cambridge University Press.

Clark, Lynn and Graham Trousdale (2009), 'Exploring the role of token frequency in phonological change: evidence from TH-Fronting in east-central Scotland', *English Language and Linguistics* 13(1), 33–55.

Collins, Beverley and Inger Mees (2003), *The Phonetics of English and Dutch* (5th revised edition), Leiden and Boston: Brill.

Comerford, R. (1989), 'The Parnell era, 1883–91', in William Vaughan (ed.), *Ireland under the Union 1870–1921 (A New History of Ireland VI)*, Oxford: Oxford University Press, pp. 53–80.

Corbett, John, J. Derrick McClure and Jane Stuart-Smith (eds) (2003a), *The Edinburgh Companion to Scots*, Edinburgh: Edinburgh University Press.

Corbett, John, J. Derrick McClure and Jane Stuart-Smith (2003b), 'A brief history of Scots', in John Corbett *et al.* (eds), pp. 1–16.

Corrigan, Karen (2010), *Irish English, Volume 1: Northern Ireland*, Edinburgh: Edinburgh University Press.

Cosgrove, Art (1987), *Medieval Ireland 1169–1534 (A New History of Ireland II)*, Oxford: Oxford University Press.

Cox, Felicity (2012), *Australian English: Pronunciation and Transcription*, New York: Cambridge University Press.

Cruttenden, Alan (2001), *Gimson's Pronunciation of English* (6th edition), London: Arnold.

Cunningham, Una (2011), 'Echoes of Irish in the English of southwest Tyrone', in Raymond Hickey (ed.), *Researching the Languages of Ulster*, Uppsala: Uppsala University Press, pp. 207–21.

de Rijke, Persijn (2015), *'[S]ince We Came across the Atalantic': An Empirical Diachronic Study of Northern Irish English Phonology*, unpublished PhD thesis, University of Bergen.

Dieth, Eugen (1932), *A Grammar of the Buchan Dialect*, Cambridge: Heffer.

Dobson, Eric (1957), *English Pronunciation 1500–1700*, Oxford: Clarendon Press.

Docherty, Gerard and Paul Foulkes (1999), 'Derby and Newcastle: instrumental phonetics and variationist studies', in Paul Foulkes and Gerard Dochery (eds), pp. 47–71.

Donnelly, James (1989), 'Excess mortality and emigration', in William Vaughan (ed.), pp. 350–6.

Dorian, Nancy (1981), *Language Death: The Life Cycle of a Scottish Gaelic Dialect*, Philadelphia: University of Pennsylvania Press.

Douglas-Cowie, Ellen (1984), 'The sociolinguistic situation in Northern Ireland', in Peter Trudgill (ed.), pp. 533–45.

Eckert, Penelope and William Labov (2017), 'Phonetics, phonology and social meaning', *Journal of Sociolinguistics* 21(4), 467–96.

Elliot, Marianne (2000), *The Catholics of Ulster: A History*, London: Penguin Books.

Ellis, Alexander (1869), *On Early English Pronunciation, Part I: On the Pronunciation of the XIVth, XVIth, XVIIth, and XVIIIth Centuries*, New York: Greenwood Press.

Ellis, Alexander (1889), *On Early English Pronunciation, Part V: The Existing Phonology of English Dialects Compared with That of West Saxon*, New York: Greenwood Press.

Evans, Emrys (1997), 'Materials for a study of the Hiberno-Scots dialect of Glinsk, Co. Donegal', in Séamus Mac Mathúna and Ailbhe Ó Corráin (eds), *Miscellanea Celtica in Memoriam Heinrich Wagner*, Stockholm: Gotab, pp. 325–43.

Filppula, Markku (1999), *The Grammar of Irish English: Language in Hiberian Style*, London and New York: Routledge.

Fischer, David (1989), *Albion's Seed: Four British Folkways in America*, New York and Oxford: Oxford University Press.

FitzGerald, Garret (1984), 'Estimates for baronies of minimum level of Irish-speaking amongst successive decennial cohorts: 1771–1781 to 1861–1871', *Proceedings of the Royal Irish Academy* 84C, 117–55.

FitzGerald, Garret (2003), 'Irish-speaking in the pre-famine period: a study based on the 1911 census data for people born before 1851 and still alive in 1911', *Proceedings of the Royal Irish Academy* 103C, 191–283.

Foulkes, Paul and Gerard Docherty (eds) (1999), *Urban Voices: Accent Studies in the British Isles*, London: Arnold.

Gillies, William (2009), 'Scottish Gaelic', in Martin Ball and Nicole Müller (eds), pp. 230–304.

Glauser, Beat (1988), 'Aitken's Context in Northumberland, Cumberland and Durham: a computer assisted analysis of material from the Survey of English Dialects (SED)', in Alan R. Thomas (ed.), *Methods in Dialectology: Proceedings of the 6th International Conference Held at the University College of North Wales*, Cleveland: Multilingual Matters Ltd, pp. 611–24.

Gordon, Elizabeth, Lyle Campbell, Jennifer Hay, Margaret Maclagan, Andrea Sudbury and Peter Trudgill (2004), *New Zealand English: Its Origins and Evolution*, Cambridge: Cambridge University Press.

Görlach, Manfred (1987), 'Colonial lag? The alleged conservative character of American English and other "colonial" varieties', *African Studies* 46, 179–98.

Gregg, Robert (1958), 'Notes on the phonology of a county Antrim Scotch-Irish dialect: Part I, Synchronic', *Orbis* 7(2), 392–406.

Gregg, Robert (1964), 'Scotch-Irish urban speech in Ulster', in G. Brendan Adams (ed.), pp. 163–92.

Gregg, Robert (1972), 'The Scotch-Irish dialect boundaries in Ulster', in Martyn Wakelin (ed.), *Patterns in the Folk Speech of the British Isles*, London: The Athlone Press, pp. 109–39.

Gregg, Robert (1975), 'The distribution of raised and lowered diphthongs as reflexes of M.E. ī in two Scotch-Irish (SI) dialects', in Wolfgang Dressler and F. V. Mareš (eds), *Phonological 1972, Akten der zweiten internationalen Phonologie-Tagung, Wien 5–8 September 1972*, Munich/ Salzburg: Fink, pp. 101–6.

Gregg, Robert (1985), *The Scotch-Irish Dialect Boundaries in the Province of Ulster*, Ottawa: Canadian Federation for the Humanities.

Guy, Gregory (1980), 'Variation in the group and the individual: the case of final stop deletion', in William Labov (ed.), *Locating Language in Time and Space*, New York: Academic, pp. 1–36.

Hargreaves, Alexander (1904), *A Grammar of the Dialect of Adlington (Lancashire)*, Heidelberg: Carl Winter's Universitätsbuchhandlung.

Harris, John (1984), 'English in the north of Ireland', in Peter Trudgill (ed.), pp. 115–34.

Harris, John (1985), *Phonological Variation and Change: Studies in Hiberno-English*, Cambridge: Cambridge University Press.

Harris, John (1987), 'On doing comparative reconstruction with genetically unrelated languages', in Anna Giacalone Ramat, Onofrio Carruba and Giuliano Bernini (eds), *Papers from the 7th International Conference on Historical Linguistics*, Ansterdam: John Benjamins, pp. 267–82.

Harris, John (1990), 'More on brogues and creoles: what's been happening to English short U?', *Irish University Review* 20(1), Special Issue, *The English of the Irish*, 73–90.

Harris, John (1991), 'Ireland', in Jenny Cheshire (ed.), *English around the World: Sociolinguistic Perspectives*, Cambridge: Cambridge University Press, pp. 37–50.

Harris, John (1993), 'The grammar of Irish English', in James Milroy and Lesley Milroy (eds), *Real English: The Grammar of English Dialects in the British Isles*, London and New York: Longman, pp. 139–86.

Harris, John, (1997), 'Phonological systems in collision in the north of Ireland', in Hildegard Tristram (ed.), *The Celtic Englishes*, Heidelberg: Winter, pp. 201–23.

Haugen, Einar (1976), *The Scandinavian Languages: An Introduction to Their History*, London: Faber & Faber Ltd.

Hedevind, Bertil (1967), *The Dialect of Dentdale in the West Riding of Yorkshire*, Uppsala: Acta Universitatis Upsaliensis.

Henry, Alison (1995), *Belfast English and Standard English: Dialect Variation and Parameter Setting*, New York and Oxford: Oxford University Press.

Henry, Patrick Leo (1957), *An Anglo-Irish Dialect of North Roscommon*, Zurich: Aschmann & Scheller.

Henry, Patrick Leo (1958), 'A linguistic survey of Ireland: preliminary report', *Norsk Tidsskrift for Sprogvidenskap (Lochlann, A Review of Celtic Studies)*, Supplement 5, 49–208.

Hickey, Raymond (1984), 'Coronal segments in Irish English', *Journal of Linguistics* 20, 233–50.

Hickey, Raymond (1986), 'Possible phonological parallels between Irish and Irish English', *English World-Wide* 7(1), 1–21.

Hickey, Raymond (1999), 'Dublin English: current changes and their motivation', in Paul Foulkes and Gerard Docherty (eds), pp. 265–81.

Hickey, Raymond (2004), *A Sound Atlas of Irish English*, Berlin and New York: Mouton de Gruyter.

Hickey, Raymond (2005), *Dublin English: Evolution and Change*, Amsterdam and Philadelphia, PA: John Benjamins.

Hickey, Raymond (2007a), *Irish English: History and Present-day Forms*, Cambridge: Cambridge University Press.

Hickey, Raymond (2007b), 'Southern Irish English', in David Britain (ed.), pp. 135–51.

Hickey, Raymond (2013), 'Supraregionalisation and dissociation', in J. K. Chambers and Natalie Schilling-Estes (eds), *Handbook of Language Variation and Change* (2nd edition), Oxford and Hoboken, NJ: John Wiley & Sons, pp. 537–56.

Hickey, Raymond (2014), *The Sound Structure of Modern Irish*, Berlin and Boston, MA: de Gruyter Mouton.

Hinskens, Frans, Peter Auer and Paul Kerswill (2005), 'The study of dialect convergence and divergence: conceptual and methodological considerations', in Peter Auer, Frans Hinskens and Paul Kerswill (eds), *Dialect Change: Convergence and Divergence in European Languages*, Cambridge: Cambridge University Press, pp. 1–48.

Hinskens, Frans, Jeffrey Kallen and Johan Taeldeman (2000), 'Merging and drifting apart: convergence and divergence of dialects across political borders', *International Journal of the Sociology of Language* 145, 1–28.

Hock, Hans Henrich (1991), *Principles of Historical Linguistics*, Berlin: Mouton de Gruyter.

Holmer, Nils (1940), *On Some Relics of the Irish Dialect Spoken in the Glens of Antrim*, Uppsala: Almqvist & Wiksells Boktryckeri-A.-B.

Holmer, Nils (1942), *The Irish Language in Rathlin Island, Co. Antrim*, Dublin: The Royal Irish Academy.

Holmer, Nils (1962), *The Gaelic of Kintyre*, Dublin: Dublin Institute for Advanced Studies.

Honeybone, Patrick (2019), 'Phonotactics, prophylaxis, acquisitionism and change: the history of *RIME-xxŋ in English', *Papers in Historical Phonology* 4, 83–135.

Hundt, Marianne (2009), 'Colonial lag, colonial innovation or simply language change?', in Günter Rohdenburg and Julia Schlüter (eds), *One Language, Two Grammars? Differences between British and American English*, Cambridge: Cambridge University Press, pp. 13–37.

Jespersen, Otto (1909), *A Modern English Grammar on Historical Principles, Part I: Sounds and Spellings*, Heidelberg: Carl Winter's Universitätsbuchhandlung.

Johnston, Paul (1997a), 'Older Scots phonology and its regional variation', in Charles Jones (ed.), *The Edinburgh History of the Scots Language*, Edinburgh: Edinburgh University Press, pp. 47–111.

Johnston, Paul (1997b), 'Regional variation', in Charles Jones (ed.), *The Edinburgh History of the Scots Language*, Edinburgh: Edinburgh University Press, pp. 433–513.

Johnston, Paul (2007), 'Scottish English and Scots', in David Britain (ed.), pp. 105–21.

Jones, Charles (2006), *English Pronunciation in the Eighteenth and Nineteenth Centuries*, Basingstoke and New York: Palgrave Macmillan.

Jones, Daniel (1909), *The Pronunciation of English*, Cambridge: Cambridge University Press.

Jones, Daniel (1922), *An Outline of English Phonetics*, New York: G. E. Stechert & Co.

Joyce, P. W. (1910), *English as We Speak It in Ireland*, London: Longmans, Green & Co.

Kallen, Jeffrey (ed.) (1997), *Focus on Ireland*, Amsterdam and Philadelphia, PA: John Benjamins.

Kallen, Jeffrey (1999), 'Irish English and the Ulster Scots controversy', *Ulster Folklife* 45, 70–85.

Kallen, Jeffrey (2013), *Irish English, Volume 2: The Republic of Ireland*, Boston, MA and Berlin: Walter de Gruyter.

Keating, Patricia and Aditi Lahiri (1993), 'Fronted velars, palatalized velars, and palatals', *Phonetica* 50, 73–101.

Kerswill, Paul (2003), 'Dialect levelling and geographical diffusion in British English', in David Britain and Jenny Cheshire (eds), *Social Dialectology: In Honour of Peter Trudgill*, Amsterdam and Philadelphia, PA: John Benjamins, pp. 223–43.

Kerswill, Paul (2007), 'New-dialect formation: the inevitability of colonial Englishes (review)', *Language* 83(3), 657–61.

Knooihuizen, Remco (2009), 'Shetland Scots as a new dialect: phonetic and phonological considerations', *English Language and Linguistics* 13(3), 483–501.

Kingsmore, Rona (1995), *Ulster Scots Speech: A Sociolinguistic Study*, Tuscaloosa and London: University of Alabama Press.

Kökeritz, Helge (1932), *The Phonology of the Suffolk Dialect, Descriptive and Historical*, Uppsala: Uppsala University.

Kökeritz, Helge (1953), *Shakespeare's Pronunciation*, New Haven, CT: Yale University Press.

Kolb, Eduard, Beat Glauser, Willy Elmer and Renate Stamm (1979), *Atlas of English Sounds*, Bern: Francke Verlag.

Labov, William (1972), *Sociolinguistic Patterns*, Philadelphia, PA: University of Philadelphia Press.

Labov, William (1994), *Principles of Linguistic Change, Volume 1: Internal Factors*, Malden, MA, Oxford and Carlton, Victoria: Blackwell Publishing.

Ladefoged, Peter and Keith Johnson (2011), *A Course in Phonetics* (6th edition), Boston, MA: Wadsworth Cengage Learning.

Lass, Roger (1976), *English Phonology and Phonological Theory: Synchronic and Diachronic Studies*, Cambridge: Cambridge University Press.

Lass, Roger (1990a), 'Early mainland residues in southern Hiberno-English', *Irish University Review* 20(1), 137–48.

Lass, Roger (1990b), 'Where do Extraterritorial Englishes come from? Dialect input and recodification in transported Englishes', in Sylvia Adamson, Vivien Law, Nigel Vincent and Susan Wright (eds), *Papers from the 5th International Conference on English Historical Linguistics, Cambridge 6–9 April 1987*, Amsterdam and Philadelphia, PA: John Benjamins, pp. 245–80.

Lass, Roger (1992), 'Phonology and morphology', in Norman Blake (ed.), *The Cambridge History of the English Language, Vol. 2: 1066–1476*, Cambridge: Cambridge University Press, pp. 23–155.

Lass, Roger (2000), 'Phonology and morphology', in Roger Lass (ed.), *The Cambridge History of the English Language, Vol. 3: 1476–1776*, Cambridge: Cambridge University Press, pp. 56–186.

Lass, Roger, Margaret Laing, Rhona Alcorn and Keith Williamson (2013), *CoNE: A Corpus of Narrative Etymologies from Proto-Old English to Early Middle English and Accompanying Corpus of Changes*, Edinburgh: The University of Edinburgh.

Livingston, Alistair (2012), 'Gaelic in Galloway: Part 2 - Contraction', *Transactions of the Dumfriesshire and Galloway Natural History and Antiquarian Society, Third Series*, Vol. 86, 63–76.

Lucas, Leslie (1979), *Grammar of Ros Goill Irish, Co. Donegal*, Belfast: Institute of Irish Studies.

Luick, Karl (1940), *Historische Grammatik der Englischen Sprache*, Cambridge, MA: Harvard University Press.

Lunny, Patrick (1981a), *Studies in the Modern English Dialect of Ballyvourney, West Cork*, unpublished PhD thesis, Queen's University, Belfast.

Lunny, Patrick (1981b), 'Linguistic interaction: English and Irish in Ballyvourney, W. Cork', in Michael Barry (ed.), *Aspects of English Dialects in Ireland, Volume 1: Papers Arising from the Tape-recorded Survey of Hiberno-English Speech*, Belfast: The Institute of Irish Studies, pp. 118–41.

Macafee, Caroline (1983), *Varieties of English around the World: Glasgow*, Amsterdam: Benjamins.

Macafee, Caroline (1996), *Concise Ulster Dictionary*, Oxford: Oxford University Press.

Macafee, William and Valerie Morgan (1981), 'Population in Ulster, 1660–1760', in Peter Roebuck (ed.), *Plantation to Partition: Essays in Ulster History in Honour of J. L. McCracken*, Belfast: Blackstaff Press, pp. 46–63.

McCafferty, Kevin (1994), 'No Prods or Fenians here! The absence of Northern Ireland social organisation in sociolinguistic studies', *Nordlyd* 21, 1–32.

McCafferty, Kevin (1999), '(London)Derry: between Ulster and local speech – class, ethnicity and language change', in Paul Foulkes and Gerard Docherty (eds), pp. 246–64.

McCafferty, Kevin (2001), *Ethnicity and Language Change: English in (London)Derry, Northern Ireland*, Amsterdam and Philadelphia, PA: John Benjamins.

McCafferty, Kevin (2007), 'Northern Irish English', in David Britain (ed.), pp. 122–34.

McColl Millar, Robert (2016), *Contact: The Interaction of Closely Related Linguistic Varieties and the History of English*, Edinburgh: Edinburgh University Press.

McCone, Kim (1994), 'An tSean-Ghaeilge agus a Réamhstair', in Kim McCone *et al.* (eds), pp. 61–219.

McCone, Kim (2005), *A First Old Irish Grammar and Reader*, Maynooth: National University of Ireland.

McCone, Kim, Damian McManus, Cathal Ó hÁinle, Nicholas Williams and Liam Breatnach (eds) (1994), *Stair na Gaeilge*, Maynooth: Roinn na Sean-Ghaeilge, Coláiste Phádraig.

McCoy, Gordon (1997), *Protestants and the Irish Language in Northern Ireland*, unpublished PhD thesis, Queen's University Belfast.

McDowell, R. (1986), 'The age of the United Irishmen: reform and reaction, 1789–94', in Theodore Moody and William Vaughan (eds), *Eighteenth Century Ireland 1691–1800 (A New History of Ireland IV)*, Oxford: Oxford University Press, pp. 289–338.

MacMahon, Michael (1999), 'Phonology', in Suzanne Romaine (ed.), *The Cambridge History of the English Language, Vol. 4: 1776–1997*, Cambridge: Cambridge University Press, pp. 373–535.

McManus, Damian (1994), 'An Nua-Ghaeilge Chlasaiceach', in Kim McCone *et al.* (eds), pp. 335–445.

Mac Póilin, Aodán (1999), 'Language, identity and politics in Northern Ireland', *Ulster Folklife* 45, 108–32.

Maguire, Warren (2012a), 'Pre-R Dentalisation in northern England', *English Language and Linguistics* 16(3), 361–84.

Maguire, Warren (2012b), 'Mapping *The Existing Phonology of English Dialects*', *Dialectologia et Geolinguistica* 20, 84–107.

Maguire, Warren (2012c), 'English and Scots in Scotland', in Raymond Hickey (ed.) *Areal Features of the Anglophone World*, Berlin and Boston, MA: Mouton de Gruyter, pp. 53–77.

Maguire, Warren (2016), 'Pre-R Dentalisation in Scotland', *English Language and Linguistics* 20(2), 315–39.

Maguire, Warren (2018), 'The origins of epenthesis in liquid+sonorant clusters in Mid-Ulster English', *Transactions of the Philological Society* 116(3), 484–508.

Maguire, Warren (2020a), 'LAS3 Revisited', in Joanna Kopaczyk & Robert McColl Millar (eds.) *Language on the move across contexts and communities. Selected papers from the 12th triennial Forum for Research on the Languages of Scotland and Ulster*, Aberdeen: FRLSU.

Maguire, Warren (2020b), 'The origins of *owld* in Scots', to appear in Joan Beal, Ranjan Sen, Nuria Yáñez-Bouza and Christine Wallis (eds), *The Eighteenth-Century English Phonology Database (ECEP)*, Special Issue, *English Language and Linguistics* 24(3).

Marckwardt, Albert (1958), *American English*, New York: Oxford University Press.

Marckwardt, Albert and J. L. Dillard (1980), *American English* (2nd edition), New York and Oxford: Oxford University Press.

Mather, James and Hans-Henning Speitel (1986), *The Linguistic Atlas of Scotland, Scots Section, Vol. 3: Phonology*, Beckenham: Croom Helm.

Mathisen, Anne (1999), 'Sandwell, West Midlands: ambiguous perspectives on gender patterns and models of change', in Paul Foulkes and Gerard Docherty (eds), pp. 107–23.

Matras, Yaron (2009), *Language Contact*, Cambridge and New York: Cambridge University Press.

Millar, Sharon (1987), 'The question of ethno-linguistic differences in Northern Ireland', *English World-Wide* 8, 201–13.

Milroy, James (1981), *Regional Accents of English: Belfast*, Belfast: Blackstaff Press.

Milroy, James (1982a), 'Probing under the tip of the iceberg: phonological normalisation and the shape of speech communities', in Suzanne Romaine (ed.), *Sociolinguistic Variation in Speech Communities*, London: Arnold, pp. 35–47.

Milroy, James (1982b), 'Some connections between Galloway and Ulster speech', *Scottish Language* 1, 23–9.

Milroy, James, Lesley Milroy, Sue Hartley and David Walshaw (1994), 'Glottal stops and Tyneside glottalization: competing patterns of variation and change in British English', *Language Variation and Change* 6, 327–57.

Milroy, Lesley (1987), *Language and Social Networks*, Oxford and New York: Basil Blackwell.

Minkova, Donka (2004), 'Philology, linguistics, and the history of [hw]~[w]', in Anne Curzan and Kimberley Emmons (eds), *Studies in the History of the English Language II: Unfolding Conversations*, Berlin and New York: Mouton de Gruyter, pp. 7–46.

Minkova, Donka (2014), *A Historical Phonology of English*, Edinburgh: Edinburgh University Press.

Molineaux, Benjamin, Joanna Kopaczyk, Warren Maguire, Rhona Alcorn, Vasilis Karaiskos and Bettelous Los (2019), 'Early spelling evidence for Scots L-vocalisation', in Rhona Alcorn, Bettelou Los, Joanna Kopaczyk and Benjamin Molineaux (eds), *Historical Dialectology in the Digital Age*, Edinburgh: Edinburgh University Press, pp. 61–87.

Montgomery, Michael (1998), 'In the Appalachians they speak like Shakespeare', in Laurie Bauer and Peter Trudgill (eds), *Myths in Linguistics*, New York: Penguin, pp. 66–76.

Montgomery, Michael (1999), 'The position of Ulster Scots', *Ulster Folklife* 45, 86–107.

Moody, Theodore, Francis Martin and Francis Byrne (eds) (1976), *Early Modern Ireland 1534–1691 (A New History of Ireland. III)*, Oxford: Oxford University Press.

Morton, Alan (1993–2005), DMAP: Distribution mapping software [Computer program], Version 7.2e, http://www.dmap.co.uk/.

Moylan, Séamas (1996), *The Language of Kilkenny*, Dublin: Geography Publications.

Moylan, Séamas (2009), *Southern Irish English: Review and Exemplary Texts*, Dublin: Geography Publications.

Mufwene, Salikoko (1996), 'The Founder Principle in creole genesis', *Diachronica* 13, 83–134.

Mufwene, Salikoko (2001), *The Ecology of Language Evolution*, Cambridge: Cambridge University Press.

Murray, James (1873), *The Dialect of the Southern Counties of Scotland*, London: The Philological Society.

Mutschmann, Heinrich (1909), *A Phonology of the North-eastern Scotch Dialect*, Bonn: Peter Hanstein, Verlagsbuchhandlung.

Nally, Eamonn (1971), 'Notes on a Westmeath dialect', *Journal of the International Phonetic Association* 1(1), 33–8.

Ní Chasaide, Ailbhe (1985), *Preaspiration on Phonological Stop Contrasts: An Instrumental Phonetic Study*, unpublished PhD thesis, University College of North Wales, Bangor.

Ní Chasaide, Ailbhe (1999), 'Irish', in *Handbook of the International Phonetic Association* (no editor named), Cambridge: Cambridge University Press, pp. 111–16.

Ní Ghallchóir, Caitríona (1981), 'Aspects of bilingualism in north west Donegal', in Michael Barry (ed.), pp. 142–70.

Ó Baoill, Dónall (1991), 'Contact phenomena in the phonology of Irish and English in Ireland', in P. Sture Ureland and George Broderick (eds), *Language Contact in the British Isles*, Tübingen: Max Niemeyer Verlag, pp. 581–95.

Ó Baoill, Dónall (1997), 'The emerging Irish phonological substratum in Irish English', in Jeffrey Kallen (ed.), pp. 73–87.

Ó Baoill, Dónall (2009), 'Irish', in Martin Ball and Nicole Müller (eds), pp. 163–229.

Ó Corráin, Ailbhe (2006), 'On the "After Perfect" in Irish and Hiberno-English', in Hildegard Tristram (ed.), *The Celtic Englishes IV: The Interface between English and the Celtic Languages*, Potsdam: Universität Potsdam, pp. 153–70.

Ó Curnáin, Brian (2007), *The Irish of Iorras Aithneach, County Galway*, Dublin: Dublin Institute of Advanced Studies.

Odlin, Terence (1997), 'Hiberno-English: pidgin, creole, or neither?', *Centre for Language and Communication Studies Occasional Paper* 49, Dublin: Trinity College Dublin.

Ó Dochartaigh, Cathair (1987), *Dialects of Ulster Irish*, Belfast: Institute of Irish Studies.

Ó Dochartaigh, Cathair (ed.) (1994–7), *Survey of the Gaelic Dialects of Scotland*, 5 vols., Dublin: Dublin Institute for Advanced Studies.

Ó Gráda, Cormac (1989), 'Poverty, population, and agriculture, 1801–45', in William Vaughan (ed.), pp. 108–36.

Ó hUiginn, Ruairí (1994), 'Gaeilge Chonnacht', in Kim McCone *et al.* (eds), pp. 539–610.

Ó hÚrdail, Roibeárd (1997), 'Confusion of dentality and alveolarity in dialects of Hiberno-English', in Jeffrey Kallen (ed.), pp. 133–52.

Ó Maolalaigh, Roibeard (1997), *The Historical Short Vowel Phonology of Gaelic*, unpublished PhD thesis, University of Edinburgh.

Ó Muirithe, Diarmaid (1996), 'A modern glossary of Forth and Bargy', in Terence Dolan (ed.), *The Dialect of Forth and Bargy, Co. Wexford, Ireland*, Dublin: Four Courts Press, pp. 17–30.

Orlova, V. G. (1970), *Obrazovanie severnorusskogo narečija i srednerusskix govorov*, Moscow: Nauka.

Orton, Harold (1962), *Survey of English Dialects (A): Introduction*, Leeds: E. J. Arnold & Son Ltd.

Orton, Harold and Eugen Dieth (eds) (1962–71), *Survey of English Dialects (B): The Basic Material*, Leeds: E. J. Arnold & Son Ltd.

Orton, Harold, Stewart Sanderson and John Widdowson (eds) (1978), *The Linguistic Atlas of England*, London: Routledge.

Ó Siadhail, Mícheál (1989), *Modern Irish: Grammatical Structure and Dialectal Variation*, Cambridge: Cambridge University Press.

Ó Snodaigh, Padraig (1995), *Hidden Ulster: Protestants and the Irish Language*, Belfast: Lagan Press.

Ó Tuathail, Éamonn (1933), *Sgéalta Mhuintir Luinigh (Munterloney Folk-tales)*, Dublin: Irish Folklore Institute.

Owens, Elizabeth (1977), *Distribution of /l/ in Belfast Vernacular Speech*, unpublished MA dissertation, Queen's University of Belfast.

Oxley, James (1940), *The Lindsey Dialect*, Kendal: Titus William.

Patterson, David (1860), *The Provincialisms of Belfast and the Surrounding Area Pointed out and Corrected*, Belfast: David Mayne.

Perceval-Maxwell, M. (1973), *The Scottish Migration to Ulster in the Reign of James I*, London: Routledge & Kegan Paul Ltd.

Pilch, Herbert (1990), 'Hiberno-English: empirical model of a phonemic substratum', *Celtica* 21, 576–87.

Poplack, Shana, Lauren Zentz and Nathalie Dion (2012), 'Phrase-final prepositions in Quebec French: an empirical study of contact, code-switching and resistance to convergence', *Bilingualism: Language and Cognition* 15 (2), 203–25.

Przedlacka, Joanna (2012), 'A historical study of Voice Onset Time in Received Pronunciation', in Joanna Esquibel and Anna Wojtys (eds), *Explorations in the English Language: Middle Ages and Beyond – Festschrift for Professor Jerzy Welna on the Occasion of his 70th Birthday*, Frankfurt: Peter Lang, pp. 67–76.

Quiggin, Edmund (1906), *A Dialect of Donegal: Being the Speech of Meenawannia in the Parish of Glenties. Phonology and Texts*, Cambridge: Cambridge University Press.

Ringe, Don and Ann Taylor (2014), *The Development of Old English (A Linguistic History of English 2)*, Oxford: Oxford University Press.

Robinson, Philip (1974), *The Plantation of County Tyrone in the Seventeenth Century*, unpublished PhD thesis, Queen's University, Belfast.

Robinson, Philip (1978), 'British settlement in County Tyrone 1610–1666', *Irish Economic and Social History* 5, 5–26.

Robinson, Philip (1982), 'Plantation and colonisation: the historical background', in Frederick Boal and J. Neville Douglas (eds), *Integration and Division: Geographical Perspectives on the Northern Ireland Problem*, London: Academic Press, pp. 19–47.

Robinson, Philip (1984), *The Plantation of Ulster*, Dublin: Gill & Macmillan.

Robinson, Philip (1997), *Ulster-Scots: A Grammar of the Traditional Written and Spoken Language*, Belfast: Ullans Press.

Rydland, Kurt (1998), *The Orton Corpus: A Dictionary of Northumbrian Pronunciation, 1928–1939*, Oslo: Novus Press.

Schneider, Edgar (2007), *Post-Colonial English: Varieties around the World*, Cambridge: Cambridge University Press.

Schneider, Edgar (2008), 'Accommodation versus identity? A response to Trudgill', *Language in Society* 37(2), 262–7.

Shorrocks, Graham (1998), *A Grammar of the Dialect of the Bolton Area, Part 1: Introduction, Phonology*, Frankfurt am Main: Peter Lang.

Siegel, Jeff (1985), 'Koines and koineization', *Language in Society* 14, 357–78.

Siegel, Jeff (1999), 'Transfer constraints and substrate influence in Melanesian pidgin', *Journal of Pidgin and Creole Languages* 14(1), 1–44.

Silverstein, Michael (2003), 'Indexical order and the dialectics of sociolinguistic life', *Language & Communication* 23, 193–229.

Simms, John (1976), 'The war of the two kings, 1685–91', in Theodore Moody *et al.* (eds), pp. 478–508.

Sivertsen, Eva (1960), *Cockney Phonology*, Bergen: Oslo University Press.

Sommerfelt, Alf (1929), 'South Armagh Irish', *Norsk Tidsskrift for Sprogvidenskap* 2, 107–91.

Staples, J. H. (1896), 'Notes on Ulster English dialect for comparison with English dialects by the late A. J. Ellis, F.R.S., with samples in Palaeotype, comparison specimen and wordlist', *Transactions of the Philological Society* 23(2), 357–98.

Stifter, David (2006), *Sengoidelc: Old Irish for Beginners*, Syracuse: Syracuse University Press.

Stockman, Gerard and Heinrich Wagner (1965), 'Contributions to a study of Tyrone Irish', *Lochlann: A Review of Celtic Studies* 3, 43–236.

Stuart-Smith, Jane (2003), 'The phonology of modern urban Scots', in John Corbett *et al.* (eds), pp. 110–37.

Stuart-Smith, Jane, Claire Timmins and Fiona Tweedie (2006), 'Conservation and innovation in a traditional dialect', *English World-Wide* 27(1), 71–87.

Stuart-Smith, Jane, Claire Timmins and Fiona Tweedie (2007), '"Talkin' Jockney"? Variation and change in Glaswegian accent', *Journal of Sociolinguistics* 11(2), 221–60.

Tanner, James, Morgan Sonderegger and Jane Stuart-Smith (2019), 'Vowel duration and the voicing effect across English dialects', SPADE Data Consortium, lingbuzz/004640 <https://ling.auf.net/lingbuzz/004640>.

Thomas, Erik (2011a), *Sociophonetics: An Introduction*, London and New York: Palgrave Macmillan.

Thomas, Erik (2011b), 'Collecting data on phonology', in Warren Maguire and April McMahon (eds), *Analysing Variation in English*, Cambridge: Cambridge University Press, pp. 7–29.

Thomason, Sarah (2001), *Language Contact*, Edinburgh: Edinburgh University Press.

Thomason, Sarah and Terrence Kaufman (1988), *Language Contact, Creolization and Genetic Linguistics*, Berkeley, Los Angeles and Oxford: University of California Press.

Thurneysen, Rudolf (1946), *A Grammar of Old Irish*, revised, edited and translated by D. A. Binchy and Osborn Bergin, Dublin: Dublin Institute for Advanced Studies.

Todd, Loreto (1975), *Base Form and Substratum: Two Case Studies of English in Contact*, unpublished PhD thesis, University of Leeds.

Todd, Loreto (1984), 'By their tongue divided: towards an analysis of speech communities in Northern Ireland', *English World-Wide* 5(2), 159–80.

Todd, Loreto (1989), 'Cultures in conflict: varieties of English in Northern Ireland', in Ofelia Garcia and Ricardo Otheguy (eds), *English across Cultures, Cultures across English: A Reader in Cross-cultural Communication*, New York: Mouton de Gruyter, pp. 335–55.

Tollfree, Laura (1999), 'South East London English: discrete versus continuous modelling of consonantal reduction', in Paul Foulkes and Gerard Docherty (eds), pp. 163–84.

Trudgill, Peter (ed.) (1984), *Language in the British Isles*, Cambridge: Cambridge University Press.

Trudgill, Peter (1999a), *The Dialects of England* (2nd edition), Oxford and Malden, MA: Blackwell Publishers Ltd.

Trudgill, Peter (1999b), 'A window on the past: "Colonial lag" and New Zealand evidence for the phonology of nineteenth-century English', *American Speech* 74(3), 227–39.

Trudgill, Peter (2004), *New-dialect Formation: The Inevitability of Colonial Englishes*, Edinburgh: Edinburgh University Press.

Turton, Danielle (2017), 'Categorical or gradient? An ultrasound investigation of /l/-darkening and vocalization in varieties of English', *Laboratory Phonology: Journal of the Association for Laboratory Phonology* 8(1): 1–31.

Vaughan, William (ed.) (1989), *Ireland under the Union 1801–70 (A New History of Ireland V)*, Oxford: Oxford University Press.

Wagner, Heinrich (1958), *Linguistic Atlas and Survey of Irish Dialects, Vol. I: Introduction, 300 Maps*, Dublin: Institute for Advanced Studies.

Wagner, Heinrich (1958–64), *Linguistic Atlas and Survey of Irish Dialects*, 4 vols, Dublin: Institute for Advanced Studies.

Wagner, Heinrich and Colm Ó Baoill (1969), *Linguistic Atlas and Survey of Irish Dialects, Vol. IV: The Dialects of Ulster and the Isle of Man. Specimens of Scottish Gaelic Dialects. Phonetic Texts of East Ulster Irish*, Dublin: Institute for Advanced Studies.

Wakelin, Martyn (1972), *English Dialects: An Introduction*, London: Athlone Press.

Watson, Seosamh (1994), 'Gaeilge n hAlban', in Kim McCone *et al.* (eds), pp. 661–702.

Watt, Dominic and Lesley Milroy (1999), 'Patterns of variation and change in three Newcastle vowels: is this dialect levelling?', in Paul Foulkes and Gerard Docherty (eds), pp. 25–46.

Wells, John (1982), *Accents of English*, Cambridge: Cambridge University Press.

Wettstein, Paul (1942), *The Phonology of a Berwickshire Dialect*, Bienne: Schüler.

Widén, Bertil (1949), *Studies on the Dorset Dialect*, Lund: C. W. K. Gleerup.

Williams, Ann and Paul Kerswill (1999), 'Dialect levelling: change and continuity in Milton Keynes, Reading and Hull', in Paul Foulkes and Gerard Docherty (eds), pp. 141–62.

Wilson, James (1915), *Lowland Scotch as Spoken in the Strathearn District of Perthshire*, London: Oxford University Press.

Wilson, James (1923), *The Dialect of Robert Burns as Spoken in Central Ayrshire*, London: Oxford University Press.

Wilson, James (1926), *The Dialects of Central Scotland*, Oxford: Oxford University Press.

Winford, Donald (2005), 'Contact induced changes: classification and processes', *Diachronica* 22(2), 373–427.

Wright, Joseph (1905), *The English Dialect Grammar*, Oxford: Henry Frowde.

Wyld, H. C. (1927), *A Short History of English* (3rd edition), London: John Murray.

Zai, Rudolf (1942), *The Phonology of the Morebattle Dialect*, Lucerne: Raeber.

Index

Aberdeenshire, 58
acoustic analysis, 79–80, 102
adult speaker, 4, 11, 19, 36, 146, 162–3, 165, 173–5, 177, 181, 183
after perfect, 157–8
aitch (haitch), 35
America, North (North American English), 2, 27–8, 43, 63, 65, 69, 71, 109–10, 156, 160, 167–8, 182, 187
Anglican (Episcopalian), 21, 28
Angus, 54, 68, 111
Antrim, 2–5, 9, 14–17, 19, 21–2, 24–5, 28, 31–3, 58, 99, 117, 135, 149, 171, 177
Appalachian English, 167
Argyll, 19, 24
Armagh, 3–5, 9, 15, 18–19, 24–5, 27, 31–3, 58, 99, 106, 111, 113, 131, 143, 149
aspiration, 92–3, 97, 154, 175
Australia, 2, 65, 69, 182, 187
Ayrshire, 19, 21, 24, 54, 68, 87, 119, 122

BAIT lexical set, 112, 163
Ballyvourney, 6–7, 136, 185
Banffshire, 58–9
BATH lexical set, 47–8, 100–3, 107–9, 115–17, 121, 126–8, 131–2, 139, 141, 166, 181, 183
Bedfordshire, 19, 162
Belfast, 1, 3, 5, 8–9, 14, 18, 21, 28, 31, 35, 36, 64, 69, 78, 107–8, 112, 116, 129, 131, 135, 166
Belfast Paradox, 35
Belfast Vernacular English (BVE), 1, 8–9, 28, 35, 95, 102, 106, 113, 132, 135, 137, 139
Berkshire, 67, 132
Berwickshire, 19, 106, 122–4
bilingualism, 5, 11, 24–6, 34, 37, 54, 62, 147, 148, 150–1, 159, 179, 184, 187
Bliadhain an Áir, 27
Bolton (dialect), 67

BOOK lexical set, 127–30, 137–8, 166
Border (Irish), 8, 29
Borders, Scottish, 19, 24, 54, 77, 94
borrowing, 42, 45–6, 55, 59–60, 85, 96, 98, 108, 126, 140, 143, 145–9, 152, 156, 158, 169, 180
Britishness, 16–17, 22, 25–6, 27, 29, 149–50, 170
broad (velarised) consonant, 6, 41, 44–5, 49–51, 55–6, 60–3, 78, 80–1, 94–6, 105, 108, 135–6
Bute, Isle of, 19, 54

Caithness, 58, 111
Cambridgeshire, 19, 77
Caribbean, 54–6, 109–10
Carrickfergus, 14–15, 18
Catholic, 9, 11, 17, 21–3, 25–30, 34–7, 58, 66–7, 70, 76, 78, 99, 150, 157, 159–60, 179, 182, 188
Catholic English, 37
Cavan, 3–5, 18, 24–5, 31–3, 55, 58
census, 5, 23–5, 30–4
Central Belt (of Scotland), 24, 43, 68, 77, 106
cherry-picking data, 11, 62, 136, 154, 156, 160, 168, 170, 182–3
Cheshire, 19, 132
CHOICE lexical set, 48, 81, 101–2, 115, 117, 127
class *see* social class
Cockney, 65
Coleraine, 14–15, 18, 99
colonial lag, 11, 146, 154, 167–70, 183
Common Scandinavian, 59
compatibility, 55, 78, 89, 92, 147, 152, 154–5
complexity, 63, 114, 116, 120, 148, 163, 170, 172, 176, 185–6
Connacht, 4–5, 22, 56, 58, 60, 73, 76
conservatism, 11, 42, 71, 91, 98, 101, 130, 142, 145–6, 156, 165–71, 180–1, 183
consonant cluster, 58, 76, 82–4, 86, 91–2, 172
consonant deletion *see* deletion of consonant

constraint (linguistic), 85, 87–8, 116, 136, 174, 180
convergence, 153, 163, 169, 171
conversion (religious), 25–7, 29, 34, 149–50, 178–9
Cork, 6, 22, 136, 185
coronal consonant, 41–2, 51, 57, 59–63, 87–8, 96, 107
Cromwellian conquest of Ireland, 21–2
Cumberland, 74, 94, 96, 134
Cumbria *see* Cumberland
CURE lexical set, 127, 130, 142

Danish, 60
debuccalisation of /θ/, 67–70, 97, 99
deletion of consonant, 46, 69, 84–91, 95, 97–9, 154, 166, 175, 177, 180
demography, 13, 20, 23–7, 146, 148, 155, 159, 164, 178–9, 182, 187
dental fricative, 2, 61, 66–73, 97–8, 148, 155
dephonologisation, 132
Derbyshire, 52, 75, 89
Derry (English) *see* (London)Derry, (London) Derry English
determinism, 45, 152, 163–5, 172, 186
Devon, 19, 111, 132, 162
dissociation, 169
Donegal, 2–5, 18, 24–5, 29, 31–4, 46, 58–9, 73, 105–6, 108, 135–6, 149, 151, 171, 177, 187
DOOR lexical set, 127, 129–30, 142
Dorset, 53, 73, 87, 132
Down, 2–3, 9, 14, 16–22, 24–5, 27–8, 30–2, 58, 99, 111, 113, 131, 135, 139, 143, 149, 171, 177
Downpatrick, 14
DRESS lexical set, 47, 49, 81, 101–3, 106, 109, 113, 115–17, 127, 130, 141–2, 172, 181
Dublin (English), 4, 14, 18, 22, 66, 71, 78, 103, 118
Dumfriesshire, 19, 106, 112
Durham, 134
Dynamic Model, 165

Early Modern English (EModE), 11, 19–20, 24, 38, 45, 51, 56, 69, 82, 88, 92, 98, 107, 109–13, 130–2, 137, 139–42, 145–6, 157, 161, 165–7, 169, 178, 180–1, 183, 185
East Anglia, 19, 43, 52, 67, 96, 106, 111–12, 142, 162
eclipsis, 41, 135
Elizabeth conquest of Ireland, 14–15, 17, 167

Elizabethan English, 8, 166–7, 183
epenthesis, 7, 10, 76, 82–4, 86, 88, 97, 152, 154–5, 172, 175, 185
Episcopalian *see* Anglican
Essex, 19, 53
ethno-religious dimension, 10, 13, 26–30, 35–8, 99, 149, 161, 179
extra-territorial variety, 1–2, 11, 43, 45, 54, 65, 69, 110, 160, 178, 183

FACE lexical set, 36, 47, 49, 81, 101–3, 111–12, 115, 117, 124, 127, 129–30, 141–2, 183, 185
Famine, Great, 27–8, 30
Fermanagh, 3–4, 18–20, 24–5, 31–2, 150
fieldworker, 9, 99, 118–19, 122, 124–5
Fife, 54, 68, 94
first language (L1), 147–8, 152–3, 156, 173–4, 176, 185, 187
FLEECE lexical set, 47, 49, 81, 101–2, 110, 116–17, 127, 134, 142
Flight of the Earls, 16
focusing, 35, 155, 163, 171–2
FOOT lexical set, 36, 101–4, 106, 109, 117, 126–30, 136–8, 142–3, 166, 173, 181, 183, 185
FOOT–STRUT split, 103–4, 129–30, 137–8, 142, 163
FORCE lexical set, 48, 127, 129–30, 142, 166
founder effect (founder principle, founding population), 23, 38, 159, 162, 163–4, 186–7
French, 37, 110

Gaelic Revival, 29
Gaelic, Scottish, 15, 17, 24–6, 33, 37, 45–6, 54, 56, 58–60, 74, 83, 89, 154–5, 178, 184
Gaeltacht (English), 5, 9, 156, 160, 187
Galloway, 14, 24, 54, 68
Galway, 58–9
geographical diffusion, 176
Germanic, 59, 83
Glasgow, 21, 54, 65, 68–9, 170, 176
Glens of Antrim, 5, 17, 32–3, 58
glottalisation, glottal replacement, 93, 97–8, 176
Gloucestershire, 19, 129, 132
GOAT lexical set, 48, 81, 101–2, 115–17, 123–4, 127–8, 130
GOOSE lexical set, 48, 56, 81, 101–3, 110–11, 116–17, 126–30, 136–8, 141–2, 144, 172–3, 181
grammar, 174
Great Vowel Shift, 134

/h/ (retention, dropping), 42–6, 68–9, 72, 96, 166, 169, 172, 175, 177, 185–6; *see also* aitch
habitual *be*, 157
Haddingtonshire, 19
hand-Darkening, 107
Hebrides, 17
Herefordshire, 77, 130
Hertfordshire, 52
Herzog's Principle, 153
/hj/, 40, 42–3, 96
Home Rule, 29
/hw/, 40, 42, 44–6, 96, 135, 166, 172, 175–7, 185–6

Icelandic, 167
identity, 25–6, 29, 35, 160, 164–5, 170
imposition, 57, 148–9, 152, 173–7, 183, 186–7
indexing (social), 158–9, 164, 182, 187
indicator (sociolinguistic), 158–9
indirect question, 157
interference, substratum, 148–9, 151–3, 156–8, 160, 187
interlanguage, 176
intermarriage, 15, 25–6, 29, 179
isogloss, 4, 126

Jacobean English, 167, 183
Jamaica (Jamaican Creole), 54–5
James I/VI, 16, 21, 23

Kilkenny, 132, 136
Kincardineshire, 19
Kintyre, 15, 17
Kirkcudbrightshire, 19, 21, 94, 106, 112, 122
KIT lexical set, 47, 49, 81, 101–3, 106, 109–10, 114, 116–17, 120, 127, 141–2, 172, 181, 183, 185
/kl/ and /gl/, 95–6, 175
/kn/, 93–4, 97
koinéisation, 11, 38, 106, 146, 162–3, 165–6, 182–3, 186

/l/, 6, 46, 50, 56, 72, 74–82, 84, 86–9, 91, 97–8, 107, 124, 166, 175–6, 180, 185
Lagan Valley, 18–19, 28, 108, 129
Lanarkshire, 10
Lancashire, 19, 52–3, 67, 71, 73, 111, 132
language shift, 10–11, 13, 34, 38, 69, 84, 89, 96, 126, 146–52, 154, 156–60, 171, 173–5, 177, 179, 181–2, 184–5, 187

Laois, 16–17, 22
learner (of English), 43–4, 70, 76, 88, 98, 134, 136, 147, 151–5, 163, 165, 173, 176, 179, 182, 186–7
Leicestershire, 19, 75, 77, 130, 132
Leinster, 4, 14, 49
Leitrim, 22, 58
lenition (Irish), 41–3, 45, 60, 76, 98, 135
levelling, 5, 29, 46, 71, 74, 157, 159, 162, 165–6, 171–2, 176, 182
lexical distribution, 11, 40–1, 44–6, 74–6, 96–7, 100–1, 103, 113, 125–7, 129–30, 132–8, 142–3, 145–7, 161, 165–6, 170–7, 180–1, 183, 186
lexical redistribution, 176, 183
lexis, 146, 148–9, 156–8, 161, 182
Lincolnshire, 52, 72, 75, 129–30
Linen Triangle, 27–8
Linguistic Atlas of Scotland, Vol. 3 (LAS3), 4, 8–10, 29, 45, 54, 58, 66–8, 73, 96, 99, 104, 106–7, 110–13, 116, 118–20, 122–4, 131, 135, 139, 143, 181
loanword, 46, 96, 156, 180
London, 18–19, 51, 68–70, 111, 165
(London)Derry, 1–5, 9, 11, 15, 18, 20, 24–5, 31–3, 139, 143, 149, 177
(London)Derry English, 35–6, 69–70, 78, 113, 160
Longford, 22
LOT lexical set, 48, 81, 101–3, 108–10, 113, 115–17, 123–4, 127–8, 130–2, 138–41, 143, 173, 181, 183, 185
Lothian, 19, 122

marker (sociolinguistic), 158
MATE lexical set, 112, 163
meaning list, 156–7
MEAT lexical set, 102, 115–16, 127, 130, 142, 166, 169, 183, 185
MEET lexical set, 166, 169
merger, 42, 57–8, 60, 63, 66–7, 69, 99, 112, 114–15, 118, 121, 123–5, 129–31, 139, 143, 148, 158, 163, 166, 169, 173
Middle English (ME), 43–5, 51, 71, 74–5, 88, 93, 103, 107–8, 112, 127–30, 133, 137, 139, 142, 163, 180
Middle Irish, 87, 89
Middlesex, 19
Midlands (England), 11, 18–19, 38, 43, 51–3, 62, 74–5, 86–7, 92–3, 98, 104, 107, 110, 112–13, 121, 126, 129–32, 137–8, 142, 145–6, 161–3, 165–7, 169–72, 178, 180–6

Modern Scots (ModSc), 104, 107, 109, 134, 137

Monaghan, 3–4, 24–5, 29, 31–3, 42, 45

Morayshire, 54, 58–9

morpheme boundary, 61, 84–8, 90, 102, 112, 116, 124, 133–4, 143, 174, 180

Morpheme Boundary Constraint (MBC), 61

morpheme-internal, 64, 83, 85, 87–91

MOUTH lexical set, 48, 81, 86, 101–3, 110–11, 116–17, 127–8, 130, 132, 139, 141–2, 166, 172–4, 180–1, 185

Munster, 4–5, 16–17, 22, 73, 76

NEAR lexical set, 47, 127, 129

New Dialect Formation (NDF), 1–2, 11, 13, 38, 62, 72, 74, 98, 120, 146, 154–5, 161–6, 168–74, 177–9, 182–7

New World, 27, 34, 54, 109

New Zealand English, 2, 43, 65, 69, 72, 162, 164–5, 182, 186–7

Newry, 14–15

Norfolk, 6, 19, 53, 67, 69, 77, 110, 162

Norman, 14–15, 37, 148

Norse, 54

North Channel, 67, 111

NORTH lexical set, 48, 127, 129, 130, 142, 166

Northamptonshire, 77, 110, 129–30, 132

Northern England (Northern English), 7, 38, 67, 71, 75, 88–9, 94, 126, 129, 185

Northern Ireland, 1, 26–9, 35, 37–8, 182

Northumberland, 58, 134–5

Nottinghamshire, 19, 75

NURSE lexical set, 48–9, 52, 127, 129–30, 142, 153, 166, 185

Offaly, 16–17, 22

Old English (language; OE), 51, 83, 88, 93

Old English (settlers in Ireland), 15, 26, 36

Old Irish, 66, 73, 76, 87, 89

OLD lexical set, 86, 127–8, 130, 142, 166, 180, 185

Older Scots (OSc), 74–5, 77, 87, 104, 107, 109, 111–12, 117, 120, 124, 133–4, 136–9

Omagh, 9, 20, 70, 140, 166

Orkney, 58

Oxfordshire, 19, 52, 110, 129, 132

Ozark English, 167

Palatal Velarisation (PV), 56–60, 97, 145, 147, 156, 180

palato-alveolar consonant, 40, 52–3, 56–7

Pale, The, 14–15, 22

PALM lexical set, 48–9, 75, 100–2, 117, 121, 127–8, 139

Partition of Ireland, 29

Pennines, 94

peripheralisation, 11, 145–6, 154, 156, 169–71, 183

Perthshire, 58, 68

phonological rule, 7, 49–50, 65, 80–1, 101, 105, 113–16, 118, 121, 132, 136, 142–3, 153, 174–7, 183, 186

phonotactic constraint, 84, 91, 100, 174–5, 177, 183

place-name, 8, 45–6, 59, 63, 96, 98, 126, 140, 143, 147, 156–7, 180

Plantation of Ulster, 1–2, 10, 13–14, 16–27, 29, 33, 36–8, 44–5, 54–5, 59, 62–3, 65, 67, 70, 72–3, 78, 93–4, 96, 104, 106, 120–1, 125, 130, 132, 134–5, 139, 149–50, 154, 159–60, 162, 164–5, 167, 169–70, 172, 176–9, 182, 184, 188

Poland, 21

polarisation, 35, 146, 169–70

Post-/r/ Retraction, 67, 70, 74, 97

Pre-Fricative Lengthening (PFL), 115–16, 120–2, 124–5, 142, 172

Pre-Palatal Raising (PPR), 48, 50, 52–3, 102–3, 141

preposition, 157

Pre-R Dentalisation (PreRD), 6–7, 10, 61–4, 67, 69–71, 73, 97, 163, 166, 172, 175, 185

Presbyterian, 20–1, 24, 27–9

prestige, 29, 146, 148–50, 155, 160, 164–6, 182

PRICE lexical set, 47, 49, 51, 81, 101–3, 112–17, 120, 125, 127, 129–30, 132–4, 141–3, 172, 174, 181, 183, 185–6

PRIZE lexical set, 102, 115, 127, 133

Protestant, 9, 11, 16–18, 20–9, 34–7, 43, 58, 66, 70, 76, 78, 99, 149–50, 157, 160, 170, 178–9, 182, 188

Protestant English, 37

/r/, 6, 48, 56–7, 61–2, 64, 66–7, 69–74, 78–9, 81, 86, 93, 95, 97, 99–100, 102, 107, 114–17, 132–3, 153, 155, 175–7

Rathlin Island, 5, 32–3, 58

Rebellion of 1641, 28

Received Pronunciation (RP), 11–12, 42, 44, 51, 56–7, 68–70, 73, 77–8, 81, 92, 103, 107–8, 111, 120–1, 125, 136, 144, 170, 175

reinforcement, 11, 42, 56, 61–2, 70, 78, 82–4, 86, 89, 91–3, 95, 97–8, 103, 110, 125, 136, 141, 143, 145–7, 151–6, 160, 169, 176, 182, 184, 187
Renfrewshire, 19
Republic of Ireland, 29
rhoticity, 47–8, 70–2, 74, 97, 99–100, 130, 153, 166, 169–70, 172, 175–7, 183, 186
Ribble-Humber Line, 126
Ring, 61–2
Ros Goill, 136
Roscommon, 8, 117, 132, 136
Roxburghshire, 19, 112, 122–3
/r/-Realisation Effect (RRE), 61–2, 74
Russian, 60

/s/, 52, 56–7, 71, 74, 84, 92, 95, 97, 115, 118, 121, 154, 172
Scandinavia, 21
Scottish Standard English (SSE), 40, 44–6, 77, 111, 119–20, 133, 137, 139, 143, 173–4
Scottish Vowel Length Rule (SVLR), 113–14, 116–20, 124–5, 132–4, 142–3, 172, 174, 181, 183, 185–7
second language (L2), 147–8, 173, 176, 184, 187
semi-weak past tense, 85, 99
SERVE lexical set, 47, 127, 129–30, 142, 166, 183, 185
servitor, 17–18, 22–3
settlement colonisation, 2, 16, 21, 24, 146, 149–50, 160, 162, 178, 187
Shakespeare (Shakespearean English), 8, 69, 131, 166–7, 183
Shetland, 58–9
short vowels in Irish, 49–50, 81, 105–6, 109, 138, 141
Shropshire, 19, 75
simplification (due to contact), 113, 138, 148, 163, 172, 174
slender (palatalised) consonants, 41, 44–5, 49–51, 55–7, 60, 62–3, 76, 80–1, 85, 96, 105, 108, 135–6
Sligo, 58
social class, 1, 35–6, 44, 69–71, 77, 99, 103, 158, 170
Somerset, 19, 132
south-east England, 75, 77, 87, 90, 108, 111
Southern boundary of Mid-Ulster English, 3–5, 66

southern England, 18–19, 52, 65, 105, 108, 121–2, 125, 137, 145–6, 162–3, 165–6, 169–70, 178, 184–6
Southern Irish English (SIrE), 2, 4, 40, 42, 47, 49, 58, 64, 66, 68–9, 72, 78, 81, 92, 99, 103, 105, 109, 111, 114, 116–18, 121–2, 132, 136, 180, 185
Southern Ulster English (SUE), 3–5, 9, 33, 49, 114, 116–18, 121–2
south-west England, 43, 52–3, 72, 75–6, 85, 88, 90, 92, 98, 106, 110, 112–13, 137–8, 142, 162
South-west Tyrone English (SwTE), 3–4, 9–11, 29, 42, 47–8, 57–60, 63–6, 69–72, 78–82, 84, 86, 95–6, 99, 102, 106–9, 112–16, 127–9, 131–2, 135, 137, 139–40, 156, 161, 186, 188
Sperrin Mountains, 5, 33
SQUARE lexical set, 47, 127, 129
stabilisation (linguistic), 155, 163, 165
Staffordshire, 19, 75, 132, 162
Standard English (StE), 10–12, 19, 38, 43–5, 52, 56, 62, 66, 75, 85, 93–4, 98, 112–13, 124, 126, 130, 134, 139, 142, 145, 161–2, 165–7, 169–70, 178, 180, 183
Standard Northern Irish English, 1, 36, 47, 84, 86, 88, 127–9, 135, 137
standardisation, 29, 86
START lexical set, 48–9, 51, 54, 127, 130, 142, 183, 185
stereotype, 35, 158
stigma, 37, 43, 164–6
STRUT lexical set, 48, 81, 101–6, 109, 114, 116–17, 126–30, 136–8, 141–3, 163, 173, 181, 183, 185
subordinating *and*, 157
substratum, 147–9
Suffolk, 19, 69, 72, 77
superstratum, 148–9
supraregionalisation, 19, 29, 36, 146, 151, 178
Surrey, 19
Survey of English Dialects (SED), 6–8, 10, 52–3, 65, 67, 69, 71, 74–5, 77, 85, 87–90, 92, 94–5, 110–11, 118–19, 131, 135, 143, 156–7
Sutherland, 58
swamping, 23, 164, 178–9
syntax, 4, 146, 148–9, 156–61, 182, 184, 187
systemic difference, 40–2, 98, 100, 102–3, 138–40, 172, 175, 177, 186

tabula rasa, 163–4

Tape-recorded Survey of Hiberno-English Speech (TRS), 4, 8

target language (TL), 147–9, 152–4, 156, 174, 176–7

THOUGHT lexical set, 45, 48, 81, 101–2, 108, 113, 115, 117, 121, 127–8, 130, 138–40, 143, 173, 181, 183

Threshold Rider, 162

TH-stopping, 66–7, 69–70, 97–8, 155

transcription, 41, 76, 105, 118–20, 122–5, 143

transfer, 132, 136, 143, 147, 183

TRAP lexical set, 47–9, 51, 54, 81, 100–3, 107–9, 115–17, 120, 123, 126–8, 131, 139, 141, 166, 172, 181, 183

Troubles, The, 29

T-to-R Rule, 65

Tudor period, 14–15

/t/-Voicing, 63–5, 97, 99, 172, 175

Tyneside, 6

Tyrone, 1, 3, 5, 18–20, 22, 24–5, 27, 30–3, 58, 69, 78, 105, 108, 150, 166

Ulster Crisis, 29

Ulster Irish, 5, 29, 31, 33–4, 46, 56–8, 62, 73, 83, 91, 94–6, 105–6, 108–10, 114, 135–6, 140–1, 151, 154, 181

Ulster Scots (USc), 2–4, 9, 20, 23–4, 32–3, 37, 45–6, 48, 55, 58–9, 66–7, 73, 75, 90, 92–3, 99, 103–4, 106–7, 109–14, 116–17, 120, 126, 131, 133–5, 139–41, 143–4, 177, 180, 185–6

Ulster Scots/Mid-Ulster English dialect boundary, 3–4, 126

undertaker, 17–20, 22

United States, 54–5

Urban Ulster Scots, 113, 133

Velar Palatalisation (VP), 47–56, 58, 60, 97, 103, 139, 154–5, 166, 172, 175–6, 185

vocabulary *see* lexis

voiced stop, 40–1, 90, 92–3

voiceless stop, 40–1, 92–3, 115, 122–3, 128, 139, 175

Voicing Effect (VE), 115–17, 120, 122–5, 142, 172, 181

vowel backing, 103, 107–8, 141

vowel centralisation, 103–6, 110, 114, 141, 181, 185

vowel diphthongisation, 112–13, 141

vowel fronting, 48, 50, 103, 108, 110–11, 141, 173

vowel lowering, 103–6, 109, 113, 131–2, 137–8, 140–1, 181, 185

vowel quality, 2, 5, 11, 41, 49–50, 80–1, 100–3, 107, 109–10, 112, 114, 120, 122, 125, 140–1, 145, 170, 172, 174, 176–7, 180–1, 183, 186

vowel quantity (vowel length), 2, 5, 11, 45, 81, 83, 87, 99–102, 107–8, 112–25, 130, 139, 141–3, 145, 153–4, 170–2, 174, 176–7, 180–1, 183, 185–6

vowel shortening, 120, 137–8, 143

vowel unrounding, 48, 100, 103–5, 108–10, 130–2, 139–42, 173, 181, 185

WALK lexical set, 48, 75, 108, 115, 127–8, 130, 139–40

Warwickshire, 19, 77, 130–1

Waterford, 14, 61

West Midlands, 19, 74, 110, 113, 162, 167

Westmeath, 22, 117

Wexford, 14, 22

Wigtonshire, 19, 21, 67, 70, 106, 112, 119, 122

Williamite Wars, 21, 29

Worcestershire, 77, 132

/wr/, 93–4, 97

/x/, 40, 45–6, 75, 96, 98, 115, 145–7, 175–6

Yod Coalesence, 56–7, 99

Yod Dropping, 56

Yorkshire, 19, 52, 67, 72, 74, 113

/z/, 56, 74, 96–7